DATE DUE			

THE FINANCE OF
BRITISH GOVERNMENT
1920–1936

THE FINANCE OF
BRITISH GOVERNMENT
1920-1936

BY

URSULA K. HICKS

With a New Introduction

OXFORD
AT THE CLARENDON PRESS

Oxford University Press, Ely House, London W. 1

GLASGOW NEW YORK TORONTO MELBOURNE WELLINGTON
CAPE TOWN SALISBURY IBADAN NAIROBI DAR ES SALAAM LUSAKA ADDIS ABABA
BOMBAY CALCUTTA MADRAS KARACHI LAHORE DACCA
KUALA LUMPUR SINGAPORE HONG KONG TOKYO

FIRST PUBLISHED 1938
REPRINTED LITHOGRAPHICALLY IN GREAT BRITAIN
(WITH A NEW INTRODUCTION)
AT THE UNIVERSITY PRESS, OXFORD
BY VIVIAN RIDLER
PRINTER TO THE UNIVERSITY
1970

INTRODUCTION TO THE 1969 IMPRESSION

THE *Finance of British Government* tells the story of the expenditure and revenue of British governing bodies in the interwar period. By 1920, my starting date, budgetary practice on current account had returned to something near normal, although the capital account was still confused by the disturbances caused by war borrowing (not that the distinction between current and capital account was then recognized). The book was finished in 1937 when the first shadows of the finance of the Second World War were just beginning to appear. This presaged a very definite end to a period; but it was then too soon to put the events recorded adequately into historical perspective, more particularly because of the world monetary crisis into which Britain found herself plunged in 1931 and which was to colour the economics of the whole of that decade.

The task I had set myself was not easy. There were few published statistics of economic relevancy. Calculations of the National Income had only been made privately and spasmodically. Such as there were had a mainly social objective: to estimate whether poverty was falling or the nation getting richer. There was no thought of using them as an instrument for fiscal decision making, until Keynes showed the way in 1939.[1] The arrangement of the budget accounts was strictly objective, with Ministries lumped together in a more or less haphazard manner and Votes arranged according to the objective classification (the classic example is 'hay for horses' in whatever part of the world the cavalry might be using them). I wanted to know how much was really being spent on different services, that is to say I wanted a functional classification. (The first official recognition of the need for this was the (Plowden) Report on the Control of Public Expenditure, 1961.) The best I could do was to go through the Appropriation Accounts, head by head, and freely transfer them on to a functional basis. It was a laborious, but

[1] 'Britain's Economic Potential', *E.J.*, Dec. 1939.

I think worthwhile exercise. I had to make my own classifications, and no doubt not everyone would agree with them in detail; but broadly they served my purposes.

For this re-issue I have not made any alterations in the text beyond inserting the official National Income statistics for the period (p. 35). Broadly I stand by what I said then. There are some topics indeed which are now of central interest, such as growth in *per capita* income, which were then not thought to be important, and are not discussed—and in any case there was no way of measuring such growth; but on the other hand several topics in which I was particularly interested have since come into the centre of discussion. I might mention two in particular, concerned respectively with the planning of road development and the economics and finance of large conurbations, 'Metropolitan Areas' as we should now call them.

I felt very strongly that priorities in road development could and should be determined on a rational calculus. I suggested that in the first place they should be based on traffic counts at different times and seasons to ascertain existing and prospective density. Starting out from this I argued that it should be possible to estimate the relative cost-saving in vehicle time from alternative improvements. Clearly this was a good long way from a modern cost/benefit analysis, but I think that it at least contained the germ of the idea. Had something of the kind been undertaken at that time we might by now have an adequate road system.

Secondly, I was much exercised by the cost and inefficiency arising from the fact that in areas of continuous urban development administration was divided between a large number of small and financially weak local authorities. Basing my argument on the L.C.C. I felt that the most promising solution was a super council covering the whole area, undertaking most services, but with sufficient responsibility reserved to the individual units to prevent their identity being completely submerged. This problem is now occupying the attention of economists, administrators, and town planners in all the advanced countries, more especially in the U.S.A. and Canada. In terms of comprehensives the G.L.C. is an improvement on the L.C.C.; and in 1969 there is little doubt that we are on the threshold of a big expansion of the idea. It is essential that something should be done quickly.

Since the publication of the *F.B.G.* (as I shall call it) a large number of books have been published dealing with particular aspects of my field[1] but none I think attempts such a comprehensive view and none carries the story up to the present. Although recent events are doubtless very well remembered it may be useful to some readers if I briefly summarize the story as I see it up to the middle 1960's by way of putting the *F.B.G.* discussion into its historical setting.

A process of change has been proceeding continuously sometimes faster, sometimes more slowly, since the last quarter of the nineteenth century: extending from the Public Health Acts, the introduction of free and compulsory primary education, and Gladstone's budgetary reforms (all in the 1860's and '70's) right up to the present day. Britain's experiences in this process have not been unique; they can be paralleled in most of the Western countries. But in a number of ways the continuity in Britain has been greater than in most. Although the pound has been devalued three times and there has been a certain amount of inflation (especially in the most recent years) there has been no collapse of the monetary system such as has occurred more than once in Germany and France and, in a different way, in the United States in 1931.

The economic outlook which lay behind policy decisions in the *F.B.G.* period differed very substantially from that on which the present generation of administrators has been brought up. Keynes's *General Theory* appeared only at the end of 1935, but much of its analysis was already familiar to students and academic economists from lecture notes, and from Kahn's 'Multiplier Analysis of 1931'.[2] But the 'Treasury View' (of the uselessness of public works expenditure as a cure for unemployment) still held sway in government circles, although in practice it was politically necessary to undertake a good deal of public works in order to appear to be 'doing something'. In the early days of the war Keynes himself was able to expound his doctrine within the walls of the Treasury itself. The message at that stage was much concerned with the importance of maintaining low interest rates as a stimulus to expansion. It was also conducted in terms of a closed economy, and had reference only to short period effects. This was not just what was

[1] Besides my own Home University Library summary *British Public Finances, 1880 to 1952*, mention should be made of *The Growth of Public Expenditure, 1890 to 1955*, Peacock and Wiseman, and *Government Finance and Fiscal Policy in Postwar Britain*, Ilersic.
[2] R. F. Kahn, *E.J.*, June 1931.

wanted for war finance. But it was the beginning of the use of an informed technique for national policy decisions, based on the Social Accounts of available resources and expected demands on them. This technique is now universally accepted. It was put to practical use in the first White Paper on National Income and Expenditure introduced with the Budget in 1941.

The basic British economic worries of the *F.B.G.* period were first the persistence of a high level of unemployment and secondly the evil economic effects which might be expected from the approach of a stationary population. The resulting stagnant economy (it was thought) could hardly fail to bring with it a still higher level of unemployment. In fact to the 'long unemployment' of the 1920's—essentially due to the decline of the basic Victorian industries of cotton and coal, and to the troubles of the war expanded 'heavies'—was added at the end of the decade the short term impact of the world slump. The combined effect of these two factors was a strongly localized long unemployment on which was grafted a cyclical sagging of demand which affected most areas.

In strong contrast, the basic worry of the '50's and '60's has been war and rumours of wars, and the cost of warding them off. This preoccupation was almost wholly absent from the inter-war mentality. The First World War had been a 'war to end all wars'; defence expenditure was allowed to drop to about 2·5 per cent. of the national income. In the 1960's by contrast a great effort was needed to force it below 8 per cent. Largely it would seem as a result of the war itself the worries of the *F.B.G.* period have vanished. The birth rate rose rapidly at the beginning of the Second World War, and has remained high. The British labour problem of the '50's and '60's has been much more of a shortage leading to an overheated economy. This tendency to a labour shortage was in fairly marked contrast to the situation in most of Britain's economic competitors: Germany, France, Japan, and the U.S.A. all had large labour reserves to draw upon: the first three especially from their old-fashioned labour intense agricultural sectors, which in Britain had already been drained.

Some degree of stagnation had indeed been present in the inter-war period. It seemed as if Britain and other countries were going through a period of temporary slackening of the pace of technological advance, and that this was reducing the incentive to fresh investment. Such temporary slackenings seem to have occurred

previously following a strong investment boom, such as that caused
by the great age of railway construction. In the inter-war period
traditional savings habits, built up when the typical small firm had
only itself and its friends to rely on for financial expansion, but still
persisting, may have aggravated the situation. Stagnation may also
have been related to the slowing down of population increase, but if
so it was a 'chicken and an egg' effect. In practice 'love on the dole'
did not lead to a high birth rate.

In spite of continuing full employment in the '50's and '60's the
spectre of the recrudescence of unemployment has continued to
haunt Britain—politicians and workers alike—particularly in the
guise of regional unemployment. This has not been without reason,
since any slackening of demand invariably showed up first in the
former depressed areas. Thus in a fully employed economy the fear
of unemployment has continued to be a major influence in British
policy decisions. This has not been so on the Continent, although
it has found an echo in the U.S.A. There, however, it has been
increasingly mixed up with the Colour Question, even where that
was not strictly at issue.

Similarly the fear of general stagnation has melted before the
whirl of technical advance set off by the demands of the war for
research and development. The pace of technical advance continued
unabated in the '50's and '60's although in some fields—for instance
nuclear physics—it has begun to show some signs of slackening.
In Britain in the '50's and '60's the fear of general stagnation was
replaced by a related apprehension: that the country was not growing so fast as other countries. Hence there arose a tremendous
preoccupation with rates of growth in *per capita* income. (In
the *F.B.G.* period the blessed word 'Growth' had not yet appeared
on the scene.) Certainly over the years 1955–66 Britain's *per capita*
income rise was not so rapid as those of Germany and France, and
was very much lower than that of Japan. In all these countries,
however, there were special explanations of previous retarded
development. Britain's growth rate compared well with that of the
U.S.A.—or for that matter with that of Switzerland—and was
besides very much steadier than that of the U.S.A. We are not
concerned to assess the importance of these differences, nor indeed
the significance of statistical growth rates, especially when unaccompanied by statistics of income distribution. But it should
be noted that the assumed ignominy of a bad place in the 'League'

affected both British policy decisions and other countries' evaluation of her prospects; I shall return to this point below.

After the Second World War neither the fear of unemployment nor of stagnation affected Britain's main continental competitors to any serious extent. But they have lived constantly with the spectre of inflation, leading to hyperinflation and a complete breakdown of confidence. In Germany especially this fear has entered strongly into policy decisions, not only in financial and government circles, but in the business and even in the household sectors. It has fostered a high propensity to save, heavy taxation, and a determination to concentrate on exports rather than on the home market. In France the fear of hyperinflation has been less intense, and the incentive to save and to tax less high. The phenomenon has showed itself rather in a distrust of credit expansion, which indeed had always been regarded with suspicion in France. Hence surpluses have tended to be invested in gold. In the 1960's government expenditure, especially on defence, accompanied by pressure on industry to expand in order to maintain a high growth rate, did much—in some ways too much—to counteract the deflationary effects of French currency policy. British Governments were of course aware that inflation was a bad thing; but in the country there was no general apprehension of it, perhaps because the horrors of hyperinflation had never been experienced.

In assessing the changes which have taken place in British public finances since the *F.B.G.* period we have to keep our eyes on three separate fields: (i) the relations of the government to industry especially concerned with the nationalization of the fuel, power, and most of the transport industries, (ii) the relations of the government and the financial sector, epitomized by the nationalization of the Bank of England, and (iii) the relations of the government to the citizen and especially the establishment of the Welfare State. All three are manifestations of the growth of the Public Sector, and especially of the central government. The effects of this showed themselves not only in these specific fields but also in the growth of a paternalistic participation by the government in the life of the ordinary citizen, even outside the confines of the Welfare State. This indeed was a species of socialism, though a very different species from the communist.

The growth of the public sector was not by any means uniquely a British phenomenon, although it took different forms in different countries. In France it was particularly prominent where the introduction of global 'indicative' planning implied in practice a good deal of government interference and participation in particular industries and extension of control over local authorities. In the U.S.A. it took the form of a great enhancement of the power of the Federal Government, very largely by such indirect means as the specification of performance and location of particular projects, more or less connected with defence, and also in increased Federal grants for social welfare and transport improvements. In Germany the constitution imposed by the Allies implied that only an indirect growth of the public sector was possible. It was, however, manifested in the expansion of state participation in a number of important industries and firms.

In Britain the more conspicuous changes depended on legislation introduced by the Labour (Attlee) government which took office at the end of the Second World War. This was true of all the nationalization Acts, including that of the Bank of England. The measures by which the welfare state was established were also due to legislation by this government: the most important were concerned with the unification and extension of the social security system, the nationalization of almost all the hospitals, and the establishment of the National Health Service. Other changes such as the growth of paternalism in industry and agriculture are less directly traceable to major legislation: but there have been frequent adjusting legislation and orders, as well as discriminatory tax concessions and subsidies, on an unprecedented scale. The Location of Industry Act of 1948 (giving the government power very largely to dictate where factories might or might not be established) has been of major importance, not perhaps so much in itself but as showing the manner in which land use and industrial development could be made to serve political rather than economic ends. The range of these changes was so wide that at first sight it looks like a revolution, and in some senses this is true. Had it not been for the great expansion of government influence and control during the war, which had accustomed the British public to regulation and interference in their private lives, it could hardly have come about so easily.

Yet if we look more closely it soon appears that the foundations in all three directions had already been laid much earlier, in some cases back to the turn of the century and beyond. The pace of change was accelerated, but only to a minor degree was its direction altered.

On the side of state ownership, the troubles of the coal industry in the 1920's had led to a general conviction that on both technical and socio-political grounds it would have to be nationalized, or at least put under unified control in respect of policy. This was practically a bi-partisan view. Electricity and gas were already substantially controlled by legislation both as to prices and profits. Local authorities already owned a substantial share of both industries. From 1926 a national Central Electricity Board took over the generation of electricity although leaving distribution to the existing operators. In respect of transport, the railways had always been closely controlled and the establishment of the London Passenger Transport Board virtually nationalized every form of public transport in the London area. Outside London many cities owned their own trams or buses. Thus in all these directions nationalization implied transfer of control with unification of policy and finance, much more than it implied change from the private to the public sector. Incidentally the nationalization of electricity removed from local budgets their one not negligible source of trading profit.

The degree of public ownership already existing in transport was much smaller than in gas or electricity, so that the effect of nationalization was more pronounced. The original intention had been to nationalize all forms of commercial transport except such vehicles as local delivery vans. This would have enabled profits to be transferred from road to rail. This proved extremely complicated, and the greater part of road haulage was subsequently denationalized, leaving the railway deficit out in the open, as in most other countries. Steel was another case in which unification under semi-public ownership had progressed far before nationalization. Apart from a greater government control in determining the location of new works the transfer does not seem to have effected great changes.

Public provision of low rent accommodation had started in a small way early in the century, as a contribution to slum clearance. From 1920 the provision of 'council houses' became by far the biggest item in public investment. Together with the needs of the Utilities the volume of investment on public account was sufficiently large in the 1930's to raise problems of its timing in relation to fluctuations in the general level of economic activity. In total, however, it was still modest in comparison with the 1950's when for a time public investment slightly exceeded the whole of investment in the private sector.

Public enterprise was thus fairly well established before the outbreak of the Second World War. It was, however, fundamentally different in effect from public enterprise in the nationalization period. In the 1930's control was disseminated. Many of the municipal undertakings were small—in some cases uneconomically so. There was no integration of policy in respect of price and output, except in so far as legislation required them to be linked. There was little common policy in respect of trade unions. Although nominal control over local authority borrowing was exercised by central Ministries there was no dictation of timing of issues nor of terms of loans, such as was exercised by the Public Works Loans Board and the Capital Issues Committee in the 1950's and 1960's.

The effect of nationalization was to establish a set of giant firms: railways, coal mines, electricity, gas, to name only the more important. Each followed a unified policy, and after an experimental period they all derived their investment finance from the Treasury apart from very small amounts which might be saved out of gross profits. Each 'firm' it is true, worked through sub-units: railway regions, hotel, steamship and catering departments, area boards in electricity and gas, and so on; but these had little power of independent decision making. Each 'firm' in turn worked closely with a sponsoring Ministry and was subject to Treasury control in respect of its annual investment programme. Such a close knit system of giant undertakings would hardly have been possible without the new management techniques which were developed in the post-war period. This is a point to which we shall have to return later.

The sequence of change in the financial sector differed very substantially from the events which we have been examining, because the fundamental revolution was already far advanced in the 1930's, as an aftermath of the massive borrowing to finance the First World War. (The story of this is analysed at considerable length below, Part III.) As a result of the war borrowing, by 1920 government debt had come to dominate all financial markets, short, medium, and long. It was, however, some time before the full implications of the potential government control thus created were recognized. The reverse side of the war borrowing was the large amount of public expenditure which had to be devoted to servicing the debt, especially as the greater part of it had been borrowed at high (5–6 per cent.) rates of interest for relatively long periods (around 10 years). In practice, however, this budgetary charge did not exercise a very restrictive effect on the economy, since the debt was largely self-financing, in the sense that debt holders were subject to income and surtax, and so to a considerable extent provided their own interest charges. In the later '20's when prices had fallen uncontrollably, the national debt interest, fixed in money terms in a period of high prices, brought the interest charge up to 7–8 per cent. of the national income, and then indeed apprehension of the stultifying effect of this section of the budget became considerable.[1]

In 1932 after the devaluation of the pound it became possible to convert the large block of 5 per cent. war loan to a 3½ per cent. basis, and thus ease the situation. After that the problem of the First World War debt sank into the background. In the 1930's, largely as a result of the experience gained in launching this Conversion operation, the authorities came to realize what considerable power they had to manipulate interest rates by adjusting the form and timing of their own issues to the anticipated demands of the different sections of financial markets.[2] That these implicit powers were recognized by the City is apparent from the speech made by the Governor of the Bank of England (the redoubtable Montague Norman) at the Mansion House dinner in October 1936 (cf. p. 377):

"I assure Ministers that if they will make known through the appropriate channels what they wish us to do in the furtherance of their policies, they will find us at all times as willing with goodwill and loyalty to do what they direct, as though we were under legal compulsion."

In the Second World War a still larger sum was borrowed. Between 1939 and 1945, £14,000 m. was added to the debt. The methods used, however, were entirely different. On Keynes's advice, and under the shelter of effective exchange control of capital movements (which could hardly have been achieved in the First World War) the policy was followed of 'glutting a closed economy with cash'. Borrowing was continuous, but very short term. By

[1] Cf. *Report (Colwyn) Committee on National Debt and Taxation* and J. E. Meads, *Economic Analysis and Policy.*
[2] Cf. Ch. xxiii below.

this method the average rate of interest on the new debt was little above 3 per cent., and actually fell as the war progressed. Thus the interest charge never reached former alarming proportions.

In spite of the even greater dominance of government debt in post-1945 markets it would be a mistake to conclude either that the control of the government in financial markets was complete or that the nationalization of the Bank of England merely registered a *fait accompli*. For instance in the early post-war years the Chancellor of the Exchequer (Dr. Dalton) found himself, in face of a strong private sector demand for investment funds, unable to force down interest rates as he had intended. In fact the low rate short term financing of the Second World War carried the seeds of its own troubles, in that the money market was repeatedly being asked to digest a larger volume of liquid resources than it could easily absorb, thus creating a tendency to undue expansion and inflation. Against this danger many devices were brought into play (mainly concerned with departmental debt carrying) so that with the aid of a little inflation the war debt as such had ceased to be a major problem by the late 1950's.

The necessities of the nationalized industries on the other hand presently posed a new debt problem. First came the need for funds to compensate former shareholders on take-over. Later when the industries got into their stride and after the Treasury had assumed responsibility for all the finance for their fixed capital formation, there was a steady stream of investment demands. In spite of the fact that such debt was not really 'deadweight' since it was represented by real assets, the mere expansion of the national debt was such as to give rise to serious doubts among Britain's foreign creditors as to whether the situation could be brought fully within the government's control—a revival of the doubts of 1931. By that time also it had become apparent that on nationalization the Bank of England had largely lost its power of independent judgement and advice. We must return to this point again in relation to the crisis of 1967-8.

The biggest expansion of the Public Sector after the Second World War was, however, in the field of social expenditure. It is not difficult to trace the beginnings of the Welfare State back to the turn of the century and further. In respect of education the establishment of the Board of Education in 1902 and the absorption of the School Boards by the local authorities marked the beginning of a national policy, for many years more closely defined and integrated than that of any other social service. But the Act of 1902 was itself building on the Forster Act of 1870 which had introduced compulsory universal primary education. The Fisher Act (1918) was the first attempt to secure some further (secondary) education for all, and to plan for the raising of the school leaving age, which was a necessary condition for a rational secondary course.

Grants to local schools, both government and independent, had been made before the middle of the nineteenth century. These were repeatedly expanded and in the 1930's especially, very great advances were made in the standard of secondary education. Whereas it was said that the First World War had been won on the playing fields of Eton it was even more true that the Second World War was won in the classrooms and laboratories of the grammar schools. From them emerged a stream of boys with a mechanical and scientific training which enabled them quickly to absorb the new techniques of such things as aeronautics, radar, and electronics. It was against this background that the (Butler) Act of 1944 was passed, promising after the war free secondary education for all according to ability; but the working of this belongs to the next chapter of the story.

The poor of course had always been with us; they were the cause of the first social legislation in the reign of Elizabeth I. The first attempt to get away from the harshness of the nineteenth-century Poor Law and to discriminate between different causes of poverty was the result of the momentous Reports of the Poor Law Commission (dominated by the Minority Report of Sidney and Beatrice Webb) which was published in 1909. Unemployment Insurance, Health Insurance, and Old Age Pensions were introduced by the bright young politicians of the period: Unemployment Insurance by Lloyd George, Health Insurance by Winston Churchill, and Old Age Pensions by their leader, Asquith.

In the 1920's and 1930's, as we have seen, the problem of poverty was dominated by the pressure of unemployment. The burden of this was too heavy to be dealt with adequately either by the Unemployment Insurance Fund or by the local authorities (up to 1929 more precisely the Poor Law Guardians) who were responsible for maintaining those who had fallen out of insurance. Gradually and most reluctantly the Treasury was compelled to shoulder this responsibility itself, although the process was not complete until after the Second World War. As a result there was a steady increase in the charge falling on the taxpayer and the ratepayer, and a by no means negligible additional burden on the contributors themselves. Even so, right up to the war it was an unequal race between outgoings and incomings of the Unemployment Fund. The burden on the local rate in different areas remained high and uneven in spite of some alleviation. The local costs of poverty are not confined to feeding and housing the indigent.

In the field of health great improvements had been made in environmental health since the realization in the last quarter of the nineteenth century that the spread of cholera and other infectious diseases was largely due to dirty urban and domestic conditions. The early researches of the local Statistical Societies[1] were much concerned with these problems, and undoubtedly hastened the advent of general water borne sewerage and clean water supplies, matters in which Britain was much ahead of continental countries. In respect of individual health, insurance gave some general assistance in times of illness. The school health service, and later school meals, were part of the general improvement in elementary schools. In the 1920's specific grants were available to local authorities for the diagnosis and treatment of tuberculosis and venereal disease. A maternity and child welfare organization was also established. The Poor Law Guardians were responsible for the care of physically and mentally sick recipients of public assistance. For this purpose some boards had built substantial hospitals which might well be superior to any other treatment centres in poor districts. On the transfer of the powers of the Guardians to the multi-purpose local authorities in 1929 not a few of the latter took over the management and development of these hospitals, which were thus the first to come completely under public ownership.

Even with these developments social health provision was not on a satisfactory basis. Insurance made no provision beyond the patient. The local clinics were very unevenly used, especially by the poorest families which needed them most. The great majority of hospitals, relying on private charity, were gradually being crushed between the falling volume of subscriptions and legacies, as surtax and death duties took their toll of private savings, and the rising cost of treatment as the new technologies became available. The former poor law hospitals were mainly in poor areas where the

[1] Especially the Manchester Statistical Society.

local authorities could not afford to develop them properly except at an intolerable burden on the rates. The fundamental revolution had yet to come in this aspect of the social services.

We have seen that low rent housing was the major item in public investment in the inter-war period that hovers on the borders of social and economic expenditure. Before the First World War its small beginnings are traceable mainly in the substitution of grim 'tenement' blocks in place of some of the worst city slums: by 1913 some £7 m. was being spent on this process. The policy was to charge sufficient rents to cover most of the costs. It was in the 1920's that the essential revolution took place, although there were still further expansions in the 1930's and after the Second World War. In 1920 capital outlay on housing had risen to £82 m.; subsequently it remained high but fluctuated in relation to the subsidy policy of the government.[1] In the 1930's there was a steady decline, partly due to a change of policy—with greater emphasis on slum clearance—under the Conservative government, partly to the decline in the need for subsidies after the conversion operation had brought down the rate of interest and stimulated a boom in the private building of small houses.

This short account indicates the social service position at the time of the establishment of the Welfare State (it is analysed in much greater detail in Ch. III). Well known as the more recent developments must be, it is desirable to chart them briefly in order to complete the picture. Turning first to education: the Butler Act of 1944 could not be implemented until the war was over. Its objective was free secondary education for all according to ability, compulsory up to the age of 15. A qualifying examination at eleven-plus would determine whether a child should go to a grammar school for an intellectual training, leading to a skilled job or the university, or would be sent to a (euphemistically called) 'Modern School' to receive a more 'practical' and less bookish training. The only alternative was a fee paying independent school. It was evident after some years that this discrimination was unacceptable, and especially that the fateful decision as to a child's future was made as early as 11. Consequently the plan was evolved by the Wilson government of changing to 'comprehensive' schools which would be large enough to cater adequately for all levels of ability within the four walls of the school. Not enough experience had by

[1] Cf. M. E. A. Bowley, *Housing and the State*.

1968 been gained of this method of working to judge whether it could indeed be applied to the whole country without immense cost on the one hand, or a dilution of standards on the other.

The more spectacular education development in the 1960's was, however, in the expansion of the universities; on the advice of Lord Robbins the British University population is being drastically expanded in order to bring it into line with the situation in the U.S.A. and some other countries. This implies the building of a number of new universities, the elevation of some existing colleges of technology to university status, and the enlargement of the smaller 'redbrick' universities. We are not concerned with the practicability of this policy if it were to be carried through smoothly and without a serious lowering of standards. The university 'explosion' is by no means uniquely a British phenomenon, and there is little doubt that the suddenness of its implementation has contributed actively to student unrest in many countries.

In Britain, however, it impinges strongly in the field of public finance, in two directions: first the sheer cost of the new buildings and equipment required, including the discovery of well qualified teachers to man them, and secondly and more importantly the cost of student scholarships. In the inter-war period and especially in the 1960's the practice had grown up of granting state or local authority scholarships to all who could pass the entrance requirements, and whose parents' income was below a certain not very high figure. This was already expensive in 1946 when the number of students was 54,600, it was becoming a serious drain by 1966 when the number had risen to 168,600. It would seem that either some cheaper method of finance (such as for instance the American student loan system) would have to be found, or a more summary method of education provided, with an inevitable lowering of standards, if indeed even then all the new universities were to justify their continued existence.

The new Social Security system, dating from the late 1940's, developed out of the war-time Report of the (Beveridge) Interdepartmental Committee on Insurance and Allied Services. A number of new benefits were introduced (most importantly Maternity, Death, Sickness, Family Allowances, and Child Care). Of these only the Sickness benefit called for large out-payments (reaching £264 m. by 1966). In the second place, as was inevitable due to the rise in the cost of living, rates of pensions were raised

and the coverage widened.[1] The monetary result of these changes
was that whereas Pensions, which in 1950 had cost £303 m. by 1956
were costing £489 m. and by 1966 £1426 m. (it is interesting and
significant that they had been running neck and neck with education, which in 1950 cost £302 m. on current account, in 1956
£492 m. and in 1966 £1446 m.). Education is a dynamic forward
looking type of expenditure and this cannot be claimed for Pensions.
Moreover the pensionable age fixed in the middle of the twenties,
has been put entirely out of date by the rise in the expectation of
life (more particularly the choice of age 60 for the retirement of
women). As a result of premature retirement it has been necessary
to gear the income tax so as to tempt back into employment some
of the many able-bodied pensioners—clearly a doubly wasteful
exercise.

The National Health Service came into operation in July 1948
with virtually 100 per cent. subsidization of medical and hospital
services. By 1950 it was costing £401 m., by 1956 £555 m.; and by
1967-8 £1,594 m. on current account, together with more than
£90 m. on capital account. No one doubts the popularity and
general success of the health service, although many who can
afford to do so prefer to continue to make their own arrangements.
To realize the success of the health service it is only necessary to
reflect on the situation, for instance in the U.S.A., where good
conditions for doctors and nurses seem to come before good conditions for patients, where a serious illness in even a well-off middle
class family can spell financial disaster, and where also the treatment available to coloured people is markedly inferior. At the same
time the British Health Service is still inadequate in many respects,
and it is doubtful if the best value is being obtained for its very
considerable costs.[2]

By 1966-7 the three big social services, Education, Pensions, and
Health, were together consuming about 13 per cent. of the national
income. In addition there were a number of other smaller social
outlays, some of which we noted above. The slogan that the state
would look after the individual from the cradle to the grave was no
idle boast. But there is another side to this, in that it implies a

[1] Contrary to the Beveridge recommendations no effort was made to build
up a fund for these, a most regrettable mistake.
[2] Cf. M. S. Feldstein, *Economic Analysis and Health Service Efficiency* (North
Holland Publishing Co.).

degree of paternalism which can easily result in a restriction of the individual's freedom and which is almost inevitably discriminatory in its incidence. Although in a sense the present relation between the state and the individual are just a development of a situation which we have observed since early in the century, it has recently been gathering momentum. A very great extension of the powers of the state (or more precisely the powers of Public Departments) can be traced to the controls introduced in the Second World War such as rationing of food and clothes, conscription, and direction of labour. It must be remembered that at an early stage of the war Britain became to all intents and purposes a planned economy. In spite of the gradual dismantling of the most irksome controls in the early 1950's, much of the mentality remained. Hence it has been deemed necessary to appoint a special officer (the Ombudsman) to check that damage is not being caused to groups or individuals by departmental decisions.

In the industrial field a parallel growth of government power to control and direct remained as a legacy from the war. This was also for the most part a development of what had occurred during the First World War and its immediate aftermath. As recorded in Chapter V agriculture enjoyed a large and expanding array of subsidies as well as an important tax concession in the removal of agricultural land and buildings from the rating system. The later stage of this policy was guaranteed prices to producers and subsidies to keep food prices low to the consumer. Insistence on cheap food was in the direct tradition of the Victorians, but was very different from the food policy of most other countries.

In the 1920's and 1930's there was also increasing aid for industry, discriminating both by type and by plant location. At that time this was motivated almost wholly by the incidence of unemployment. An example was a protective tariff awarded to a small pocket of unemployed button makers, whose market was in fact narrowing due to a sartorial change. It would appear from the Appropriation Accounts that virtually every department was encouraged to show at least some small outlay designed to relieve unemployment; similar pressure was brought to bear on Local Authorities.

Quantitatively much more important were the efforts to assist the 'Special Areas' (see Chapters XII and XIII). Although at the time these efforts were largely ineffective, the precedent set was of first importance. For the full rehabilitation of such areas as South Wales and the North East Coast the upsurge of demand in the Second World War was required. Although in the '30's some miners found employment in the Kent mines and some in the Cowley motor works, many left Wales only to become curb musicians in London. Through the 1950's and 1960's regional policy was carried very much further, partly by tax concessions to firms setting up in selected areas, partly by refusals of Permits to firms which wanted to set up elsewhere, or even sometimes to extend an existing plant in a prosperous area. It is not our concern to evaluate the social implications of such a policy. Economically it can too easily force business into the adoption of 'second best' decisions. There is also the danger of arbitrary decisions, with the inevitable expansion of the personal element in awards.

In the middle 'sixties, in addition to taxation required to pay for the social services, and the cost of agricultural and industrial policies, service of the national debt was also giving some trouble: from a low point of 1·8 per cent. of the national income in 1960-1 it had risen to over 3 per cent. This was partly due to the rise in interest rates, partly to the expansion of debt caused by the demands of the nationalized industries on the Treasury. In principle this should have been no burden on the exchequer, but in practice the charge was by no means negligible, especially in respect of the railways and coal mines. In both these respects Britain was worse off than her competitors who had more completely floated off their war debt burdens by inflation, and who appear to obtain a better result from their public undertakings.

Until the middle 1960's when Britain's balance of payments got into serious trouble this expansion in outlay was financed by tax adjustments and alterations within the economy. We must consequently turn to examine the distribution of the very considerable tax increases, first of the inter-war period, and secondly of the years since 1945. There have only been a few changes in the types of taxes used in Britain, so that we still have to keep our eyes mainly fixed on the development of the large revenue earners of early in the century, that is to say (i) income and surtax on individuals and companies, and including social security contributions, (ii) the traditional customs and excise duties on tobacco and alcohol, and in recent years on oil, including motor fuel. Into this class go also some other miscellaneous customs duties, and more importantly

Purchase Tax, introduced early in the Second World War. Lastly we must consider the two most recent taxes (a) Capital Gains tax and (b) Select Employment Tax which latter first became payable in the autumn of 1966.

When in 1909-10 the Chancellor of the Exchequer added 2d. in the £ to the 1s. income tax, he expressed considerable apprehension concerning its effects on industry; a greater case could be made for this on the 1968 levels of 42½ per cent. on corporations and an all time high (in time of peace) of a standard rate on personal income tax of 8s. 3d. in the £. Surtax has moved faster than the standard rate. In 1920 when the standard rate was still at the wartime maximum of 6s. in the £, 50 per cent. of income was already taxed away on the higher incomes[1] (at something under £23,000). In 1966-7 the 50 per cent. level was reached at the more modest income of £14,240 (and that consisting of much depreciated £s).

Social insurance in 1914-15 required a total weekly stamp (for an adult male worker) of 1s. The additional benefits, especially non-contributory pensions, in the middle 1920's raised this to 2s. 9d. The Welfare State sent it up from 9s. 1d. in 1949-50 to 18s. 2d. in 1960-1 and to 31s. 10d. in 1966-7. Finally liability to Select Employment Tax brought the total tax cost of employing an adult male worker to 37s. 6d. a week. In respect of workers in 'productive industry'—broadly not services—refunds of S.E.T. were, however, available at various rates differing according to the type of industry and to the location of the factory (better conditions in bad areas); there was also a substantial but varying lag between paying the tax and receipt of the repayment.

All of this added greatly to the uncertainty of entrepreneurial planning. The net result on the revenue was that of the revenue collected by S.E.T. about 30 per cent. was expected to be returned, a somewhat wasteful exercise. The objective of S.E.T. was to tax services, which were held to be undertaxed, and perhaps by this means to free labour for industry. In practice many of the firms in the service trades were extremely small and their directors were already paying income and surtax. It is doubtful if much of the labour released finds its way into industry. The capital gains tax owed its origin to the tendency of investors in time of inflation to

[1] Taking the tax limit of a married couple with one child of 10 years. All figures are taken from The British Economy, Key Statistics 1900–1966 except 1968-9 forecasts which are from Financial Statement, 1968.

seek for appreciating stocks rather than for a steady income. In the 1968 budget it was hoped to collect £44 m. by this means; up to that time revenue had been negligible.

The result of all these changes was that the budget estimate for 1968-9 forecast a total revenue of £7,142 m. from 'direct' taxes (including the net figure for S.E.T.). This compares with a forecast of revenue from taxes on outlay of £4,012 m. This was also a very great expansion over the 1936 figure. It was achieved very largely by drastically increasing tax rates on the leading specific duties: tobacco, alcohol, and more recently oil. In addition the field of more general *ad valorem* taxes was widened: in 1932 by the tariff (as recorded in *F.B.G.*) and in 1941 Purchase Tax (a selective sales tax).

In 1914 the rates of tobacco taxes were very light (no more than 3s. 8d. per lb. on the raw material). During the First World War they rose to 8s. 2d. and continued to rise gradually. The sensational change came in the Second World War: from 13s. 6d. in 1939-40 to 35s. 6d. in 1945-6. In the 50's they reached 61s. 2d. By 1967-8, 87s. 4½d. had been attained with a further small increase announced in the 1968 budget. The rise in alcohol duties was hardly less spectacular. By 1965-6 the 14s. 9d. of 1914 had become 292s. The relative increase in beer duty was even steeper. Petrol tax first appeared in 1909/10 at 3d. a gallon. At the end of the First World War (as recorded in *F.B.G.*) it was allowed to lapse completely, reappearing in 1928-9 (at 4d.). In 1950 it became 1s. 6d. and in the 1968 budget 3s. 11d. Complementary with petrol and oil taxes are the motor vehicle duties (one on the usage and the other broadly on the size of the vehicle). As the number of motor vehicles increased the revenue automatically responded. In fact, however, rates were allowed to drop in the 1950's and it was not until 1968 that they were fully restored.

Although the abandonment of free trade for a general tariff was a momentous step in British tax history,[1] in practice the revenue effect has not been very great, first because of Britain's adherence to G.A.T.T. (the General Agreement on Trade and Tariffs) and secondly because the yield of the new customs duties has been overshadowed by that of purchase tax. When this tax was first introduced its revenue was held down by rationing and trading difficulties (in 1946 it was no more than £161 m.). During the

[1] See below, pp. 240 ff.

1950's the (*ad valorem*) rates were kept high and the revenue rapidly expanded. From the middle 1960's, however, there was a general move to simplify and reduce rates, even perhaps to the extent of substituting a general sales tax at lower rates. This might indeed be a better instrument for the control of consumption than the highly selective purchase tax.[1] Policy was, however, reversed in the 1968 budget and it was planned to collect £877 m. from purchase tax—£140 m. higher than the previous record.

How effective were these increases in the rates of taxes? In 1913 tobacco taxes yielded not much more than a quarter of the alcohol duties, but from that point they gradually came together. By 1936 alcohol revenue was only half what it had been in 1920 while tobacco was 50 per cent. higher. The big change came, however, with the Second World War. In 1946 alcohol brought in £364 m., tobacco £438 m. By 1956 alcohol had reached £416 m. but tobacco revenue had jumped to £685 m. In 1965 it topped the £1,000 m. mark. The relative change in the experience of these types of taxes is largely to be explained by a change in tastes and in particular to the spread of smoking among women. Alcohol revenue is unlikely to touch the £1,000 m. mark, although in the most recent period there has been some revival of the demand for wines and spirits. The rise in the revenue from oil duties has been spectacular. Over the ten years from 1956 to 1966 the revenue climbed from £333 m. to £856 m. For 1968 it was forecast that it would exceed £1,000 m. In most years the out-turn has been above the estimate, a sure sign of an expanding revenue source. But there is another side to this success story.

In many countries the taxation of motoring goes to improve the roads. This was the original idea in Britain and a Road Fund was established into which the taxes would be paid. In the 1920's, however, the combined effect of petrol tax and vehicle duties exceeded what was thought necessary for road finance; hence Churchill was able to 'raid' the accumulated surplus of the Road Fund in order to present a nominally balanced budget. In spite of this exercise at this period expenditure on roads was less than tax receipts on motoring: it was not until 1933-4 that they became equal (see p. 145). During the depression years road-building was a form of expenditure favoured by the Labour Party—in the interests of employment, not of road users. Hence the location of road works was determined by

[1] Such is the view of O.E.C.D. economists.

the state of local unemployment, not of traffic needs. By the early 1950's, with minimal unemployment, Labour had lost interest in road works while the costs of the establishment of the Welfare State left scant resources for other improvements. Expenditure on roads in 1950 was no more than £85 m. (in depreciated pounds) compared with £79 m. in 1931: by 1956 outlay still had not exceeded £90 m. It was not until the launching of the Motorway programme that expenditure on roads really began to expand (1960 £111 m., 1966 £242 m.). Meanwhile the number of the vehicles on the road was growing fast. In 1936 it had been no more than 2,146,000; by 1960 there were 7,090,000, and by 1966 10,850,000. Nevertheless taxation continued to run ahead of road works (£912 m. in 1966, and an estimated £1,238 m. after the budget changes of 1968).

The idea that motor taxation should be ear-marked for road expenditure has not indeed much to recommend it. Motor vehicles as such are a perfectly eligible subject for general taxation. But the existence of a separate account does encourage the formation of a rational road development programme. When the rapid rise in the number of vehicles took place there was no co-ordinated plan and virtually no research, either into techniques or into desirable priorities. The Motorway programme has made a certain amount of research inevitable; but much still remains to be done, especially in respect of the co-ordination of motorways and entrances to city street systems. As already stated I foresaw the necessity for a co-ordinated plan for road development, and endeavoured to sketch a rational method of determining priorities—a sort of primitive cost/benefit system (cf. Chapter VIII).

From the point of view of both economic and social policy it is interesting to compare the performance of the group of taxes on income and capital with that of the taxes on outlay, or as I called them then Commodity taxes (this was a bad name as one must also include taxes on the services of durable goods, such as houses and motor vehicles). Table A shows this for selected years for the whole period:

TABLE A

(£ million)

Taxes on:	1913	1923	1928	1936	1950	1956	1966	1968	1968[1]
Incomings[2]	88	440	407	429	1,847	2,364	4,479	6,430	6,657
Outlay	76	279	278	352	1,589	2,086	3,617	3,734	4,012
Local rates	80	163	191	197	338	556	1,353	?	?
Rates + outlay taxes	156	442	469	549	1,927	2,642	4,970		

In respect of both types of tax Britain is in a very similar position to Germany, but in France direct taxes are very much lower and outlay taxes higher.[3] It is notable that neither Germany nor France put so much weight on a few leading levies as Britain. France gathers most of her revenue from the tax on Value Added; Germany has been using a straight turnover tax, but in conformity with the policy of the European Community must change over to Value Added.

Before we leave these questions a word must be said concerning the local rate. This sole independent tax source of local authorities is a levy on the occupancy of land and buildings (with as we have seen exemption for agricultural land from 1929). It has had a peculiar career. In 1913 when government grants to local authorities were negligible local rate receipts exceeded the whole of central government outlay taxes. A heavy burden had been thrown on local authorities by the Education Act of 1902. As will be seen from Table A rate receipts doubled between 1913 and 1923. The Local Government Act of 1929 afforded some temporary relief, and in 1934 local authorities lost some of their responsibility for public assistance. This process of transferring responsibility of what was at once the heaviest and most disequalizing charge on local authorities was completed in 1948. At the same time a new Equalization Grant was introduced which gave sub-normal local authorities the opportunity to spend up to the national average. Other grants were also extended; nevertheless as late as 1950 rates (at £338 m.) exceeded grants (at £298 m.). In the 1960's, however, grants have regularly exceeded rates as a source of local revenue.

This relative failure of the rate to stand up to the complexities of modern local government raises the whole question of the future

[1] After budget changes.
[2] Including death duties, minor Inland Revenue duties, and for the last year Capital Gains.
[3] Cf. National Accounts of O.E.C.D. Countries, 1957–66.

of democratic local government finance and organization. Already in the 1930's, as we have seen, difficulties were apparent, due to the small size of many local jurisdictions, more particularly in continuously built up areas such as South-east Lancashire and Tyneside. Some improvement was brought about by concentrating responsibility for Education in the Counties and County Boroughs; but this did not touch the general problem. On the other hand the London County Council was already pointing the way to a means of dealing with organization and finance in a 'metropolitan' area, although its very limited size became increasingly inadequate for the purpose as London continued to spread. In this respect the substitution of the Greater London Council was a decided improvement, although it equally did not solve the problem of overspill. Problems of metropolitan areas have now become of increasing concern in all the advanced countries. Clearly every nation must tackle them in accordance with its own traditions and ideology. So far as Britain is concerned it may well be that the answer will be found in a more or less 'federal' authority covering a complete urban complex and its surroundings.[1] (The G.L.C. is already more 'federal' than the L.C.C.)

So far we have been concerned almost entirely with Britain's internal finances; but we cannot altogether neglect her position in the world economy, especially since this was raised in an acute form in 1931 and again in 1967-8. How far, we should briefly ask, is the world a different place for Britain today from what it was in the 1920's and 1930's, and how does this affect her finances? Since the inter-war years two changes of general economic importance have occurred, amounting almost to revolutions. These have affected different countries in different ways, but on Britain the alteration in her world position to which they contributed has been particularly important. The revolutions are respectively (i) that in transport and communications and (ii) what has become known as the managerial revolution. The two are related, since it is largely the revolution in communications which has made modern managerial methods possible.

In the 1930's the communications revolution was only beginning to make itself felt. In the U.S.A. the generalization of the automobile had already taken place. The long distances to be travelled implied that good roads, 'turnpikes', had to be constructed for it.

[1] Cf. pp. 178 ff.

In Britain by the early 1930's most middle class people had a family car and a good deal of freight was also going by road. The railways were already suffering from competition, but neither this nor the parking problem were serious. As we have seen, serious road building to meet the new situation did not begin until the middle 1960's.

The big transport revolution which occurred between the middle '30's and the '60's was, however, in air travel. In the early '30's it was an adventure to fly even to Paris; longer flights, probably by flying boat, required frequent overnight stops. The war was the cataclyst which, starting from the simple propeller plane led to the faster turbo-prop and the still faster jet, bringing speeds from some 250 m.p.h. to over 600 (not to anticipate supersonic speeds). Far distant places came close together; international conferences of all sorts became daily occurrences and business management found that it could control the activities of plants and firms all across Europe (and increasingly also across the Atlantic).

There had indeed been some very big firms before the Second World War, especially in the U.S.A., notwithstanding the anti-trust laws; but in Europe also there were giants like the Anglo-Dutch Unilever, which assumed its present form in 1928. But the organization of these giants was essentially the same as that of many other, smaller, integrated many-process firms. The modern multi-national organization is essentially different. Affiliated firms in different countries produce components which are then brought together for assembly elsewhere, not necessarily in the country in which any of the components are manufactured. Something like 30 per cent. of British exports appear now to represent transactions between such international affiliates.

This new pattern of international trading implies that the operations of an affiliate within a country are much less within reach of government controls (fiscal and monetary) than those of an un-affiliated national firm. Two factors in particular have made this revolution possible: first air freight, enabling such things as mach-ine parts to be flown quickly and economically from the country where they can most efficiently be made to the country where it is most convenient to assemble them. In such circumstances one step in the process cannot be stopped or slowed down without en-dangering the entire output, and inflicting much greater losses than would be the case with a national firm. The second and interlocking factor is the managerial (or administrative) revolution. With the general improvement in statistical techniques and above all with the development of the computer—a matter of hardly more than twenty years—it has become possible to keep detailed track of all relevant transactions, wherever in the world they may occur, and so to take efficient and co-ordinated policy decisions, which at the same time need not be stultifying at the unit management level, since it too can have all the relevant information.

The new management techniques are equally applicable to public undertakings, and it would seem urgent to apply them to the British very large and multi-product nationalized industries. It is essential that these should make a better economic showing than they have done in the past, or than they are doing today in comparison with the success of other countries, notably Sweden and Germany.

With her long tradition of skilled workmanship and largely successful switching to a new industrial structure in place of the nineteenth-century coal and cotton economy, Britain should have the possibility of maintaining a strong position in the world. Inevitably the British economy has been the victim of a slow process of relative shrinkage of stature. To this several causes have contributed: on the financial side the emergence of New York as a premier world financial centre dating from the establishment of the Federal Reserve system in 1913, on the economic side the delayed development of other countries, especially Germany, which was already cutting into British trade by the turn of the century, and more recently of Japan. This process has thus been a long period affair, but there is little doubt that of recent years it has been gathering momentum.

The emancipation of her colonies and the consequent weakening of the sterling area and of the overseas markets for British goods has been an important contributory factor, although it should be noted that few if any of the Colonies (and certainly not India) were still 'paying' propositions. British policy in cutting the Colonies uncompromisingly adrift much more drastically than for instance France (at least in Africa), has hastened the process and led to a decline in British invisible exports of services, which traditionally paid for her necessary imports of food. With the change in the channels of trade due to the transport revolution and to changes in relative growth rates this situation was bound to become more marked. Britain's position in the world had already begun to decline by 1920. The character of the sterling crisis of 1967-8 compared with that of 1931 is in some sense a measure of the further decline that has taken place. The manner in which the government sought to meet the crisis on the two occasions is also of interest from the point of view of the development of internal policy.

The crisis of 1931 was set off by the collapse of an Austrian bank, not in itself very important although it was effectively the credit centre for middle and eastern Europe. Had there been a strong world monetary leader, as London had been in the 1890's, there is little doubt but that it could have organized a consortium of international finance houses which would have contained the trouble until it could be effectively dealt with. Exactly this was done in the Baring crisis of 1890. But in 1931 London was no longer the undisputed financial leader, and Britain was herself under grave international suspicion on account of what was then regarded as large scale international borrowing to finance unemployment pay. New York was in no position to help; Americans had been lending heavily in Latin America, with very poor cover, and at home everyone seemed to be in debt and illiquid. The Federal Reserve System had not the flexibility to expand its lending that was available to the Bank of England through the possibility of a 'Treasury Letter' authorizing it to do so. And so the failure of the little Credit Anstalt became a disastrous world wide monetary collapse.

The reaction of the British government was quick and decisive (cf. pp. 14 ff.). The situation was sufficiently serious: there was a prospective current account deficit of £75 m. with one more than double that size looming up for the following year. A second budget was introduced in the second week of September, with provision for completing all its stages within ten days. Taxation was heavily increased, 70 per cent. of this fell on direct taxes and the remainder on the big outlay taxes: beer, tobacco, petrol, and entertainments. Income tax went up from 4s. 6d. in the £ to 5s. and surtax 10 per cent. throughout its range. All allowances were reduced. At the same time the devaluation of the £ within a short period was announced.

Opinions differ as to the wisdom and success of this policy. Unemployment only gradually declined, and in some ways the internal situation recovered more slowly than the international. But it was scarcely conceivable that Britain could stage a full scale recovery on her own, while the rest of the world, and particularly the U.S.A., remained in chaos. Important merits can, however, be claimed for the policy. Maximum use was made of the 'impact' effect, and the nation responded magnificently. Tough measures were taken on the chin and national self-confidence quickly restored, so that no further deflationary action was necessary. To illustrate this I may perhaps be allowed to quote Snowden's words (cf. p. 14):

"Old age pensioners have returned their pension books, war pensioners have offered to forego their pensions for a year, National Savings Certificates have been returned cancelled, Postal orders large and small pour in. Children have sent from their savings boxes shillings and half crowns to help the nation in its need."

As a result of this prompt action no further deflationary measures were necessary; it may well be that the total amount of deflation required was thereby minimized.

All this was in strong contrast to the policy followed in 1967-8, when a delay of six months was allowed to elapse between the announcement of deflationary measures and their implementation. The intervening 'spending spree' not merely caused a further deterioration in the international situation, but also made it much more difficult to persuade the public that the position was serious. Hence further doses of deflation were unavoidable, as might not have been necessary if strong measures had been taken immediately.

At the same time the difference between the position in which Britain found herself in 1931 and 1967 must not be overlooked. In 1931 the crisis on the Continent and in the U.S.A. *preceded* the British troubles. Once British internal confidence was restored and it was seen that the government had the situation in hand, international confidence returned quickly. In relation to other countries Britain appeared to be uniquely strong. Her international prestige was higher than ever in a world that continued to crumble. The effect of the devaluation was consequently immediately successful. In 1967 the U.S.A. was in the midst of an intense war boom. Britain's place in the Growth League was poor relative to the E.E.C. countries; although they had their difficulties these had not shown up seriously at the time of the British crisis. Confidence in the British economy was sadly lacking and in spite of high interest rates London had only a very weak drawing power. The effects of devaluation were clouded, and government spending continued at a high rate.

The second budget of 1931 was based on no more than an intelligent hunch that something drastic had to be done, and done quickly. Action in 1967-8 was delayed in order to evaluate from the National Accounts the exact degree of inflation that would be required. Given the inevitable lag in obtaining the figures and the dynamic symptoms of the disease, such an exercise had not a very high chance of definitive success. A lesson may perhaps be drawn from these experiences: in a crisis even the best system of accounts may not be a perfect substitute for commonsense and intelligent thought.

This is not to decry the usefulness of the—essentially Keynesian —practice of social accounting, which as we have seen was introduced in Britain in 1941 and has since spread to (at least) all the advanced countries. It merely suggests that in itself social accounting methods do not provide a quick enough instrument to deal with a crisis. In order to meet this difficulty Sweden has adopted the system of voting alternative budgets at the beginning of the year to look after every eventuality. It may be that this would be an improvement in Britain, but the greater complication of the British economy as compared to the Swedish must be borne in mind. There is also the unsettled state of the world in 1969 to reckon with. However, if countries behave themselves, with the present degree of willingness for international co-operation, especially on the monetary side, and the much greater statistical knowledge of the situation, only serious mismanagement could again plunge the world into the monetary abyss of 1931.

URSULA K. HICKS

Oxford, February 1969

PREFACE

THE attempt to include within a single volume the whole of the field of Public Finance during the eventful years which intervened between the end of the War and the beginning of rearmament, calls for some explanation and perhaps for some apology. It is now generally agreed that the great extension of government influence on the economic system necessitates a much more thorough treatment of the economic aspect of public finance than was called for in the nineteenth century. It has become essential to pay much more attention to expenditure policy on the one hand, and secondly, to the economic—as distinct from the social—effects of taxation. Further, public borrowing and monetary policy are now an essential part of public finance, and cannot successfully be divorced from fiscal and expenditure policy.

Many of the effects of public finance can only work themselves out over a considerable period. Economists have always been aware of this, and so there is probably little new to say here, except in so far as the extension of public activity has led to an acceleration of change. On the other hand, the great amount of recent research on the trade cycle has brought into the light many short period problems in the field of public finance which were only half perceived before. Every one wishes to see recent theoretical discoveries embodied in a new and far-seeing economic policy; but a necessary preliminary to formulating such a policy is a realization of the features of the existing situation. To do this thoroughly it will be necessary to accumulate a corpus of studies of individual aspects of the subject—regional surveys of such matters for instance as the timing of public works or the internal finances of local authorities. Already a beginning of such studies has been made at centres of economic research—enough to reveal the importance of regional differences. But it has seemed to me that there is much to be gained, particularly at the present stage of inquiry, from a conspectus of the whole economy, and consequently from the examination of total figures, which are at the same time relatively easily available.

I am well aware that such a study properly calls for an official investigation, or at the least for the concerted efforts of a research group. I therefore take this opportunity of apologizing in advance for any shortcomings or inaccuracies, either of arithmetic or of technical details, which may have survived revision. Many things in this country which should be the subject of official investigation unhappily get left to private enterprise—such, for instance, as the calculation of the National Income. And it is in the hope that this survey will fill a gap that I have embarked on it.

Since my field was necessarily so extensive, I have taken what steps I could to limit it. Especially on the expenditure side where the mass of available material is almost limitless, severe selection and compression have been inevitable. This means probably that most readers will find some subject, which is dear to them, omitted or summarily dealt with. I can only plead that I have devoted attention to those subjects which seemed to me most important or most interesting. But two particular limitations require to be specially mentioned, since they are fundamental to the whole book. In the first place I have confined myself to those aspects of public policy where money actually passes—from public to private hands or vice versa. On the expenditure side this implies, for instance, that the beet sugar subsidy receives fuller treatment than the agricultural marketing boards. On the taxation side I do not attempt to make an evaluation of the quota system, although naturally it cannot pass unnoticed. My second limitation is that I confine myself strictly to the activities of governmental bodies. This absolves me from examining the ways of such public or semi-public boards as the B.B.C., the Central Electricity Board, and the London Passenger Transport Board. This limitation is the less serious since a number of useful investigations of such bodies have recently been published.

Finally I should say that I have throughout concentrated as much as possible on straightforward economic considerations. Such a proceeding makes it necessary to omit many questions which, although primarily administrative, have also an important economic aspect. I have in mind discussion of the internal administration of public departments such as that contained in the reports of the Committee on Public Accounts and the Cadman Commission of Civil Aviation. Many of these subjects urgently require investigation, but they do not strictly belong to my field.

I have endeavoured to refrain from the use of economic jargon, and to use even such unavoidable terms as 'inflation' and 'deflation' as sparingly as possible, and only where their obvious meaning as expanding (or contracting) the national income in money terms was quite evident. I have also avoided the use of abbreviations, except well known ones such as the initials of the *Economic Journal*, the *Journal of the Royal Statistical Society*, and the *Journal of Political Economy*. I have tried to keep the text reasonably clear of obstructions by relegating most of the figures to the ends of the chapters, or to the appendix.

I should perhaps say that the substance of this book was written before the end of 1937—consequently before Sir John Simon's budget of 1938 proceeded to put into practice several of the suggestions in Part II, before the announcement of the Ministry of Health's scheme for public works plans by local authorities, and before the publication of the Bressey Road Plan for London. But much still requires to be done.

It only remains to thank the many friends who have assisted with this work at various stages. Originally undertaken as a piece of research with a Leverhulme Grant, at the London School of Economics, the work must acknowledge a first debt to Professor L. C. Robbins, my supervisor there. To Mr. D. H. Robertson, of Trinity College, Cambridge, I am very grateful for having been kind enough to read through the whole of Part III, in manuscript, and to Mrs. Tappan Hollond, of Girton College, for performing a similar office for Part II. I have also to make acknowledgements to Mr. R. F. Bretherton, of Wadham College, Oxford, for a number of useful suggestions, particularly concerning local investment; and to Professor Erik Lindahl, of Göteborg, for allowing me to make use of his taxation studies, and for information on the reform of the Swedish budget. The debt which I owe to my husband, Dr. J. R. Hicks, is too wide to be acknowledged in detail, but there are two points which I should specially like to mention, since they impinge directly on the book which he was simultaneously writing —namely the discussion on consumer's surplus which is involved in chapter XV, and that on the effects of public borrowing in chapter XX. Owing to the highly controversial nature of many of the subjects with which I am concerned, none of these people can be held in any way responsible for the views I have expressed.

U. K. H.

May 1938.

CONTENTS

INTRODUCTORY

PART I. EXPENDITURE

PART II.   TAXATION

CONTENTS xli

LIST OF DIAGRAMS

INTRODUCTORY

'But a fuller and a fairer symbol of Taxation, both in its possible good and evil Effects, is to be found in the Evaporation of Waters from the surface of the Planet. The Sun may draw up the moisture from the River, the Morass, and the Ocean, to be given back in genial Showers to the Garden, the Pasture, and the Cornfield, but it may likewise force away the moisture from the fields of Tillage, to drop it on the stagnant Pool, the saturated Swamp or the unprofitable Sand-waste. The gardens in the South of Europe supply, perhaps, a not less apt illustration of a system of Finance judiciously conducted, where the Tanks or Reservoirs would represent the Capital of a Nation, and the hundred Rills hourly varying their channels and directions under the Gardener's spade, give a pleasing image of the dispersion of that capital through the whole Population by the joint effect of Taxation and Trade. For Taxation itself is a part of Commerce, and the Government may be fairly considered as a great manufacturing house carrying on in different places, by means of its Partners and Overseers, the Trade of the Ship-builder, the Clothier, the Iron-Founder, &c., &c.'
COLERIDGE.

I

THE BUDGETS AND THE CHANCELLORS

IN the financial sphere the war ended not in 1918 but in 1920. The decisive engagement opened with the announcement by the chancellor of the exchequer, Austen Chamberlain, that the 1920 budget must and would be balanced. This was not the first step which had been taken to restore order out of chaos. The previous December for instance a maximum had been fixed for the note issue. Nor was it by any means the end of the campaign. In spite of economies, the total budget in 1920 reached the enormous figure of £1,195 m., or more than six times that of 1913–14. For the time being inflation proceeded little less rapidly than it had done in the previous year. The cost of living did not pass its maximum until November 1920. The price of consols touched its nadir in December, and the floating debt continued to expand until June 1921. Nevertheless, at the end of the financial year the budget was balanced, with a (nominal) surplus of £230·6 m. It is true that the items composing this remarkable figure would not all bear a close scrutiny from an orthodox financier; but it was a conspicuous change from the deficit of £326·2 m. realized in April 1920. The budget speech of 1920 was a highly significant reassertion of the principle of orthodox finance—a principle that was to be flouted not a little by certain of the post-war chancellors, but which in the end has always been confirmed as the foundation of British tradition.

This then is the starting-point for our story. It may appear at first sight that the events of 1920 have as little relevance to the conditions of the 1930's as those of 1913. In one sense this is true. The economic and financial situation underwent considerable modifications between 1920 and 1936. Indeed, the period breaks up rather easily into three sub-periods—1920–4, 1925–31, and 1931–6—each of which has markedly different characteristics from the others. By 1924 the real national income per head had roughly recovered to the level of 1914.[1] Other statistical evidence also indicated that the immediately disturbing effects of the war had passed over. Thus 1924 may be considered as the end of the reconstruction period. The re-establishment of the gold standard in April 1925 emphasized the return to normal conditions, but it also marked the beginning of a new period in which the economic and financial alinement of the post-war world became more apparent than it had been in the chaos of the earlier years. This sub-period ended decisively with three disturbing factors—the depression of 1931, the abandonment of the gold standard, and the conversion of the war debt. For a period of national strain and international ease was substituted one of international strain, but at home a return to something like pre-war prosperity.

In an important sense, however, we were still in the post-war world until 1937. The decisive break occurred when the community came under the influence of rearmament. This was a new force of first-rate, although of incalculable, importance. But if the period 1920–36 is essentially one, it does not stand alone. Not only do the events of the early twenties cast their shadow on the later years, but account must also be taken of the pre-war world. Up to 1914, in spite of the political volcano towards which the country was drifting, economics and finance remained much as they had been for generations. The armaments race had not seriously disturbed either general or relative price- and wage-levels. The tax structure had only been slightly modified since Victorian days. If we look carefully, however, often as far back as the nineties we can discern in some, perhaps in most directions, the beginning of changes which blossomed with disconcerting suddenness as soon

[1] Cf. Bowley and Stamp, *The National Income 1924.*

as hostilities ceased. We have only to think of the growth of municipal activity before 1900, and the expansion of social expenditure by the central government from 1906. In social policy development was continuous, although the war caused a certain irregularity. In the economic and financial spheres, however, the break made by the war was decisive; and from the relations established during and after the war there has been comparatively little return to those existing in 1914.[1] For instance, wage statistics show that while there had been by 1936 some small return to the prewar relation between skilled and unskilled labour, by and large relative rates had remained as established during the war. And what concerns us more nearly, in spite of the fall in prices, budgets and taxes were still of war dimensions. There has been no return to the levels of 1914.

If there is something to be said for writing political history in terms of the prime ministers, an even better case can be made for writing financial history in terms of the chancellors of the exchequer. Financial history in these fifteen years presents a personal problem of exceptional interest. If we neglect for a moment the two budgets of Sir Robert Horne and the one of Mr. Baldwin, both in the reconstruction period, we find that financial history since 1920 is written round the names of Churchill, Snowden, and Chamberlain.[2] In interest it is at least comparable to the days of the great Victorians, in incident it is incomparably richer.

The budgets of the reconstruction period need not detain us long. They were presented in turn by Austen Chamberlain in 1920 and 1921 (on the latter occasion acting for Sir Robert Horne, who was, however, said to be the real author of the budget), by Sir Robert Horne in 1922, by Mr. Baldwin in 1923, and by Snowden in 1924. At the beginning of the period finances were in such a chaotic condition that estimates were frequently wild. Receipts on particular items might differ by millions in either direction. In these circumstances normal budgeting was impossible, and financial administration cannot be criticized very closely. Moreover, the rapid turnover of chancellors militated against the development of any particular line of policy. Such matters of interest as emerge from the early budgets are mainly significant as pointers rather than themselves of much importance.

[1] 'The Course of Wage Rates in the U.K. 1921–34', E. C. Ramsbottom. *J.R.S.S.* iv, 1935.   [2] Including both Austen and Mr. Neville Chamberlain.

In 1920 Austen Chamberlain was presenting his fourth and last (personal) budget. It was therefore his own policy of the previous year that he was implicitly condemning in announcing that the budget must be balanced. In spite of its high resolutions, however, this was still mainly a war budget. The estimated bill for military services (including war pensions) was well over £600 m., or more than three-quarters of the entire budget ten years later—and 1930 was not itself a year of small spending. Chamberlain was taking no risks with the revenue. He continued to exploit the wartime best payers—a 6s. income tax, an increase of super-tax for the direct payer, and of beer and tobacco duties for the indirect.

But the revenue side of the budget contained four innovations of future portent. 1919–20 had witnessed boom conditions over the whole industrial field. It was in the hope of turning some of these profits into the exchequer, as well as those 'war fortunes' which were still available, that the excess profits duty was raised from 40 to 60 per cent., a new corporations profits duty was imposed, and the stamp duties on stock exchange transactions raised. This was an interesting attempt to tax the boom, although it was made too late. Secondly, the petrol duty was abolished and the system of licence duties on motor vehicles was increased and revised. Thirdly, the basis of income tax was changed for the smaller incomes. The Royal Commission on the Income Tax[1] had recommended that not only should allowances be given for children and other dependants on a more ample scale than previously, but that a differential in favour of earned income should be introduced. The extension in the post-war period of this principle of ability to pay goes far to explain the curious form which the British tax structure now assumes.[2] Finally, although there was in 1920 no question of a general tariff—no one then doubted the feasibility of rebuilding Britain's overseas markets on the free-trade system under which they had grown up—Austen Chamberlain did not disguise his liking for protection. His impassioned speech on the advantage of a tariff, both as a means of redressing the relations between direct and indirect taxes and as a stimulus to production, was indeed a portent. For the time being, however, the only result of his championship of the principle of protection was a continuation of the war-time 'McKenna' duties, and a crop of stillborn safeguarding duties.

[1] Royal Commission on the Income Tax, 1920.   [2] Cf. Chap. XVI, pp. 269 ff.

In the budget discussions of 1920 there was little talk of the need for economy, and little direct retrenchment occurred during the year. Since all taxes had proved resilient it was confidently expected that they would continue to bring in good returns. When Lord Rothermere complained that two such budgets would destroy the Empire, Chamberlain retorted that they would redeem the whole of the national debt. But the post-war boom proved a great deal shorter than any one—including the chancellor—had anticipated. Its collapse was hastened by a swift rise of Bank Rate to 7 per cent. in the spring of 1920. The index of ordinary share values had already begun to decline in the early months of the year: it was followed some six months later by the index of physical production.

The two somewhat timid budgets of Sir Robert Horne which followed contained nothing new in principle and little of interest. It was not his fault that excess profits duty had produced over £70 m. less instead of (as had been hoped) some £10 m. more than the year before, or that the corporations profits tax had brought profit to no one but the accountants. It is significant, however, that the chancellor could think of no better method of overcoming economic difficulties than giving a large direct subsidy to the coal industry. He further decided to assist production by taking 1s. off the income tax. In principle this was a wise step in depression. At the same time it was doubtful whether the moment for large tax reductions had yet arrived. The budget was still a long way short of being balanced out of revenue. Ominously also at this moment the shadow of the war-debt service began to disturb the country's finances. The early cheap war borrowings were beginning to mature. Some at least of them had to be transferred to a long-term security, although to do so necessarily added to both the principal and interest of the debt. As long as the boom lasted it had been possible to neglect the claims of economy, but with tax receipts everywhere lagging behind estimates, some definite action had to be taken. Through the activity of the Geddes Committee, which presented a number of recommendations, culminating in a final report in 1922, the civil service was reduced to a peace-time footing, and by these means the budget was scaled down to more reasonable proportions. In 1920 the total had been nearly £1,200 m. In 1922 it barely exceeded £810 m. In the meantime, however, prices had fallen heavily (the index of wholesale prices had fallen from 326 to 160), so that economy was more apparent than real.

The financial year 1923 was chiefly notorious for the somewhat unfelicitous settlement of the American debt. Although the terms were stiff, the reduction in uncertainty which the settlement achieved was a good in itself. Judged by standards which had ruled up to the war the terms were not ungenerous. It could not, and probably should not, be judged on the basis of the sort of terms debtors were obtaining at the end of the decade. In most respects, however, Mr. Baldwin's financial administration was both lucky and clever. The recovery from the depression—almost as rapid as had been the down swing—had allowed him to inherit a handsome surplus which considerably smoothed his path. As might be expected, the budget was the least provocative of the whole post-war series. Small concessions were made both in income tax and in some commodity duties. A determined and highly successful drive to recover tax arrears was made. As the *Economist* remarked, firms had no better use for their idle funds during depression than to pay them over to the exchequer. Thus the causes both of financial integrity and of reducing idle balances were served. Expanding exports and increased confidence brought the price of consols to near 60. It was to be eight years before they again touched such a point. In one respect, however, Mr. Baldwin misjudged the temper of the country. In spite of Austen Chamberlain's rebuff two years previously there were undoubtedly large interests in the country which saw in a tariff the only hope of reducing the burden of direct taxes. But the country as a whole was not yet prepared to abandon free trade, and on this rock the conservative government foundered.

We may either view Mr. Snowden's first budget in 1924 as a continuation of the Baldwin régime of financial orthodoxy, or as the first act of his own later more extended régime, for it is both. If we consider both the tax and expenditure sides it is on balance rather the former, and necessarily so since the labour party was in a minority position. In indirect taxation the reductions made by Mr. Baldwin were carried further—notably in entertainments tax and beer duty. But in increasing the allowances for housekeepers in income tax and more importantly in his short shrift with 'breakfast table' duties, the only genuine free-trade chancellor of the post-war period appeared in his true colours. It will be more convenient, however, to deal with Snowden's policy as a whole in connexion with his second term of office, and to pass on immediately to Mr. Churchill's administration.

Mr. Churchill presented five consecutive budgets, for which as a series, and even individually for the dullest of them, the only epithet is dramatic. New measures of first-rate importance such as contributory pensions and the reform of the system of local taxation, as well as suggestions for new tax experiments and devices of unprecedented ingenuity for balancing the budget, fell in quick succession on the ears of a fascinated House. Among the larger innovations small fry, such as the first appearance of that old man of the sea, assistance to the sugar-beet industry, and a batch of unrelated import duties, attracted relatively little attention. And this even though their author avowed some of them to be 'shamelessly protective'. (It will be recalled that he had been returned as the free trade member for Epping in the parliament of 1924.) But the greatest event of the administration was after all a purely monetary measure—the return to the gold standard in April 1925. This was the dramatic secret which Mr. Churchill selected to open his series of budgets.

The Contributory Pensions Act also saw the light in 1925. In itself no new idea, the moment chosen for the introduction of so large an extension of the social services was, to say the least of it, audacious. Further, like the derating scheme introduced two years later, it proved a pig in a poke in the sense that its full cost considerably exceeded the original estimates. Unforeseen difficulties of definition and anomalies of treatment both played a part in this. In 1926, although no spectacular measures were introduced to compare with those of 1925, expansion in a number of lines were foreshadowed. It is worth briefly examining these, since they illustrate aptly the scope of Mr. Churchill's activity.

The budgets of 1925 and 1926 go together in the sense that the expenditure started in 1926 was a continuation of the policy already announced in 1925. These two budgets set the pace for the rest of Mr. Churchill's régime, and indeed for that of his successor. 1925, however, was the decisive year, since it saw, on the one hand, a measure—the restoration of the gold standard—which at best was likely to be mainly restrictive in its operation, and on the other, the inauguration of a large programme of expansion. Thus at the outset of Mr. Churchill's administration the internal contradiction which was to dominate British public finance until 1931 was already established.

Increases in expenditure, 1926–7, due to the parliament of that year

	£ m.
Contributory pensions	5·7
Increase in State share of unemployment insurance .	3·8
Beet-sugar subsidy	1·75
New cruiser campaign	3·7
Coal-mining subvention	4·1
Unemployment insurance in Northern Ireland . .	0·87
Marketing empire produce	0·55
Police pay revision	0·4
Steel houses in Scotland	0·37
New drainage scheme	0·2
Tithe Act, 1925	0·15
Training the unemployed	2·15
	£ m. 23·6

Increases due to previous parliaments

	£ m.
Royal Air Force	2·5
Old Age pensions	1·25
Health insurance	1·93
Housing subsidy	0·57
Land settlement revaluation	0·56
Teachers' pensions	0·5
Oversea settlement	0·5
Imperial War Graves	0·3
Police pensions	0·15
	£ m. 8·3

It is not difficult to find a quite impersonal explanation of the sudden move towards expansion. Economy had seemed necessary in 1922, but it is rarely practised in a community for anything other than very short periods. By 1925 there was a growing pressure for a change of policy. The quick recovery after 1921 had caused depression to be replaced by moderate optimism: high hopes were entertained of the expansion of international trade as a result of the re-establishment of the gold standard: the findings of the Colwyn Committee which drew up its report in 1926, although it was not actually published until the next year, probably acted as a stimulus to optimism.[1] Although they included vague warnings such as that of the probable evil effects of heavy death duties on the rate of saving, the general impression given was that

[1] Committee on National Debt and Taxation.

neither the tax structure nor the war debt were a serious burden on the country. On the contrary the report suggested that the process of income redistribution in favour of the lower classes had made less progress than had usually been thought. Under certain assumptions as to the consumption of a few very highly taxed commodities among the working classes, the tax structure was shown to be heavily regressive at the lower end.[1] These points were ably exploited by labour leaders such as Dr. Dalton and Mr. Pethick Lawrence. The possible effect of heavy taxation on saving was argued to be irrelevant, since it appeared that expansion was in practice being financed out of company reserves. This phenomenon was regarded as a new condition, peculiar to the postwar world. It is probable, however, that the phase which the trade cycle had reached was at least partly responsible for it.

Thus in presenting expansionist budgets Mr. Churchill was swimming with the tide. But on the whole he was gaining on it.

By the time the 1927 budget was introduced the outlook had decidedly changed for the worse. The *Economist* described it as sombre. The coal strike had broken out on 30 April 1926, and was followed by the general strike from 4 to 12 May. Trouble in the coal industry lasted throughout the year. By the third quarter general production had fallen almost to the lowest levels of the depression. In these circumstances the chancellor's policy was viewed with apprehension in more than one quarter. Mr. Hilton Young, Sir Alfred Mond, and a few others had already in 1925 urged that the contemplated expansion of expenditure was incompatible with the gold standard, and the force of this contention was now becoming realized. The industrial troubles of 1926 had made every one aware of the more obvious financial difficulties. In addition far-seeing members of the labour party were already suggesting that a general price fall was probable. Hence, given the apparently inevitable rigidity of interest rates, they rightly argued that the burden of the war debt would shortly become a question of first importance. The idea of a capital levy suggested by the labour party was evidently generally unacceptable. Indeed, the time for the confiscation of windfall profits due to the war was in 1926 already long past. Hence the only way to lighten the debt

[1] Prof. Bowley has recently reminded us that the estimates of consumption were based on a 'not very well informed guess'. Cf. his review of C. Clark, *National Income and Outlay*, *Economica*, Aug. 1937, and Chap. XVI below, pp. 271 ff.

was by genuine economy. Even the chancellor had been forced to take notice of the criticisms of his expansionary programme. The king's speech of December 1925 had foreshadowed a reduction of expenditure, and a cabinet committee was appointed to consider possible victims for the axe. Snowden once remarked that Churchill's economy was the best joke ever perpetrated in the House. The measures which were now suggested—of which the most important was the suppression of certain government departments started in the war—resulted in rearrangement rather than in any net reduction of expenditure.

In 1928 Mr. Churchill introduced his second large-scale extension of budget liability—the derating clauses of the Local Government Bill. The derating scheme, being mainly a transfer to the budget of funds formerly raised by the local authorities, imposed only a slight additional tax burden on the community as a whole. It added, however, some £29 m. to the budget. Judging from the 1929 budget it was Mr. Churchill's intention to launch out once again on a large programme of expansion, had his party remained in office. A scheme for the extension of the rural telephone system was proposed. £6·5 m. was to be devoted to the development of railway transport. The budget was, however, plainly an election manifesto. These measures were never seriously debated. Discussion on the second half of the budget was postponed until the summer, and when the labour party came to office no more was heard of them.

The question that inevitably presents itself is how was it expected to finance these schemes, particularly in the rather unfortunate period in which they were launched? It is here that the true genius of the chancellor, who delighted above all in a 'series of balances nicely adjusted', emerged. It must be borne in mind that he inherited a revenue reduced by over £25 m. through the tax concessions of his predecessor. He further increased his own difficulties by taking a full 1s. off the income tax in 1925. The intention was to finance contributory pensions out of the continuation of the McKenna duties, and derating out of a tax on petrol. While the expansion of the latter proved it in the long run to be one of the best performers on the revenue sheet, at the time the two were quite inadequate for their tasks. Nor were other new experiments, such as the betting tax or various small excursions into the protective field, able to fill the gap. In the circumstances it proved impossible to allow at all fully for the automatic expansion of the new expenditure. The most ingenious devices were required even to cover current needs. The notorious (but later fashionable) 'raids' on the Road Fund (or appropriation of earmarked receipts of past taxation), the use of capital assets to balance current revenue—such as repayments of war debt from our late allies—the anticipation of future tax receipts (by altering the dates at which instalments became due), and even such purely monetary devices as the amalgamation of the treasury and banknote issues—all were grist to the mill.

When labour took office in June 1929 affairs were working up to a crisis in America. Even had the troubles which in September followed quickly on the Hatry crisis and the stock exchange crash not occurred, it was fortunate that the country's finances were to fall once more into the hands of a careful husbandman. Snowden was profoundly opposed to Churchillian financial methods, both temperamentally and as a matter of doctrine. From the outset the new chancellor took a gloomy view of his prospects. He wrote in his *Memoirs*: 'The miracle of the loaves and fishes was a comparatively little thing compared with what I was supposed to do.' Labour members naturally expected their first chancellor to carry out the party programme as expeditiously as possible. But in 1924 his hands had been tied by labour's minority position. And in 1930 it was plain that economy must come first. Although schemes of expansion, mainly directed against the unemployment problem, were pushed on right up to the crash of 1931, Snowden never had a chance to show his ability as a constructive statesman. In no year of his administration could the financial situation have fairly been described as normal. And at the end he had to face the extraordinary task of opposing his lifelong associates in the final struggle for economy. A contemporary comment suggested that 'Martyr or hero is in his make-up'. For a brief moment he had an opportunity given to few statesmen of starring in the double role.

Both Churchill and Snowden rose to their full height in the face of difficulties. But their reaction was very different. For Snowden, the greater the difficulties the greater the orthodoxy. The sinking fund must be maintained actually and not only nominally, whatever the state of trade. The balancing of the budget by temporary expedients should only be used in the direst necessity. There is a phrase which occurs in his *Memoirs*, on his return to the Chancellor's office in 1929, which will serve to sum up his attitude to the national finances: 'I found that Churchill had altered the position of all the furniture in the room. I at once had it replaced.' In general, however, there is no doubt that Snowden was in the best tradition of Victorian finance. We have seen that in the late twenties the labour party was taking a strong line about debt repayment, and this no doubt accounted in part for his highly orthodox attitude to the sinking fund. But in spite of his party affiliations he was never anxious to increase expenditure at a faster rate than the country could afford, much less to introduce new services with an eye to election effect. As he wrote, 'The State has no right to tax any one unless it can show that it can use the money more beneficially and more economically', or, again, 'I am fully aware of the psychological effect of increased taxation, even where no material burden is imposed. Recognizing this I am convinced that an essential factor in ameliorating unemployment is a restoration of a spirit of confidence and enterprise among those now responsible for conducting industry and commerce.' At the same time he looked to a stream of consumer-purchasing as the surest foundation of industrial stability. His chief argument for repealing the 'breakfast table' duties in 1924 was that it would add some £30 m. to the spending power of the community. This, and the labour tradition of cheap food, confirmed him as the most intransigent of free traders, as much as his realization of 'one of the gravest dangers of the tariff system—namely its corrupting influence on politics'. Had the alternative system of quotas been as developed when he wrote these words as it is to-day, there is little doubt that it would have come equally under his censure.

We have seen that the main relaxation of the 1924 budget was on the indirect taxation side. In 1930 not even this was possible. Income tax, super-tax, estate duties, and the beer duty were all raised. Except for the beer duty (and Snowden never had any sympathy for alcoholic consumers), this increase fell almost entirely on the higher incomes. Business and conservative circles, who had in fact got off very lightly under the Churchill régime, were seriously alarmed. High taxation was loudly denounced— the depression was fast gathering momentum, bringing general 'deflation' in its course. It was asserted—and not indeed denied— that the death duties, particularly on agricultural estates, were ruinous. More significant, a proposal to allow in the income-tax return a deduction for the full amount of industrial re-equipment undertaken was only just defeated. Mr. Hilton Young, who had criticized Churchill's expenditure heavily enough at the time, now discovered that his deficits had been illusory. But Snowden had done his worst for the moment. It was evident that without change of national feeling taxation rates could not well be raised. The chancellor's main concern was now to defend social expenditure, and to excuse the rapid cyclical expansion which was taking place in it. He seemed almost unconscious of the significance of the Treasury minute in January 1931, that 'Continued state borrowing on the present vast scale without provision for repayment by the (Unemployment) Fund will quickly call in question the stability of the British financial system'. At the economy debate in February he was strangely abstracted, and boasted that he could write the report of the committee in a day. Nor did the interim report of the Royal Commission on Unemployment Insurance appear to move him. It was now Snowden's turn to declare that current deficits were illusory, and despite previous denunciation he proposed to balance the budget by highly Churchillian methods, optimistically assuming that there would be no further rise in expenditure. The exchange account, a relic of the war, was to provide £20 m., and the acceleration of the remaining income-tax schedules together with another 2d. on the lucrative petrol tax was to do the rest. Most significant of all he allowed and even encouraged a red herring of the most generous dimensions to develop during the budget debates. It is surprising to find that by far the greater part of the discussions at this time of crisis were occupied with the proposed land-value tax. The whole question was debated in a highly abstract and doctrinaire manner, liberal and labour members making full use of the opportunity to ride their favourite hobby horses. This left little room for a considered discussion of the financial situation.

It was in such an atmosphere that 1931 unrolled its ominous course. The publication of the final report of the Commission on Unemployment Insurance, the collapse of the Austrian Credit Anstalt and of the German banks, the Hoover moratorium, and the relentless May report on national expenditure, followed each other in quick succession. After this last event the centre of financial alarm was transferred from the Continent to England, with results that are too well known to require either recapitulation or comment at this stage. Once more Snowden emerged as the champion of the most puritanical economy. Finance (No. 2) Act of 1931 was the budget of 1930 over again but infinitely more drastic. Sacrifices (calculated to be as nearly proportionate to income as possible) were now demanded from all classes in the community, including even those who as subsidy receivers were actually negative taxpayers. It was a bitter end to a labour chancellor's career. Yet it is plain from Snowden's *Memoirs* that the introduction of Finance (No. 2) Bill was the greatest moment in his life. In spite of the break with the majority of his friends which it entailed, and the indefinite postponement of schemes which he had advocated for years, he knew himself to be the national hero, engaged in a task of supreme difficulty, which nevertheless was not entirely uncongenial. With the triumph of a martyr rejoicing in the deaths of the faithful he extolled:

'Old Age Pensioners have returned their Pension Books, War Pensioners have offered to forego their pensions for a year, National Savings Certificates have been returned cancelled, Postal orders large and small pour in. Children have sent from their savings boxes shillings and half crowns to help the nation in its need.'

The nation took its medicine, but it is not a diet on which a country cares to live for long. The next doctor had a new remedy up his sleeve, and on the whole it was accepted with alacrity.

It is tempting to speculate what would have been the effect on the country's finances if, the course of world events being as it was, labour had remained in power in 1924, and the country had had its series of Snowden budgets *before* it was treated to Mr. Churchill's fireworks. In the first place it is very probable that the return to the gold standard would have been less precipitate—if it had been more considered might not the form have been different? Secondly, there is a great likelihood that expenditure would have increased no faster than it actually did under Churchill, though to be sure it would have been more 'social' and less 'economic'— tending directly to increase the purchasing power of small incomes rather than aspiring to increase the profits of industry. It is practically certain that the budget would have been well and truly balanced during those relatively normal years. From the policy expressed in the minority report of the Colwyn Committee it can hardly be doubted that considerably greater efforts would have been made to pay off debt. This should have had a beneficial effect on interest rates, even in the very difficult situation of the late twenties. On the other hand, had Mr. Churchill been at the helm in 1931, as a successor to four years of careful finance, there might have been no internal crisis. His genius was particularly adapted to steering the country's finances through depression with an appearance of balance in the budget, but with a minimum of additional tax burden and deflation.

Still waters succeeded to the dramatic events of 1931. Although recovery from the crisis was slow—unemployment figures did not recede below the two-million mark until October 1933—some improvement was noticeable almost from the moment of the abandonment of the gold standard. The main reason for this was no doubt that the essential step for the restoration of confidence in British finances had already been taken by Snowden in the second budget of 1931. The job had been done so thoroughly that the most conservative chancellor could hardly have wished to amend it. The only important fiscal change introduced by Mr. Neville Chamberlain was the general tariff, opposed to the last by Snowden.

It can scarcely be hoped to give a mature account of events so recent as the administration of Mr. Chamberlain at the exchequer. It is, however, possible to notice certain broad and highly significant ways in which public finance 1931–6 differed from the years preceding it. Broadly Finance (No. 2) Act of 1931 established the war-time taxes at considerably more than war-time rates. Income tax, it was true, was 1s. less than it had been in 1920, but surtax,[1] estate duties, beer and petrol taxes were all substantially higher. The first striking point about the tax structure since 1931 is that in the main these increases were suffered to remain. Income tax after a brief period at 4s. 6d. moved up again to 4s. 9d. in 1936. There was also some relaxation in indirect taxation, but of a minor order, such as a reduction in vehicle licence duties and in the tax on the cheaper seats at entertainments. By far the most important change, however, was the increase in the weight of the indirect tax schedule, caused by the imposition of a general tariff. Since this method of raising revenue has important indirect effects on the power of the community to export, it is not possible to measure its full burden in the same way as that of a self-contained tax. The long-continued fall in the prices of foodstuffs, and the devaluation of the currencies of countries from which

---

[1] The change in name from super- to surtax occurred in 1929.

we mainly import them, served to conceal the direct effect for a considerable time. But it is clear that there was a substantial restoration of the pre-war relation between direct and indirect taxes. A somewhat parallel development took place on the expenditure side. Again the balance was shifted by the development of a new line rather than by the curtailment of existing services. The chief beneficiaries of expansion in the 1924–31 period were consumers of the wage-earning class. The new expenditure was directed to the aid of particular classes of producers. It can hardly be maintained that the standard social services suffered very seriously from this shift of interest. The cuts in unemployment pay were restored at an early date. The administration of the Unemployment Assistance Board appears in practice to have been less restrictive than was originally feared. There has even been a tardy revival of an expansionary programme in the social services.[1] There was a very marked difference, however, between the volume of new social legislation introduced between 1931 and 1937 as compared with the previous five years. Moreover, defence interests as well as social policy may perhaps be detected in certain extensions.

The expansion in economic expenditure in the thirties occupied a smaller place in the budget than did the expansion of social expenditure in the twenties. Direct subsidies to industry totalled £20 m. in 1933. By 1935 they had risen to £28 m.[2] For the class of 'Trade and Industry' in the civil accounts expenditure for 1935 amounted to £17·1 m., as against an original estimate of £11·4 m. The final estimate for 1936 was £18·9 m. The economic programme was in full swing by 1935. The new expenditure budgeted for in that year sufficiently indicates its nature:

	£ m.
Directly included in estimates:	
Tramp shipping	2·0
Ministry of Agriculture	2·1
Milk for children	0·3
Milk subsidy	1·9
Development	1·5
Anticipated:	
Beet sugar	4·0
Cattle subsidy	4·0
Herring ,,	0·5

Expansion continued in 1936. The original estimates for 1937 showed a slight reduction, mainly due to saving on subsidies based

[1] Cf. Chap. IV, pp. 41 ff.   [2] Cf. Chap. IV, p. 66, and Chap. V, p. 90.

on the selling price of commodities. Within four months of the budget, however, these had been fully negatived by new expansion in substantially identical lines.

The importance of an economic programme of the type introduced by the national government far transcends its comparatively small weight in the budget. It must be viewed as part of a widespreading policy of assistance to production, supplementing the work of tariffs, import quotas, and processing taxes (such as the wheat quota payment). Within the country its effects are intentionally sectional, and hence almost necessarily opposed to those of the whole body of consumers[1]—except in so far as they may be generally welcomed as a necessary part of a defence programme. The new orientation of public expenditure is also a further development of a movement which has been apparent ever since the war—the substitution of home interests and investment for international trade and foreign lending. In the early post-war years strenuous efforts were made to revive both international trade and foreign lending. During Mr. Churchill's administration there was a marked slackening off in this policy. For instance the trade facilities guarantees were discontinued on grounds of economy. Since 1931 the cutting of international ties has been so marked as to constitute almost an active policy of isolationism. The decay of international trade has been striking, but the change is even more marked in the sphere of foreign lending. The effect of concentration on the home market undoubtedly simplified the problem of internal financial management, but at the price of an incalculable loss in international relations, both political and economic.

The change in sentiment in public expenditure must also be viewed in relation to similar movements abroad. That it has taken the form it has in Great Britain, and been able to develop within the framework of the democratic machine, may partly be accounted for by the budgetary resources available. Budgeting from 1932 to 1936 was a straightforward matter compared with the problems confronting chancellors in the twenties. By the simple means of maintaining taxes at crisis rates, and by utilizing some of the savings in the war-debt charge due to conversion, ample funds were available for development. This was, moreover, compatible with a steady decline in the real tax burden as long as incomes were rising.

[1] See discussion in Chap. IV, below.

It thus appears that if there was general agreement over a wide field there was also a considerable individual divergence between the policies of the three chancellors who made history in our period. Is this to be explained mainly on party or on personal grounds? Let us put ourselves for a moment in the place of the chancellor. Broadly the fiscal situation is a datum. He inherits all the results of the actions of his predecessors, and must make allowance for the obligations undertaken by them. If he is active and progressive he will certainly not want to present a passive budget, quite apart from the pull of election pledges. The scope for financing new lines of expenditure by economies in existing lines is usually very small indeed, the saving of interest on the war loan in the thirties being a notable exception. There is perhaps more possibility of finding resources on the revenue side, since it is easier to increase taxes than to cut down expenditure. There is also some choice as to the rate of debt repayment, no matter how assiduously previous parliaments may have sought to impose sinking-fund obligations. This implies that the possibility of innovation is strictly limited, even for the chancellor whose administration coincides with the upswing of a boom when there is revenue to spare. On the whole the hard facts of the budget curtail individual initiative.

Another factor usually making for continuity of policy is the trend of social philosophy, which tends within a relatively short period such as we are considering to move in the one direction. It exerts an extra-parliamentary pressure of some force, although no doubt the intensity differs considerably from one period to another. During the post-war period fundamental unanimity of purpose between the different parties was probably exceptionally great, owing to the gruelling experience which the nation had just undergone. Just as the whole nation had been united in the determination to fight the war, so it was united in the desire to undo some of the evils which had resulted from the development in the nineteenth century of large-scale production and the free play of economic forces. In the sphere of social expenditure for instance, not merely general lines of policy, but particular measures, were common to the different parties. All again were united in extending assistance to agriculture on a quite unprecedented scale. The labour party had in preparation a number of schemes which were subsequently launched by governments mainly conservative, such as the national electricity grid, and the London Passenger Transport Board. Other schemes of an essentially similar nature, however, came directly out of the conservative box. Again, there was an extraordinary degree of unanimity on the two changes of exceptional importance made in 1931—the economy campaign and the tariff. It is significant that the national government was not returned on a specifically protectionist ticket, and that the adoption of the tariff was only obtained by an unprecedented break in the tradition of ministerial solidarity. Yet there can be no doubt that the change was universally acceptable to the country. Mr. Baldwin was as right in holding that he had an implicit mandate for protection in 1931 as he had been wrong in 1923.

On the other hand, the office of chancellor allows a considerable scope for individuality, possibly more than in the case of other cabinet members where the supporting ministries are larger. The play of individuality is perceptible in general lines of policy. Mr. Churchill's social policy belonged to post-war philosophy, but the youthful hand of 1906 is clearly traceable. Mr. Chamberlain's economic experiments were essentially an elaboration of the policy enunciated years ago by his father, and more recently by his brother. There is opportunity also for individual decisions of great importance on particular points. Perhaps the time chosen for the return to gold and the first form of the National Defence Contribution of 1937[1] are the most interesting examples of this since the war. The history of the post-war chancellors suggests indeed that there is no very close correspondence between conservatism in politics and in financial administration. The most conservative chancellor of the twenties belonged to the labour party. Will his successor be found in the liberal chancellor of to-day?

But it is beyond the scope of our study to follow up surmises of this nature, however intriguing. We are not called on to inquire either into the formation of social philosophy or into the relative importance of the different factors governing financial policy. Our task is to examine the problems created by their impact on the economic situation.

[1] On the latter point Dr. Dalton secured an explicit avowal of responsibility (cf. Report on debate on N.D.C. in *The Times*, 1 June 1937). Sir John Simon's apparent lack of enthusiasm for the first form of the measure 'increased the suspicion of the Opposition that in its original form the N.D.C. was an example of individual enterprise by the present Prime Minister' (Dr. Dalton). Mr. Chamberlain nodded assent.

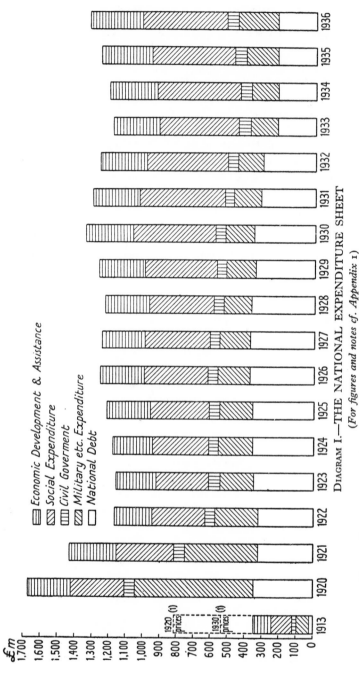

DIAGRAM I.—THE NATIONAL EXPENDITURE SHEET

(*For figures and notes cf. Appendix 1*)

(1) 1913 figures expressed in 1920 and 1930 prices on the basis of the Cost of Living Index Number.

II

THE NATIONAL ACCOUNTS—A REVIEW OF THE PROBLEMS

ALTHOUGH policy is made at the centre, neither the chancellor, nor for that matter parliament, controls the whole of public expenditure. Some of the spending of local authorities is entirely outside the jurisdiction of parliament, more of it is only indirectly controlled by the central government, for instance through the conditions attached to grants. Again, the expenditure policy of the social funds—National Health Insurance, Unemployment Insurance, and Contributory Pensions—is regulated as to its broad lines by statute. Many minor variations in detail are, however, possible from year to year. The same is true on the taxation side. Individual local rates are the affair of the individual local councils. The rates of contribution to social funds is fixed by parliament or by independent bodies (for instance, the Unemployment Insurance Statutory Committee) subject to parliamentary confirmation. Hence to get a complete picture of how the nation spends its public income and covers the expenditure we must include besides the budget accounts, first the funds independently raised and spent by local authorities, and secondly the contributions to and payments from the social funds.

It is clear that for many problems nothing short of such an inclusive account will be sufficient. Only complete figures will show net contraction and expansion. On both sides of the account there has been variation in the proportion due to the different spending and taxing authorities—considerable in the case of the relative shares of central and local government, and far from negligible between the central government and the funds. Secondly the effect of public action is obviously the effect of the whole. Only the complete account will give a satisfactory idea, for instance, of the relation of public finance to private industry, or to the total resources of the community. Thirdly, although the different parts of public expenditure are related to central policy and control in different degrees of directness, there is scarcely any part which is not so related in some degree. Only the total account

represents the full possibility of a consistent socio-economic policy
—if such a thing were ever to come into being.

Total figures for expenditure by public authorities in Great
Britain for our period are shown in Diagram I.[1] In order to get
some idea of the relative valuations which the community puts on
its needs—as evidenced by the amounts it spends on them—expenditure has been arranged in five groups. These are: National
Debt Services, Military Expenditure, Civil Government, Social
Expenditure, and Expenditure for Economic Ends. The exact
composition of the groups is naturally a matter of individual taste
and judgement, since many of the items are on the borderline
between two or more. The arrangement adopted here therefore
requires some explanation and justification.

The first group is quite unambiguous. It includes the total
budget outlay[2] (interest, management, &c.) of the 'deadweight'
debt, that is to say, the debt of the central government not held
against assets. As can be judged by comparing the size of this
block in the pre- and post-war periods, over 90 per cent. of this
expenditure is due to the war debt.

Just what, in addition to the annual expense of the defence
forces, should be included in group II is a matter of individual
preference. Since our period, and especially the early years, was
dominated by the effects of the war, it has seemed better to err on
the comprehensive side. So far as it can be isolated therefore, all
expenditure directly connected with the war and the aftermath of
fighting is included in group II. One of the most serious effects of
war is after all the vast legacy of obligations it leaves in its wake, in
addition to the cost of paying interest on the expenditure financed
by borrowing. In the early years therefore the figures in this group
are much swollen by expenditures of three different types: (i) the
Middle East services which were mainly military in character, and
were virtually a conclusion of the war in those parts; (ii) a number
of unclassified miscellaneous war expenses of considerable amounts,
representing the liquidation of armament and other liabilities; and

---

[1] In the case of National Health Insurance the actual spending is carried out
by the friendly societies acting for the state. Irish services have been omitted
throughout, mainly because of the difficulty caused by the change of territory
after the separation of the Irish Free State. The only year, however, when
Ireland imposed any serious weight on the British budget was in 1921 at the
time of 'The Trouble'.

[2] For actual cost of the Debt cf. Chap. XXII, p. 360.

(iii) a group of small expenditures arising directly out of the war such as the cost of the Imperial War Graves Commission, the training and transfer of soldiers to civilian life, and the relief of war victims. The £6,900 which the Cenotaph cost is also included.[1] For the greater part of the period, however, the figure for this group is dominated by two items—the cost of the Services and of war pensions.

Group III attempts to show the cost of being governed. Roughly it covers the classes in the civil accounts now described as 'Central Government and Finance', 'National and Foreign', 'Home Department, Justice and Law', and 'Common Services'. The miscellaneous group of 'other Consolidated Fund Services', and, so far as they can be isolated, the police service and the administrative expenses of local authorities, are also included. In a number of cases it has been necessary to transfer to other groups small items such as the educational work of the Home Office, and the Empire Marketing Board (which appeared under 'National and Foreign').

The main item in group IV is local expenditure on public health, education, and housing. This comprises practically the whole of the work of local authorities, except for police, roads, and trading services. The two other important sub-groups are: (i) direct expenditure by the Ministry of Health, including Old Age Pensions, and by the Ministry of Education, including grants to voluntary bodies; and (ii) payments from the social funds. In addition there are a few small items transferred from other groups (as above), including also some housing experiments carried out directly by the Office of Works. Miscellaneous grants for public works are also included here, as their nature shows them to have been social rather than economic in intent.

Group V comprises all expenditure for economic purposes, either where public authorities are themselves entrepreneurs, such as the Post Office and the trading services of local authorities, or where the state merely acts as a fairy godmother to entrepreneurs. Assistance of the latter type may be given either by direct money grant (whether obtained from the budget or not), or by service. It may accrue to industry as a whole, or to particular groups of producers. Economic expenditure therefore includes the whole of group VI (trade and industry) in the civil accounts. Road

---

[1] It is regrettable that one cannot get total figures for expenditure on war memorials up and down the country.

expenditure also finds its place here, since its purpose is economic rather than political or social. These four items cover most of the expenditure, except in the early years when a few large temporary grants were given (mainly to the coal industry). There are a few small items transferred from other groups such as the cost of the Empire Marketing Board, the Trade Facilities Committee, the Export Credit Department, and the Economic Advisory Council, and finally some recent additional grants to different parts of the agricultural industry.

A diagram of this type is necessarily based primarily on current account expenditure. To include expenditure on durable equipment from loan funds would hopelessly obscure the real continuity of development that exists, since loan expenditure takes place in relatively large amounts, and discontinuously. This omission makes it inevitable that in social and economic expenditure, where durable investment is of considerable importance, total expenditure is in almost any year somewhat larger, and in some years very much larger, than the amounts here shown. We shall return to this point in our more detailed investigations of these groups.[1] On the other hand, a considerable amount of capital expenditure is financed out of revenue. The most important item here is roads, but there are others.[2] Hence the diagram is not entirely a current account sheet: from the British method of accounting it appears quite inevitable that it should be a hybrid.[3]

Before we turn to examine the relative movements of the different groups, the course of expenditure as a whole suggests some interesting points. It cannot of course be expected when the quantities represented are so large and the scale necessarily so small, that small variations will show up, even if they are economically quite important. A different apparatus is required for dealing with them. We are, however, now in a position to compare total public expenditure with other community totals—with the growth of population on the one hand, and on the other with the national income.

In Great Britain the population grew by about 9 per cent. between 1913 and 1935. Expenditure in the same period expanded by nearly 270 per cent. We must, however, allow for the change in the value of money. If we increase the 1913 figure by 50 per cent. the expenditure increase is reduced to about 245 per cent., which is sufficiently formidable. The pre-war rate was equivalent to a little

[1] Cf. Chaps. III, and VI to VIII. [2] Cf. Chap. VII. [3] Cf. Chap. XVII.

over £7 10s. per head. The post-war is over £25. On the other hand, expenditure has not grown steadily in the post-war period, but has moved in well-defined waves. The first of these lasted from 1925 to 1932. The second began in 1934, and it is noticeable that its rate of increase has been considerably faster than that of the earlier movement. Since this depends on a number of causes it is not inconceivable that each successive wave may carry total expenditure to a higher point. In that case, even in the absence of another national catastrophe, the secular trend of the level of expenditure from 1920 onwards may easily prove to be moving up more steeply than the increase of a population which is fast becoming stationary. This question, however, obviously requires investigation in relation to the different lines of expenditure.[1]

A number of calculations of the national income have been made, giving—so far as they overlap—results varying by amounts up to £400 m. This divergence arises both from the methods of calculation adopted, and from differences of opinion as to the most useful definition of the national income. For our purpose, however, the variation is not important. On any calculation the change between the pre- and post-war relation comes out about the same. For year to year movements we are not concerned with absolute amounts, so that any series consistently calculated will serve. In 1913 the national income was estimated to be about £2,000 m., so that public expenditure at £325 m. was about 16 per cent. In 1924, on the other hand, with income at something like £3,800–4,000 m., and spending at £1,110 m. the proportion had risen to 27–9 per cent. It is evident that the community has had to make a very formidable readjustment in the relation between public and private spending. As in the case of population it is difficult as yet to say anything definite about the secular trend of public expenditure in the post-war years, in relation to the national income. It looks as though they were keeping very close together.[2] It is at any rate clear that the trend is very different from that of the nineteenth century, when the national income was increasing considerably faster than public expenditure.

[1] Cf. especially Chap. III.
[2] Bowley and Stamp conclude that the national dividend (real national income) increased more rapidly than population in the generation before the war. Real income per head accordingly increased by about 33 per cent. between 1880 and 1913. Between 1924 and 1935 it increased by 20 per cent. according to Mr. Clark (*National Income and Outlay*).

The variations in the relation between public expenditure and the national income are extremely suggestive. The first official calculations of the net national income were published with the Budget of 1941. In the 1930's there were available only private calculations and even the method of procedure was not agreed, hence it was not possible to make any but the broadest generalizations. Income rose from 1924 to 1929, with a temporary recession in 1926 which was more than compensated in 1927. After 1931 income dropped sharply to a point below the 1924 figure, and finally recovered again in 1935. On these general trends authorities are agreed, but on details—for instance the timing and degree of recovery in the thirties—there is considerable divergence of opinion.[1] According to Professor Bowley the 1924 level was not attained before 1936, so that over the decade 1924–34 a fall of about 5 per cent. was realized. According to Mr. Clark, on the other hand, a rise of about 4 per cent. was achieved. Table 1 gives Mr. Clark's figures since they represent the only continuous series for the period. It should be borne in mind that they appear to be somewhat optimistic for the later years.

Even with the rough material at our disposal it is still possible to say something about the relation between changes in public expenditure in relation to changes in the national income. There is obviously a rough correlation between good years and high spending. But it is noticeable that very bad years also tend to be years of high spending. Thus expenditure in 1926 and 1927 exceeded 1925 and 1928; and 1931 and 1932 were greatly in excess of 1933 and 1934. Even allowing for the effect of price changes this divergence is sufficient to suggest two lines of explanation. In years when tax revenue is good, new services tend to be introduced. The greater part which the state now takes in social and economic life has enormously increased the opportunities for these.

---

[1] The best available sources were Colin Clark, *National Income and Outlay 1937* and A. L. Bowley, *Wages and Income in the U.K., since 1860*.

At the end of the chapter, p. 35, a table (1) gives the official calculations for the entire period 1921 to 1937. It will be seen that according to the official estimate the national income fell over the depression years 1931 to 1934 but recovered in 1935.

On the other hand, in bad years when the national income is low and unemployment high the state has expensive obligations to fulfil. The first movement appears to be one accentuating the boom, the second may tend to offset the depression. This is obviously a point which we shall have to investigate.

When we turn from total expenditure to examine the movement in the different groups, great divergence is at once apparent. The greatest changes, both between 1913 and 1920, and within the post-war period, are in the cost of the national debt. The smallest item of all before the war, it exceeded social expenditure in the early twenties, and did not substantially fall below it until the expansion of the latter in 1929–30. On the other hand, after the conversion operation of 1932, outlay on the debt fell to not much over half its cost in 1926 and 1927, the most expensive years. Military expenditure also shows a large degree of variation. Apart from the sudden drop between 1921 and 1922, due to the liquidation of war undertakings, there was a gradual decline in the cost of the Services until 1932, and a continuous decline in the cost of war pensions throughout the period. In the diagram the latter movement partly masks the increase in the cost of the Services since 1932. The steady expansion of the social services from 1925 is notable even on this small scale. The expansion in the depression due to the increase in emergency services is also evident. The growth of 'economic' expenditure from 1932 is less obvious, partly because of its smaller amount, and partly because new investment which provides the heavier items in this group was kept almost stationary on grounds of economy for some years after 1931.

Since our main concern is with factors influencing the size and distribution of the national income, the different lines of expenditure obviously have very differing claims on our attention. Neither expenditure on civil government nor expenditure for defence is concerned in intention with socio-economic policy. They do not therefore call for our detailed investigation. On the other hand, they are not necessarily entirely passive agents in relation to the national income.

The cost of civil government might become an active factor from our point of view, if either the cost of being governed were changing at a different rate from expenditure in general, or if the remuneration of civil servants could be shown to affect the wages and salaries of other workers. The increase of government control during the war naturally led to a great extension of the civil service. Not a little of this was of a permanent nature—such for instance as the reorganization of local government under the Ministry of Health, and the establishment of the Ministries of Labour and Transport. We are more governed, and we must expect to pay for it. It appears, however, that the Geddes Committee succeeded in pruning away unnecessary war-time growths, since no subsequent inquiry—not even the May report—was able to suggest substantial economies in administration. Moreover, on the whole, except for temporary movements (such as that in the National and Foreign vote in 1923, mainly due to the American debt negotiations), the cost of government does not appear to be growing faster than total expenditure. The numbers in the central service fell steadily until 1934. Total expenditure on administration was very little different in 1929 in relation to public spending from what it had been in 1922. On the other hand, the national government's economic policy has thrown a considerable additional weight on the central civil service. It is too early yet to see the full effect of this change.

During the war there was also a very considerable increase in the pay of civil servants. According to Professor Bowley[1] the increase between 1914 and 1922 was of the order of 81 per cent. on small salaries and of 42 per cent. on larger. It is clear that there was nothing exorbitant about this, considering the rise in prices and the increase of industrial remuneration. The May Committee was of the opinion that 'on the whole the remuneration of the civil service is (not) out of scale with that determined on the principle of fair wages'.[2] It does not therefore seem likely that the central civil service can exert an active influence either on the other expenditure groups or on the labour market. There has, however, been a very remarkable growth in the local civil service, which has continued steadily throughout our period. The increased activity of the local authorities and the new services which they have had to develop has had two effects. Personnel has expanded all down the scale, but there has been a relative increase in the highly paid officials. In 1934 the central civil service was less than a third of the size of the local. This is a factor which cannot be adequately represented on our table, because of the difficulty of isolating the

---

[1] Bowley, *Economic Consequences of the Great War*.
[2] *Report on National Expenditure*, p. 81.

establishment expenses of local authorities. The point will call for further discussion at a later stage.[1] Military expenditure may exert an active influence on the national income in two ways. The distribution of war pensions is similar in effect to the other social services, being in part a substitute for some of them. It will therefore call for discussion in relation to the social services in general, following the practice of the official return. Secondly, expenditure on durable military equipment is, economically considered, a form of public works. It tends to increase direct and indirect employment as do other forms of public works, so long as it is additional to, and not merely a substitute for, other investment. But the amount of such expenditure is determined on political and technical grounds, without reference to social or economic conditions.

Is it then quite impossible to bring military expenditure into the economic calculus of the needs of the community? One method of 'rationalizing' military expenditure is to regard it as an insurance premium against international risks. On this basis the 'premium' paid for most of the post-war period was certainly lower than that paid at the beginning of the century. In the last quarter of the nineteenth century the cost of the Services (which is the only expenditure here relevant) was 2 per cent. of the national income. By 1913 it had risen to $3\frac{1}{2}$ per cent. By 1925 it had fallen to 3 per cent., and was steadily reduced until 1932. It did not rise again to over 3 per cent. until 1936. Moreover, a progressive reduction of personnel, such as was taking place in the twenties, implies a relatively high proportion of rigid costs (such as pensions on retirement). The growth of expenditure on effectives was less than 60 per cent. of total military expansion. Further, the period has been one of exceptionally rapid change in the form of armaments, and hence expenses on equipment have been particularly heavy. When these considerations are taken into account in connexion with official statements since the beginning of rearmament, it appears probable that defence provision was subnormal during the post-war period. So far as military expenditure stood in the way of the development, for instance of social expenditure, it was the result of the last war. Post-war military economy may be regarded as a gamble on the success of collective security.

The main part of our problem then is to be found in the groups

[1] Cf. pp. 51 ff. and 150 ff.

of social and economic expenditure. Besides the points which have already emerged, the investigation of these will be found to entail discussion of a number of related problems which will occupy us for the next eleven chapters (Part I). The most important addition to the problems suggested by the general survey is the place of public investment (Chapters VI and VII). This we may define as the ownership and working by public authorities of enterprises requiring durable equipment, whether profit-earning or not. It presents both a long-period problem of the relation of public investment to private industry and a short-period or cyclical problem of the variations of public investment in relation to the trade cycle. This in turn brings us to the problem of unemployment and the extent to which it may be controlled by public expenditure, either on current or on capital account (Chapters XI, XII, and XIII). But both the central government and the local authorities have a share in social and economic policy. We shall find that we cannot deal fully with the possibilities either of long period development or of varying expenditure with cyclical conditions, unless we have first explored the relation between central and local finance (Chapters IX and X).

But expenditure is only half the problem of public finance. Since different methods of raising revenue have different social and economic effects, the tax structure is also an active influence on the size and distribution of the national income. We can proceed to map out the broad movements on the fiscal side as we have already done for expenditure, by examining the variations over our period, compared with the situation before the war. Diagram II, the National Taxation sheet, thus corresponds to Diagram I. There are a number of ways in which taxes can be grouped.[1] The one chosen here aims at distinguishing broadly personal levies and other taxes. Thus rates are a property tax, and the indirect section mainly consists of commodity taxes. On the other hand, surtax, death duties, and social insurance are all personal, and income tax mainly so. (Both employers' and workers' insurance contributions are included, since we are at the moment occupied exclusively with the resource side of public finance.) It must be noticed that this arrangement does not give a very good approximation to a division between the shares of the rich and the poor, since some of the

[1] Cf. Chaps. XIV and XV, where a classification of greater economic significance is used.

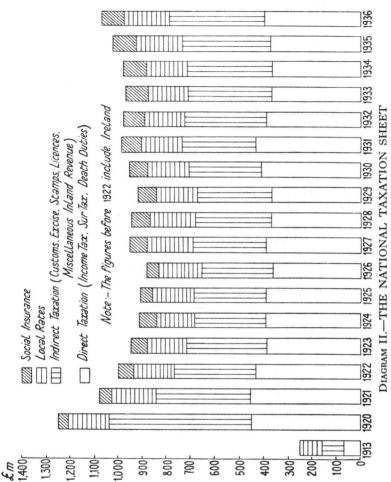

£m

Social Insurance
Local Rates
Indirect Taxation (Customs. Excise. Stamps, Licences.
    Miscellaneous Inland Revenue)
Direct Taxation (Income Tax. Sur-Tax. Death Duties)

Note:—The figures before 1922 include Ireland

DIAGRAM II.—THE NATIONAL TAXATION SHEET
(For figures of individual taxes cf. Appendices 7 to 9)

non-personal taxes, such as excess profits duty and stamp duties, are primarily connected with the ownership of property. Also the part of income-tax receipts paid out of undistributed profits is in effect a profits tax, although it is always included in the direct group. This arrangement, however, is a convenient way of showing up the most important post-war variations.

Obviously Diagram II cannot be expected to balance Diagram I, for the taxation totals are considerably short of the expenditure ones. Several factors account for this divergence. The most important additional item in revenue consists of the receipts from local trading services, but in addition we must allow for the fact that the budget may be balanced—or unbalanced—to a greater or less extent. The greater the amount of the true sinking fund the nearer will tax receipts be to covering expenditure. The central government also receives some assistance from trading services. For instance, the Post Office is at present not merely covering its cost but contributing some £11 m. a year to the general expenses of the exchequer. Further, there is the effect of the current-capital account confusion to consider. In the early post-war years considerable capital sums were brought in to balance the budget, and the practice was not unknown in later years. Normally, however, tax revenue put to investment exceeds sums from capital accounts applied to balancing the budget.

There is naturally less to say about the changes in the tax sheet than on the expenditure side, since they are derived directly from the bill to be met. There is therefore no need to comment here on the fact that the post-war tax structure is more than four times as large as that of 1913, as compared with a national income no more than double. It follows from the expansion of expenditure. It must concern us later, however (Chapter XV), since it implies a magnification, which cannot be neglected, of certain tax effects. Before the war the tax structure was divided into three parts which were roughly equal—direct and indirect taxation by the central government, and local rates. Since the war the first two have grown relatively to the third. This is a change of great importance. It does not represent any lack of pressure on local rates. On the contrary, the pressure was so great that it had to be relieved by a reform of the local taxing system. This is a matter which we shall already have investigated, since it bears on the whole question of the relation between central and local finance. The change in the

relation of the other two groups is quite as significant. Neglecting
the swelling of indirect receipts by the excess profits duty in
1920-1, it is evident that the war burden was heavier on direct
than on indirect contributions. The extent to which this situation
was gradually intensified, up to 1931, is clearly indicated. The
reductions on commodity taxes by Mr. Baldwin and Mr. Snowden
in 1923-4 shows up on the diagram; so also does the extra weight
put on direct contributions by Snowden in 1929-31, and the
reversal of this trend by the imposition of a general tariff
from 1932.

The problems on the fiscal side have in their turn both a long-
period or secular, and a short-period or cyclical aspect. The
economic effects of different taxes and the burden of the tax structure on different incomes are chiefly concerned with the former.
Social and economic influences of this type take some time to work
themselves out. But the real tax burden depends on the size and
distribution of the national income, and varies with the different
phases of the trade cycle. Thus the effort to balance the budget
has different economic effects according to the state of trade. How
far is it possible or desirable by varying taxes on the one hand and
the extent to which the budget is balanced on the other, to take
account of these variations? This is a matter which requires much
detailed research. In Chapters XVII and XVIII we shall attempt
to map out the ground.

One item in the expenditure group still remains to be accounted
for in our investigation—the cost of the national debt. This outlay
differs from others in that it is wholly a transfer, or redistribution
of income, and not a purchase and distribution by the state of
goods and services. The same is true of some social expenditure,
with the important difference that this has, and the national debt
service has not, a basis in socio-economic policy. Hence we have
to examine the consequences of the double process of public income and outlay in connexion with the debt.

The most important aspect of the debt, however, is in the
monetary rather than in the social or economic field. Its management requires the state to undertake vast borrowing and repayment operations on the stock exchange and in the money market.
The state of the debt has an important effect on the monetary
situation, and so monetary policy forces itself into the sphere of
public finance via the national debt. Once, however, monetary

policy has passed beyond the stage of keeping the national currency in line with an international standard, as it has done in the post-war world, it is already in the field of public finance on its own account. The volume of cash and securities of various types is manipulated directly by the government. Whether this occurs more or less accidentally in the course of debt management or forms part of a conscious policy is to some extent irrelevant. Monetary management affects the size of the national income and can no longer be a matter of indifference to public finance. We cannot therefore leave our study without examining the implications of monetary policy for public finance in our period.

When we include in a single view the large proportion of the community's resources which passes into the coffers of public authorities and out again, we can be under no illusion as to the immense importance of public action in the economic field. Of this volume of resources the greater part is collected and disbursed by the central government, and is hence under the control of a single form of policy. Although local authorities are responsible for spending some 30 per cent. of the total, only about 7 per cent. is due to their independent powers of taxation. And the direction of rate expenditure itself is largely determined by the government grants available. Moreover, the effect of public finance stretches out beyond the limits of the activities of the public authorities with which we are here concerned. By paying part of the tune, the state can also direct the energies of voluntary effort—for instance in the fields of education and public health. Even more important, the growing body of influential public boards, such as the Central Electricity Board, the B.B.C., and the London Passenger Transport Board, are bound to the state much more closely than public utilities of the pre-war type. On the one hand, their financial arrangements make them contingent liabilities of considerable importance. On the other, the state has power to influence the tempo of their activities, and thus to turn them into instruments of public policy.

It has for some time been realized that to study economics under the assumption of perfect competition can give only a very approximate idea of conditions in the real world to-day. To study the working of private industry without taking into account the effect of public finance is certainly no less unreal.

TABLE I

Net National Income

	£ m.			£ m.
1921 . . .	4,662	1930 . . .		4,149
1922 . . .	3,766	1931 . . .		3,763
1923 . . .	3,634	1932 . . .		3,614
1924 . . .	3,757	1933 . . .		3,704
1925 . . .	3,979	1934 . . .		3,975
1926 . . .	3,764	1935 . . .		4,146
1927 . . .	3,981	1936 . . .		4,355
1928 . . .	4,006	1937 . . .		4,599
1929 . . .	4,147			

PART I

EXPENDITURE

'Tis easy conduct when Exchequers flow
But hard the task to manage well the low.

DRYDEN

III

SOCIAL EXPENDITURE

SOCIAL Expenditure is the natural starting-point for an investigation into the effects of public expenditure. If we except the
temporary expansion of military expenditure and of the cost of
the debt, both due directly to the war, social expenditure was by
far the largest group both before and after the war. It is, moreover,
the service which has most definitely and continuously expanded
in our period. This movement followed a very considerable
increase of social expenditure during the war period itself, in spite
of the more insistent claims of the military departments. Moreover the establishment of the Ministry of Labour, the reorganization of local government under the Ministry of Health, and the
inauguration of important new health services (such as the maternity and child welfare service) during the war, laid the foundation
for the post-war development.

It is curious that no official definition of the social services has
ever been given. Since 1920 an annual return of expenditure
has been published,[1] but the items included in it are not fully
comprehensive. They cover, however, the main lines—education,
public health, housing, public assistance and unemployment
payments, and pensions. The education group does not include
the provision of public libraries, museums, and picture galleries
by local authorities (together costing about £2·5 m. a year), or of
miscellaneous educational work sponsored by government departments other than the Board. More important, the public health
group does not include such community health services as the
construction and maintenance of the sewerage system, the collec-

[1] Known as the Drage Return, because it was inspired by Sir Geoffrey Drage
and the Charity Organization Society.

tion and disposal of house refuse, the provision of baths, wash-houses and bathing places, as well as of parks and open spaces. Expenditure on the welfare of the blind, which had only just come under official care at the time the return was started, is also missing. If we are discussing the effects of social expenditure it is obvious that we should include all outlay by public bodies which is social in intent. This may be defined as services provided or financed by public authorities mainly out of taxation,[1] for the purpose of improving the welfare, health, or education of the population. This would leave to be considered as trading services such undertakings as waterworks and cemeteries, which are of undoubted benefit to the health of the community, but normally cover their costs.

The most important borderline case between social and economic expenditure is housing. Before the war it was customary to charge something like an economic price (or rent) for such few houses as were provided by local authorities. Immediately after the war the rents which could be charged (if the right sort of tenants were secured) covered such a small part of the cost that the provision of working-class housing grew up as almost purely a social service. As the cost of building fell, however, it approximated once more to a trading service. It is probably unlikely that it will ever become wholly one, as the process of rehousing tends to move down the social scale. At the same time the application of methods of large-scale production is progressively tending to lower the cost of building materials, and it is possible also that local authorities may be able to cover a greater proportion of their costs by charging discriminating rents—on the same principle by which it is customary to make discriminating charges for certain monopoly services, such as electricity. But in our period housing has been overwhelmingly a *social* service. Indeed, the development of municipal housing has been the dominating movement in the social services since the war.

We have already observed the general lines of development of social expenditure (Chapter II, Diagram I). Diagram I below gives the social services proper in more detail, divided into groups, and with the addition of war pensions. The grouping of

---

[1] Loan finance plays a not unimportant part in the social services, but in so far as the interest charges are not covered by receipts, the services are ultimately financed out of taxation.

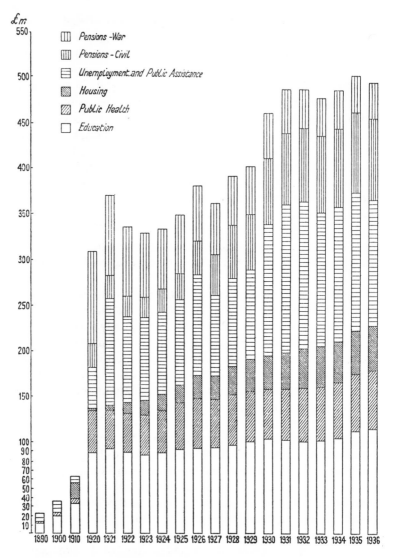

£m

⊞	Pensions -War
⊞	Pensions - Civil
⊟	Unemployment and Public Assistance
▨	Housing
▨	Public Health
☐	Education

DIAGRAM I.—EXPENDITURE ON SOCIAL SERVICES—GROSS
(Great Britain) Excluding Loan Expenditure
(*For notes and figures cf. Appendix 6*)

the services·has been based on the purpose of expenditure, since this is the most relevant factor from the point of view of economic effect. Three of the divisions—education, public health, unemployment and public assistance—are, however, omnibus groups, comprising services which differ both in type and in the source from which they derive their funds. These differences have also some economic relevance. The Board of Education parliamentary vote includes not merely grants to local education authorities, and to privately owned elementary and secondary schools, but also contributions to the universities and to other adult educational and research bodies. This last sub-group is quite small. In 1936 the universities received £2·3 m. from public funds, scientific investigation and museums, &c., about £0·8 m. between them. Finally, we must also include here the subsidy to the B.B.C. (some £2–3 m.). Practically all educational benefits are given in the form of services, not money grants. Except for a very small amount of fees, &c., the funds for the expenditure here shown are provided wholly from taxes and rates. The other two omnibus groups include payments both in money and in services to the beneficiaries. In these services public funds are supplemented to quite a considerable extent by insurance contributions, and to a small extent by fees, &c. (mostly in payment for medical services).

This diagram, as we have said, does not cover the whole field of social expenditure. In the first place we must add some £20 m. —rising to about £30 m. by the end of the period—in respect of the educational and health services not included in the official return. There is further the question of capital expenditure to be considered. An addition has lately been made to the Return giving capital expenditure both from grant and loan, in respect of the social services. It is more complete than any other source, and therefore useful although the period covered is very short. The figures are summarized in Table 1 (p. 60). Capital outlay varies considerably from year to year. The economic significance of this can be discussed more conveniently in relation to other forms of public investment (Chapter VIII). Here we need only observe that the addition to be made for capital account is quite considerable. It brings the total of social expenditure up to nearly £550 m. in normal years. The enormous growth of capital expenditure on the social services can be realized by observing the

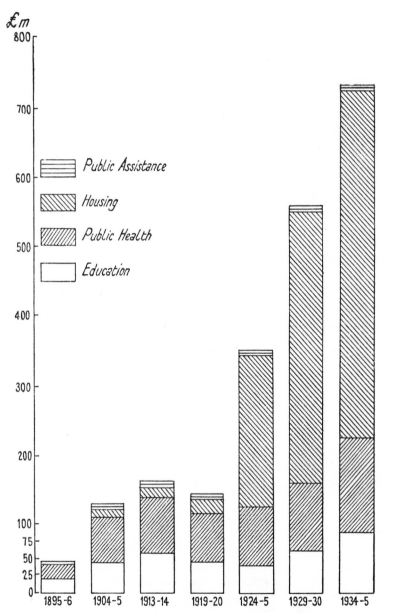

£m

▦	Public Assistance
▨	Housing
▧	Public Health
▢	Education

DIAGRAM II.—OUTSTANDING GROSS DEBT FOR SOCIAL SERVICES
OF LOCAL AUTHORITIES IN ENGLAND AND WALES

(*From Statistical Abstract*)

expansion of local debt in respect of the services during the last forty years (Diagram II).

The long-period expansion of social expenditure is evidently all part of the same movement, dating in fact from the completion of the representative system of local government in the nineties. Taking 1913 as the mid-point between 1895 and 1931 (the end of the first post-war period of expansion), and expressing the whole in 1913 prices, expenditure grew by about 1·8 times in the first half and about doubled in the second. The post-war expansion, although undoubtedly an acceleration, has not been so great an innovation as appears at first sight. Far the biggest general increase, allowing for price changes, took place in the years 1925–31. There is, however, a marked divergence between the periods in which the development of the different services was accelerated. Education did most of its growing between 1900 and 1910. Housing, on the other hand, expanded most rapidly in the early twenties, pensions not until after the introduction of Mr. Churchill's contributory scheme. As we should expect, war pensions is the only group to show any continuous decrease. On the other hand, education, the poverty services, and pensions show well-marked short-period fluctuations. It hardly requires emphasizing that the rate of growth of all services has been far in excess of the increase in the population.

The main forces determining the rate of expenditure on the different social services may be grouped under five heads: legislation (including statutory orders), economy campaigns, trade fluctuations, population movements and changes in the degree of utilization of services. Two of these depend on policy and three on more or less uncontrollable causes. Housing and pensions are the best illustrations in the post-war period of the effect of legislation, which is quantitatively by far the most important cause of expansion. As a result of the 'Addison' Housing Act local expenditure on housing trebled between 1920 and 1921, and more than doubled between 1921 and 1922. The incidence of the later housing acts is also evident, and more particularly the accelerating effect of the announcement of the reduction of the subsidy in 1927–8. The effect of legislation on the pensions service is equally striking. During the post-war period the proportion of the population over 70 increased steadily, at a rate which varied between 0·3 and 1·7 per cent. per annum. Between 1924 and 1925, however, pensions expenditure increased by 4·8 per cent. (the effect of the Old Age Pensions Act of 1924), and from 1925 to 1926 by 7 per cent. (the additive effect of the Contributory Pensions Act). The Act of 1929, which extended the scope of unconditional pensions, largely by clearing out some anomalies in the contributory pensions scheme, caused expenditure to exceed estimates by 5·8 per cent. As against these increases the expansion of pensions expenditure due to the depression did not exceed 2 per cent.

Not all legislation is equally effective in causing changes in social expenditure. Since new services which are to be administered by the local authorities inevitably put some additional burden on the rates, the rate of expansion of such services depends primarily on the extent of financial inducement offered by the central government. The great extension of the social services since the war can be traced to the abandonment of 'permissive'[1] legislation in favour of a system of extensive grants and subsidies. In Diagram I the incidence of all three economy campaigns appears in the education service much more clearly than in any other. There may be special opportunities for economy due to the decline of the school population, but some at least of the reduction seems to have been at the cost of parents. It is unfortunate that this service appears to offer the best scope for economy in social expenditure.

The most important uncontrollable cause of the expansion of expenditure has undoubtedly been the extra demand for the social services during depression. Public health is affected to a small extent—the incidence of sickness is greater. Pensions are affected rather more severely. But the main weight falls naturally on public assistance and the unemployment services. Thus the increase in these between 1928 and 1929 was 0·7 per cent. In the next year it was over 40 per cent. and the following year a further 17 per cent. Some of this can be accounted for by a change of policy after the labour party took office, but this affords only a partial explanation since it was not found possible to make any considerable reduction in the following year. It seems probable that the financial crisis of 1931 was largely due to the failure to realize in advance the extent to which social expenditure had become increasingly vulnerable to depression on account of the

[1] On the effectiveness of different types of stimulus cf. Chap. X, pp. 172 ff.

steady expansion of the unemployment services. Cyclical sensitivity is a matter which should properly be taken into account when new social legislation is introduced. Although the exact timing of the increase cannot be foreseen, it should be possible to make a reasonably good estimate of its extent. On the other hand, changes due to population movements can be foreseen with some degree of accuracy. The rate of decline in birth and death rates is known and the relative change in the different age groups can be calculated at least a generation in advance. The services most affected are those which deal with the ends of life where change is taking place most rapidly, particularly education and pensions. We must return to this point in a moment.

A considerable number of the social services are either on a voluntary basis, or it is possible for workers who are not compulsorily included in a scheme to qualify for benefits by making regular payments. Thus services exist which are used by only a small part of the eligible population. It has been stated, for instance, that the maternity and child welfare service is used by little more than half the possible beneficiaries. Only 46 per cent. of the expectant mothers who might visit antenatal clinics do so, and only 59 per cent. of mothers take their babies to infant welfare centres.[1] On the other hand, there are large numbers of voluntary contributors to National Health Insurance and this fringe tends to increase in times of prosperity. The increase in cost if all optional services were as fully used as they might be would undoubtedly be very considerable, although there would probably be some saving in overheads.[2]

The cost of total social expenditure in the future cannot be foreseen with any accuracy. After six years of relative stagnation 1936–7 apparently ushered in a new period of heavy expansion. The measures of chief financial importance were the Education Act (passed in 1936 but not operative until 1938–9), and a voluntary addition to the contributory pensions scheme. Other new services proposed or announced included additional health inspection in factories, some closing of the gaps in medical attention by extending medical inspection to pre-school children, and health insurance

---

[1] Cf. *P.E.P. Report on the Social Services*, p. 194.
[2] Estimates of the cost of the Contributory Pensions scheme introduced in 1937 differed by £20 m. according to the assumptions made as to utilization, cf. Gibbon, 'The Public Social Services', *J.R.S.S.*, 1937.

to young workers. Further additional grants were announced for improving physical training and for milk distribution under cost to mothers and children. This sudden reawakening of interest in the development of the social services is striking, but it is not difficult to account for. Social expenditure is popular with all parties, and the expanding tax receipts of the early thirties promised a better opportunity for development than was vouchsafed in the twenties. Further, the fear of another war and the realization of the difficulties of a declining population, no less than the example of the achievements of other countries, have drawn attention to the desirability of improving physical fitness. It is too early to foresee the cost of most of the new services already announced. The continuance of the revival of expansion, however, depends ultimately on the continuance of tax receipts in excess of requirements. It is not unlikely to suffer from the rearmament campaign.

Of the probable development of particular services it is possible to speak somewhat more definitely. In the case of the pensions service fairly precise estimates of future cost have been made. It is estimated by the Government Actuary[1] that the contributory pensions service which cost £39·8 m. in 1935–6, will cost £62·4 m. in 1955–6. On this, however, the exchequer liability will have increased by 50 per cent. to £25 m. This is a formidable sum for a single service. It may prove, moreover, that the calculations on which it is based are too favourable in several respects. In the first place the average rate of unemployment assumed is 14·5 per cent. Secondly, other calculations of the future population put the age group of 70+ from 5 to 12 per cent. higher than those used. Changes in cost might also be introduced by changes in the rate of interest, or in the numbers who continued their voluntary contributions after the expiry of their compulsory insurance. This estimate assumes that no new pensions legislation is introduced, but as mortality rates fall, and the probability of an old age beyond working life increases, is not this just the service which there will be a demand to expand? The pensions service may well become the largest group in social expenditure in twenty years time. On the other hand, there will undoubtedly be some reduction of pressure in other lines. There is likely to be ultimately some small saving on the education service (depending, however, on what

[1] Cf. First Decennial Report of the Government Actuary on the operation of the Pensions Acts (1935), and Gibbon, loc. cit.

policy for the improvement of the service is adopted). More immediately there is no need to assume that the next depression will make anything like so heavy a demand on the current funds of the poverty services. There is no necessity to suppose that future depressions will be so severe as that of 1931, and already there is a substantial accumulation of funds to meet the inevitable expansion when it comes.

The growth of social expenditure has been so rapid and general that, considered merely from the point of view of outlay, it would appear inevitable that it should have very serious economic repercussions. From the social point of view, however, the enormous improvement in the health and education of the population and the decline in mortality rates at all ages is surely enough justification in itself. Although much of the field still remains untilled, the story of the development of the social services is both fascinating and enlivening. It is, however, outside our province either to follow it in detail here, or to estimate how far it has fulfilled its purpose in the social sphere. Both tasks have been very adequately performed elsewhere.[1] We are, however, very much concerned with the economic consequences of the large expansion in our period. Social expenditure may affect the national income both immediately, and more extensively as processes work themselves out, by causing the channels of spending by members of the community to run in particular lines. Three different aspects of this process call especially for consideration. First the effect of the services supplied, secondly the effect of the fact that funds are transferred from one set of pockets to another, and thirdly the repercussions of public expenditure on related private effort. In the absence of much detailed research it is not possible to do more than explore in outline the principal movements which may be anticipated.

In the main, social expenditure is designed for the benefit of the wage-earning classes. Hence an important aspect of its economic effects is its influence on the supply and price of labour. To attempt to ascertain this in any comprehensive manner would involve estimating its social as well as economic effectiveness. There are, however, two points of particular relevance to our problem. In the first place it is clear that so long as social services are only partially used the improvement in the quality of labour

[1] Cf. for instance *P.E.P. Report* on the social services.

is much less than it might be. Secondly, the optimum improvement can only be obtained if there is no counteracting factor working to the detriment of the beneficiaries.

The excess of the provision of certain voluntary services over the use made of them has already been mentioned. But 'over-capacity' may also arise through the provision of overlapping or parallel services by different departments. Attention has frequently been drawn to the parallel health services of the public health and education departments. But although some overlapping and no doubt consequent waste takes place in this respect, the right solution does not appear to have been found. If the educational health services are to be administered by the health department it is clearly necessary to guarantee to the education department that they can be as closely integrated with their own services as they are at present. There are many borderline services such as physical education which are properly part of the education service, although they are concerned with the child's physical rather than with his mental development.

A much more serious case of excess capacity grew up under the régime of the boards of guardians. With the steady improvement in the standard of relief given, the provision, for instance, in poor law hospitals and mental institutions came to attract not only the people for whom it was intended, but also large sections of the wage-earning population. There was a real danger of the growth of a health service parallel to and partly in rivalry with those normally provided by the public health departments. With the abolition of the guardians this development was arrested, although it must be some time before the institutions taken over can be integrated with the work of the health departments, and over-capacity eliminated. Moreover, the abolition of the boards of guardians has by no means put an end to the overlapping of the health and poverty services. The unemployment assistance committees seem to find themselves compelled to provide much more than mere money payments for their clients. They are required to treat the family as a unit, and this may imply no little health provision. It appears that the problem of the over-lapping of the health services of the assisted and non-assisted parts of the population has not been solved but merely altered from one between rival local departments to one between local and centrally controlled organizations. It is to be hoped that some means of solving it may be found without having recourse to the creation of new institutional provision.

For the services to have the optimum effect it is obviously necessary that the benefits of one set of workers should not be offset by losses to others. It is clearly desirable that if there is any discrimination between beneficiaries it should be in favour of the most needy, and not distributed in a regressive or even in a haphazard manner. It has been asserted that these conditions are far from always being fulfilled. Let us examine a few cases.

In the first place, there is the question of the cost of pensions, which already (counting civil and war pensions) exceeds expenditure on education. There is a real danger that as the proportion of the elderly in the community increases, the cost of maintaining them may bear so heavily on the working population that some of the benefits of social expenditure are undone. The older section of the population is accidentally tending to exploit the younger. Workers are now paying over £25 m. a year in sickness and pensions insurance. It is true that whatever may have been the case at first the contributory system is now popular. This is shown both by the existence of voluntary contributors and by the demand of agricultural workers to be admitted to an unemployment insurance from which they were unlikely to benefit greatly. It must be remembered, however, that since the insurance contributions are a flat rate, they form a regressive tax on the lowest income groups. The benefits received, on the other hand, are only very little if at all progressive down the income scale. There is thus a real danger that contributions which may be easily borne by well-paid workers should become too heavy a strain on the poorest. While it would be absurd to condemn the contributory system on this ground alone, it would obviously be well to take care that if flat-rate contributions are necessary they do not form too heavy a part of the wages of unskilled workers. An alternative would be to make an adjustment in contribution so that workers with a large number of dependants paid less.

Another cause of uneven incidence of charge and benefit arises from the exploitation of the unemployment insurance system by certain occupations. It is said[1] that workers in some occupations— for instance, the South Wales tin-plate industry, the Lancashire cotton industry, and dockers everywhere, habitually draw out

[1] Cf. *P.E.P. Report*, p. 163.

more than they pay in. In the case of dockers the difference is said to be as much as 3s. 3d. a week. While industrial risks can never be evenly spread—and this is indeed the whole basis of insurance—a different situation arises when whole industries habitually benefit at the expense of others, merely on account of their short-time arrangements. Workers in these industries are receiving an income partly derived from the taxation of their fellow workers. Employers are enabled to keep wages low because their workers are partly supported by the state. Certain individual anomalies which the inquiries of the Royal Commission on Unemployment Insurance revealed were set right in 1931, but it appears that these industrial anomalies continue to persist.

A third counteracting influence occurs when a worker's family budgeting is, owing to social expenditure, forced to take a form which he does not really desire but which he can hardly escape. There was to start with a tremendous outcry against the compulsory levy for National Health Insurance. A similar trouble appears frequently to arise when a family is forced—by lack of alternative housing accommodation—to move into a new council house at a very much higher rent than that which they were paying previously. While the better house will undoubtedly have a good effect upon health, if rent becomes too large a proportion of income there is a tendency for the more flexible items of expenditure such as food to be cut down, which in the short run at any rate may have a greater counteracting effect. This seems to provide an additional argument for attempting to enforce differential rents.

There is little evidence that social expenditure has any effect on the supply of labour—as distinct from its quality—except in so far as it lowers the mortality rates of the under 60 age-groups. A great amount of legislation has recently been enacted in countries abroad aiming at increasing the birth-rate, both by expenditure and by differential taxation. So far the evidence does not point to any very considerable success from this effort.[1] It is worth noting, however, that there is an almost complete absence of such encouragement in England. Except for the allowances for children given by the Unemployment Assistance Board and the Public Assistance Authorities, and the widows' section of contributory pensions, there is no differential in favour of large families.[2] On

---

[1] Cf. Glass, *The Struggle for Population.*
[2] Apart from the Income Tax Allowances.

the other hand, rents cost more and the risk of dependants' sickness is greater. The burden of indirect taxes and of rates is heavily regressive on large families. In view both of the additive effect of the powerful social and other factors which are making it steadily less attractive for a citizen to rear a large family and of the known economic difficulties of a stationary population, it would seem desirable to consider whether the situation might not be considerably improved by comparatively simple means. For instance contributory pensions cover dependants. Might not some similar arrangement be possible in health insurance?

The improvement in the quality of labour which has undoubtedly resulted from the social services, necessarily has some favourable effect also on its cost to industry by increasing industrial efficiency. There are in addition a number of ways in which social expenditure affects wages more directly. The repercussions are difficult to disentangle, and as far as economic effect is concerned, they do not all work in the same direction. There appear to be two principal factors in social expenditure which tend to depress wages. Firstly, there are the cases mentioned above, of the subsidization of certain wages from unemployment pay. Secondly, the payment of unconditional pensions possibly has an effect in allowing older candidates for jobs to underbid younger men. On the other hand, there appear to be two groups of factors which would mainly tend to make wages higher than they would otherwise have been. The great increase in the number of workers who depend for their incomes on public enterprise—particularly the direct and indirect employees of the local authorities—implies that a much larger proportion of the population than formerly derives its income from bodies not directly subject to the economic calculus. Moreover, this group forms a large sheltered industry, and one that is not highly subject to cyclical influences. In such occupations wages tend to be both higher and more rigid than elsewhere. Besides affecting costs in general, this probably tends to encourage a similar development in wages in comparable industries—for instance the electrical engineering trades.

A second factor arises from the existence and manner of administering unemployment and poverty payments. It is clear in the first place that the incentive for trade-union leaders to consent to a reduction in money wages with a view to increasing the total volume of employment is very much reduced when the unemployed will be maintained by the state.[1] The objective of policy comes to be the maintenance of money wage rates rather than of employment. Secondly, it has been asserted that the system of labour exchanges, however beneficial it may be, does tend to diminish both local and industrial mobility. The former effect was emphasized by the Unemployment Grants Committee.[2] The extent of the latter differs very considerably from industry to industry; it is said to be especially noticeable in the Lancashire cotton industry. It must be recognized that the high hopes entertained at the time of the establishment of the unemployment exchanges have not entirely been fulfilled. They have done little or nothing to abolish casual labour and they have not proved a very useful medium for the direct filling of jobs. At the same time it would seem doubtful whether the enormous migration of labour which took place in the twenties could have been so easily accomplished if they had not been in existence.

But the most important effect of unemployment insurance on wages is undoubtedly the approximation of the total allowances made in benefit and assistance relative to the lower wage scales. The following figures have been quoted as typical of a South Wales miner with a large family:[3]

Wages (in average working week) . . 45s. 0d.
Unemployment Assistance . . . . 46s. 0d.

Similar conditions exist among unskilled workers all over the country. The trouble largely arises because benefits are, and wages are not, apportioned to needs. Under these circumstances, and allowing for the possibility of short time and other deductions from earnings, unemployment is a much more reliable way of acquiring an income than work. Where scales of relief attempt to provide subsistence and not merely to supplement savings, this tendency for assistance rates to get mixed with the lowest wage rates is extremely hard to avoid. It has also given trouble in America. The danger could only be completely eliminated by raising the general level of unskilled wages or apportioning them to needs by means of family allowances.[4]

[1] Cf. Beveridge, *Unemployment a Problem of Industry*, 2nd ed.
[2] Cf. *Final Report of the Unemployment Grants Committee*, 1933.
[3] Cf. *P.E.P. Report*, p. 163.
[4] The cost of such a scheme need not be prohibitive, since an allowance beginning at the fifth child would be sufficient to eliminate the worst clashes.

Since social expenditure is a net transfer from the rest of the community to (broadly speaking) the classes below the income-tax paying level, it imposes a net tax burden on the wealthier part of the community. This is indeed its intention. It must be noted, however, that if this burden is not wisely distributed it may have a far from negligible effect on the demand for labour. This is a matter which we must discuss at a later stage (Chapter XVII). The tax effect of the employers' contributions to social insurance is, however, so closely related to social expenditure that some notice of it must be taken here. The contribution is, briefly, a poll tax per worker employed. Although small in relation to other costs it amounts to some £4 10s. to £5 per worker per annum, and thus is by no means negligible, particularly in bad times. The incidence of the tax is, however, very uneven, both as between industries which employ or do not employ a large proportion of labour relatively to capital, and between those in which the proportions of workers to machines is rigidly fixed and those in which marginal workers can be dismissed without upsetting the organization of production. Except in the very short run, there is in most businesses a normal tendency to shift the real burden of the tax on to other shoulders. Some firms may add the tax to the price of the product they sell. Others may squeeze the suppliers of their raw materials. Others again may pass it on to their own workers in the form of reduced wages.

The contributory system is now so well established in this country, and is so obviously popular with beneficiaries of all classes, that it would need a revolution to overthrow it. But it is by no means certain that equally useful benefits cannot be obtained by other financial methods which have less direct economic effect. American experiments in this respect are especially worthy of study. In view of the rapid enlargement of the field of contributory insurance the economic disadvantages of this tax on production deserve more attention than they have received.

The importance which should be attached to the various factors which affect the price of labour differs very considerably according as we have long-period or normal conditions in mind, or are chiefly concerned with the immediate repercussions of the trade cycle. In the very long run most effects are probably adjusted by changes in other phenomena, in the sense that an old tax is no tax. The most important effect of high wages is in relation to selling power in competitive international markets. Even this may be compensated by a change in the international value of the currency, although at the cost of considerable internal and international disturbance. In the somewhat shorter period it seems probable that if the national income is relatively stationary (as it was 1925–31) a sudden increase in social expenditure may add seriously to the difficulties of the exchequer. The certain prospect of the automatic increase of important social services and the very uncertain prospect of the future of the national income suggest that this is a problem which may require careful attention in the future.

It is in depression that the economic effects of social expenditure are most marked, and its cross-currents most important. On the one hand, it is clearly desirable to maintain the volume of spending in order to prevent prices falling. Social expenditure contributes to this directly, since considerably larger sums than in normal times are distributed through the social services. To some extent its influence in maintaining wages works in the same direction. On the other hand, the real tax burden on industry rises as business incomes fall. An increase in insurance contributions such as occurred in the last depression may well turn the scales in favour of dismissing a worker. Alternatively in the early stages of recovery it may tend to retard an increase in the demand for labour. There are undoubtedly cases where a greater flexibility of wages would tend to extend employment and so raise total pay rolls and incomes.[1] The problem therefore is to maintain the social services without increasing the tax burden, and if possible to reduce the cost of labour to industry without destroying workers' purchasing power. This is a matter of considerable complication to which we shall have to return at a later stage (Part II, especially Chapter XVIII). The most important point at this stage is that the automatic expansion of social services which we have seen to be such a striking aspect of bad times is not a phenomenon which should cause alarm, but which if properly foreseen and financed, is itself a useful tool for fighting depression.

The economic effect of social expenditure may be profoundly influenced by the extent to which the funds accrue directly to

[1] The argument that a fall in money wages cannot increase employment is only completely true in a closed economy. It is not therefore very applicable to the British situation.

workers' incomes—either in the form of money or services—or are absorbed by other payments on the way. The social insurances are gradually building up considerable reserves under the management of the Treasury. The order of magnitude of these at the end of our period was: National Health Insurance £136 m., Unemployment Insurance £43·7 m., Treasury Pensions Account £20·9 m. In so far as these amounts exceed the necessary provision for foreseeable risks, there appear to be three alternative policies which the government may follow in their disposal. First, it may invest the funds so as to maximize their value, using any net capital gains for the benefit of the workers, in the form of reduced contributions or additional benefits. Secondly, it may use the funds as an additional weapon for smoothing out trade fluctuations by building them up in prosperity and allowing them to run down to the bare minimum in depression. Thirdly, it may apply the funds to what it considers to be the general interest of the community, and make use of them in its general monetary policy. On a priori grounds the second alternative would appear to be the most desirable, particularly in view of the uneven incidence of the benefits of social insurance. We shall have to investigate its possibilities fully at a later stage (Chapter XVIII). There is evidence that some use of the third alternative has been made. This is also a matter which will call for investigation later (Chapter XXIII). The objection to this last alternative from the point of view of the social services should, however, be mentioned here. It is doubtful if the Treasury is under any obligation to make good to the funds any losses which they may sustain in the course of their use in monetary policy. In view of what happened to the Road Fund, it is not even certain that the Treasury would be particularly merciful in the matter of interest on losses. It seems desirable to reserve social funds for social purposes, in one way or another.

It would be a long, though not unprofitable, task to examine in the case of each service the extent to which the wealthier classes in the community benefit from social expenditure rather than those for whom they are intended—for instance in administrative or professional salaries. This problem is obviously closely related to that of over-capacity to which reference has already been made. There are, however, two particular services in which a somewhat conspicuous rise in the cost per head suggests that it would be worth inquiring to what extent increasing expenditure has been passed on to the beneficiaries in improved service. Elementary education cost £5 2s. per child in 1913, £12 4s. in 1922, and in 1936, in spite of the considerable fall in prices, nearly £15. There are of course a great number of contributory causes to this increase, such as the increased cost per head of educating a smaller school population, and the expenses of the reorganization of the curriculum introduced during the period. These, however, hardly seem sufficient to account for such a large expansion. It is worth noting that the May Committee[1] were of the opinion that the great increase in teachers' salaries had played an important part. This may or may not be fully passed on to the children in improved teaching. There are also grounds for believing that considerable economies might be effected by the abolition of the system of dual responsibility among local authorities and by a consequent drastic reduction in the number of independent education authorities. In 1936 there were 351 education authorities in Great Britain. Of these 170 were responsible for local education only, while the larger authorities supplied secondary education in their areas, besides being responsible for the entire education service elsewhere. The abolition of the education authorities with limited powers was recommended by the May Committee in 1931. It was not carried out, and has since become more urgent. The pressure on all education authorities to provide improved services for the older children is leading in some places[2] to competition between the elementary education authorities as purveyors of senior schools, central schools, and junior technical institutes, and the county authorities as providers of secondary education. Competition of this type is both wasteful and undesirable on technical grounds. It would be serious if the education service, which is such a desirable part of social expenditure and which appears to have reached a relatively stationary stage of development, did not make the best use of its funds.

Costs per head in National Health Insurance increased from £1 2s. per annum in 1920 to about £2 in 1934—again with much lower prices. As the number of beneficiaries has steadily though not alarmingly increased, there should have been some possible economies in spreading overheads, but the contrary

[1] Cf. loc. cit., pp. 191 ff.
[2] Cf. *P.E.P. Report*, p. 68.

appears to have been the case. To what causes should the increase be ascribed? The May Committee were of the opinion that the remuneration of panel doctors was definitely too high (it worked out at an average of 9s. 4½d. per patient).[1] They were most emphatic that the high remuneration had increased the cost of medical officers to the public authorities. It was, however, decided in 1937 to continue the rates of payment unchanged. Another curious phenomenon is the extraordinary increase in the number of prescriptions.[2] In twelve years these rose from 38 million to 62 million and the cost from £1·2 m. to £2·1 m. This phenomenon is apparently confined to England, which suggests that the southerner prefers his medical service in bottle form. It does not necessarily follow that he gets the best value.

The most wasteful factor in health insurance is, however, the extraordinarily anomalous position which has grown up among the approved societies through which the scheme is administered. This system was originally introduced because it offered an attractive means of getting the service started quickly, without setting up complicated and expensive administrative machinery. The advantages to be derived from a worker being free to join the democratically managed society of his choice were also emphasized. In practice this freedom of entry has not been realized. All might have been well if the societies had possessed reasonably equal resources, and had been really democratically managed, but neither of these conditions was fulfilled. Hence the power of the stronger societies to insist on good employment and health prospects in their members has led to the absurd position in which societies vary in membership from over 2 million to under 50. The Royal Commission on National Health Insurance[3] found that at one end of the scale 70 societies had less than 100 members, while at the other 24 had over 50,000. The stronger the society, the better the health record of its members, and the greater the additional benefits it can afford. It has been estimated that at present about two-thirds of insured workers receive additional benefits up to 5s. a week, while over one-fifth, who probably need them most, receive no additional benefits at all. This is a situation somewhat analogous to the exploitation of one set of workers by

---

[1] Cf. loc. cit., p. 159.   [2] Cf. Gibbon, loc. cit.
[3] Cf. *Royal Commission on National Health Insurance*, 1928, p. 96, and *P.E.P. Report*, p. 112.

another under the unemployment insurance system. It cannot result in the maximum health benefit being derived from the service.

The extent to which the social services imply a redistribution of the national income from the richer to the poorer part of the community naturally differs very much from one service to another, as it does from one country to another. Thus the British education service is more redistributive than for instance the Dutch, where all classes use the state-provided schools, both for elementary and secondary education. It is not possible to get a highly accurate picture of the extent to which workers (or members of the community with incomes below £250 a year) do in fact pay for their various benefits. An approximation can, however, be made by deducting from the figures of Diagram I, workers' contributions to social insurance, fees, &c., paid for education, and rents, &c., for houses. (Since the last two entries in the official return also include interest payments, they are not entirely net figures.) The results are shown in Diagram III. (There are in addition some small payments made for public health (hospital) services.) This diagram gives an approximate measure of transfer expenditure. Although all the expenditure may be said to be for the benefit of workers, their net receipts are of course smaller than the amounts shown. Some £25 m. a year is absorbed in administrative expenses. On the other hand, additions of some £20–30 m. a year have to be made for other public health expenditure, not shown in the Return of Public Social Services. At least half of this should probably be allotted to the benefit of workers, on the basis of the share of working-class houses in rate contributions. A further sum, differing from year to year but mainly accreditable to workers, since housing is the largest item, should be allowed for fresh expenditure out of loan. This would make a total (for 1933) of about £393 m. net—with additions of about £20 m. For most years the proportion of transfer to gross expenditure on the social services is about 80 per cent., but, as we should expect, the proportion of transfer increases slightly in bad years. Thus in 1926 it was 88 per cent. compared with about 84 per cent. the year before. In 1931 it was 85 per cent. compared with 83 per cent. in 1934. This slight swing-over is an additional assistance to the favourable economic repercussions of social expenditure in depression,

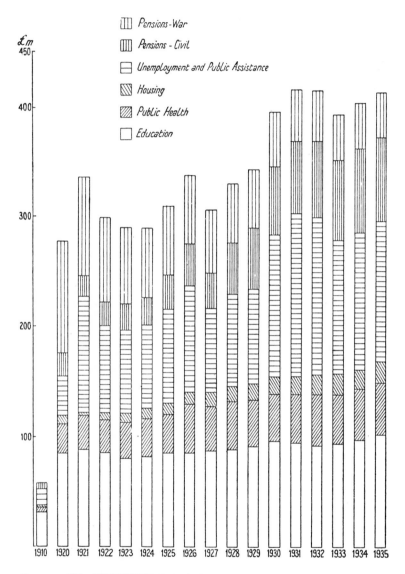

DIAGRAM III.—EXPENDITURE ON SOCIAL SERVICES—TRANSFER
(Great Britain) Excluding Loan Expenditure
(*For notes and figures, cf. Appendix* 6)

particularly if it is not financed by an increase in the current tax burden (as was indeed the case in 1931–2).

The question is often asked how far social expenditure is a net redistribution to workers in the sense that it is a net receipt not merely over specific contributions to particular services, but over their share of national and local taxation. To determine the proportion of total taxes paid by workers (that is by people with incomes under £250) is an extremely hazardous business. Not only are the statistics of working-class consumption of taxed goods inadequate and out of date,[1] but no statistical apparatus has yet been devised for determining the final incidence of indirect taxes and of rates. The main variable on the tax side is undoubtedly the extent of commodity taxes on articles of food, and on the two heavily taxed groups of tobacco and alcohol. In the thirties the trend of indirect taxation has been upwards, but it is not so high as it was before the war, particularly on commodities of ordinary consumption. On the expenditure side the proportion of transfer to gross expenditure appears now to be fairly steady. Any increase in the proportion of contributory services tends to lower it slightly. The small difference noted above between 1925–6 and 1931–4 can be accounted for by two factors. The social legislation of 1925–31 was predominantly of the contributory type, and war pensions, which is almost wholly a transfer service in this sense, had considerably declined. On the other hand, although the difference between gross and transfer expenditure tends to increase as social expenditure increases, the absolute amount of transfer expenditure is steadily growing. Before the war practically the whole of the social services were redistributive on the expenditure side, but the total did not exceed £70 m.

The situation is thus fundamentally different from what it was before the war. On any calculation of the incidence of indirect taxation the working-class population made a net contribution to national and local revenue in 1913. In the post-war period there has been a redistribution of increasing importance in their favour. Unless we are willing to make assumptions as to the final incidence of taxation, it is not possible to say what the order of magnitude of the redistribution is. Mr. Clark is prepared to

---

[1] The position will be very much improved when the revision of the Cost of Living Index Number (undertaken in 1937–8) has been completed.

maintain that it amounted in 1935 to £91 m.[1] He was using a series of expenditure figures which are apparently a little less comprehensive than those on which our diagrams are based. If for the moment we accept[2] his tax assumptions, but continue with our expenditure figures, we may conclude that redistribution was of the order of £80 m. in 1925–6, and £100 m.[3] ten years later (with additions of £10 m. to £15 m. to allow for other public health expenditure). To estimate the complete long-term economic effect of this it is of course necessary to take into account the taxes from which the funds were obtained. As long as indirect taxation does not increase faster than gross social expenditure the upward trend in redistribution is practically bound to continue.

The public social services are far from exhausting the whole tale of expenditure of the national income on behalf of the working classes. There are in addition voluntary social services[4] spending annually many millions of pounds, and employing thousands of workers, paid and unpaid. Some of these services are entirely independent of public expenditure, although they are actually carrying out very similar tasks to some of those operated by local authorities. Their work thus implies a similar redistribution of income to that of the public services. The chief examples of this type are the Charity Organization Society, and large numbers of small independent charities. Many of the voluntary services are, however, connected more or less directly with public work. Thus they may act as paid agents for public authorities (as the voluntary hospitals do); or they may be grant aided, either in respect of their general policy, or for the performance of specific duties. One type of increasing importance is really an extension of public work in cases where rather more freedom of action and flexibility of finance is required than is thought proper for public authorities. Conspicuous examples are the Nuffield Trust and the Land Settlement Association, both working in conjunction with the

[1] Cf. Clark, *National Income and Outlay*, p. 148.

[2] But see further discussion in Chap. XVI, and Bowley's review of Clark, *National Income and Outlay*, in *Economica*, 1937.

[3] Using Mr. Clark's figures for the wage bill, this would imply that the social services led to an expenditure for the benefit of workers equivalent to about 5 per cent. addition to wages—rather less in 1925, rather more ten years later.

[4] Cf. *P.E.P. Report*, pp. 132 ff., for an account of the relation of voluntary to public social services. They have not, however, examined the vexed question of the relation of public health services to the medical profession and the voluntary hospitals.

Commissioner for Special Areas. Finally, there is a very large body of voluntary workers attached to the public social services, such as the co-opted members of education, &c., committees, managers of voluntary schools, and workers in the various organizations connected with child welfare. All these voluntary organizations form in fact an extension of the public services, and their policy and scope of operations is to some extent determined by the state. The field of influence of the social services is thus considerably larger than that covered by expenditure out of public funds.

It is evident that the extent of the social services makes them a powerful factor from the purely economic point of view, as well as from the social standpoint. Their effect is, moreover, one of steadily increasing weight in the community. The motive behind the expansion of the social services now appears to be a definite, if still only implicit, programme of redistribution of income. It is thus primarily political in character. This provides a much more solid basis for expansion than the more purely charitable motives which dominated the nineteenth century. It is essential both for their own sake and for the realization of a unified socio-economic policy that the economic aspect of the social services should not only be fully realized, but properly co-ordinated with the other departments of public finance.

TABLE I

Social expenditure on capital account in Great Britain

(£ m.)

	1931	1932	1933	1934	1935
Education . . .	9·9	5·7	4·6	4·8	†
Public Health . . .	2·2	1·9	2·2	2·2	†
Housing:					
England and Wales . .	32·2	20·9	21·0	18·7	†
Scotland . . .	4·9	4·9	7·4	†	†
Public Assistance . .	1·1*	0·6*	0·8*	0·7*	†
Total . . .	50·3	34·0	36·0	36·4	

* These figures refer to the following year.
† Not Available.

(From *Return of Public Social Services*.)

IV

STATE AID TO INDUSTRY AS A WHOLE

IN surveying social expenditure our task was relatively easy. A number of different services had to be considered, and it was necessary to take account of both central and local spending. But we were examining a whole, more or less unified in purpose, closely related if not actually co-ordinated. The economic section in our consolidated expenditure account (Diagram I, Chapter II) is by no means so unified. In the first place it includes outlays of two entirely different types. By far the largest part is represented by enterprises in which public authorities are themselves entrepreneurs. This consists of three big sub-groups—the trading services of local authorities, highway expenditure, and the Post Office. (The last is the only large trading service under the direct control of the central government.) The second type consists of those outlays (practically all from the central budget) which aim either at assisting industry as a whole or at giving aid to particular groups of producers. This section represents policy directly, and is the most variable. It has therefore an interest far exceeding its actual bulk. We shall be concerned with it in this chapter and the next. The three large sub-groups in the first type comprise what is generally termed public investment. This is an aspect of economic expenditure which raises very important problems, both of a long period and of a cyclical nature. We shall be occupied with them in chapters VI to VIII.

A block diagram illustrates the distribution of the different items of economic expenditure (Diagram I). It has, however, somewhat less significance than the companion piece in the last chapter. It is necessarily confined to current expenditure but it is impossible to avoid including a certain amount of capital outlay. This is responsible for some irregularity. Moreover, current expenditure is of course only a very limited part of total expenditure when capital works have to be provided. This is a more important item here than in the case of social expenditure.[1] Further, economic expenditure is in general considerably more variable than social expenditure. The

---

[1] Cf. discussion in the next chapter.

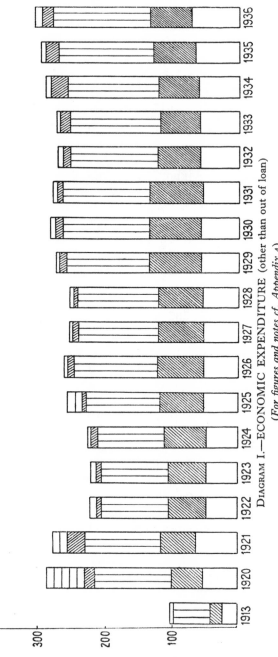

Aid to Industry and Trade
Aid to Agriculture
Local Trading Services
Roads
Post Office

£m

400
300
200
100

1913 1920 1921 1922 1923 1924 1925 1926 1927 1928 1929 1930 1931 1932 1933 1934 1935 1936

DIAGRAM I.—ECONOMIC EXPENDITURE (other than out of loan)
(For figures and notes cf. Appendix 4)

first two items in particular consist of a number of small scattered grants, any of which may suddenly be put on or discontinued. Their separate movements are sometimes additive and sometimes compensatory. Nor again is direct expenditure a useful guide to the importance or significance of a service. A sudden increase in a particular line may only indicate that the policy has been a failure and that unexpected losses have to be covered (as was the case with the trade facilities guarantees and the milk subsidy). Further economic expenditure frequently affects other industries almost as vitally as those it is designed to assist. If the secondary reactions are very violent they may in their turn lead to fresh expenditure, otherwise they will not figure in the expenditure account. Far more important than these considerations, however, is the fact that actual economic outlay is only a part, and in general, a very small part, of economic policy. The expansion of economic expenditure is an important but only a partial reflection of the move towards public control and paternal economic policy which has been characteristic of the post-war world.

Even with these reservations, however, the diagram does reveal certain interesting movements. The direct interests of public authorities in the economic field are now of very considerable importance. Annual expenditure amounted to 60 per cent. of social expenditure in 1936 and absorbed 23 per cent. of total public outlay. This is of course a very small proportion compared with countries where there is a long tradition of public ownership and where in addition to the activities of the local authorities the central government may own important natural resources and mining rights as well as transport and other services. Nevertheless, for a country which is founded on a *laisser-faire* tradition, the steady expansion and present total are alike striking. Economic purposes are becoming an important candidate for the taxpayer's money. Public investment absorbs an ever-increasing part of his savings.

The year to year variations are, as we should expect, broadly the same for economic as for social expenditure. The effect of economy campaigns is, however, more noticeable. Economic expenditure is less automatic and contractual than social. The economy years—1922, 1923, 1928, and 1932–3—show up even more clearly if we isolate the Trade and Industry Vote (the heading under which the majority of miscellaneous economic expenditures to be found):

Trade and Industry (Class VI) Vote (Gross Exchequer Issues)

£m. (Financial years)

1913	1920	1921	1922	1923	1924	1925	1926	1927
1·2	13·5	11·1	4·9	7·5	4·4	5·6	8·5	9·9

1928	1929	1930	1931	1932	1933	1934	1935	1936
9·1	10·2	12·6	14·9	9·2	9·3	16·3	17·1	17·8

Broadly, expenditure increases with tax receipts, and the outlying parts are abruptly cut off when there is difficulty in balancing the budget. But although the period is too short to draw very definite conclusions, and comparison with pre-war situations is not very helpful because the scope of such expenditure was very much more restricted, it appears that the timing of economic expenditure in relation to the trade cycle tends to differ slightly from that of the social services. The latter expand automatically at the beginning of depression, and this leads to an effort at economy at a later stage. Economic expenditure, however, can more easily be restricted at once, but as soon as tax receipts begin to show any sign of a turn there is a tendency for it to expand to assist particular groups of producers out of the pit. This tendency continues at an accelerated pace, so that the maximum public expenditure may easily coincide with the boom. The 1937 estimates were somewhat lower, but this did not represent an economy so much as a transfer of energy —on the one hand to rearmament, and on the other to greater highway expenditure by the central government on the assumption of responsibility for trunk roads from April 1937. The timing of economic expenditure is a question which we must investigate in detail later, both in relation to budget votes and to public investment.

Our first task is to survey economic expenditure designed to aid industry as a whole. To do this we must search out the nooks and crannies of the national accounts. Not only may items be found almost anywhere, but the same item is apt to change its place from year to year, depending sometimes on the technical form in which the vote is presented or on the manner of making up the national accounts.[1] One great difficulty with economic expenditure is that there is no co-ordinating department[2] parallel to the Ministry of

---

[1] The classification of the Civil Accounts was completely altered in 1927 and it is not always easy to trace what became of particular votes.

[2] The Board of Trade would be the natural nucleus of such a department.

Health for the social services. This, however, makes it all the more desirable to attempt to undertake the task of bringing the various items together. Table 1 shows the 'Trade and Industry' class broken up into its various items, together with votes collected from other parts of the accounts, excluding assistance to the agricultural industries, which is analysed separately (Table 1, p. 90). The greater part of this expenditure was designed to assist industry as a whole. It was supplemented by tax concessions of a more or less general nature, which should properly be treated with it.

Assistance to industry as a whole falls roughly into six groups:

   (i) General Services.
  (ii) Research.
 (iii) Interest Guarantees.
 (iv) Credit Insurance.
  (v) Economic Development.
 (vi) Tax Concessions (Derating).

Of these, the first two are more or less completely general, the benefit to one firm or industry is as great as to another, and the assistance is in the nature of an 'external economy'. Expenditure in the third, fourth, and fifth groups accrues to particular firms, but the assistance is available to all or a number of industries. The last group is from the budget point of view a new expenditure, dating from the Local Government Act of 1929, as local authorities had to be compensated for the loss of rate receipts. From the point of view of the taxpaying community it is, however, a transfer, not a new burden. From the point of view of entrepreneurs it represents a direct saving similar to a reduction in rent. Assistance accrued to industrial and agricultural entrepreneurs, and eventually to the railways.

(i) In the first class we have the routine services of the central departments concerned with industry—mainly under the Board of Trade, such as the Weights and Measures, and the Standards Departments, and the Mercantile Marine services. It is a matter of definition whether certain services of the Ministry of Labour such as the maintenance of employment exchanges should also be included. In their original intention they certainly should have had the effect of widening the labour market and lessening frictions, and thus have been of economic assistance; but as they have developed, their main functions are now social rather than

TABLE I

Expenditure in Aid of Industry and Trade (Excluding Agriculture)[1]

(£ m.)

	1920	1921	1922	1923	1924	1925	1926	1927	1928	1929	1930	1931	1932	1933	1934	1935	1936
Board of Trade (General Services)	1·5	1·7	0·6	0·4	0·5	0·5	0·5	0·5	0·2	0·2	0·2	0·2	0·2	0·2	0·2	0·2	0·3
Mercantile Marine Services	0·6	0·4	0·3	0·4	0·4	0·4	0·4	0·4	0·4	0·4	0·4	0·4	0·4	0·3	0·3	0·4	0·4
Assistance to British Shipping[2]	0·4	··	··	··	··	··	··	··	··	··	··	··	··	··	··	1·9	2·0
Department of Overseas Trade	0·4	0·4	0·3	0·3	0·3	0·2	0·3	0·3	0·3	0·4	0·4	0·4	0·4	0·4	0·4	0·4	0·5
Export Credits	0·5	0·2	0·1	0·2	0·04	0·3	0·1	0·1	0·1	0·07	0·04	0·8	0·7	0·2	0·3	··	0·3
Overseas Settlement and Colonial Development	0·7	1·0	0·7	0·4	0·4	0·6	1·1	1·2	1·1	0·6	1·4	0·8	0·7	0·5	0·5	2·9	0·9
Empire Marketing Board	··	··	··	··	··	··	0·5	0·4	0·5	0·6	0·6	0·5	0·3	0·3	··	··	··
Trade Facilities Payments	··	··	··	··	··	··	0·1	0·1	0·1	0·2	0·2	0·5	1·0	1·7	1·4	0·1	0·1
Mines Department	0·04	0·2	0·2	0·2	0·2	0·1	0·1	0·2	0·1	0·2	0·2	0·2	0·2	0·2	0·1	0·1	0·1
Ministry of Transport	0·9	0·3	0·3	0·1	··	0·4	0·1	0·4	0·2	0·4	0·5	0·4	0·1	0·6	0·6	0·6	0·9
Department of Industrial and Scientific Research	0·4	0·2	0·1	0·3	0·3	0·4	0·4	0·4	0·4	0·4	0·5	0·4	0·5	0·1	0·1	0·2	0·1
Development Grants (Public Utilities)	0·1	··	··	··	··	··	··	··	··	··	··	0·4	0·1	0·1	0·1	0·2	0·6
State Management Districts	0·03	··	··	··	··	··	··	··	··	0·2	0·02	0·2	0·5	0·8	0·9	0·9	0·2
Civil Aviation	0·3	0·7	0·6	0·6	0·6	0·6	0·6	0·6	0·6	0·6	0·6	0·5	0·6	0·8	0·9	0·9	0·9
Coal Industry—subsidies, &c.	15·0	0·8	3·8	0·8	··	19·0	4·2	0·1	0·5	0·7	0·4	0·04	··	··	··	··	··
Australian Zinc Concentrates[3]	··	0·8	1·2	1·3	··	0·2	0·5	0·6	0·9	0·2	0·4	0·2	··	··	··	0·1	··
Miscellaneous[4]	35·4	9·3	1·2	0·8	0·02	··	··	··	··	0·3	0·3	0·2	0·1	0·1	0·2	0·1	0·3
Total Net Expenditure	56·1	15·9	9·5	5·4	2·4	21·9	8·6	4·7	5·1	4·5	5·2	4·5	5·0	5·7	5·3	9·0	7·7

[1] From Appropriation Accounts, Net Issues. Where fees, &c., are a substantial part of revenue, their value is shown in small type. Trade Facilities payments from Finance Accounts.
[2] Including the Coastwise Shipping subsidy, and the Tramp Shipping subsidy. The Cunard-White Star advances are not shown.
[3] Contracts of 1916 and 1917.
[4] Including the Bread Subsidy (1920) and contribution to the Railway Rebates Fund (1920). The cost of the Economic Advisory Council is not given separately in the accounts, and is not included.

economic.[1] In addition there are the special post-war services—
the Department of Overseas Trade, the Empire Marketing Board,
the Colonial Development Fund, &c., and the Economic Advisory
Council. Of the first of these we need say little here, as we shall
be concerned with one of its most useful functions in connexion
with export credits. It is universally acknowledged that difficult
as was the position of exporters among the many fresh unknowns
of post-war overseas markets, it would have been still worse
without the expert advice of the D.O.T. This is the type of economic service that the government of a powerful country, having
agents in every important town in the world, is in a unique position
to provide for its exporters.

The Empire Marketing Board was established in 1926, during
the Churchill régime, to assist in the marketing of Empire goods,
and abolished on the recommendation of the May Committee in
1931. It was understood that funds up to £1 m. per annum would
be available for it. Actually it never received a grant much above
£600,000, and in every year net expenditure was considerably
below the sum allotted.[2] Less than half its funds were devoted to
marketing and publicity, the remainder being either absorbed by
administrative expenses or passed on to other departments as subsidies for research, &c. It appears that such extraordinary economy
of resources was due not so much to good management as to a
difficulty in finding means to fulfil its purpose. A possible explanation of this was that the work of the E.M.B. overlapped with that
of several other departments, but that it was not itself in a position
to be a co-ordinating body. There is an obvious limit to the amount
which can profitably be spent on publicity, specially of the very
general nature which the board undertook. It has been maintained[3]
that towards the end of its career the board performed useful work
by laying the foundation for the (home) agricultural marketing
boards, but this was hardly within its original purpose. The failure
of the E.M.B. to find any work of lasting importance to perform is
of interest in view of the projected establishment of a Colonial
Marketing Board.

The Economic Advisory Council proved a similar misfit, although
its life has been shorter and its total expenditure a quite negligible
sum. It was established as an effort to deal with the sudden crisis

[1] Cf. Chap. III, p. 50.   [2] Cf. *May Report*, p. 132.
[3] Cf. Venn, 'State Control in Agriculture', *E.J.* 1935.

of 1930. It may be remarked that when the patient is *in extremis* it is usually too late to call in a doctor. Under the circumstances it was not surprising that his advice was neglected. There can be no two opinions as to the necessity for greater attention to economic factors in public finance and government. An external advisory council without prestige, power, or even definite functions is, however, hardly sufficient to secure it.

Quite considerable sums have been expended in one way or another in promoting trade with the overseas dominions. Actual disbursements form only a small part of policy in this direction. Tariffs and quotas have played a much larger role. The expenditure is, however, worth examining for its own sake. Immediately after the war funds were used for setting up ex-soldiers and others overseas. Another group of expenditures is connected with the Colonial Development Fund, established in 1929. Its purpose was to develop agriculture and industry in the non-self-governing colonies and mandated territories, and thereby to promote commerce and industry in the United Kingdom. The fund may have played some small part in promoting the development of tropical territories which has been a striking feature of the post-war world economy. The May Committee[1] were, however, of the opinion that the second part of the aim—which was indeed the prime cause of its establishment—was only very remotely served by the type of grants awarded. These tended to turn into additional subsidies to the local authorities in the colonies in respect of public health, &c., expenditure. After 1931 expenditure was somewhat curtailed, but it does not appear that the objects assisted underwent any modification.

The greater part of expenditure under these heads had its origin in legislation passed during Mr. Churchill's tenure of office. They are notable for paying particular attention to promoting overseas trade, and in that respect were a continuation or substitution of the policy of interest and credit guarantees which had been started in the early post-war years. It cannot be said that any of these schemes had a very brilliant career, and all had their activities much curtailed as a result of the May investigation. The economic policy of the 'National' government, partly no doubt as a result of this experience, has run on more specific and hence more manageable lines.

[1] *May Report*, p. 133.

(ii) *Research.* The research expenditure shown in Table 1 is that co-ordinated under the Department of Scientific and Industrial Research. Actually, however, research is carried on by a great number of departments. It is not possible to isolate the actual sums spent, but a more or less complete list of the channels of research expenditure can be made:

    i. Research and grants by central bodies (Medical Research Council, Department of Industrial and Scientific Research).
    ii. Grants by other government bodies (Development Commission, Empire Marketing Board).
    iii. Grants to scientific bodies for research (Royal Society votes of £11,050–£12,050 are the most important).
    iv. Agricultural research, sponsored by
        (*a*) The Ministry direct.
        (*b*) The Development Commission.
        (*c*) Empire Marketing Board.
        (*d*) Forestry Commission.
        (*e*) North Sea Fisheries grant.
    v. Research by other government departments:
        (*a*) Ministry of Transport.
        (*b*) Mines Department.
        (*c*) Post Office.
        (*d*) Fighting services.
        (*e*) Board of Trade (Standards Department).

The questions which arise in connexion with research are three: (i) the extent to which research should be increased; (ii) the type and amount of research which the state itself should undertake, and (iii) the best methods of co-ordination. There can be little doubt that the general tendency is to spend too little on research, and particularly on what is almost certainly the most important part from a scientific point of view—that which does not offer immediate answers to particular questions, but where fully trained permanent workers are engaged on problems of their own finding. The May Committee, the time and terms of whose appointment predisposed them towards retrenchment, were emphatic[1] that research should be an expanding service. In view of this it is disturbing to find that, like other educational services, it tends to be cut down during depression. While there may be no immediate and apparent loss in results, continuity is essential for the production of first-class work.

[1] *May Report*, pp. 99–102.

When the May Committee discussed the type of research which the state should undertake, their reasoning became rather obscure. The state, they argued, should not undertake 'the burden of ordinary industrial research which has become one of the essential costs of production', but should seek to 'maintain the incentive to individual manufacturers to embark on research which is of direct benefit to themselves'. The state should therefore concentrate on research 'which is of direct benefit to the community', it should above all avoid research 'which however interesting does not afford the prospect of benefit to the country commensurate with the cost'. There are certain services which obviously fall within this criterion, a good example being those which the Ministry of Transport undertakes, in connexion with road surfaces, the wear and tear of different kinds of vehicles, braking, &c. But in the main, research which is of direct benefit to the community and not to particular firms is so because in the first instance it is of direct benefit to public enterprise. In this case its benefits should also be extended (with due precaution as to payment) to similar private industry. But it seems clear that the research which the state can most usefully undertake (or subsidize in suitable hands) is just in those lines which do not offer any immediate result, and which are therefore most likely to be neglected by individual firms or specific industrial research bodies.

The effectiveness of research is naturally much enhanced if co-ordination (both of public and private research) is secured, and overlapping avoided. When the May Committee wrote, although there were two[1] co-ordinating bodies and the prospect of a third, co-ordination was obviously far from complete. Both in respect of the grants made by the Development Commission and the Empire Marketing Board for instance, the committee speaks of 'assistance being granted to a service by two or three different channels, thus making Treasury or Privy Council control very difficult'. When we contemplate the variety of research bodies at the beginning of the section, the task of co-ordination is obviously formidable.

We may say then in conclusion that although public grants for research were very much extended during the post-war period, the

---

[1] The Department of Scientific and Industrial Research and the Medical Research Council. The formation of an Agricultural Advisory Council was contemplated, and took place a few months later.

type of research which the state should properly assist had not been adequately thought out, and the expenditure (partly no doubt because of its rapid increase) was very imperfectly co-ordinated.

(iii) *Interest Guarantees by the Government.* The guarantee of principal and interest on certain types of borrowing is a method of assistance (by cheapening production costs) which has been much practised since the war. If all goes well the public outlay is negligible, but as this has not always been the case, we should review the service as a whole. There have been two distinct periods of interest guarantees. The first was the era of the 'Trade Facilities Acts 1921–6', initiated by the immediate post-war coalition government, the second a series of guarantees under various acts, to promote investment, sponsored by the 'National' government. The contrast between the methods and results of the two is an interesting study both of the process of learning by experience and of the re-orientation of economic policy which took place during the period. The object of the trade facilities scheme was to overcome the restrictive effects on investment of the very high interest rates ruling immediately after the war. Although of quite general application it was primarily intended to assist the export industries, especially heavy engineering (there were a great number of ship-building grants). In the years of its operation (1921 to March 1927) £74·3 m. was guaranteed as to principal and interest. As the government itself was not in a position to borrow very cheaply the loans could not be floated at less than 4½–5 per cent. and were generally for 20–30-year periods. The assistance was given to a large number of different firms, it being quite exceptional for the same firm to receive it for more than one or at most two loans. The loans were for the most part in very small amounts, sums over £1 m. being altogether exceptional, the majority being less than £100,000. The distribution[1] was roughly as follows:

i.	Transport	15	per cent.
ii.	Shipping and shipbuilding	14	,,
iii.	Miscellaneous heavy industries	11	,,
iv.	Electric power	10	,,
v.	Beet-sugar factories	5	,,
vi.	Other home industries	6	,,

[1] The Committee on Industry and Trade estimated that the distribution of the operations of the assisted companies was: Home guarantees £49·2 m.; Empire £8·3 m.; Foreign £7·4 m. At the time of the report guarantees amounting to £63.9 m. had been given.

The subsequent financial history of many of the assisted companies has been unfortunate,[1] particularly in the shipping and heavy industry groups. The sugar companies have had their profits secured (and hence the means of paying interest) only by the beet sugar subsidy.[2] The government, i.e. the taxpayers, has had to pay substantial sums to the debenture holders. In view of the subsequent fall in interest rates it would have been very desirable to convert the loans to lower rates, so that the interest charge might be within the means of the companies themselves. Permission to convert was indeed obtained in the budget of 1934, but owing to the rigidity and length of life of the loans there was very little scope for putting it into effect.[3]

The second period of government guaranteed issues began in July 1935 with a loan for the purpose of electrifying suburban lines in London. The chief issues which would strictly speaking be included in this period are:

London Electric Transport Finance Corporation £32 m. 2½ per cent. deb. (at 97), issued 1935, repayable 1955, plus £9·65 m. issued in Jan. 1937 at 92½.

Railway Finance Corporation, £27 m. 2½ per cent. deb. (at 97), issued 1936, repayable 1951-2.

British Sugar Corporation, £750,000 2¾ per cent. deb., 1936.

The first two are Treasury companies formed in order to relend the funds to certain private companies—the big railways, for the purposes laid down in the relevant acts—mainly for electrification. The new corporations thus stand as middlemen between the companies on the one side and the investors and the government on the other. The spending companies are otherwise as independent and free from control as before. They are, in fact, in a very similar position to those that took advantage of the Trade Facilities Acts 1921-6, but in other respects there are important differences between the two schemes. In the first place the loans are wholly for home investment, and there is therefore more opportunity for judg-

[1] A typical history is that of the Newfoundland Power and Paper Co. which received a T.F.A. guarantee in 1923. It had an unfortunate career and its assets were acquired by the International Paper Co. of Newfoundland in 1927. This company paid no dividends before 1935, but was then able to convert its T.F.A. loan from 4½ per cent. to 3 per cent.

[2] Cf. p. 101 below.

[3] In 1934 conversion was only possible in the nine cases in which optional redemption dates had been provided for. Only seven of these occurred before 1941.

ing the future prospects of the beneficiaries. These are in themselves much stronger than most of the companies who received the earlier guarantees. The purpose of mitigating the effect of high interest rates is less important than in the earlier period, and the aim of encouraging investment in a time of slackness bulks more importantly. They are thus essentially part of a depression 'Public Investment' policy. The question of subsequent conversion is of little importance when interest rates are low, and it is naturally of advantage to make the loans for as long a period as possible. Railway electrification is an investment the profitability of which has long been debated. The Southern Railway has found it a definitely paying proposition without any assistance. It is thus possible that the railways are being aided to do what they could have done unaided and would probably do later, but apart from the trade cycle argument of speeding up this form of investment, there is a very strong amenity argument for proceeding with electrification (and smoke abatement) at as quick a rate as possible.

Obviously, as far as industry is concerned, this type of assistance may have two disadvantages. To assist one line of investment 'discriminates' unjustly against others. There is perhaps less substance in this argument when applied to such general services as transport than in other cases. Secondly, the fact that money can be borrowed at 'gilt-edged' rates, without reference to profits, may encourage slack administration on the part of the assisted companies. Both the existence of the regulating Treasury companies and the fact that the loans are in a few large issues does something to lessen the danger of money being wasted, but again the case of railways is perhaps particularly favourable. From the point of view of the government (and hence the taxpayers) the largeness and infrequency of the loans is a definite advantage, since it enables the government to 'rig the market', and to float the loans at a particularly cheap rate.[1] It was clear that some of the special causes of failure of the earlier loans, such as borrowing for long periods at high rates, and assisting companies whose prospects were both unknown and uncertain, have been avoided in the most recent loans. In these days of managed currencies[2] the unfortunate

[1] Cf. *Economist*, 18 and 25 Jan. and 1 Feb. 1936.
[2] But even managed currencies can rarely be managed without any reference to the level of the foreign exchanges.

conjunction of high interest rates and depression are much less likely to recur. Generally speaking high rates are a boom symptom, and a clear signal for the government to avoid pushing on public investment. Given the absence of the special difficulties of the early post-war years, it seems that this form of government assistance might play an extremely useful part in depression policy.

The British Sugar Corporation is in a rather different position. The capital was subscribed by the constituent companies, under the compulsory amalgamation of the 'Sugar Industry Reorganisation Act', 1936.[1] The British sugar-beet industry is in the peculiar position of existing only on the taxpayers' suffrance. That implies that although profits depend partly on efficiency of management, their ultimate source is the annual subsidy. The corporation's rate of profit is limited to 7 per cent. Under the circumstances this appears to be largely a matter of book-keeping. Nevertheless, the organization of an industry under a public commission, with some sort of government control, suggests a new method which is capable of numerous modifications, whereby industries might be virtually passed into public control while retaining some of the advantages of private management and equity.

When we consider the whole history of interest guarantees during our period the device looks much better than it did in 1927 when the trade facilities scheme was discontinued. There has been, however, no second attempt to revive the export industries by this method, and this must be set down partly to the change, already noted, in government policy. Economic self-sufficiency and exports are incompatible. On the other hand, the revival effect on home industry of the big railway loans was undoubtedly substantial.

(iv) *Credit Insurance.*[2] The insurance of credits in export trade was, like the trade facilities guarantee scheme, a product of the immediate post-war years—another example of the anxiety of the coalition government to revive the export industries. The first period of operation of the scheme came to an end in 1926, but unlike the trade facilities guarantees it was not then abandoned. Experience had already pointed to a way in which it might play a permanent part in state assistance to industry. As refounded the

---

[1] For the terms cf. *Economist*, 1 Aug. 1936.
[2] For the whole question of credit insurance, cf. Shenkman, *Insurance against Credit Risks.*

scheme differed materially from the earlier somewhat grandiose conception. In the early post-war years considerable sums were lost by attempting to provide cover against exchange depreciation. It was found that this was not a suitable risk for insurance.[1] After 1926 the scheme was gradually put on to a paying basis. Although a token vote of £100 is annually allowed, the venture has operated at a profit since 1931. The statutory limits to the credits outstanding were limited to £25 m. (until 1937), but the service provided was more extensive than this would suggest. Since insurance is usually on a 75 per cent. basis, the fund could finance transactions amounting to about £35 m. simultaneously. In so far as cover was demanded for quickly liquidated transactions, such as in consumers' goods, or indeed many raw materials, it could provide the basis for a revolving fund, which covered a substantial proportion of total exports.[2] In practice it was found possible to provide cover also for somewhat longer export transactions, and in the case of 'machinery and other capital goods' special arrangements are made 'on the merits of the case'.

Since the refounding of the scheme in 1926 two extensions have been introduced which are worth noting although they do not lie wholly within our period. From the end of 1935[3] it became possible to insure against delays of payment in countries where exchange restrictions are in force, and where consequently a perfectly solvent debtor may have difficulty in acquiring the requisite foreign exchange at the due date. Under the Export Guarantees Act, 1937, a further enlargement of the field of operations was made possible. The statutory limit of the fund was raised from £25 m. to £50 m., and the time limit for credits abolished. Further cover was provided on the one hand for re-exports, and on the other for expenditure incurred abroad. It was announced that in four years the fund's turnover had increased from £7·5 m. to £35 m., and that (up to the first half of 1937 presumably) a profit of £2 m. had been made.

[1] Besides dealing with an unpredictable risk, currency depreciation insurance is concerned with a biased sample: depreciated currencies tend to further depreciation. While normally losses can be covered on the forward market, this device is only too likely not to be working freely.
[2] At some £370–£450 m.
[3] Announced in *The Times*, 25 Oct. 1935. Normally the guarantee is for 75 per cent. of the *sterling* value of goods, but it may be refused if there is little likelihood that sterling will be forthcoming at the due date.

The main reason for the success of the export credits scheme is no doubt the fact that it deals with an unbiased sample, good debts as well as bad being insured, and by strong firms as well as weak. In this respect it differed from the early trade facilities guarantees where on the whole strong firms were conspicuous by their absence. At the same time, a very important part of its work is the unrivalled information which the D.O.T. can supply to the Treasury through the consular and diplomatic service. The actual finance is provided by the banks, who in this case perform an office similar to the Treasury corporations under the second trade facilities scheme. This may also be a contributory factor to success, since the banks are in closer touch with their own clients than a government department could be. The extension to longer period transactions constitutes a species of middle-term foreign lending. This is particularly useful. In a period when there is little encouragement and to some extent an actual embargo on foreign loans, it does something to keep alive the basis of international trade. Moreover, medium-term credit is notoriously a difficult form of borrowing to arrange, either for home or for foreign transactions.[1]

(v) *Economic Development.* There is very little to show in the way of direct expenditure on economic development if we except the beet-sugar industry, which is more conveniently dealt with under agriculture. Certain relatively small sums have been allocated to particular firms under the powers given to the Development Commission to assist rural industries, inland navigation, &c. The Development Commission was a pre-war inheritance, created in 1909 at the same time as the petrol tax was allocated to road development. In accordance with the liberal policy which was responsible for its establishment, its energies were mainly directed to rural betterment. Like the Empire Marketing Board it devoted considerable sums to subsidizing agricultural research. Further grants of a broadly similar type were made under the Development (Loans and Grants) Act of 1929. This was, however, mainly an employment measure. Its principal aim was to extend the field of public works beyond the rather restricted area in which public authorities could operate. From the economic point of view grants offered in this manner tend to suffer from the same disability which was experienced by the early trade facility guarantees. The terms

---

[1] It was explicitly stated by the parliamentary secretary of the D.O.T. that the Act of 1937 was intended as a stimulus to international trade.

appeal mainly to those firms or industries which have difficulty in raising funds through the normal channels. This is usually because their financial prospects are not particularly rosy. Hence the return on the public funds tends to be decidedly below the current industrial return.

The only other series of grants which need be considered here are the civil aviation subsidies. Imperial Airways Ltd. was created in 1924 primarily to develop air routes to the Continent. But from 1927 Empire rather than European development was given first place. Subsidies took the form both of capital grants and of annual payments. Although Imperial Airways was the chief recipient of grants (in 1934 it received £0·481m. of a total £0·561m.), other companies connected with civil aviation also received some assistance. The general policy was one of coupling subsidy with the right to operate a particular route. On *a priori* grounds it might perhaps have been doubted whether this policy would provide sufficient incentive for development.

No investigation of the effect of the subsidies was made during our period, and it was not until the end of 1937, as a result of questions in the House, that a Royal Commission was appointed to examine the state of civil aviation. In their report, issued in March 1938, it was stated that not merely had the development of European routes been sacrificed to imperial connexions, but that the policy of Imperial Airways, and of the Air Ministry in respect of civil aviation, had been seriously deficient. We need not concern ourselves in detail with the reforms suggested,[1] since they lie outside our period. It is worth noting, however, that the extension of the monopoly subsidy system was advocated, in spite of its failure to secure adequate development. It may be asked whether it would not have been wise to attempt to devise some alternative method of grant, which by embodying the principle of paying by results—per unit of service provided—might not afford both a greater incentive for development and an ultimate saving to the taxpayer.

(vi) *Derating.* The derating provisions of the Local Government Act of 1929[2] gave rise to the largest exchequer disbursement for any one purpose in connexion with economic expenditure

---

[1] Cf. Cadman Report and *Economist*, 12 March 1938.

[2] The derating scheme was introduced in the budget of 1928, but was not available to industry until 1929.

during our period. The essence of derating was the transfer of part (or in the case of agriculture the whole) of the existing liability of industrialists for local taxation, to the shoulders of the general body of taxpayers. Industrialists had their tax burdens lightened to an extent which was estimated at £29 m. The exchequer made good the consequent deficits of the local authorities by means of a Block Grant distributed on a formula which was intended at the same time to be a reform of local finance. The process of derating thus had two aspects. We shall be concerned with the change in the position of the local authorities in Chapter IX. Here we have to examine the effect of the tax concession on industrialists.

The process of derating included three separate measures applying respectively to 'productive industry', the railways, and agriculture. The extent of the tax concession differed between these three parts, and also the extent by which it was intended that they should benefit. Productive industry was relieved as to 75 per cent. of its rate liability. On existing assessments this was equivalent to an exchequer subsidy of about £21 m. The railways were credited with a subsidy of about £4 m., but in the first instance they were forced to pass this on. Agriculture also received a subsidy of between £4 m. and £5 m., and in its case relief from local taxation henceforth amounted to 100 per cent. The provisions of 1929 were in respect of agriculture the last stage in a process which had been going on since 1896. The arguments in favour of derating were mainly based on the improvement which might be anticipated in the heavy industries, for derating was on the industrial side essentially an employment measure. It was estimated that the heavy industries contained 75 per cent. of all insured workers, and their percentage of unemployment was known to be very high.

In applying industrial derating, however, no direct attempt was made to single out the heavy industries. Under the provision of the Act the 75 per cent. relief was awarded to production of all types. Production was defined as including any premises where a definite process was applied to material. This gave rise to an extraordinary number of borderline cases, to take such random examples as cold storage and rag-picking of which the first was not derated but the second was. Garages which undertook reconstructional work were also difficult to place. The definition thus created a curious dichotomy between the productive and other parts of the economic process. Offices, business, and storage premises were not derated. The concession was discriminatory in favour of certain parts of the industrial field, but the benefits were meted out in these parts to the prosperous and the needy alike. Needless to say, these ambiguities of definition led to a considerably greater outlay of exchequer funds than had originally been intended. It need hardly be remarked that the dichotomy between productive and non-productive industry has no economic basis. In addition to their own derating, certain branches of the heavy industries and agriculture received part of the proceeds of railway derating in the form of freight rebates. This was particularly advantageous to loadings of coal, ore, and agricultural produce.

As a sheltered home industry the railways were not expected to require or receive any direct benefits from derating, but the opportunity was taken of altering their method of assessment to rates. 'Freight transport hereditaments', as they were called in the Act,[1] were in future to be assessed on the basis of receipts for the lines as a whole, instead of on the supposed letting value of the property, piece by piece, as it occurred in the territory of different local authorities. When the assessments under the new arrangement were announced it became apparent that the interpretation of the act by the new Railway Valuation Authority had substantially increased the rate liabilities of the railways.[2] They thus found themselves, in contrast to industry, decidedly worse off under derating than before. Against this state of affairs the railways not unnaturally lodged a complaint. After appeal it was finally decided in 1936 that during the first (quinquennial) rating period under the new arrangement they had been overtaxed to the extent of some £15–£17½ m. Of this some £10 m. had gone to the Rebates Fund, and the remainder to the local authorities. The matter was finally settled by a compromise whereby the railways received for the first period about two-thirds of this amount. The money was found by the issue of a Treasury loan—the greater part of which was taken up by the railways themselves. Thus the railways made good their claim to a degree of derating at least equivalent to that which had already been awarded to industry.

In contrast to the railways agriculture received under the Act

[1] Railway Rating and Valuation Act, 1930.
[2] See note at end of chapter.

of 1929 a larger benefit than any of the previous steps in the derating of the farming industry. The process of agricultural derating
had been as follows:

Year	Nature of relief	Estimated relief (£m. p.a.)
1896	50 per cent. on agricultural land	1·3
1923	,, ,, of remainder	3·8
1925	agricultural buildings	0·7
1929	remaining 25 per cent. on land	4·1

As in the case of industrial derating the benefit accrued equally to
the prosperous and the needy, and many branches of agriculture
were by no means depressed. From the point of view of local
administration the unfortunate situation was created in which
a large class of local government electors were almost totally
exempted from payment for the services which they received and
helped to control.

Agriculture does not appear to have been in any particular need
of assistance at the time: it seems clear that the needs of industry,
and specially of the 'heavies', was the principal motive which lay
behind the adoption of derating. It was frequently argued during
the parliamentary debates[1] that rates were an especially heavy
burden on the constructional industries because the tax 'entered
into' costs again and again as the raw material underwent various
processes on its way to becoming goods of final consumption.
Since rates, which must be paid as long as the premises are occupied, are as clear a case of overhead costs as it seems possible to
find, they cannot, economically, enter into costs except in the sense
that firms may be driven out of business as a result of the levy. It
is possible, however, that rates did constitute a heavier burden
on the constructional industries than on some others, in the sense
that heavy industries tend to inquire large and hence heavily rated
premises in relation to the value of the turnover. But a much
stronger case might be made out for the damage caused by high
rates to the building industry for instance—as an important factor
depressing the selling price of the product.

It is not therefore surprising that derating provided little stimulus to the 'heavies'. Indeed, the subsidy was too widespread and
too arbitrarily distributed to make any noticeable difference to
industrial costs in any particular industry or area. Moreover, in

[1] Cf. Debates on Derating, summarized in Mallet and George, *British
Budgets, 1920–1930*.

the longer period the net gain was not so large as had been hoped on account of the rising tendency of rate poundages.[1] To this derating itself in part contributed. Nevertheless, the subsidy was a genuine and important one. Moreover, without it the task of attracting new firms to depressed areas would have been much more difficult. But it can hardly be contended that the taxpayers' money was laid out to the best advantage.

A Note on Railway Rating

The traditional practice of railway assessment was to allow the hypothetical tenant (the railway in its aspect of owner of the rolling stock, &c.) a return on his capital *before* ascertaining the amount due from him as rent to the 'landlord' (the railway in its capacity as owner of the fixed capital). This allowance was thus deducted from the total assessment. The new Railway Rating authority took the opportunity of an ambiguous clause in the Act of 1930 to abolish this tenant's priority. The result was that under the new arrangement railway assessments were scaled up by £3·4 m. for the first quinquennium. The basis of assessment was the relatively good years 1928–9, so that the extra weight falling on railway revenues during depression was a double one. The railways appealed in the first instance to the Railway and Canal Commission, which set aside the Assessment Authority's interpretation of the act on the ground that the clause was only permissive. Returning to the old method of assessment the Authority then scaled down railway liability to allow for the decline in receipts during depression. Their action was subsequently confirmed by the House of Lords. The figures for the different railways and the subsequent agreements with the local authorities is shown below. Cf. *Economist*, 1 Feb. 1936.

Railway	Original Assessment	Assessment under new method	Assessment by Rail and Canal Com.	Agreement between Railways and local authority	
				1st quin.	2nd quin.
	£m.	£m.			
L.M.S.	3·7	5·0		1·75	1·5
L.N.E.R.	2·6	3·5	nil	1·1	1·1
G.W.R.	2·3	2·8		1·65	1·4
S.R.	1·8	2·1	1·1	1·1	?

[1] Cf. Chap. IX, pp. 163 ff.

V

STATE AID TO PARTICULAR INDUSTRIES

MUCH of the economic assistance which we have hitherto examined benefited—in fact if not in intention—particular industries rather than industry as a whole. This must always to some extent be the case even when impartiality is aimed at; the opportunities offered can be more conveniently grasped by some industries than others. But even in the early post-war period some measures offering more specific assistance were passed, and after 1931 an extensive series of enactments, avowedly specific and discriminatory in intention, was introduced. These supplemented and, to some extent, supplanted the older type of general assistance, which had become somewhat discredited because of its apparent want of success. Specific assistance is frequently more effective in achieving its immediate object than measures whose scope is wider, but its very success is a danger, since it tends to obscure the possibly less advantageous secondary effects, on the assisted industries and on other parts of the industrial field. It is only too easy to set up a new inequality of opportunity in place of those the policy is designed to correct. There is thus a particular duty on economists to draw attention to the possibility of secondary and long period effects.

In this part of our study we have to face a certain difficulty. In attempting to survey state aid to particular industries it is no longer feasible to confine our attention narrowly to expenditure, since this formed only a small part of the programme. To give anything like a full account of policy would, however, take us far beyond the field of expenditure, and hence of our inquiry. We must therefore be content with a rather brief summary which will serve to relate expenditure of this type to the rest of the field of public finance. It will be convenient to group the economic aid given to particular industries according as it affected on the one hand the heavy industries, and on the other the different branches of agriculture.

Throughout the post-war decade the heavy industries were the special concern of the government. They had enjoyed abnormal prosperity and undergone considerable expansion, not only during the war period but in the post-war restocking boom. But through-out the post-war period they were steadily depressed except for a very partial recovery in 1928–9. During these years every branch of the heavy industries received a certain amount of state assistance.

The coal-mining industry was the first to benefit. It received in the early post-war years a series of direct grants, which practically amounted to an annual subsidy.[1] The only exception was 1923, the year of adventitious prosperity due to the occupation of the Ruhr. When in 1925 an attempt was made to bring this type of assistance to an end it resulted in—or materially contributed to —the disastrous strikes of 1926. It was by that time realized that the changed conditions had come to stay, and must be met by some other method than by repeated subvention. Except therefore for the routine expenditure of the Mines Department and the assistance awarded by derating (including a share in railway freight rebates) the mining industry dropped out of the picture of economic expenditure.[2] The domestic coal industry experienced some revival with the recovery of the early thirties. At the end of our period a small recovery was visible even in the export trade, but these signs of improvement can only very partially and in-directly be attributed to public finance, and not at all to expenditure policy.

Iron, steel, and general engineering received little pecuniary assistance in the early post-war years, except such as individual firms secured from the trade facilities guarantees. But as we have seen, derating was largely designed for their relief, although its results in this respect were somewhat disappointing. After the depreciation of the pound and the introduction of tariffs the position of these industries gradually began to improve. In the early thirties the combined effect of recovery and the anticipation of rearmament expenditure restored them to something like their pre-war activity. The process of emergence of the various sections of the heavy industries under these successive stimuli can be observed by comparing the quotations of the ordinary shares of typical companies over the period from 1931.[3] Values in all cases

[1] Cf. Table 1, Chap. IV.
[2] There was substituted for it in 1930 the somewhat futile assistance of the Coal Mines Reorganization Commission.   [3] Cf. Table 2, p. 103.

rose very much faster than either the general index of ordinary shares or the index of physical productivity. Firms working for the home market recovered first, then those directly connected with rearmament. These were followed by firms more remotely connected with rearmament, and finally, but to a lesser degree, by the coal-exporting concerns. While elaborate statistical analysis would be required to isolate the part played by protection, there is at least an *a priori* case for believing that it was considerable.

In the immediate post-war period the railways were considered to be outside the pale of government assistance, since they were naturally a sheltered industry; but in fact the newly amalgamated railways had not emerged from government control in a very prosperous condition, and as the post-war situation developed definitely unfavourable factors began to appear. On the one hand, the rapid development of road transport—both passenger and commercial—led to a heavy transfer of traffic away from the railways. On the other, the decay of international trade reduced total traffics compared with pre-war days. As might be expected, the railways did not remain unaided, but soon received assistance both in the form of taxes on rival services and of tax concessions on their own. In 1926 the licence duties on commercial road vehicles were sharply increased. In 1928 the petrol tax, repealed in 1919, was again imposed[1] (in the form of a duty on hydrocarbon oils). Further, the result of the decisions of the Railway and Canal Commission under the Road Traffic Acts of 1930-3 appears to have been to stabilize the number of public hauliers and passenger transport undertakings at the level of those years, thus leaving the railways free to enjoy the benefit of any traffic expansion which occurred. Finally, the railways received a share of the derating concession, retrospectively to 1930, which is at least commensurate with that enjoyed since 1929 by the other heavy industries. It should also be remembered that they have had one opportunity, and are likely to have more, of borrowing money for development at gilt-edged rates, with Treasury guarantee.

In the early thirties, moreover, events turned definitely more favourable to the railways than they had been in the previous decade. The revival of home trade brought more traffic to the railways, both because industrial activity was greater, and because a larger part of it was directed to home markets. This is parti-

---

[1] On the taxation of road users cf. Chap. VIII, pp. 142 ff.

cularly true of agricultural freights, where an important effect of government assistance has been to increase the amount of cash sales, and hence the carriage of farm produce.

In long-distance passenger traffic also some turn back to the railways was observed, after the experimental period of bus transport was over. The result was a not inconsiderable improvement in the position of the railways, in which the most important factors were the derating decision and the general improvement in trade.

Of all the heavy industries, shipbuilding and shipping have been most frequently in the pocket of the government (or the taxpayers) during the period. Immediately after the war there was a boom in shipbuilding to replace war losses and to make good the years of inactivity. Such was the world shortage of tonnage that it seemed as if demand must be almost insatiable, and this was no doubt one of the reasons behind the large number of trade facilities guarantees for shipbuilding. Except for the relatively good years 1927-9, however, British shipping has not been in a really good position since the war. The volume of international trade has throughout been smaller than in the pre-war decade, and less of it has been carried in British bottoms. Two main causes of this were the high cost of British shipping services during the gold standard years, and the determination of other countries, as a result of war experience, to build up their own merchant fleets for safety. The first was a passing trouble, but it largely accounted for the spectacular collapse of British shipping after 1929.

Foreign subsidized shipbuilding and shipping is a factor the effect of which it is more difficult to assess. During the twenties (except for the quasi-boom years) the position of British shipping seemed to deteriorate steadily, and it certainly appeared that the enormous growth of subsidized foreign building must be largely responsible. This condition endured far into recovery. Even in 1935 it was assumed that there was a substantial world over-capacity of shipping.

Thus, although government assistance secured temporary profits to shipbuilding firms, it was of little value to the shipping industry.[1] For some years after the cessation of new trade facilities guarantees the two industries received no assistance, if we except the govern-

[1] Cf. the criticism both of the trade facilities guarantees and of the scrap and build scheme by Lord Essendon at the annual meeting of Furness Withy & Co. in 1936 (*Economist*, 1 Aug. 1936).

ment insurance guarantee awarded to the Cunard Co. for the
building of their giant liner '534' (the *Queen Mary*), laid down in
1930. In 1934, however, mainly as an employment measure, advances were given to the combined Cunard-White Star Co. for the
completion of this boat, work on which had been suspended at
the end of 1931.[1] A more general measure of assistance was the
Tramp Shipping Subsidy worked in connexion with a scrap and
build scheme under the British Shipping Act of 1935. As a
condition of receiving a subsidy for building, a ship-owner was
required to break up a certain proportion of old tonnage. The
scheme was thus similar to the Slum Clearance Act. It was intended to ensure a process of gradual reduction and modernization
of the entire merchant fleet.

In 1936, however, in spite of only a very partial recovery of
international trade, the shipping situation apparently underwent
a profound and somewhat unexpected modification. The shipbuilding yards revived. Ships were rapidly brought out of retreat
and put into commission once more. Freight-rates rose substantially and there were even signs of a shortage of bottoms in
some services. The scrap and build programme had to be abandoned in February 1937 because owners had no ships to scrap, and
it became impossible to buy them in the scrap market at a reasonable price. If world trade were fully to revive it seemed possible
that a genuine world shortage of shipping might be apparent. It is
therefore extremely difficult to form a judgement on the merits of
public expenditure in aid of shipping in our period. As late as the
summer of 1936 it appeared that a permanent subsidy both for
building and for operating might be necessary if the British
merchant fleet was to retain its quota of world trade. The indications of shortage depend partly on the extent of the revival of
international trade, and partly on the competition of naval rearmament in the shipyards, but other factors may also contribute. The
supply of new ships is in any case somewhat inelastic in the short
period. It is possible that the revival of demand coincided with the
technical obsolescence of a large number of ships of about the
same age. It seems not inconceivable that periods of prosperity

---

[1] The assistance included advances both for the completion of the liner and
towards the working capital of the merger. The interest on these (at rates below
those current in the gilt-edged market) was secured by a mixture of profit-sharing
and claims on the assets of the merger. Cf. *Economist*, 16 Dec. 1933.

may occur rather infrequently in shipbuilding because ships are relatively durable equipment, just as they do in the case of house building. In any case, post-war experience in this and other countries has made it clear that state assistance to shipping and shipbuilding is fraught with unsuspected difficulties. If the state goes to the aid of the most highly fluctuating part of the industrial field, it must expect to be confronted with some of the risks to which entrepreneurs in these industries have grown accustomed.

State aid to the heavy industries thus appears to have become a regular part of the British economic programme. Although the aid given cannot compare in scope or variety with the assistance afforded to similar industries in some other countries, it reveals an extraordinary and highly significant turn in the affairs of the great Victorian industries. In our period there have been strong social as well as economic arguments for such assistance, since the heavy industries were highly localized. But this is insufficient to justify permanent assistance. And the prospect is indeed serious if permanent assistance is required on purely economic grounds. This does, however, appear to be a real danger in the case of shipbuilding and shipping if a full revival of international trade fails to materialize. There is also some reason to fear that as assistance becomes more established, and the methods of giving it more varied, secondary reactions will also grow in importance. Thus in our period the stabilization of road transport after 1930 probably contributed not a little to the revival of the railways. Again, monopolistic influences in the iron and steel industries have certainly not diminished as a result of the easier marketing conditions secured by the tariff. These secondary effects go some way to nullify, as far as the community as a whole is concerned, the benefits of specific aid.

Assistance to agriculture may be regarded as the very type and pattern of post-war economic aid, so large and varied have been the favours bestowed. Depression in agriculture, and some measure of assistance, are long-standing features of the British situation. They are not the creation of the war or even of the twentieth century, but the increasing speed and efficiency of methods of packing and transport of overseas products in our period further curtailed whatever remaining advantages the British farmer still possessed over his foreign and dominion rivals. It is not strange, therefore, that the period has seen a quite unprecedented extension both of pecuniary aid and of tax concessions. The three political parties vied with each other in their attempts to restore permanent profitability to British farming. The methods used varied from time to time, according to the temporary dominance of particular forms of socio-economic policy.

The first in the field were the liberals. Mainly under the influence of Mr. Lloyd George an extensive programme of land settlement was inaugurated first under the Small Holdings and Allotments Act of 1908 and later under a new Land Settlement Act of 1919. Meanwhile, existing branches of agriculture were kept alive by large emergency subsidies paid direct to producers, and by the extension of agricultural derating. The labour party first concentrated on improving the condition of the agricultural labourer by reforming the war-time agricultural wages boards (1924). In their second period of office they introduced a system of marketing boards with the primary object of reducing the profits of the middleman, and thus raising the income of the farmer without raising prices to the consumer. The 'National' government set themselves the task of directly restoring the profits of the farmer. The extraordinary fall in the prices of farm products which preceded and accompanied the depression of 1931 made this appear a matter of urgency. The principal methods used were a combination of marketing boards—taken over from the labour party but with the important modification of limitation of supply—and a variety of direct subsidies to different branches of production. This period coincided with Mr. Walter Elliot's tenure of office at the Ministry of Agriculture.

Although the growing cheerfulness of farmers and the steady rise in home prices testified to the success of this policy in achieving its primary object, after some years difficulties began to appear. The policy of some of the control schemes came in for widespread criticism on the ground of rising prices. One scheme broke down completely, owing to lack of price adjustment. The growing expensiveness of agricultural policy began to cause the government some anxiety in view of the expected budget strain on rearmament account. The long-period benefit of the changes in production which had been brought about by the new incentives also began to be questioned. It is therefore not surprising that at the end of our period some fresh orientation of agricultural policy was announced. Neglecting this, there were thus three distinct phases of agricultural expenditure during our period. At the same time, tax concessions have continued to accumulate, both as the result of fresh legislation and of other changes from which the farmer has been able to draw unexpected benefits.

There is considerable difficulty in collecting and classifying the scattered disbursements which have from time to time been made to the various branches of the agricultural industry. An attempt is made to bring them together in Table 1. The Ministry vote covers a variety of services. It comprises agricultural education, including research and scholarships; expenditure for the improvement of live stock and the elimination of disease; improvement of land cultivation and drainage, a contribution to the provision for small-holdings and encouragement for improved methods of agriculture. The composition of the vote and the relative amounts spent on the different services tends to change very considerably from one year to another, hence the total is also fluctuating. Many of the ser-vices—for instance land drainage and settlement and research—have also been aided out of other votes.[1] The wheat 'quota' pay-ments are in a different class from other subsidies, since the funds are derived from a processing tax on milling, and not from the budget. The operations of the marketing boards, which became the chief instrument of agricultural policy under the 'National' government, do not figure directly in the table, since normally they do not give rise to any outlay of public funds. An exception to this is the milk board. Milk policy has given rise to expenditure of several different varieties. Chief among these are advances to producers (nominally repayable) and a subsidy (estimated at about £2 m.) under an Act of 1934 to make good the difference between realized milk prices and the guaranteed price.[2] Public monies have also been spent on propaganda to increase the consumption of liquid milk and on the distribution of cheap milk to mothers and children.

But although the marketing boards lead only to a small amount of direct expenditure, it is necessary in any survey of agricultural policy to draw attention to the main characteristics of this method

[1] Land settlement was provided for from the Consolidated Fund, 1920–4; since 1933 it has been assisted by the Special Areas Fund. Research was financed by the Empire Marketing Board and by the Development Commission.

[2] The fundamental cause of this divergence was the increase in the supply of milk as a result of the stimulating effect of the guaranteed price.

TABLE I

*Expenditure in aid of agriculture**

(£ m.)

	1920	1921	1922	1923	1924	1925	1926	1927	1928	1929	1930	1931	1932	1933	1934	1935	1936
Ministry of Agriculture:																	
England†	4·8	2·6	1·5	4·1	2·2	3·0	2·8	2·0	2·1	2·9	2·2	2·3	2·0	2·0	2·9	2·2	2·3
Scotland†	1·7	0·5	0·3	0·4	0·4	0·4	0·7	0·6	0·5	0·6	0·7	0·6	0·5	0·5	0·6	0·7	0·7
Forestry Commission	0·4	0·2	0·02	0·2	0·5	0·3	0·4	0·6	0·5	0·6	0·8	0·5	0·5	0·5	0·5	0·5	0·8
Land Settlement‡	6·9	2·6	1·2	1·2	0·7	0·8	..	..	..	..	..	..	..	..	..	..	..
Home Grown Wheat Guarantee	..	1·7	..	..	..	..	..	..	..	..	..	..	..	..	..	..	..
Corn Production Guarantee	..	18·0	..	..	..	..	..	..	..	..	..	..	..	..	..	..	..
Wheat Quota	..	..	..	..	..	..	..	..	..	..	..	..	4·5	7·2	6·8	5·6	2·4
Agricultural Credits	..	..	..	0·5	..	..	..	..	..	..	..	..	(0·01)	(0·04)	..	(0·1)	(0·1)
Development	..	1·0	0·2	0·3	0·2	0·1	0·2	0·3	0·4	0·3	0·6	0·5	0·4	0·8	0·5	0·5	0·7
Land Drainage	0·9	0·9	0·9	1·0	1·0	1·0	1·0	1·0	1·1	1·1	1·2	1·4	1·5	1·8	1·9	2·0	2·2
Small Holdings & Allotments	0·8	0·8	0·8	0·8	0·8	1·0	0·8	0·9	0·9	0·8	0·8	0·9	0·9	0·8	0·9	0·9	0·8
Beet Sugar	..	(0·1)	(0·01)	(0·01)	(0·5)	(1·1)	3·2	4·3	2·9	4·2	6·0	2·1	2·4	3·3	4·4	2·3	3·0
Milk	..	..	..	..	..	..	..	..	..	..	..	..	..	..	2·2	1·8	1·0
Cattle Fund	..	..	..	..	..	..	..	..	..	..	..	..	..	..	2·1	3·3	4·1
Totals of above	15·5	28·3	4·9	8·4	5·8	6·6	9·1	9·7	8·4	10·5	12·3	8·3	12·7	14·9	22·8	19·8	18·0

* Exchequer grants are net issues; services for which a charge is made (i.e. small holdings and allotments) show expenditure of local authorities less receipts from producers. Figures in brackets are included in the Ministry vote.

† Including Fishery assistance.   ‡ Charged on Consolidated Fund. Land Settlement from special areas is not included.

of assisting the farmer. The Marketing Act of 1933, under which the boards were established, differed from the labour measure of 1931 by the inclusion of power to limit both imported supplies (by means of quota agreements), and surplus home production. These measures were perhaps necessary in order to secure the success of the aim of improving farming profits, but they have fundamentally altered the significance of the boards. Like the Act of 1931, the 'National' government measure is permissive. The existence of the boards depends on the majority opinion of producers. There have been some complaints on the supply side of the operation of the boards, mainly by low-cost producers who hold a different opinion from their fellows of the possibility of increasing sales by a low-price policy. But on the whole these price-fixing and profit-distributing organizations are so obviously in the interest of producers that their use spread rapidly after the passing of the act to the hop, pig and bacon, potato and milk industries. Definite steps have also been taken to bring other commodities under control, such as eggs and poultry, sugar, live stock, and certain kinds of fruit.[1] The group of milk boards is far the most important of these organizations, both because of the vast scale of its operations—it markets close on a billion gallons of milk a year and has an income of some £33 m.—and because it has been more in the public eye than the other boards. The attempt to organize the marketing of this complicated and highly interrelated group of products has encountered difficulties which are probably implicit in the operations of the other boards, but which are less obvious in the case of such modest enterprises as the hops control for instance.[2]

Before leaving the expenditure side some account must be given of two sub-branches of the agricultural industry which gave rise to fairly regular annual subsidies throughout the period—namely, land settlement in its various forms, and reafforestation. Both of these industries derived support from a number of interests, and

---

[1] For a useful summary cf. A. F. Lucas, *Industrial Reconstruction and the Control of Competition*, chap. x.

[2] Space does not permit of an account of the troubles of the pig and bacon scheme (but cf. Lucas, loc. cit.). Fundamentally they arose because farmers found it more profitable to dispose of their pigs to the pork butchers than to the bacon curers. The relation of pork prices to those of other (competitive) types of meat affected by one or more of the government's schemes is also relevant.

the fluctuations in annual outlay are partly due to the changing
dominance of different arguments. The continuance of war fears
of timber and food shortage led to a considerable development of
both in the early post-war years. They were also recommended
as a form of long-period national development in the liberal programme. More immediately they found favour as employment
measures, particularly for ex-service men whose health might make
them unfit for urban life.

A number of types of land settlement were attempted. Small-
holdings, which had long been regarded as a means of rehabilitating rural life, were provided at an accelerated pace after 1919,
when the Ministry of Agriculture assumed responsibility for the
whole of the losses occurred by local authorities in their provision.
Up to 1926, when policy was somewhat modified, over 1,200[1] men
had been settled at an average capital cost of £433. Land settlement of other types was also regarded at this period as primarily
an outlet for ex-service men. During these years 1,600 were settled
at an average cost of £953. The annual loss on their holdings
was nearly £850,000. In 1926 the Ministry wisely reduced its
financial responsibility to 75 per cent. of realized losses, but as the
bulk of the holdings were then let fully equipped they were
naturally more expensive. Nevertheless, the improvement in
equipment and the gradual fall in costs gave the later schemes a
much better chance of financial success. Although the capital
cost under the 1926 Act worked out at an average of £1,356, losses
were considerably less than on the earlier settlements.

The moment chosen for the earlier scheme was singularly unfortunate, since both interest rates and the costs of land and agricultural equipment were very much inflated. Land settlement
expenditure was not viewed with favour by the May Committee,
and indeed the precarious profits of established farmers suggest
that it is extremely doubtful whether the settlement of inexperi-
enced men on the land will ever enable them to be self-supporting.
Doubts on this head and the expense of existing schemes were
probably instrumental in introducing considerable modifications
into the scheme started by the Land Settlement Association in
conjunction with the Special Areas Reconstruction Association.[2]
The aim of this scheme is considerably more modest, little more
than assistance towards family maintenance being anticipated by

[1] Cf. May Committee, pp. 115 ff.   [2] Cf. Chap. XIII, p. 211.

way of direct return. It is, however, frankly an unemployment measure, designed at the same time to assist families from depressed areas, and to increase the supply of juvenile labour in areas where it is short. With the aid of supplementary family earnings it may become an economic as well as an admirable social proposition.

The Forestry Commission also had its origin in the first enthusiasm of the post-war world. An elaborate eighty-year planting programme was drawn up, and provision made for guaranteed resources of £3·5 m. in annual grants spread over ten years.[1] But no arrangement was made for securing that the annual sums available corresponded with the technical necessities of the programme. Consequently grants tended to be cut down whenever the budget was in a poor state, and made up when the crisis was over. Thus in 1922 the vote was suddenly reduced from £260,000 to £20,000. For the second decade (beginning in 1931) it was decided to pay £900,000 annually, but after a year the vote was scaled down to £450,000 on the recommendation of the May Committee. In 1936 it was again increased to £750,000.

Such violent fluctuations in available resources would make it extremely difficult to carry out any long-period programme. For tree planting, which requires a definite quota of workers and materials yearly, it is disastrous. At one moment there is a surplus of seedlings and no means of planting them, at the next a surplus of workers and no trees to plant. In both cases waste of funds is inevitable. The most solid justification of reafforestation is as a long-period insurance against denudation and soil erosion. But this is too distant a matter to be taken seriously by individual governments. The defence argument rouses little enthusiasm when the international situation seems reasonably secure. Forest workers' holdings are even less effective in providing employment, and more expensive than land-settlement holdings. There are thus normally no immediate and pressing arguments in favour of afforestation, and it falls an easy victim to economy campaigns. It is possible that with low interest rates the service might be put on a profit-earning basis. It may well be that the country cannot afford to let its forests disappear. In circumstances such as have existed since the war it does not seem likely that private planting will be very effective. If, however, a long-run public policy is to be

[1] Cf. *Public Enterprise*, ed. W. A. Robson, chapter 3.

carried out, it does appear that a different system of finance must be devised. For instance, if long-term borrowing by the government were adopted, expenditure would be both less at the mercy of current budget needs and more likely to bring in an economic return.

If we sum up the various forms of pecuniary aid awarded to the different branches of agriculture, it appears that producers received direct money payments of the order of £9 m.[1] during the twenties. Under the 'National' government, however, a maximum of about £20 m. was reached.

The benefits which the farming community derives on the tax side have yet to be considered. These have been of two sorts: (i) concessions on existing taxes, and (ii) benefits derived from the introduction of new taxes which discriminated in favour of their products. The process of agricultural derating was completed during our period, in two steps, in 1923 and 1928–9. It is estimated to relieve the industry[2] of taxes of some £15 m. per annum. Frequent concessions as to the payment of tithe have been made since the war. Dr. Venn has calculated that under the Acts of 1918 and 1925 relief had amounted to about £11 m. by 1935. Further relief will be available under the Tithe Act of 1936.

The most important tax concession enjoyed by farmers is, however, in the field of income tax. This arises from the fact that in making a return the farmer has three alternatives to choose from.[3] First he may choose to be assessed (under schedule D) on the annual value of the premises—a conventional figure derived in the same manner as the schedule A assessment on property. Secondly, he may choose to pay on the profits of the preceding year (under schedule B) like any other business man. Thirdly, he may in fact choose to pay on the profits (or lack of them) of the current year, since under rule 6 of schedule B he may claim a reduction to their figure, or an offsetting of loss, according to circumstances. Since the schedule D assessments are only adjusted every five years, and

---

[1] Dr. Venn ('State Control in Agriculture', *E.J.*, 1935) estimates that about one-third of the beet-sugar subsidy should be imputed to growers. For an account of this expenditure as a whole, see below, p. 101.

[2] There are no adequate data for determining in what way the incidence of derating was divided between landlords and tenants. Agricultural rents are notoriously sticky, but it is probable that landlords secured some of the benefits by curtailing the rent rebates which had become very usual. It should be remembered that over one-third of agricultural land is now farmed by owner-occupiers.   [3] Cf. Edwards, 'Farmers and Income Tax', *Economica*, 1937.

in any case bear but a very rough relation to profits, it is clearly to his advantage in years of normal or rising profit to choose this alternative. It has been calculated[1] that on the basis of the income-tax allowances in force in 1928, a married man with a farm up to 150 acres was totally exempt from income tax, while with a small family he might be exempt on a 300-acre farm. The choice of the other alternatives is more subtle, and depends on the farmer being alert enough to take advantage of fluctuating profits. If he has a bad year it is clearly best for him to choose alternative 3 for that year, and to have his tax payment scaled down to his current income. The next year, if things improve, it will pay him to switch over to alternative 2 and continue to pay on the bad year. It is not possible to estimate the pecuniary importance of this concession since farm accounts are only sent in to the Inland Revenue in bad years, when alternatives 2 or 3 are chosen. The importance of the option has, however, increased during the period. Before income-tax assessment was altered from a three-year to a one-year basis the fluctuation in profits was hardly sufficient to make the switch over worth while. Moreover, the rise in farming profits due to the other parts of the agricultural programme are continually increasing the value of the schedule D concession.

The Royal Commission on the Income Tax in 1920 strongly criticized the regulations under which this choice was available to farmers. They considered that farmers should be made to keep accounts and be assessed on profits in the same way as other businesses. But the difficulties of farm accounting have not yet been overcome. It is important at least that the community should realize that farmers enjoy this valuable privilege, in addition to more direct tax discrimination in their favour.

A further sum must be added to the farmers' credit account in respect of the effect which the various import duties and quotas have had in raising the prices of farm products. In the two years, 1931-2 to 1934-5, the prices of commodities sold by farms rose by from 7 to 8 per cent. Since changes in world wholesale prices were not an important feature during these years, the rise must mainly be attributed to the effect of the long series of market restrictions. Beginning with the Horticultural Products Emergency Duties Act of 1931, a series of measures virtually secured British market and fruit garden products from competition from foreign sources

[1] Cf. Venn, 'The Incidence of Taxation in Agriculture', *E.J.*, 1928.

during their own season. A similar series of measures limited the market of practically every farm product, either by tariff or by import restriction. It appears that if we total these various forms of assistance meted out to British farming, the farming community must benefit to the extent of some £50 m. a year. There has, it is true, been a considerable rise in labour costs, and some of this should properly be imputed to the effect of the wages boards. Dr. Venn estimates it at £10 m. On the other hand, since the rural exodus appears to be persisting unabated, there must be some upward tendency in wages, even in the absence of wage-fixing arrangements. This may become a serious problem in the future.

What, it must be asked, is the economic justification of such varied and extensive aid to agriculture, and how far has it attained its object? The argument has been put forward that assistance is necessary because the technical conditions of the industry make it unresponsive to the ordinary economic stimuli of price changes. The extension of cereal cultivation in America as prices fell is cited as an example of this. A more relevant one to this country is the case of milk prices, which may serve as an example of the economic arguments on which agricultural assistance is based.

The sequence of events appears to have been something as follows. Owing to the development of cheap road transport, coupled with the fall of beef prices during the depression of 1931, London and the great urban areas of the south began to draw supplies from a much larger area than previously. The result was a sharp fall in the price of milk. This threatened to ruin the near-at-hand producers whose costs were higher than those of the newcomers from the north and west, both on account of rents and technical conditions. In order to 'restore equilibrium' guaranteed prices for liquid milk were offered. This indeed saved the high-cost producers, but had the effect of stimulating milk production not merely in the north and west but all over the country. This movement may have most undesirable effects, apart from the financial embarrassments of the milk boards already alluded to. (i) Cows tend to be bred for mere quantity production and to be overmilked, thus shortening their lives[1] (and hence reducing their total milk yield), and increasing the incidence of disease, particularly tuberculosis. (ii) Calf production, which is largely a rival

---

[1] The average life of a cow is said to be several years longer in Denmark than in England.

product to milk, tends to be curtailed. The result to be appre-
hended from this is first a shortage of store cattle,[1] and later and
much more disastrously a shortage of milch cows.

The course of production suggests not that the British farmer is
insensitive to price changes, but that he is too sensitive. In this
case there is no reason to suppose that once the new sources of
supply for the urban milk market had been established, a new
equilibrium would not have been reached without interference.
Admittedly it might have taken some time, but the farther milk
prices had fallen initially the less incentive would there have been
for a substantial change over to milk production, and consequently
the less violent would the movement have been in the long run.
(Incidentally lower prices might have stimulated increased demand, an end so much desired by the government.)[2] The argument that lower prices stimulate supply is more likely to be true
in the case of specialized one-crop agriculture, such as dominates
the American situation. The change in production on British
farms, as one form of assistance after another has made particular
crops relatively profitable,[3] shows clearly enough that the typical
British farmer is not a specialist and that he is highly sensitive to
changes in relative prices.

Assistance to agriculture can be much more readily justified on
political or social grounds. The economist must take these for
granted. But he has the right to ask the politician and the lover of
country life two questions. Firstly, are they satisfied that the sums
spent on agriculture, relative to those spent on other industries
and on the various social services, are justified? In answering this
question, counteracting effects such as the decline in international
trade through the limitation of imports, and the fall in the real
incomes of the working classes, on account of the rise in food
prices, must naturally be taken into consideration. Secondly, are
the net results of assistance (allowing for counter influences within
the industry) those most desired for the industry itself?

---

[1] A shortage of store cattle had already appeared by the summer of 1936,
but it was temporarily made good by imports from Ireland.

[2] It must be doubted whether the aim of increasing milk consumption is
either very necessary or very practical, except for nursing mothers and young
children. The British public has long preferred to take the relevant vitamins
in the form of butter. Cf. Booker, 'Parenthood and Poverty', *Economica*, 1937.

[3] Cf. Carslaw and Graves, 'Recent Changes in the Physical Output of Arable
Farms', *E.J.* 1935.

The statistics suggest that the main results of assistance given by the 'National' government have been: (i) a slight absolute increase in physical output (but it must be remembered that the harvests of 1933, 1934, and 1935 were all exceptionally good); (ii) a smaller decline in arable than would otherwise have occurred; (iii) reduction in the number of workers, but improved standard of living for those who remained (this was accompanied by a marked increase in mechanization); (iv) an increase in the profitability of farming, of which the largest part was undoubtedly due to the price manipulation schemes (nevertheless, the increase has hardly restored agricultural profits to the pre-war rates);[1] (v) a redistribution of crops and a greater sale of crops off the farms[2] in order to gain the benefit of government prices.

If this is a correct judgement of the matter there are three possible sources of danger. The most obvious is that consumers' interests are being neglected. There is considerable evidence that this has indeed been the effect of the operation of the marketing boards.[3] It has only proved possible to secure an increase in farm prices by very considerably curtailing imports. Since home supplies fluctuate this is one source of a potential price rise. More important, however, is the fact that it has not so far proved possible to do without the services of the middleman distributor. Hence the rise in farmers' profits has tended to be at least proportionately passed on to the consumer in higher retail prices.

The second danger is that the various subsidies and changes in subsidies will upset the nice balance of customary crop distribution and sequence. Particularly in mixed farming, almost every crop has a double purpose—its own yield and as a preparation for another crop. A subsidy which changes rotations may damage the future yields of subsidiary crops.

A distinction must, however, be made between the effect of different forms of subsidy in this respect. The danger of a sudden

[1] Cf. Venn, op. cit. 1935. Farm products were then fetching slightly higher prices than pre-war. Labour was estimated to cost 100 per cent. more, other costs being 60 to 70 per cent. more. This would leave a deficit of some £60 m. compared with pre-war figures, which assistance at about £50 m. only partially bridges. Prices of farm products have since risen further.

[2] The increase in cash sales is stressed both by Venn and by Carslaw and Graves.

[3] Cf. especially the Report of the Food Council for 1936, and Lucas, loc. cit. It is hardly necessary to draw attention to the inconsistency of endeavouring at the same time to raise prices and increase consumption.

change over and the consequent flooding of the market and over-working of productive resources would seem to be greater the less permanent the assistance is expected to be. Hence, where the government's policy is to initiate a long-period policy, for instance of stock improvement, or an increase of acreage under a particular crop, it would seem necessary to offer some long-run guarantee. Farmers have to re-plan their lay-out of production for the whole of a complicated rotation. This will mean considerable preliminary expense. The wheat deficiency payment type of subsidy, which aims at giving a guaranteed price for a crop of a certain size and quality, not much in excess of what may normally be expected, is probably more effective in achieving a long-run improvement than the milk subsidy, which gives an absolute guarantee of a price very attractive to low-cost producers. The cattle breeders were emphatic that no real improvement in the quality of meat could be expected unless a guaranteed price were forthcoming. They also preferred a tariff to restriction of imported supplies by a quota, because they believed it was more likely to be permanent. On the other hand, if it is merely the government's intention to give temporary support to prices during depression, the quota system offers definite advantages on account of its proved flexibility. For this purpose a guaranteed price for a maximum crop with definite tapering of the subsidy as prices improve is probably also useful. But the experience of the wheat scheme suggests that there is some danger of over-stimulating production even by this method, and also that there is likely to be heavy pressure to extend the operation of the subsidy. It must be remembered that the government is not necessarily free to choose the type of subsidy which is best calculated to achieve its object, particularly if this is a long-period one. Direct subsidies lead to budget difficulties. Processing taxes are chiefly useful where, as in the wheat and flour industry, there is a convenient stage at which the tax can be imposed. Open food taxes such as tariffs are still (fortunately) politically difficult.

The third danger is related to the second. It may be put in the form of a question. What provision is there in the programme for assuring that long-run measures, such as land drainage and cleansing, which are necessary to preserve the fertility of the soil, will be more efficiently carried out than they have been in the past? Questions of long-run fertility were worrying experts long before the inauguration of the present programme. Land drainage in particular has frequently been examined and always pronounced to be deteriorating. The farmer does not make as good profits as he did before the war, even with the assistance which he receives: on the other hand, death duties and other taxes weigh more heavily on landlords than before the war.[1] It was, no doubt, considerations such as these which prompted the government to offer additional subsidies for the long-run needs of both land and stock maintenance in their programme of 1937. While this will presumably require a considerable extension of agricultural expenditure, it may well be a necessary step to secure the long-run success of the rest of the programme. To keep a declining industry in as good a condition as a prosperous one is necessarily expensive. Although it is to the ultimate interest of both landlords and farmers, it is not a task which they can be expected to undertake. If it is to be done it must be done by the state.

The difficulties which surround the provision of state assistance to agriculture are not wholly peculiar to that industry. They are typical in different degrees of all methods of aiding particular industries. Agriculture is especially rich in products which are closely related in production, and all of which consequently are strongly affected by assistance given to one. But all industry is to some extent interrelated, and most firms already make, or are prepared to make, a number of products. Consumers may be able to get some of them cheaper as a result of the assistance, but they are likely to have to pay more for others. The total effects of assistance require to be analysed in each case; they cannot be stated generally.

The aim of assistance is normally to increase the profits of a certain group of producers—those in a particular line of production. Should not the community demand some definite recompense for this? Reorganization is frequently demanded as the price of government help, but it happens only too often that reorganization is postponed once assistance has been given (cf. the coal, and iron and steel industries). Fundamental reorganization requires surplus profits, and these can usually not be realized until some degree of assistance has already been given. Too often reorganization is interpreted as the introduction of 'more orderly marketing' in the sense of limiting supply and allotting production quotas. Without this there is a danger of increased profits leading to the expansion of output, as happened in the milk market. But besides

[1] Cf. Bowley, *Economic Consequences of the Great War*.

tending to raise prices, restriction of supply carries with it another danger. It apparently tends to reduce the elasticity of supply in the short period.[1] Hence prices may fluctuate even more violently than they would have done in the absence of control. Moreover, control tends to enhance the power of the producer's committee, and the question arises whether it may not be necessary to provide safeguards against the abuse of this power, if indeed such a step is possible. These are problems which lie beyond the scope of our inquiry, but it is clear that they are in urgent need of investigation.

The second great danger of particular economic assistance is the creation of the vested interest. There has been a remarkable example of this in the post-war period in the case of the sugar-beet industry. Although the facts are well known,[2] they are so striking that it is worth recalling them. On *a priori* grounds the case for assisting the cultivation of beet is weak, since the British crop normally has a low sugar content compared with the continental product. It is also a rival to cane sugar, which is extensively grown in the tropical Empire, in whose economic prosperity we are deeply interested, since it forms one of our best overseas markets. On the demand side a product of ordinary working-class consumption, such as sugar, normally has a rather inelastic demand. Hence an expansion of beet sugar, even if it were to lead to lower prices, would not be likely to make a great difference in the total amount sold, and hence in the profits of the sugar industry. Given these conditions, the subsequent history of the industry has been exactly as might have been expected. The incentive for beet production was provided by the high prices which ruled for sugar immediately after the war. There appeared to be a possibility of introducing an important new crop for the rehabilitation of British agriculture. A small subsidy was given to encourage the infant industry, but the high prices soon called forth an immense world over-supply and prices fell sharply. Sugar factories had been set up to refine the British product, but it soon became apparent that no part of the process was capable of economic independence. To secure capital for the industry the profits of the factories had to be

[1] Cf. Rowe, *Markets and Men*, and Eastham, 'Rationalization in the Tin Industry', *Review of Economic Studies*, 1935.

[2] The literature on the beet-sugar question is enormous. Cf. especially the (1935) Report of the Greene Committee. Every independent inquiry has condemned the subsidy, cf. also the recurrent fulminations of the *Economist*.

guaranteed. To secure raw material for them the subsidy to producers had to be continued. Thus upwards of £50 m. (excluding
the small early grants to growers, but including the excise rebate
on sugar refining) was paid in twelve years,[1] to the benefit of
farmers in the eastern counties, and shareholders in sugar-beet
factories (and later of all the sugar refining firms), but to the direct
detriment of international trade relations with tropical countries
and of the British consumer.[2]

It was considerations such as these which led the Victorians to
distrust partial economic interference by the state. In taking up
this attitude they overlooked many important hindrances to free
exchange to which attention has since been drawn. Their bogies
were nevertheless founded on fact, and there is little evidence that
any method of rendering them innocuous has yet been found.
Moreover, as specific aid extends, another danger comes to light.
Entrepreneurs tend to rely more and more on having their markets
prepared for them by the government. Entrepreneurial energy
tends to be transferred from its proper function of anticipating
economic forces to one of predicting—and creating—the policy of
governments. And it must be remembered that government prepared markets are of necessity mainly home markets. In the long
run anything which diminishes the ability of entrepreneurs to
compete in overseas markets is of doubtful benefit to a country
which has traditionally depended for its high standard of living on
a large volume of international trade.

[1] For the financial reorganization of the industry at the end of our period,
cf. Chap. IV, p. 72.
[2] The experience of later awarded grants is somewhat more reassuring. The
wheat, tramp shipping, and meat subsidies have all shown a definite tendency
to taper off as prices rose. It may be suspected that anticipated budget stringency
has played some part in bringing about this desirable result.

TABLE 2

*Quotations of ordinary shares of typical firms in the heavy industries**

Firm	1931	1932	1934	1936
Baldwin .	3/9 to 1/2¼	3/8½ to 1/10½	4/- to 4/3	11/10 to 7/8
Barrow Haematite . .	-/3¾	-/6 to -/5¼	7/1½ to 2/6	16/6 to 8/9
Beardmore .	-/9 to -/1	-/4 to -/1¾	2/- to -/3	10/- to 5/9
Cammell Laird	2/9 to -/6	1/10½ to -/6	3/6 to 2/1½	15/6 to 5/3
Consett Iron .	9/- to 2/5	7/1½ to 4/4½	7/10½ to 5/5½	15/1 to 8/4
Dorman Long	6/3 to 2/-	5/6½ to 3/3	2/4½ to 1/6	39/10 to 20/-
Ebbw Vale .	1/9 to -/1	1/6 to -/10½	1/0¼ to -/3	1/3 to -/3
Guest Keen .	24/3 to 9/9	17/4 to 9/11¼	19/6 to 14/9	39/6 to 31/-
Hadfields .	8/4½ to 3/-	5/10 to 4/7½	13/6 to 8/3	34/- to 18/-
Ocean Coal and Wilsons .	12/7½ to 6/3	9/6 to 6/-	14/6½ to 10/1½	10/- to 5/5
Pease and Partners . .	3/1½ to -/6	2/- to 1/4½	12/6 to 7/3	9/9 to 4/7
Powell Duffryn	9/10½ to 3/4	7/1½ to 4/-	21/10½ to 16/4	21/7 to 17/-
Ruston and Hornsby .	4/6 to 1/3	3/- to 1/10½	6/1½ to 3/10½	28/3 to 20/-
South Durham	27/6 to 8/9	24/7 to 19/-	27/9 to 21/7½	64/3 to 48/1
Richard Thomas .	3/3 to -/6	2/- to 1/3	4/10½ to 2/8½	15/9 to 13/-
Weardale .	23/9 to 14/1½	11/6	33/- to 27/-	34/9 to 27/-
Gen. Index of Industrials†	84·7	102	125	161
Index of Physical Production†	84·3	84·9	101·7	116·4

(From Stock Exchange quotations (highest and lowest.)

* It must be remembered that differences in capital structure and other casual factors often account for wide differences in the prices quoted for the shares of similarly placed companies.

† London and Cambridge Economic Service, annual averages

VI

PUBLIC INVESTMENT

THE term 'public investment' is generally used to cover all public operations which require the use of durable equipment, and where, consequently, it is customary to meet part of the expenditure from loan funds. There are, however, two sorts of public investment, corresponding to the two divisions of expenditure with which we have been dealing. The first, which we may call 'Economic' public investment, would include all enterprises operated by public authorities, where a specific charge is made for the services, with the object of covering costs, or even of making a net profit. 'Social' public investment would consist primarily of those services for which no specific charge is made, and where consequently current expenses and debt interest have to be met out of taxation. These two types of public investment are economically quite distinct, although there are naturally, once again, a number of border-line cases. Where a fee is charged which covers only a small part of the cost, for many problems it is a matter of convenience only which class we consider a service to belong to. Although for most of our period housing belonged definitely to the class of social investment, its large volume and astonishing growth since the war make it convenient to consider capital expenditure on housing alongside of that for the purely trading services.

For some problems the distinction between social and economic investment is of very little importance: it is the movement of total investment which counts. Investors do not generally trouble to find out what proportion of the municipal stock which they intend to buy as a trustee security is represented by trading services, or what, for instance, by a sewage farm—although the distribution of debt may influence their choice in the case of a new flotation. The movement of public investment as a whole is not without importance if we are considering the very long-period accumulation of equipment by the community. This is particularly true if, as has been asserted, changing distribution of income and of social habits are tending permanently to decrease the volume of private investment. But more immediately it is the behaviour of total public investment which is a factor of prime importance in the short-period movement of the trade cycle. One type of borrowing and spending is as good as another if it is equally effective in depression in dispersing overgrown bank balances and stimulating the demand for labour and equipment. The erection of town halls in the boom may be as competitive with the erection of factories, as the construction of municipal power stations. Moreover, the building of battleships and other forms of durable military equipment must logically be included in public investment from the trade-cycle point of view. And, finally, it is necessary to take account also of such semi-public investment as the operations of the Central Electricity Board, and the railways borrowing under trade facilities guarantees, since the *tempo* of their activities is to some extent controlled by the government.

But economic history fortunately does not consist entirely of trade cycles, at least not of violent peaks and troughs. There appear to be considerable periods when production is running on a fairly even keel, and when consequently it is possible to sit back and review the development over a longer period. It is then that the distinction between social and economic investment cannot safely be neglected. The extent of social public investment which the community desires depends only on the subjective valuation of its satisfactions in relation to other ways of spending money. Social public investment is desirable on social grounds. It may, as has been said, also be desirable on economic grounds. But it must be borne in mind that each extension increases the amount of debt interest which has to be met out of taxation. Not only does the investment itself involve the sacrifice of alternative forms of spending, but debt service leads to a redistribution of income, the effects of which have to be taken into account[1] in the final evaluation of the net advantages of the investment. The desirable rate of economic investment as a whole depends likewise on subjective grounds—on the extent to which the community is prepared to apply its resources to durable equipment bringing in a return only over a course of years, rather than to present satisfactions. But the fact that the interest charge is covered by receipts means that there is no further burden on the community.[2] Further, more

---

[1] Cf. discussion in Chap. XXII.

[2] As to the relative merits of financing investment from loans or from current receipts, cf. Chap. VII, p. 122.

objective economic criteria are available for determining the correct allocation of resources between different types of investment, analogous to those used in private investment.

Since the scope of public investment differs enormously from country to country it is necessary in the first place to realize the types which predominate, or indeed are possible, in Great Britain. The most significant feature of British practice is that the central government has practically no borrowing powers[1] for long-term investment, except on behalf of the Post Office. In fact the central government operates no other trading service of any importance, although it finances out of taxation some small semi-social forms of public investment such as afforestation. It does, however, contribute to the financing of local investment of a semi-social nature, such as housing, and, exceptionally, other public health works. On the other hand, the local authorities carry on a large and varied amount of public investment. Normal trading services include water, gas and electricity, trams and buses, baths and washhouses, markets and cemeteries. In addition, there are such rarer birds as Birmingham's Bank, Hull's telephone, Colchester's oyster fishery, Doncaster's race-course, Bradford's wool conditioning house, and Wolverhampton's cold storage. Watering-places frequently own pavilions and piers; municipal aerodromes are becoming increasingly common. In short, there are no limits to the variety of local investment except those set by the imagination of town councillors and their ability to get parliamentary sanction for experiments.

The proportions of expenditure on economic investment met from loans and from current receipts—such as taxes or fees—differ very considerably from one form of public investment to another. For the most part this variation is based on fortuitous institutional regulation rather than on any economic criterion. It has the disadvantage, from our point of view, that in order to get a complete idea of the relative importance of the different forms of public investment, it is necessary to pay attention to expenditure both from current receipts and out of loan funds. As far as current account expenditure is concerned, the importance of public invest-

[1] Small exceptions to this policy have been made from time to time, as for instance, the Land Registry (New Buildings) Act, 1900, Finance Act, 1908 (Public Buildings), Finance Act, 1911 (Sanatoria, &c.), and Housing Act, 1914. Little use of any of these acts has been made since about 1923.

ment—both as a whole and in different directions—is apparent
from the three lower sections of the blocks of Diagram I, Chapter
IV. While there is some possibility of varying the amounts of
such expenditure in the short run, except in the case of roads the
greater part of it is naturally of a routine nature and represents
indispensable outlay on working capital and maintenance charges.
The most important and variable part of public investment
expenditure is obviously that financed out of loan. The main lines
of economic capital investment and their development in our
period are shown in Table 1 (p. 117). It is clear at once that
both as regards expenditure out of current receipts and out of
loans, public investment is dominated by the action of the local
authorities. (It will be remembered that total current expenditure
on the Post Office services is about equal to that on roads, and
together they are about equal to the local trading services, including housing.) But Post Office expenditure met by borrowing is very
moderate—it is actually less than investment in the local electricity
services. The outstanding feature of the table is the dominant
role played by housing. It is clear that as far as our period is concerned, the factors determining housing expenditure were powerful
enough to overcome any others in the field of public investment.

To attempt a detailed investigation of the policy under which
these various types of public investment have been conducted
would be beyond the scope of our study. In the first place, since
both the extent of public ownership and the price and output
policy followed differ from one locality to another, a comprehensive account calls for an investigation of individual practice as
revealed in council minutes and accounts. Secondly, in every
case except roads, the provision of the services is shared between
the local authorities and public utility companies which are
privately owned but publicly controlled (in varying degrees). One
of the most important aspects of the investigation of the financial
policy of local authorities should, therefore, be an evaluation of
the course pursued by the two types of provider and of the
effect of such divided responsibility on the development of the
services. The responsibility for the operation of the different
services as a whole and in each locality depends on no general
policy, but on historical accident. It is clear, however, that the
policy followed by the publicly owned service must—and no
doubt should—vary according to the extent of public ownership

in the locality. A municipal electricity department, for instance, will tend to have a different cost schedule and a different selling policy according as the gas and/or transport services are also publicly owned. These considerations are clearly outside our field, however interesting they may be in themselves.[1]

During our period a specially complicated example of the relation of municipal enterprise to other forms of supply has been afforded by the electricity service. Although capital invested in local authority electricity supply is actually less than that sunk in waterworks, and only slightly more than investment in docks, harbours, &c., since the war electricity has climbed into the first place in municipal trading services. But during this period of rapid development the whole industry has been undergoing a revolution in organization and control. The business of electric supply consists of three processes—generation, mains trans- mission, and retail distribution (including sales promotion). After a struggle lasting from 1919 to 1926 the first two of these were placed on a national footing as regards operation and control, under the auspices of the Electricity Commissioners and the Central Electricity Board. But the terms on which the final round of the struggle—for the rationalization of distribution—will be fought were in 1936 only beginning to emerge—as a result of the report of the McGowan Committee published in June of that year. Apart from the future of that part of the industry which has always been under public ownership, the C.E.B. itself represents an experiment in public control which is full of presage for the future.[2] But this, too, lies outside the scope of our study.

As soon as it was established, the C.E.B. proceeded to erect a national transmission system for the supply produced by certain 'selected' stations. The effect of the 'grid' on local authority 'undertakers' has been somewhat complicated. On the one hand, local consumers have been protected from an increase of price, whatever the previous policy under which the council supply was marketed. This is obviously only a temporary arrangement. On the other hand, as far as selected or reserve (marginal) council

[1] The only official examination on the relative position of public and private enterprise in the trading services in recent years is the 40 pages devoted to public trading enterprise in the Report of the Committee on Industry and Trade (Balfour Committee), in *Further Factors in Industrial and Commercial Efficiency*, 1928, covering experience up to 1925–6.

[2] Cf. T. H. O'Brien, *British Experiments in Public Ownership and Control*.

suppliers are concerned, it appears that the increased availability
of power transmission has resulted in a considerable saving in new
investment. It has been stated[1] that 'the initial effect of the construction and operation of the grid has been to enable individual
generating stations to meet the steady annual increase in demand
and to earn revenue with plant which it had formerly been
necessary to hold in reserve'. In other words, the first effect of the
grid was greatly to increase the short-period elasticity of supply.
The cost of expansion during the period (from about 1929 to 1935)
was therefore thrown on the C.E.B. Owing to this and other
economies resulting from the grid working, the total new investment was probably much less than would have been required
under conditions of independent ownership to meet the 70 per
cent. increase in demand which took place contemporaneously.
From 1935, when the grid came into approximately full working,
the position has returned to a more normal trend. Given the
continuation of the present trend of expansion of demand, since
the reserve is now fully occupied, it appears that a new expansion
of power production will be required. It is clear that neither the
costs or receipts of local electricity supply have followed the trend
which was established in the war period as a result of the rapid
extension of the uses of electricity. Hence local investment in
electricity can hardly be regarded as normal during our period.

It is not possible to say what the ultimate effect of the rationalization of retail distribution will be. What economies accrue must
depend to a considerable extent on the thoroughness with which
the process is carried out. The McGowan Committee noted that
(in 1935) there were 635 'authorized undertakers',[2] of which about
60 per cent. were local authorities. Since the field of operations
of the public undertakers is limited to their administrative areas,
the average size of their undertakings tends to be considerably
smaller than that of the non-public concerns, particularly than the
power companies, which have been steadily expanding since early
in the century. While efficiency is no doubt not uniquely correlated to size,[3] there is abundant evidence to show that there are
serious technical 'diseconomies of small scale'.[4] It can only be

[1] O'Brien, op. cit., p. 65.
[2] About 40 more than recorded by the Balfour Committee.
[3] The writers of the *P.E.P. Report on Electricity*, published in 1936, consider
that the McGowan Committee overstressed the relation between size and
efficiency.   [4] Cf. remarks of Balfour Committee, loc. cit.

surmised therefore that any method of rationalization will decrease the importance and independence of municipal suppliers. The change in position of the largest trading service cannot fail to react on the finance of the other trading departments to which it is related.

The analysis of the financial aspect of municipal trading and its relation to other organizations supplying similar services is thus in itself a study of wide dimensions. While we must renounce any attempt to undertake it here, it is nevertheless possible to make some general deductions which are not without relevance for both normal and cyclical policy, on the basis of figures of total investment. The main lines of policy—or lack of policy—in the development of municipal trading services are well known. The reasons which have prompted the granting of permission to start new services have been based rather on current socio-economic arguments than on any consideration of the suitability of the service for municipal enterprise, or the appropriateness of the administrative area in relation to technical requirements. Thus a smaller proportion of the gas industry than of the electric is in public hands,[1] mainly owing to the accident that the first development of electricity supply in the early eighties coincided with a wave of 'collectivism'. In the present century, and particularly in the post-war period, a considerable enlargement of the field of municipal enterprise has taken place, which is no doubt principally to be traced to the increasing weight of labour opinion. On the other hand, non-political motives are also apparent. In recent years the central government has encouraged the establishment of municipal aerodromes—partly, no doubt, as a useful form of public works. While these should properly be a trading service, there seems little prospect that the development of internal civil aviation will turn them into a remunerative investment within any short period.

The technical appropriateness of the local government area for trading services has only been seriously challenged in the case of electricity and roads.[2] In both of these services it has been found necessary to modify the original system of control very substantially.[3] With the progressive expansion of urbanization similar

---

[1] About 20 per cent. according to the Balfour Committee.
[2] There has also been discussion in respect of water and drainage areas.
[3] Cf. Chap. VIII, p. 144.

difficulties are likely to arise in other spheres. This has already occurred in the case of the transport problem in the metropolitan area. Analogous troubles have arisen where local authorities have established housing estates outside their own areas. The whole problem is closely related to that of local administration and finance in complex urban areas. If some method of solving the administrative problems can be found, the prospect of finding a technically suitable unit for different trading services will be considerably improved.

The want of attention on the part of the central government to technical and economic considerations in the development of municipal enterprise[1] does not augur particularly well for the conduct of the services on the most economical lines. Is it possible to say anything in general terms as to the price and output policy which has been followed in public investment?

It is clear that, broadly speaking, British public trading is not remunerative in the sense that it brings in large net returns. In the case of the Post Office at least it is possible to speak with some generality, since the accounts are unified. The commercial accounts give an accurate picture of Post Office finance, comparable to the profit and loss accounts of private firms. The Post Office, with a staff of 241,500 employees, is said to be[2] the largest commercial undertaking in the country. It conducts a large savings bank, and various minor activities on behalf of the central government, besides its three main 'industries' of the Postal, Telegraph, and Telephone services. Of the three main services— which, it must be noted, are more or less competitive with each other—the postal department is relatively stationary in output and profit. The number of postal packets carried expanded by only 20 per cent. in the twenty years 1913 to 1933.[3] The telegraph department is declining. Less than half the number of wires are now sent as compared with pre-war days. On the other hand, the telephone is rapidly expanding. The number of (local and trunk) calls put through increased nearly five times between 1913 and

---

[1] Probably the most serious consequences are to be found in the electricity industry, where the encouragement given to public enterprise and the rights awarded to councils over private companies not only resulted in the development of the small and uneconomic unit, but seriously restricted the expansion of the industry as a whole. Cf. Balfour Committee, loc. cit.

[2] Cf. J. Dugdale's contribution in *Public Enterprise*, ed. W. A. Robson·

[3] Figures from *Statistical Abstract*.

1934. Over this relatively long period the profit per postal packet sent appears to have increased by 50 per cent., the loss per wire by 12 per cent., and the profit on telephone calls by over 600 per cent.

The net profit on the services as a whole has steadily expanded since the early post-war years, when for a short period net losses were made. By far the largest share of the surplus is accountable to the postal department. Most of the net profit is transferred to the exchequer, and this constitutes a tax on the community: the amount of the tax is about double the pre-war levy.[1] The telegraph department has shown a continuous loss over a long period, the maximum loss being £3·7 m. in 1920–1. In 1927 a committee investigated American methods of sending wires, and as a result the annual loss was reduced,[2] but it still amounted to £0·7 m. in 1934. On the other hand, the telephone service has been steadily remunerative. Over our period it earned interest at 5 per cent. on the capital invested, and in addition a net profit of some £2 m. Since 1932, when telephone profits first exceeded telegraph losses, the younger service has definitely borne the older on its back. It is not possible to say to what extent the fear of loss on the capital invested in the telegraph may have retarded the development of the more modern service.

In 1933, as a result of the report of the Bridgeman Committee,[3] the whole organization of the Post Office was overhauled and placed on a more commercial basis. The secretariat was turned into a functional board, analogous to a board of directors. More important from the point of view of finance, the old system of separate accounts under the Treasury, for receipts and expenditure, was abandoned. Although the Post Office continues to pay over the whole of its surplus to the Treasury, only a standard sum is passed on to the exchequer, the remainder being handed back to the Post Office for its own commercial development. In 1933, of a net profit of £11·9 m., the Post Office was allowed to keep £1·1 m.

In spite of the criticisms made by the Bridgeman Committee, the general opinion of the investigators was that the standard of efficiency shown by the Post Office was very satisfactory. As far as the carriage of letters is concerned, it is important to realize how large a proportion of that charge consists effectively of the tax due to the exchequer. The reduction in the charge for letters in 1922

[1] Cf. Diagram I, Chap. XIV.   [2] Cf. Dugdale, loc. cit.   [3] Cmd. 4149.

(from 2*d*. to 1½*d*.) led to a loss of net revenue of £5 m. (Business only increased by 5 per cent.; thus demand appears to be very inelastic.) It is estimated that a further drop from 1½*d*. to 1*d*. would reduce net revenue by one-half. In the telegraph service, on the other hand, over-investment is evident, and at least up to 1927 there is evidence of inefficient working. A point that would well repay investigation is the cost of the special facilities afforded to the Press. The telephone figures suggest that investment and hence output has not been on a scale sufficient for the market, particularly since this is eminently a service in which there are enormous economies of large-scale production.

So far as local investment is concerned, in the absence of general and uniform cost accounting, it is almost impossible to derive any trustworthy conclusions as to the precise policy followed. The two most important services from this point of view are gas and electricity. At the time of the Balfour Committee's investigation the municipal gas service was already undergoing the slow but steady shrinkage relative to electricity, which has been common to the whole gas industry. The committee found that in 1913, 36 per cent. of the municipal concerns had made a net profit (in the form of a contribution to rates). In 1925 only 11 per cent. were doing so. The aggregate contribution of £134,500 had fallen by 71 per cent. in the twelve years. This trend appears to have continued since 1925.[1] In 1913 there was a net profit on municipal electricity services of £278,594. On the other hand, some concerns were making net losses (contributions being required from rates) to the extent of £123,274. By 1925 the aggregate profit had risen to £760,267, and the loss had shrunk to £18,236. But the average profit per concern had slightly fallen over the period—from £7,105 to £6,962. Since 1925 there has been a slight increase in the contribution of trading services to rates, and most of this is due to the increasing importance of the relatively profitable electricity service.

The aggregate net profits of the two most commercially managed trading services are thus quite negligible in relation to the total turnover of local trading. And the average, if not the aggregate, profit is declining. It appears that the gas service is being conducted in such a way that, on the average, total receipts just cancel costs. Electricity is evidently operated to give a small but steady

[1] Judging from the Local Taxation Returns.

profit. Intermittent profits are shown by other services, but these appear to be mainly the result of casual fluctuations. No doubt the rise in costs, and particularly labour costs, is a partial explanation of the change observed between 1913 and 1925. Further, the Electricity Supply Act of 1926 limited the contribution which might be made to rates from the electricity service.[1] This has probably influenced the policy of local authorities, even where their profits were well within the maximum.[2] In the slight backward swing of the pendulum since 1925 there is little evidence of any large or concerted effort to cover depression deficits out of trading profits, such as has been observed abroad.[3] On the contrary, some of the larger local authorities have decided to abandon entirely the practice of making contributions to rates from trading services.

It is frequently stated that the aim of public investment should be to give the largest possible output at the lowest possible price—that costs should just be covered but that no profit should be made. Something like an approximation to such a policy appears to be an increasing feature of British public investment. It is, indeed, exactly what we should expect from contemporary socio-economic opinion. It is therefore of some interest to inquire what the meaning and probable effects of such a policy would be if it were actually carried out. This is a matter which has been somewhat neglected by economists, although there is a growing literature on the kindred problem of price and output policy in a fully socialized community.[4]

The nature of the problem is given by the fact that almost all public investment is monopolistic in character. Either the public authority is responsible for the entire supply of the commodity in the district, and the ratepayers have no opportunity of supplying their needs—at least as efficiently and cheaply—elsewhere, or the supply of the public authority is large in relation to the demand for this and closely related commodities. We need not discuss the fact of monopoly—in most cases it is dictated by the technical conditions of the service—but for determining policy it is impor-

---

[1] Balfour Committee, loc. cit.

[2] It has also been suggested that the liability of profits to income tax has limited their realization.

[3] Cf. *Unbalanced Budgets*, ed. Dalton, especially the German section by Dr. Brinley Thomas.

[4] Cf. bibliography in Lerner, 'The Statics and Dynamics of Socialist Economy', *E.J.*, June 1937.

tant. In the first place it gives the public authority the opportunity of regarding its trading services as primarily a means of
raising revenue. Tobacco and match monopolies are frequently
operated on this basis abroad. In that case the public authority
naturally acts in exactly the same manner as a private monopolist
would in similar circumstances. It endeavours to make its total
net profits as large as possible, and adjusts price and output with
that end and no other in view. The Post Office services are partially
operated in this way. It would be the natural course for a local
authority to adopt in respect of services which are mainly used by
other than its own ratepayers—swimming pools, car parks, &c.,
at sea-side resorts for instance. At the other end of the scale the
local authority may decide to provide free, or at nominal cost,
services for which an economic fee might be charged—picture
galleries, museums, and, indeed, houses have been so provided.
Price and output policy is then determined mainly by social considerations. The policy of extending output only as far as the
point where cost is just covered is intermediate between these two.
The argument most frequently used in advocating the transfer of
services to public control is that they will be cheaper—the public
authority requires no profit motive for its functioning. The
questions which have to be answered are, what exactly is meant by
covering costs? Does this provide a criterion of price and output
to which the public monopolist can work as surely as the private,
and is there any real advantage to the community in substituting
public control and policy for private?

The spectre that haunts every monopolist entrepreneur in
contrast to purely competitive producers is that every additional
unit of product sold forces down the price and hence reduces the
profit per unit on his whole turnover. The monopolist will therefore reduce his total profits if he puts on the market any unit which
does not more than cover its costs. The public authority, however,
is satisfied if it covers costs on balance. This policy, therefore,
implies selling as large an output as possible, consistent with
covering (long-period) average costs. So long as demand is the
same, the amount to be produced and the price charged are not
a matter for arbitrary decision. There is only one amount and one
price (with given costs and demand) which will satisfy the condition of covering average costs on the largest possible output. If
it follows this policy, the public authority is deliberately neglecting

its monopoly power. Hence public control will (owing to the difference in policy) frequently give a larger output at a lower price than would private enterprise under such competitive conditions as the nature of the service allows.

The policy of making neither profit nor loss on trading services which are not conducted as primarily social enterprises should thus be the cheapest method of giving the community the largest possible real income in the particular line of investment, and should also be completely neutral as between different consumers. It must not be assumed, however, that it will always—or even generally perhaps—produce the economists' ideal output. It will only give even a bare approximation to this if average costs are minimized in the sense that the market could not be supplied more cheaply by a plant of a different size. Even then the particular market may not be sufficient to support a plant of the optimum size from the technical point of view, if there are important economies of large-scale production.

Note

It may be that average costs are falling. In that case the economists' criterion (that price should equal marginal costs) involves selling at a loss (since marginal cost will be less than average). This difficulty may sometimes be got over by making a fixed charge or rental (proportionate to house rent or other evidence of ability to pay) to cover overheads, including (economic) obsolescence, and charging for individual units at average variable cost, which in this type of enterprise is a close approximation to marginal cost. There are also more difficult complications which would have to be considered in a full treatment of the theory of public investment, such as the criterion for the amount of socially desirable investment in any particular line, and the criterion for the renewal of plant.

Our investigations do not suggest that the size of local areas will always or perhaps even commonly enable the full advantages of such a middle or normal policy to be realized. Practice may also frequently diverge from this norm, either deliberately or accidentally. If output is habitually pushed to a point where costs have to be covered out of grants or rates, and if the consumers of the service are the poorer members of the community (as in the case of housing), public investment becomes a tool of social policy. But if consumption is proportionate, or more than proportionate to income, as may for instance be the case with electricity, no social benefit accrues. In this case social considerations would suggest an approximation to a monopolistic policy, perhaps with some element of discrimination. But if policy diverges on either side from the middle way, the likelihood of public management being cheaper to the community as a whole tends to be diminished.

TABLE I

'Economic' Public Investment—Capital Expenditure

England and Wales

(£ m.)

Note. Figures of local investment in 1928 (lower line) and subsequently include small amounts financed from grant.

	1913	1920	1921	1922	1923	1924	1925	1926
Housing . . .	0·7	52·2	81·7	29·6	11·3	24·0	47·0	65·3
Electricity . . .	1·2	8·4	11·5	9·3	8·5	9·7	11·8	12·1
Gas	0·9	1·9	2·9	2·0	1·2	1·4	1·9	2·8
Transport . . .	1·3	2·8	3·5	2·5	2·2	2·6	2·6	2·7
Waterworks . .	2·0	6·0	5·5	5·4	5·2	6·7	6·5	5·3
Roads	*	3·7	6·2	9·0	8·3	9·9	10·0	9·5
Other local trading services	3·2	5·7	3·6	2·4	2·3	3·2	4·2	2·8
Post Office† . . .	4·0	6·0	8·0	7·0	7·7	9·7	12·0	11·0

	1927	1928	1929	1930	1931	1932	1933	1934
Housing . . .	66·2	38·1 / 42·9	42·8	37·4	39·6	28·2	30·6	29·3
Electricity . . .	13·1	14·4 / 14·6	15·3	14·3	13·6	10·9	11·4	12·7
Gas	2·3	1·5 / 1·6	1·5	1·7	1·4	1·2	1·2	1·2
Transport . . .	2·6	2·4 / 2·8	2·4	2·6	2·7	1·6	1·1	1·8
Waterworks . .	4·9	4·6 / 4·9	5·1	4·9	5·5	4·2	3·7	3·9
Roads	8·4	8·0 / 11·9	16·2	18·9	18·9	10·2	8·7	7·2
Other local trading services	4·9	3·9	3·7	3·2	3·4	2·7	2·5	2·4
Post Office† . . .	9·9	10·6	10·5	11·0	9·7	7·5	6·5	7·5‡

* Not given separately.   † Great Britain.   ‡ 1935 = 10·5.

(From *Statistical Abstract*.)

VII

THE TIMING OF PUBLIC INVESTMENT

IN order that the community may derive the fullest possible benefits from public investment it is clearly necessary that it should be conducted with at least as much efficiency and attention to economic considerations as private enterprise. This applies as much to financial policy as to the more technical aspects of production and organization. Public authorities start with a preliminary advantage over private industry in that they can borrow at practically gilt-edged rates, whether or not their stock commands full trustee status. But this does not necessarily ensure that they use the most economical methods of raising funds, since for one thing they may choose the times of borrowing badly. The distribution of public investment over time is also a matter of great importance on other grounds.

Before 1914 it was a matter of indifference to all except its own ratepayers whether a local authority conducted its finances wisely or not. But in our period public investment has increased to an extent which makes it a formidable rival to private industry for the nation's savings. This becomes evident if the volume of public (local authority and public board) new issues, and loans from the Public Works Loans Board is compared with non-government borrowing on the stock exchange (Table 1, p. 130).[1] It was quite exceptional for the volume of public investment not to be large enough to make an appreciable difference in the market. Thus public policy is now in a position to exert an influence on the general economic situation. If the whole volume is considered, it is almost certainly sufficiently large to be the cause of a change in the rate of total investment or in business activity.

A glance at the growth of outstanding loan debt (Table 2, col. 1, p. 130) suggests that there has been no reluctance to borrow for local investment—indeed, it was widely held in 1931 that there had been serious overborrowing—but in spite of the unprecedented rate of growth it is hard to support the contention that British

---

[1] This does not, of course, comprise the whole of local borrowing. A very important part is also played by bank advances, mortgages, and a small part by bills. Total new borrowing is reflected in the growth of outstanding debt (Table 2).

local authorities are seriously burdened with debt. It is evident on general grounds that there has been no overborrowing on the scale which caused severe embarrassment to German and American cities during the depression. It is only here and there in depressed areas (particularly in Glamorganshire)[1] that the debt charge can be regarded as embarrassing to local finances. And this local problem clearly has a particular cause—expansive optimism generated by abnormal prosperity during the war, followed by a heavy decline in population and rateable value. It must be admitted that the small burden of debt falling on local finances is partly due to the assistance which is received from the exchequer. A substantial part of the charge on the housing debt, by far the largest item of non-trading debt, is borne by the general body of taxpayers.[2] The absence of overborrowing must partly be ascribed to the supervisory powers of the Ministry of Health. In this respect there is no administrative parallel in countries where severe overborrowing seems to have taken place during the twenties. But, finally, credit must be given to the factors making cheap borrowing possible—the cautious policy of the majority of local authorities themselves, the steady increase of rateable value, and the confidence of investors.

Moreover, it must be remembered that a not inconsiderable amount of the community's capital investment—even of the most durable nature—is regularly financed from current revenue. Of the central government's activities, the Forestry Commission is financed entirely out of taxes in the first instance. The large sums transferred yearly from the Road Fund to local authorities for the construction and maintenance of highways are also derived wholly from taxes. In addition, exchequer grants of some £3 to £4 m. for capital purposes[3] are made annually to local authorities (excluding Scotland). Before the war, borrowing by the central government for purposes other than the Post Office was practised to some extent—small in the aggregate, but not inconsiderable in relation to the pre-war volume of public investment. Since the war this has been much less common.

Local authorities have the opportunity of financing capital expenditure by means other than borrowing from two sources—

[1] Cf. *Report of Commissioner for South Wales*, 1934, and discussion in Chap. XII.

[2] According to the Ministry of Health Annual Report of 1931, the rate burden of outstanding debt did not exceed 2s. 3d. in the £.

[3] Exclusive of housing subsidies.

directly out of rates, and by 'internal user' of the various funds which they are forced or desire to accumulate. The larger local authorities (and notably the London County Council) tend to adopt the policy of setting aside a definite proportion of rate receipts annually for capital purposes. In addition there is a movement in favour of establishing rate equalization funds. While these aim primarily at mitigating the rate burden in depression, in effect a fund is created which may be partially applied to capital purposes. It is obvious, however, that even in the case of the larger authorities it cannot be hoped to finance any but a small proportion of capital expenditure from rates.

Both tradition and the stringency of sinking fund regulations in certain forms of borrowing—notably in the Public Works Loans Board mortgages—cause local authorities to work with rather large nominal sinking funds. The volume and growth of these is shown in Table 2, col. 2. In addition there is a rapidly growing volume of other funds. At 31 March 1935 the total of these reached £95·34 m.,[1] of which rather over half consisted of superannuation funds, and about a quarter of trading service reserves, including house-repair funds. Although there is a limitation to the accumulation of reserves in electricity departments,[2] in general all these funds show a tendency to increase. The superannuation scheme has only been in existence since 1922, hence the funds are still in the accumulation stage.[3] Similarly, nominal sinking funds are bound to accumulate during and immediately after a period of heavy new borrowing. Thus the trend cannot be reversed for a considerable period. It is therefore a question of considerable interest to discover to what extent the funds are used internally for capital purposes, both normally and in the stress of the trade cycle.

There are, unfortunately, no data for a comparative examination of 'internal user' at different times, but a sample inquiry carried out in 1934[4] enables certain broad but definite conclusions to be drawn as to recent practice. The inquiry covered roughly one-quarter of the gross debt of local authorities (including Scotland),

---

[1] Cf. *Ministry of Health Annual Report.*

[2] Under the Electricity Supply Acts.

[3] Moreover, the Act of 1922 under which superannuation schemes have been set up is only permissive. Were the practice to be made compulsory for local authorities, there must be a very rapid accumulation of funds.

[4] *The Use of Sinking Funds, &c., for Capital Purposes,* by Long and Maxwell, published by the Institute of Public Administration, 1936.

but more than one-third of the principal funds. Of this apparently some £30 m., or rather more than 50 per cent., was used internally. It must be noted, however, that the L.C.C. was responsible for nearly two-thirds of the funds used. The larger funds contributed in the following proportions: superannuation 37 per cent., trading reserves 28 per cent., and sinking and redemption funds 26 per cent. Differences in practice as to loan pooling make it difficult to attach any precise meaning to the last figure.[1] It also emerged from the inquiry that liquid reserves in the sense of cash or maturities to meet forthcoming liabilities did not exceed 11 per cent. of the debt maturing in the following five years (which represented about 50 per cent. of total obligations). The provision which could thus be regarded as truly liquid was about £1·1 m., which represented little more than enough to meet six months' maturing liabilities (on the assumption that these were distributed evenly over the five-year period). In some cases complete reliance was placed on new borrowing to meet maturing liabilities.

It appears, therefore, that the local authorities covered by the inquiry do not work with very high liquid balances, and that in addition to their holdings of trustee stocks they do invest a considerable proportion of their spare funds in capital works. It must be remarked, however, that 1932, the year for which the returns were made, cannot be regarded as fully representative. It is not improbable that there was an abnormal demand on funds, both on general cyclical grounds and on account of the special circumstances of the financial crisis of 1931–2. More important, the inquiry which was naturally answered by the more active and progressively managed local authorities must represent something of a biased sample. The report strongly supports the inference that 'internal user' is increasing, but whether at a faster rate than the accumulation of funds it is impossible to say. Forty per cent. of the authorities making returns operated loan pools, which are conducive to the full employment of redemption funds (or rather true sinking funds are abolished by the system). The number of such authorities was increasing. As regards the cyclical movement, it is the opinion of the Ministry of Health that funds tend to run down (be raided) during depression.[2] This is what might be expected.

---

[1] Since, if a loans pool exists, there is no true sinking fund.

[2] Cf. Gibbon, 'The Expenditure and Revenue of Local Authorities', *J.R.S.S.*, 1936.

Firms usually attempt to increase their liquidity during depression owing to the increase of uncertainty, but this motive is almost entirely lacking in public investment. Also there is a natural incentive for local authorities to use every available means to avoid raising rates during depression, whether or not a specific rate equalization fund has been established.

Although the volume of capital expenditure financed out of taxes is small, it is of some economic significance. It is clearly the cheapest method in the long run, by the amount of the accumulated interest charge which would be necessary if the borrowing method had been used. For this reason local authorities have frequently been urged to attempt to finance part of their durable equipment out of rates, particularly during the period of high interest rates. Apart, however, from the considerable difficulty in doing so, particularly for the smaller authorities,[1] and the consequent danger that desirable works will be postponed, the possible alternatives require to be carefully weighed. For the public authority to invest current income in durable equipment is in fact to raise a forced loan from the taxpayers. It may well be that this is a convenient way of financing investment. But the burden which is imposed upon the taxpayer depends upon the difference between the yield of the public investment, and the yield on any other investment to which he might have devoted his funds, whether directly or through the medium of the stock exchange. In this connexion the 2 per cent. estimated by the May Committee to be the yield of forestry investment will be recalled. It must be recognized that the use of revenue to bring in so small a return lays an uncompensated burden upon the taxpayer unless the return is in fact enhanced by some advantage or amenity which accrues to the community but is not charged for.

The cyclical significance of investment out of taxation is of more immediate importance. It seems probable that the larger local authorities can here play an important part in general cyclical policy, just because they have a wider field of public investment readily available than the central government. Economically it is clearly desirable that as large a proportion as possible of any local investment taking place during booms should be financed from rates. It would, however, require a detailed examination of local

---

[1] Since rates flow in a small regular stream, and investment requires large but intermittent spending.

accounts to ascertain what, if any, cyclical variation does actually take place. The rigidity of local rates and the difficulty of increasing receipts during depression make it probable that so far as the depression is concerned, at any rate, the movement is in the right direction. On the other hand, the practice of the central government in giving grants for public works in depression out of taxes is clearly a movement in the wrong direction.

There appears to be no particular economic significance in the mere *fact* of 'internal user'. It makes no difference whether a local authority finances capital expenditure out of its own reserves or borrows the reserves of another authority. In general the use of reserves gives local authorities more freedom in matching their borrowing needs to the opportunities of the market, and it saves the trouble and expense of floating a loan. Against these advantages must be set the limited true availability of the funds, particularly those of a semi-trustee variety. Their too enthusiastic employment may lead to unexpected and expensive borrowing to restore the necessary liquidity. 'Internal user' also raises some pretty problems of accounting and imputation for the financial expert,[1] but as long as funds continue to accumulate, the amount of capital investment which may—and no doubt will—legitimately be financed internally will continue to increase. But if the volume of total new local investment were to decline, new borrowing would also tend to shrink. A position is then not inconceivable in which local authorities might become entirely self-financing. In the absence of some direct control of capital expenditure the *tempo* of public investment would in that case be considerably more independent both of the central government and of the movement of interest rates than it is (or might be) at present.

But during our period the greater part of public investment was necessarily financed out of loan. Table 3, p. 131, shows, for the period when new borrowing was proceeding rapidly, the distribution of borrowing from the more important sources for which statistics are available, according to interest due and length of loan. The largest amount of stock borrowing was made when the long-term rate of interest was 5 per cent. Substantial amounts were also borrowed at 6 per cent. The greater part of this debt runs to the middle of the century without opportunity for conversion. In the

[1] Long and Maxwell, loc. cit., are of the opinion that 'relatively few authorities appear to have appreciated the theory of a loans pool'.

early post-war years about 90 per cent. of the sums borrowed from the Public Works Loans Board, at average rates of nearly 6 per cent., were for the longest possible period—50 to 80 years. But as the decade wore on shorter loans became somewhat more popular.

It is worth noting that the borrowing policy for public investment followed by the central government was very similar to that of the local authorities. Just after the war, Post Office annuities were arranged for the twenty-five-year periods which had been customary up to 1914. The heaviest borrowing took place when rates were at a high level (viz. $4\frac{7}{8}$ and 5 per cent.). Later, the usual annuity period was reduced to nineteen years. The policy of the Central Electricity Board was also similar. £7 m. 5 per cent. stock (at 95) was issued in February and £10 m. $4\frac{1}{2}$ per cent. (at 96) in June 1932, when the long-term rate of interest was exceptionally, but very temporarily, high.

Admittedly market conditions in the twenties presented a very awkward problem to all borrowers. Public authorities were not alone in landing themselves with a heavy burden of unconvertible debt. It must be asked, however, whether some better distribution of local debt might not have been achieved. It is one of the disadvantages of divided responsibility that the general body of taxpayers is compelled to shoulder the lion's share of the shortcomings of local finance, through its liability in connexion with the housing debt.

The possibility of diminishing the annual interest and amortization charge when budgets are tight no doubt provides some explanation of the large volume of long-period borrowing (it must, however, be remembered that the medium-term housing bond was also available). But it is clear that spreading the burden of a sinking fund actually increases the ultimate charge on the rates. If interest rates are abnormally high, long-period borrowing may become a very expensive luxury. A more important factor in determining the choice of borrowing periods was probably the survival of traditional sinking-fund practice. Statutory borrowing periods tend to be for the 'lifetime' of the equipment to be financed out of the loan, and sinking funds are arranged to amortize it by the end of the period. On a number of occasions in the early twenties, however, this practice was (wisely) discarded, and fifteen- or twenty-year loans were arranged within eighty- to ninety-year amortization periods, thus abandoning the possibility of amortizing the loan by the time it was due for repayment. It would appear that this practice might have been indulged in more frequently and the majority of loans during the years of high interest arranged for these or even shorter periods. Not only is such traditional sinking-fund policy largely obsolete, but the nominal 'lifetime' of the equipment has little or no economic significance. The economic criterion requires merely that the equipment should be fully written down within its economic life, which is determined by such factors as technical obsolescence, and changes in the size of the market.

During the early post-war period the practice of pooling loans was only beginning to develop. It did not become in any way general until after a general sanction was implied in the Accounts Order of 1930. Even after that, progress in adopting a modern policy was probably delayed by the indefiniteness, if not actual contradiction, of legislative enactment.[1]

The want of skill shown in selecting borrowing periods up to 1932 can thus be partly accounted for by special circumstances, some of which have passed away or are in course of improvement. In the period which succeeded the drastic fall in interest rates, the volume of new local borrowing shrank to negligible proportions. Most of the capital raised was applied to conversion operations rather than to new investment. In 1935 some recrudescence of local activity was apparent. In that year £31·1 m., and in 1936 £62·6 m., was raised on the stock exchange (excluding public boards and Scotland), but by no means the whole was available for new investment. These loans were (quite rightly) all floated for a long period. Thus the restoration of pre-war market conditions once more brought traditional local borrowing policy into line with economic criteria. There is no definite evidence of a change of heart on the part of the public borrowers. Moreover, this new wave of public borrowing has its own problem. The coincidence of maturity dates of local borrowing since 1932 with each other and with those of central loans, may raise a conversion problem of some difficulty.[2] The local loans of the twenties came after the war borrowing, and had longer maturities; thus this particular eventuality has so far been avoided.

---

[1] Cf. Long and Maxwell, loc. cit. The Local Government Act of 1933 made no mention of the general permission granted in 1930, and it was couched in terms which took no notice of modern practice.

[2] Cf. Chap. XXIII, p. 374.

It is clear that the timing of new borrowing was not merely unfortunate from the point of view of capital market conditions, but in relation to general trade activity. Cyclical policy requires that borrowing should be pushed ahead in depression and when interest rates are low, but cut down in boom when borrowing is expensive and the competition for loan funds severe. Such a policy is also that which will pay the local authority the best by enabling it to get its funds at the cheapest possible price. But the practice of local borrowing in our period has pursued an almost exactly opposite course. The drop in stock exchange issues from £41·7 m. to £8·0 m. (Table 1) between 1930 and 1931 was particularly unfortunate, and it is worth noticing that it was greater than the drop in non-public borrowing. The depression decline in local stock borrowing amounted to 80 per cent. as compared to 53 per cent. for public works loan mortgages and 60 per cent. for non-government issues.

A number of causes have contributed to the fluctuations in borrowing, but obviously the most important factor is the variation in spending. The course of local expenditure on capital equipment is shown in Table 2, col. 7. Between 1919 and 1921 local expenditure out of loan rose from £23·9 m. to £94·5 m., the largest increase of the post-war years. 1921, 1926, 1927, and 1930 were all years of high spending. The periods from 1921 to 1923 and from 1931 to 1933 were economy periods. Very similar movements are apparent in road expenditure.[1] In 1910, the first year of the operation of the Road Improvement Act, expenditure was £14 m. In the succeeding boom years it expanded, but sank again during the war. The post-war road building boom coincided with the return to prosperity. 1919, 1920, and 1921 were all years of rapidly increasing investment: in the three years total expenditure was doubled. This period coincided with the first activity of the Ministry of Transport. Expenditure grew steadily though slowly until 1929, except during the later years of Mr. Churchill's chancellorship, when the funds were put to other uses. The next rapid expansion coincided with the boom and the labour government. After that came economy with depression. The Post Office figures show the same movement. There was a decline of loan expenditure in 1922, but it began to rise *pari passu* with general expenditure in 1924. It remained at a high level through-

[1] Cf. Chap. VIII, p. 145.

out the Churchill régime and the second Snowden period of office, but declined steadily from 1931 to 1933.[1]

These are, however, gross accounts. If allocations to sinking fund are subtracted a very much smaller figure is obtained. In the twenties net new expenditure was well in advance of repayments, but in the thirties this has not been the case. In 1932, English local authorities placed the sum of £46 m. to sinking-fund account. On the other hand, some of this was spent on capital equipment— probably about £12 m. The figures are subject also to certain internal deductions. Transfers of sums varying from about £1 m. to £1·5 m. are made annually from capital account to sinking funds, or to repayments of balances to lenders. In addition larger sums are occasionally so allocated for special accounts. Thus in 1933, £9·4 m. was transferred on account of payments for tramways by the London Passenger Transport Board. (This, however, was quite exceptional.) Further, although the figure is inclusive of expenditure concerned with capital works, it must be remembered that only a proportion is actually spent on the works themselves, the remainder going in the purchase of land, buildings, trading undertakings, &c. The figures are thus not a very reliable guide in detail to the course of net capital expenditure. Even with these limitations, however, the general movement is clear. Expenditure tends to mount in prosperity and fall in depression. And the same movement is observable in the capital expenditure of the central government.

There are, as we know, a number of factors determining the variation in public investment. In our period the most important single cause has been changes in the conditions of housing subsidies. These had a political and social, but no economic, significance. Roads appear to have been partly a political matter, or rather perhaps the explanation is that they never appealed particularly to Mr. Churchill, and he was glad of the opportunity which the Road Fund gave him of balancing his budgets. On the other hand, their high employment value made them an investment naturally favoured by the labour party. In the fluctuations of Post Office investment the influence of political expansion and economy campaigns is more evident than in the fluctuations of local investment. This is as we should expect, since Post Office expenditure is

---

[1] On the other hand, it happened that the expenditure of the Central Electricity Board was much more happily timed; cf. Chap. VI, p. 109.

more directly under control than that of the local authorities. An investigation into local variations in the timing of investment would undoubtedly reveal important local peculiarities and divergences. While these must largely resolve themselves into those due to local political causes, and those depending on local industrial conditions, it is not unlikely that they would shed an interesting light on the relative importance of factors affecting investment as a whole.

It must be emphasized that in all the figures a cyclical movement of considerable strength is apparent, working not in the opposite, but in the same direction as the trade cycle and fluctuations of private industry. Thus, throughout the period, so far as public investment is influential in the trade cycle, its weight has been thrown into the balance on the wrong side. It is easy to understand how this has occurred. Councillors, many of them connected with industry, are not immune from the waves of optimism and pessimism which play such an important part in industrial fluctuations. There is also undoubtedly widespread misapprehension as to the effect of the reduction of expenditure by public bodies. It is not realized that while to increase spending out of tax receipts during depression may be deflationary in its effects on total spending, to increase it out of borrowed funds when they would probably otherwise have lain idle will almost certainly increase incomes in general.[1] Finally, expenditure out of loan entails also some increase in the tax burden, both locally for the provision of working capital and loan charges, and centrally, since it not infrequently implies an increase in government grant.

Until the depression of 1931 it is true that attention had hardly been called to possibilities of using public investment policy as a means of fighting depression. 1920 was the first year in which expenditure on capital equipment reached a figure sufficiently large to be of any economic weight. The Post Office was not organized on a commercial basis until after 1933. In the last few years, however, the part of public investment in both boom and depression has been widely canvassed. It might therefore be anticipated that some improvement in the time distribution of investment would be evident in the boom years of 1935–7. There was, unfortunately, little sign of a change of policy. The beginning of the process of the transfer of main roads to central control provided in itself—as indeed it was inevitable that it should—an exceptional

[1] Cf. the statement of the argument in Pigou, *Economics in Practice*, chap. 2.

THE TIMING OF PUBLIC INVESTMENT 129

stimulus to new investment. A five-year programme beginning in 1937 was announced, involving annual expenditure of £100 m., much of which must synchronize with the strain of rearmament expenditure. In addition the completion of many subsidiary works—some of them standing over from 1930 to 1931—was also announced.[1] Other illustrations of the same policy may be taken at random from the daily press. The Post Office announced in January 1937, for instance, a scheme for laying underground telephone cables in Yorkshire, estimated to cost £1 m., in addition to £0·5 m. works already in hand. Expansion also extends to quasi-public investment, such as the London Passenger Transport Board, where it might be assumed that the government could, if it would, exert some restraining influence.[2]

In the actual process of investment the part played by local authorities is still more important than anything the central government can achieve by direct action. Nevertheless, in the new road and Post Office policies established since 1933 the government has considerably more scope than it had some years ago. And essentially it is the central government which is the director of policy for the local authorities. If the community is to get the best out of public investment, not merely in the trade cycle but in the way of normal development, there must be some such conscious direction. At a later stage[3] we shall have to investigate the prospects and possible obstacles to such a unified policy.

[1] For instance, a Thames tunnel at Dartford, estimated to cost £3·5 m.

[2] For instance, Railway Electrification in North East London to cost £14·5 m. The tardy appearance of this was no doubt due to the dating of the Treasury guarantee.   [3] Cf. Chap. X.

TABLE 1

Local Authority Borrowing (G.B.) compared with Industrial Issues

£ m.

	1920	*1921*	*1922*	*1923*	*1924*	*1925*	*1926*	*1927*
L.A. stock borrowing	49·6	19·0	5·6	..	10·3	21·3	41·8	27·1
P.W.L.B. . .	31·2	50·5	13·6	6·6	15·9	29·2	37·2	39·7
Together . .	80·8	69·5	19·2	6·6	26·2	50·5	79·0	66·8
Non-govt. issues .	268·5	82·5	111·5	93·1	85·8	130·5	121·0	183·8

	1928	*1929*	*1930*	*1931*	*1932*	*1933*	*1934*	*1935*
L.A. stock borrowing	14·9	8·3	41·7	8·0	28·8	24·6	36·1	51·1
P.W.L.B. . .	20·7	21·4	18·3	19·9	9·8	8·1	8·6	13·9
Together . .	35·6	29·7	60·0	27·9	38·6	32·7	44·7	65·0
Non-govt. issues .	208·7	177·0	87·1	51·0	33·6	42·1	80·5	94·2

Stock Exchange calendar years. P.W.L.B. financial years.
(From *Economist* and P.W.L.B. Annual Reports.)

TABLE 2

Debt, Loan Charges, Capital Expenditure: Local Authorities in England and Wales

Year	Gross loan debt, end of year	Sinking funds end of year	Loan charges	Proportion of loan charges to outstanding debt, at beginning of year			Capital expenditure during the year
				Total	Interest	Repay-ment	
	(1) £ m.	(2) £ m.	(3) £ m.	(4) per cent.	(5) per cent.	(6) per cent.	(7) £ m.
1914–15	570·8	37·5	35·3	6·3	3·4	2·9	21·8
1920–1	657·8	62·3	41·7	7·5	4·4	3·1	94·5
1921–2	768·6	64·6	51·5	7·8	4·8	3·0	128·7
1922–3	803·9	62·4	57·6	7·5	4·7	2·8	71·6
1923–4	820·3	61·8	59·8	7·4	4·6	2·8	50·0
1924–5	864·9	63·1	61·5	7·5	4·6	2·9	70·3
1925–6	934·7	62·8	68·8	8·0	4·7	3·3	100·7
1926–7	1027·9	67·8	74·2	8·0	4·8	3·2	117·4
1927–8	1121·3	69·8	83·4	8·1	4·8	3·3	120·0
1928–9	1175·0	67·6	89·4	8·0	4·7	3·3	102·8
1929–30	1224·7	66·8	93·2	8·0	4·8	3·2	108·9
1930–1	1303·8	88·5	99·6	8·1	4·8	3·3	110·9
1931–2	1356·8	91·1	102·1	7·8	4·6	3·2	116·8
1932–3	1393·8	93·3	106·8	7·9	4·6	3·3	84·8
1933–4	1404·4	†	117·9	†	†	†	89·3

1929–30 and later expenditure includes outlay from grants as well as loans.
(From Gibbon, *J.R.S.S.* iii, 1936.)
† Not stated.

TABLE 3

Long-term borrowing of Local Authorities

(a) Public Works Loan Board: Duration of Mortgages on Local Rates (England and Wales)

Year	Total £ m.	Per cent. for each period of years					Av. rate per cent.
		−20	20–30	30–40	40–50	50–80	
1920–1 .	30·1	2·6	4·7	0·1	3·6	89·0	5·5
1921–2	47·5	2·6	3·7	0·01	2·8	90·5	6·2
1922–3	12·4	7·6	10·9	0·5	4·3	76·6	5·4
1923–4	5·8	16·0	35·0	..	2·0	46·0	5·0
1924–5	14·5	36·8	25·8	2·9	1·3	33·2	4·9
1925–6	28·1	37·4	26·3	3·1	1·6	34·4	5·0
1926–7	35·4	35·8	20·2	5·8	1·4	36·8	5·0
1927–8	37·3	36·2	20·7	5·8	0·8	38·3	5·0
1928–9	19·1	38·3	22·4	6·7	0·3	32·7	5·0
1929–30	19·8	38·0	26·0	5·0	0·1	31·0	5·1
1930–1	17·4	25·0	30·0	6·0	1·0	38·0	4·9
1931–2	18·8	17·0	35·8	7·0	1·7	38·0	5·0
1932–3	8·8	16·0	33·1	14·4	1·5	35·0	4·5
1933–4	8·0	19·7	15·8	21·7	0·7	42·0	3·75

(From Annual Reports of the P.W.L.B.)

(b) Amounts and dates of maturity of stock debt of Local Authorities and Public Boards (excluding the Central Electricity Board), England and Wales, contracted before 1934

Repayable in period	Interest payable per cent.									
	2½	2¾	3	3½	4	4½	4¾	5	5½	6
	£ m.	£ m.	£ m.	£ m.	£ m.	£ m.	£ m.	£ m.	£ m.	£ m.
Before '34 .	10·4	2·1	99·1	29·6	13·1	..	..	..	1·4	..
'34–40	..	..	1·7	2·6	2·0	3·9	6·6	18·9	1·3	37·0
'41–5	..	..	8·3	2·2	..	34·8	12·2	22·3	8·8	..
'46–50	..	..	1·9	7·0	..	11·4	4·8	56·3	..	1·0
'51–5	..	..	2·3	..	..	9·6	..	2·1	..	..
'56–60	0·6	..	..	..	..	..	..	..	..	..
'61–5	..	..	0·4	6·2	..	..	..	..	..	..
'66+	..	..	2·7	11·7	3·2	..	..	0·5	..	0·3
Totals £ m. .	11·0	2·1	116·4	59·3	18·2	59·7	23·9	100·0	11·5	38·3

Notes: (i) The total outstanding stock debt at January 1934 was £430·4 m.
(ii) During 1934 Local Authorities and Public Boards in England and Wales raised £41·85 m. on the stock exchange (£29 m. excluding the Port of London), at an average of 3 per cent. Roughly 80 per cent. of the total was applied to funding short-term debt.

VIII

ROADS

WHILE the necessary limitations of our field prevent us from investigating fully the finances of public trading services, no such handicap exists in the case of road expenditure, which is purely a government affair. On several grounds an excursion into the economics of highway development may be of particular interest and importance. Road works have long been considered a highly convenient form of public works. There is no doubt that they may be both convenient and useful as an instrument of cyclical expenditure policy, particularly if they are planned to fit in with a general scheme of development. In the circumstances of modern traffic they probably have an important part to play also in any long-period scheme of public investment. Of the three or four lines of National Development suggested in the liberal programme of 1929,[1] roads appear to be both the most urgent and the most feasible.

The urgency of the British road problem is immediately apparent if we consider only its two most striking aspects—danger and delay. There are nearly thirteen times as many vehicles on the roads in the United States as in Great Britain, but less than six times as many people are killed in a year.[2] The British car is slower than the American, and it seems hard to believe that British road users are more careless to this extent. These figures in themselves provide an *a priori* case for examining the condition of road development. The analysis of accidents has not yet been carried out with sufficient detail to enable precise conclusions to be drawn as to the relative importance of the different contributory factors. In official inquiries the road factor is given a remarkably small weight (less than 1 per cent.), but it appears that the condition of the roadway is only reported as a cause if particular obstructions such as slippery surface or blind corners are present. The results of a local inquiry held with the approval of the Ministry of Transport[3] suggested on the contrary that in more than 75 per cent. of fatal road accidents the road was partly to blame. It would seem

---

[1] Cf. Chap. XIII, p. 219.   [2] Cf. *The Economist*, 21 Aug. 1937.
[3] In Oxfordshire. It was followed by extensive experimental improvements, with a 75 per cent. grant from the central government. Even over a short period the resulting decline in accidents appears to have been very encouraging.

more logical when investigating accidents to start from the other end, and instead of asking, 'Was there any particular road obstacle present?' to inquire, 'Could any road improvement be made which would diminish the likelihood of accidents of this type recurring?' Such an attitude would certainly lead to a more intelligent road policy.

The question of delay is closely related to that of danger. Compulsory delay is imposed in the 30-mile limit because the roads are recognized as unsafe. Further voluntary delay must be self-imposed by every careful driver in order to reduce the danger of accidents which the condition of the roads makes only too great. And delay is costly. Besides the universal appeal of the social burden of road accidents, delay has an economic aspect which, if less obvious, is none the less a real burden on the community. The improvement of the road system is not merely a humane, but a paying, proposition.

The fundamental cause both of the danger and the delay on British roads becomes immediately clear when the traffic problem is viewed in relation to that of other countries. There are 50 per cent. more vehicles per mile of road in Great Britain than in the United States. In other words, our roads are much more crowded than those of the country where motor transport is more fully developed than anywhere else in the world. While we have stretches of modern roadway which can compare with the best standards of America or the Continent and many miles of secondary road which are fully adequate for the traffic they have to bear, there are bottlenecks, blind corners, level-crossings, narrow streets through market-towns, in bewildering confusion—not to mention such more refined obstructions as bad gradients and inadequately banked corners. In these circumstances it is not impossible that the 50 per cent. difference in traffic density may give rise to a considerably more than proportionate degree of danger and delay. Any impartial observer of the road problem can hardly fail to conclude that the British road system is seriously out of date. This is scarcely to be wondered at when we consider that—except for a short period between the perfection of the express stage-coach and the building of the railway—the last government to be interested in through road communication was the Roman.[1]

[1] In this respect we are in a much less fortunate position than the French, whose road system was thoroughly overhauled by Napoleon.

But it need not therefore be concluded that the satisfactory solution of the British road problem demands the scrapping of the present road system—or its relegation to non-motor traffic—and the substitution of an entirely new system of motor-ways. The traffic problem differs enormously between one country and another. The British road system can only be made adequate if the particular place which road transport does, and should, take in the economy is fully taken into account. It is obvious on general grounds that the special advantages of road transport as contrasted with rail lie in the ease and speed with which fairly light goods in small consignments, and also passengers, can be transported for fairly short distances. It is clearly more economical to use rail transport for heavy goods, especially where there is no particular urgency in delivery, and for long hauls. Rail is also probably more comfortable and speedy for long passenger journeys than motoring. Air transport, on the other hand, has particular advantages for the rapid transport of passengers and very light goods for long distances. In the present state of technique the difficulty of finding suitable landing-grounds near the ultimate destination seriously limits its usefulness for short distances.

A wise community will obviously not limit itself in the matter of transport, but will develop each particular type to the point where, on strictly economic grounds, costs are equalized at the margin. It appears to emerge from the consideration of British conditions that there is an exceptionally high proportion of journeys for which road transport is the most economical type of conveyance. This is owing, on the one hand, to the smallness of the country and, on the other, to the high degree of urbanization. It pays to make a heavier use of road transport in Great Britain than in America or even in most parts of the Continent, because the time occupied by handling is large relatively to the time spent on the journey, and because consumers' markets are wealthy and extensive. It also follows that the commercial and business use of the roads tends to be heavier in relation to the private pleasure use than in countries where long hauls predominate, and consequently commercial road transport has few advantages to offer. These considerations suggest the essentials of an adequate road system for Great Britain. A first necessity is that it should be adapted to carrying commercial traffic quickly and easily for a large number of small consignments in every direction, not merely along a few main routes. The course of uncontrolled road development has provided the country with a network of roads unparalleled abroad. The English roads are a consequence of the special characteristics of the country, and they do the work, however inadequately. The reserved motor-ways of the continent are particularly adapted for fast traffic with few junctions and long journeys. In so far as they are suited for commercial traffic at all they are particularly advantageous for relatively long hauls. In Great Britain this need is probably fully met by the exceptionally thorough railway system. It would seem then that the highway needs of Great Britain are not so much the construction of a new system of motorways, even if it were physically and financially feasible, as the reconstruction and rationalization of the existing routes. The British road problem exists not because there are not enough roads but because there are a great number of points where the road service provided is inadequate, in the sense that normal traffic cannot proceed at a safe and steady pace. The solution implies the progressive elimination of these points.

If once this principle is accepted, a rational, if somewhat rough-and-ready, method of determining the amount of road development which it would pay the community to undertake could easily be worked out. The process consists in calculating the degree of transport-cost reduction which would accrue from any 'unit of road improvement', and arranging these in order of urgency, down to the final or marginal unit, where the cost reduction would only just balance the cost of making the improvement. The cost of bad roads in this country may be assumed mainly to be due to overcrowding at different points. Most of these can be ascertained by a very cursory inspection. The normal volume of traffic at these different black points can be obtained from traffic censuses, giving the number and weight of vehicles passing at different times and seasons. (For bad corners, &c., the delay caused by obstruction can be calculated on an analogous method, such as multiplying the delay caused to a single vehicle by the number of vehicles passing within a chosen period.) Choosing any agreed speed as normal (for the sake of argument let us say 40 m.p.h.), it would then be necessary to calculate on the one hand the cost of the time lost during a particular period under present conditions, and on the other the cost of improving the road so that the given volume of traffic would pass at normal speed. Time lost would naturally be calculated in terms of wages and petrol consumption—approximate conventional rates for these in terms of particular types of traffic could fairly readily be arrived at. The standard of surface and durability required would be determined by the volume and type of traffic to be accommodated. All units of improvement where the difference between these two costs was positive would be included in the road plan. The order of the urgency of the different units would be given by the degree of difference between the two costs.

There are, however, a number of difficulties to be overcome before the plan would be complete. Improvement schemes are both rival and complementary to each other. While improvements must naturally be costed separately in the first instance, their full value depends on freeing the whole of a particular length of road from obstruction. The decision to proceed with one improvement automatically puts those on the same route farther up the list and those on alternative routes farther down. A single plan for large areas would enable the importance of these factors to be gauged—so far indeed as is practical. (It should be noted that it is not sufficient to plan a single route in an area: it must be considered in relation to possible alternatives.)

A much more serious difficulty arises from the essentially dynamic nature of the problem. Some period must necessarily be selected within which it is expected that a road improvement will 'pay for itself' in transport-cost reduction. But the selection of the period is more or less arbitrary. The *order* of urgency of improvements can be determined by any intelligent investigation, but the *total* amount of paying investment differs enormously according to the amortization period chosen. Apart from the question of obsolescence, road works must all be considered as fairly durable. Even mere surface repairs are said commonly to remain good for at least six years—if the right mixture has been used. Major improvements and new constructions are very much more durable.

If the road traffic position could be regarded as stationary—in other words, if there were no danger of an improvement becoming obsolete—it would be reasonable to choose a very long amortization period, corresponding to the usual practice of borrowing for very permanent works. But while the volume of road traffic is rapidly increasing there is considerable danger of obsolescence. To some extent this can be guarded against by building with initial excess capacity, having in mind the trend of population and industry. Where obsolescence is inevitable it would frequently be desirable to choose a shorter period—something, for instance, between ten and thirty years—corresponding to the period for which local authorities usually borrow for less permanent works. The selection of a period much shorter than this would certainly give a false impression of the amount of paying road development. It is perhaps hardly necessary to point out that the borrowing should be undertaken by the authority to which the increase in tax receipts from greater road usage and increased industrial efficiency will accrue. That is to say, loans must be raised by the central government and not by the local authorities.

Ultimately the volume of road work which can be undertaken during a short period depends on the possibility of getting workers and materials without seriously running up their prices. This sets a practical limit to the speed with which the programme can be put into operation. It does not, however, detract from the usefulness of the calculation as a long-period plan.

The road plan just outlined is not quite comprehensive, but its completion is not a difficult matter. We have so far spoken only of road improvement. There is also the question of maintenance: this, however, raises much less difficult problems. Maintenance may be defined as keeping the roads in such a state of repair that they continue to carry their normal traffic load with undiminished efficiency. With expanding traffic this in fact includes a certain amount of minor improvements, and the line between maintenance and improvement cannot be clearly drawn. Nevertheless, the expenditure required for maintenance does not tend to change violently from year to year. It would seem desirable to allow for this before determining the improvement programme for the season, and subsequently to make adjustments where improvements will take the place of repairs.

The different uses for which roads are required give rise to a more substantial complication. The basis of the road plan is the argument that commercial traffic, including the use of private cars for business purposes, is the most important part of modern road usage in this country, but the claims of pleasure motoring and of miscellaneous local traffic have also to be met. The problem of pleasure traffic can be solved in a manner analogous to that of commercial traffic if we assume that motorists are willing to pay for improvements which would bring the roads up to a certain standard.[1] Improvements necessary to meet the pleasure-motoring demand would therefore find their level in the road plan without more ado. Local traffic, however, is another matter. It covers what the Conference on Rail and Road Transport[2] called the Community Use of roads, and must allow for pedestrians, horse-drawn vehicles, cycles, and parking facilities. The community use of roads is partly social, and the standard of development, including all the appurtenances of the road system, such as footpaths, grass verges, and trees, is obviously one for local decision. From the point of view of the road plan the essential condition is that local authorities should be sufficiently freed from responsibility for through roads, to carry out and finance their proper sphere. The problem of fitting in the claims of the minor uses of roads is thus more a matter of finance than of plan, of price rather than of output.[3]

In the case of trading services, the public authority covers its costs by making a direct charge to customers. The same object is attained in the case of roads, but the charge is made indirectly in the form of rates, licence duties, and petrol taxes. The cost of roads thus falls in the first instance on local communities and on the owners of motor vehicles. The relative contributions which different motor owners should pay can be quite objectively determined. In equity it is clearly desirable that contributions should be proportionate to the wear and tear caused, but neutral between different types of vehicle. There is no justification for discriminatory taxation except where it can be shown that particular types of vehicle cause exceptional obstruction, danger, or discomfort to other road-users. A combination of licence duties based on weight or horse-power, plus a fuel tax, appears to fulfil these requirements perfectly. It is in fact the nearest possible equivalent to a toll, the licence duty constituting a charge for the right of using the road, and the petrol tax being roughly proportionate to usage. This theoretical solution of the problem was not, however, fully enunciated until the report of the Conference on Rail and Road Transport in 1932.

The distribution of charges between motor owners on the one

[1] Price and standard could be arranged to fit in with the road plan in conjunction with the powerful associations representing private motorists.

[2] 1932.

[3] On some routes military interests would probably require to be considered, with a consequent reimputation of financial responsibility.

hand and local communities on the other is not so easy to determine, and no satisfactory formula has yet been evolved. The
definition of community use must necessarily be a matter of agreement rather than objective test. Motor traffic developed in a situation in which, owing to the long reign of the railways, the roads
had fallen into disuse as a system of through communication. Such
minor repair works as they required were naturally financed by
the local communities which used them. It was not until after the
passing of the Road Improvement Act in 1909 that any central
funds were regularly applied to road development. But in modern
traffic conditions it is clearly inequitable that 'community use'
should bear a major proportion of road expenditure. If once a
suitable definition were agreed upon, traffic censuses might well
supply information which would enable an intelligent division of
responsibility to be made. In the meantime it might be suggested
that the charge for community use should be equivalent to the
cost of all maintenance and development of other than first- and
second-class roads. This would mean a total expenditure of some
£17 to £18 m. a year,[1] or about 25 per cent. of total expenditure
on the basis established in 1932.

In carrying out the road plan the public authority is apparently
doing no more than the enlightened self-interest of road-users
would lead them to do for themselves if they had the opportunity.
From this point of view it is only a matter of convenience that the
work should be undertaken by the state. Improvements of this
kind, which are in the interest of all but too expensive to be undertaken except by combined efforts, are in the nature of an 'external
economy' to the industry. It has been asked what justification
there is for the government to extend its favours to one industry
only,—because it is obviously a favour even if the full cost of the
improvement is charged up to the industry. The answer to this
argument is that, given competition between transport owners (not
merely road-users), the benefits of decreased transport costs will be
passed on to the community, and emerge as a reduction of the cost
of production in general.[2] Ultimately the gain accrues to the com-

[1] For England and Wales.
[2] Cf. Adam Smith, *Wealth of Nations*, Book V, part i: 'As the expense of
carriage is very much reduced by such public works (roads, etc.) the goods
notwithstanding the toll come cheaper to the consumer than they would otherwise have done; their price being not so much raised by the toll as it is lowered
by the cheapness of the carriage.'

munity, not to the transport owners. It is clearly a somewhat dangerous assumption that the full benefit of cost reduction will be passed on to the community in these days of large-scale control. But the competitive field is fortunately not confined to road-transport owners. In the rivalry of the railways[1] they have a strong incentive to keep rates as low as possible. Nevertheless, the possibility of monopoly must be regarded as a grave danger-point, particularly since the trend of recent judicial action seems to be in favour of confirming local road monopolies in the name of co-ordination or the elimination of surplus capacity.[2]

We must now examine how far actual road policy has been in accordance with these common-sense suggestions. Table 1, p. 145, shows total expenditure on roads in our period compared with 1913. Owing to changes in the licensing system it is not possible to give comparable figures for the number of vehicles for the whole period. Between 1922 and 1935 the number considerably more than doubled: it probably increased threefold over the whole of our period. It is somewhat ominous that road expenditure at the end of the period was less than double what it was before the war, and only six or seven millions more than in 1922. The decline since 1931 is even more serious. In August 1935 there were about 354,000 more cars on the roads than there had been in the summer of 1931, but gross expenditure had fallen by about £18 m. between the two years. If loan charges are deducted actual expenditure on the roads was little more than £50 m. at the end of the period. Naturally the greater part of this was required for mere maintenance (cf. Table 2, p. 146), leaving only about £13 m. for major improvements and new works. Expenditure of this order will clearly not solve the road problem.

It is clear that for most of the period there was not even a rough approximation to an economic plan. The Conference on Rail and Road Transport which tried to answer the question of how much should be spent on the roads put forward the figure of £60 m. on no better grounds than that a sum of about that amount had been

[1] The controversy between rail and road transport lies outside the scope of our inquiry. It must be noted, however, that every change in the public benefits conferred on railways shifts the margin of remunerative road investment. Probably this is irrelevant in the present infra-marginal state of road development.

[2] Cf., for instance, the case of the *Railways* v. *Bouts Tillotson Transport* in 1936, and discussion in Chap. V, p. 84.

spent for several years running before they made their report. As it happens, the years they selected were not entirely in line with the trend because they were just those in which Mr. Churchill had been helping himself to the Road Fund. On the whole, and in view of the increasing congestion of traffic, it seems very probable that road expenditure has been considerably below the total profitable amount. One effect of this is to make it appear necessary to restrict traffic, on grounds merely of overcrowding, not of exceptional obstruction. Restriction of this sort is undesirable both because it tends to increase monopolistic control among road-users and because it is difficult to avoid it becoming discriminatory when there are strong vested interests in other forms of transport.

On the one hand, it seems probable that the money was not laid out to the best advantage. All committees[1] which reported on the subject were unanimous in stating that there had been a relative over-development of cheap and easy (but actually less remunerative) rural road works, while urgent urban improvements were neglected. For many years the benefit of a considerable number of road improvements was nullified by the neglect of bridges. To this several causes contributed. Many of the bridges were in the hands of the railways, and lengthy negotiations were necessary before works could be started. Further, as there were no specific grants for bridges, local authorities had little incentive to make the effort. A proper consideration of highway economics would surely have led to an earlier solution of this sub-problem. The elimination of level-crossings proceeds even more slowly.[2] But the most serious gap in the road plan was the neglect of community development. Footpaths were omitted on important highways for want of a grant that would cover them. Ribbon development was permitted for the whole of our period for want of adequate preventive legislation. It is probably this neglect which is the major factor in road danger and—since it has led to the institution of the 30-mile per hour limit—in delay.

It seems reasonable to conclude that many of the shortcomings in road development were due to the absence of an economic plan. But the allocation of financial responsibility was undoubtedly an

[1] For instance, Royal Commission on Transport 1930, Committee on National Expenditure 1931, Conference on Road and Rail Transport 1932.

[2] During 1935 two schemes for replacing level-crossings by bridges were examined by the Ministry of Transport. Cf. *Annual Report on the Administration of the Road Fund.*

important contributory factor. The distribution of road charges is shown in Table 3. It was suggested above that the share equitably imputable to local funds might be of the order of 25 per cent. But even in the years of the central government's utmost generosity, the local authorities were asked to foot 50 per cent. of the road bill. For most of the period their contribution was considerably higher.

This disproportionate burden on local funds seems to have had three unfortunate results. In the first place, it contributed to the break-down of the system of local finance by putting an undue burden on counties and non-county boroughs.[1] In the second place, it was an important cause of the neglect of subsidiary road works such as footpaths and service roads for which there was no grant. Thirdly, it is very probable that the unwillingness of local authorities to undertake new road works and the tardiness of the government in increasing the proportion of grants restricted the total amount of investment. At the same time, it gave the road fund a false air of repleteness which made it an easy prey for raids by needy chancellors. Hence arose an uncertainty as to the amount of central funds that would be available, which was undoubtedly prejudicial to planning. This was the more unfortunate since the budget debate tended to synchronize with the opening of the road-work season.

It cannot be said that the taxation of motorists has been carried out on any rational basis (see Table 1). In the early post-war years their contribution to total road expenditure was less than 25 per cent. From 1922 to 1928 the petrol tax was suspended, so that there was no charge whatever for wear and tear, and during these years motorists certainly benefited at the expense of the railways and the taxpayers. In 1926, however, licence duties were heavily increased. The average paid by commercial vehicles (lorries) rose from £21 to £28, and by hackneys (buses and taxis) from £33 to £46.[2] In 1928 the petrol duty was reimposed, although the intention was that it should pay for derating and not for road development. Only a small amount of additional funds therefore became available for roads as a result of the taxation of motorists. Nor was this position improved as a result of the tax recommendations of the Conference of Rail and Road Trans-

---

[1] Cf. Chap. IX, p. 158.
[2] Change in the size of vehicles was partly responsible for the rise in average tax paid.

port. But up to 1932 considerably more was being spent on the roads than was contributed in taxation by the motorists. Then, as a result of increased taxation and falling outlay, the contribution of motorists was raised to a point at which it was roughly equal to total expenditure on the basis established in 1932. With returning prosperity, tax receipts since 1934 have tended to exceed expenditure, in spite of a small decline in licence duties.

It thus appears that since 1932 there has been a tendency to keep expenditure roughly at the £60 m. figure suggested by the Conference. But over 60 per cent. of the bill is met, not from motor taxation, but from rates. The government has, of course, as much right to tax motoring without guaranteeing a specific *quid pro quo* as it has to tax any other form of expenditure. The motoring taxes are, in fact, a useful and, on the whole, innocuous part of the revenue.[1] This, however, does not provide an argument either for overcharging the local authorities or for failing to give the motorists and the community an adequate road system for which they are quite prepared to pay. In one respect in particular the motorist might reasonably complain that road finance is wanting in foresight—in the small proportion of expenditure financed out of loan. Reference to Table 2 shows that in all forms of road works loan finance plays a very minor part. As regards maintenance and minor improvement, this is no doubt justifiable, but there is no evidence of any distinction being made, such as is common in other trading services, between running repairs and durable works of major improvement and new construction.

It is pertinent to ask whether with the available statistical material it would not be possible to improve road planning, and some steps in the right direction have indeed been noticeable under the 'National' government. Although there is no direct central planning, local authorities have been asked to arrange their schemes in order of urgency. (There is no evidence, however, that the criterion for determining urgency is very definite or has any specially economic basis.) Periodic traffic censuses which were carried out intermittently in the twenties have been held more regularly and intensively, and have been backed up by special observations. Research on surfaces, &c., which was almost entirely lacking before 1928 is, after a period of economy, being gradually extended. Special attention has been given to footpaths and

[1] Cf. Chap. XIV, p. 244.

service roads, at least on important improvements. Most important of all, a small beginning has been made at the problem of road improvement in heavily built-up areas. Finally it seems possible that effective preventive legislation against ribbon development has at last been obtained.[1] In other respects, however, little progress is apparent. There was no co-ordinated route policy between the abandoned trunk roads scheme of the second labour government and the scheme of central administration of 1936–7. Thus while information on road problems is accumulating, attempts to put a rational plan into operation have been very meagre. As long as increased funds are not available they are naturally mainly abortive.

It is not yet possible to foresee the effects of the transfer of road accounts to the budget and of trunk roads to central management, which came into operation in April 1937. Everything depends on the manner of administration. It is much to be feared that the fact that they will have to compete directly with other needs which may appear more urgent will increase the vulnerability of highway finance to the necessities of the budget. On the other hand, the change in control has tended to bring into prominence some of the more glaring omissions of previous road policy. Hence the first effect was considerably to increase the incentive to expand investment. This trend—if it turns out to be one—may continue as long as tax receipts are rising. The best safeguard against a subsequent recession in development is improved planning, which should be to some extent facilitated by the new arrangement. On the other hand, the transfer of trunk roads may increase the difficulties of regional planning. It appears that in future the central government may be prepared to shoulder a larger proportion of expenditure than in the past. The plans announced for 1937–8 contemplated expenditure ultimately amounting to some £100 m., of which the exchequer will find £66 m. This is still some way short of the proportion suggested above. And it must be noted that it only includes large works for which grants are usually relatively favourable. It should be remembered that the trunk roads to which the new arrangement refers are far from covering even the first-class roads.

But the change brings no alteration to one fundamental weakness of British road administration—the small proportion financed out of loan. In this respect road development is quite out of line with other types of economic public investment. In the case of elec-

---

[1] In the Prevention of Ribbon Development Act of 1935.

tricity, for instance, loan expenditure represents some 25 per cent. of the total. For roads it is of the order of 10 to 12 per cent. only. The effect of this disparity in practice must necessarily be to make road development appear relatively more expensive than other forms of long-period investment. It also seriously limits the usefulness of road works as a form of public works. And such borrowing as has taken place has been wholly the work of local authorities for whom it constitutes a net addition to the interest charge. This is an aspect of road finance which has a wider significance than even the provision of an adequate road system.

TABLE I

Relation of road expenditure to vehicle taxation: Great Britain

	Expenditure					Taxation		
	Expenditure by LAS*			Min. of Transport direct	Total expenditure	Vehicle taxation	Petrol duties	Total taxation‡
	Rates and Grants		From loans					
Year	Eng. and Wales	Scotland						
	(1)	(2)	(3)	(4)	(5)			
1913–14	17·0	1·4	3·6†	..	32·0	0·6	0·4	1·0
1920–1	38·5	3·5	4·1	0·02	46·1	7·8	2·6	10·4
1921–2	41·4	3·9	7·0	1·4	53·7	11·1	0·2	11·3
1922–3	40·2	4·2	9·8	1·3	55·3	12·6	..	12·6
1923–4	41·4	4·7	9·3	0·9	56·3	14·6	..	14·6
1924–5	45·8	5·3	10·9	1·1	63·1	16·5	..	16·5
1925–6	48·8	5·7	11·1	0·8	66·4	18·1	..	18·1
1926–7	49·5	5·9	10·5	0·9	66·8	21·4	..	21·4
1927–8	52·1	6·1	10·1	0·6	68·9	24·5	..	24·5
1928–9	51·4	5·9	8·8	0·3	66·4	25·5	9·6	35·1
1929–30	50·9	6·3	17·5	0·1	74·8	26·6	11·2	37·8
1930–1	52·4	6·6	19·9	0·04	78·9	27·8	11·9	39·7
1931–2	51·9	7·2	20·2	0·02	79·3	27·3	22·6	49·9
1932–3	46·8	6·0	10·9	..	63·7	28·0	26·4	44·4
1933–4	46·3	5·5	9·2	..	61·01	31·1	30·3	61·4
1934–5	47·5	§	§	..	61·1	30·9	23·1	62·0
1935–6	§	§	§	..	63·9	30·9	33·6	64·5
1936–7	§	§	§	..	§	32·7	35·9	68·6

(From *Statistical Abstract*.)

Before 1929 figures include capital expenditure met from grants or receipts.

* Including loan charges, which amount to about 12 per cent. of total expenditure.

† In 1913 expenditure on ferries included.

‡ A small deduction should be made for N. Ireland Reserved Revenues. The petrol duty is reckoned at three-quarters of hydrocarbon oils tax receipts.

§ Not available.

TABLE 2

Distribution of expenditure on road works (G.B) (ex loan charges)
(Excluding contributions by frontagers, &c.)

(£ m.) (*Financial Years*)

Year	I. Maintenance and minor improvement			II. Major improvement			III. New construction		
	Rate	Grant	Loan	Rate	Grant	Loan	Rate	Grant	Loan
1932	22·3	7·6	0·7	0·1	3·1	2·6	0·2	2·6	1·5
1933	21·9	7·9	0·6	1·3	1·9	2·0	0·2	1·9	0·9
1934	21·9	8·2	0·7	1·5	2·1	2·3	0·1	1·3	0·8
1935	22·2	8·3	0·6	1·8	2·8	3·7	0·1	0·9	0·9

(From *Road Fund Reports*.)

TABLE 3

The distribution of road charges: England and Wales (including loan charges)

(£ m.)

Year	Amount met from			Total	% falling on rates
	Rates	Grants (RF)	Loans		
1913–14	15·5*	0·6	3·4	19·5	80
1920–1	31·2	4·7	3·7	39·6	78
1921–2	30·2	8·8	6·2	45·2	66
1922–3	28·2	9·8	9·0	47·0	59
1923–4	27·9	11·0	8·3	47·2	59
1924–5	30·5	13·0	9·9	53·4	58
1925–6	32·2	14·0	10·0	56·2	60
1926–7	32·9	13·9	9·5	56·3	60
1927–8	33·7	15·0	8·4	57·1	60
1928–9	33·9†	14·2	8·0†	55·1	62
1929–30	34·8†	18·8	16·2	69·8	50
1930–1	37·8†	19·2	18·9	75·9	50
1931–2	38·0	18·9	19·0	75·9	50
1932–3	35·4	13·6	10·2	56·2	62
1933–4	35·4	12·1	8·7	56·2	62
1934–5	35·8	12·6	7·2	55·7	65
1935–6	‡	‡	‡	‡	‡
1936–7	‡	‡	‡	‡	‡

(From *Statistical Abstract*.)

* Including ferries.

† Prior to 1929 deductions in aid of rates were included, post 1928 figures include grants for capital works.

‡ Not available. The figures for Great Britain (which are available for the later years) show a slight rise in total expenditure in 1935 and a slight fall in the proportion met from rates.

IX

RATES AND GRANTS

Every country which is not prepared to adopt complete centrali-
zation, that is to say, the absolute control of local administration
and finance by the national government, inevitably has to face a
dilemma in the relation between the centre and the parts. The
more central control there is the less will it be possible to enjoy
the benefits of local initiative. The more freedom is allowed, the
more difficult does it become to secure uniformity of development. The fruits of a tradition of sturdy local freedom are solid
and not lightly to be disregarded. Responsible local government
has proved an admirable training-ground in administrative and
political balance. It has provided a useful safety-valve for local
divergences. And the close contact between government and
citizen which local administration promotes has helped to preserve
the human element in the social services, even in vast modern
communities. On the other hand, the growing importance
attached to a progressive and unified socio-economic policy makes
a very considerable degree of central control inevitable. The
problem of central and local finance is therefore to discover the
best method of overcoming this dilemma.

Social policy as part of a political and economic programme is
a comparatively modern development, and its essentials have not
always been made clear. It is necessary once again to distinguish
between policy which is part of a programme of long-period
development and which should be applied steadily in any normal
economic conditions, and short-period exceptional policy, aimed
specifically at reducing the violence of trade fluctuations. This
would supervene on normal policy at moments of economic crisis,
either at the top of the boom or at the bottom of the depression.
Experience suggests that in spite of certain interesting examples
of local initiative it is usual in this country for the policy of the
central government to be more progressive than that of the smaller
communities. For long-period policy therefore it is desirable to
have a mechanism of central control which will secure steady and
even progress, with the emphasis on the progress rather than on
the evenness. The basis of exceptional policy is the fact that

theoretical analysis provides a strong *a priori* case for believing that—given the modern degree of importance of public, as against private spending—considerable alleviation may be imparted to booms and depressions by varying the *tempo* of public spending. The mechanism required for carrying this out is a type of central control which secures rapid joint action by all public authorities. Our tasks in this and the following chapter are to consider first, how far the British method of dealing with the fundamental dilemma of local government is itself a solution of the problem, and secondly, how far it assists or hinders the task of carrying out these two aims of socio-economic policy. Our period has witnessed very considerable modifications in the relation between central and local finance, so that the system we have to observe has not been a stationary but a rapidly changing one.

In England the fundamental dilemma of local government first became apparent when the relations between central and local finance and administration were established in the last quarter of the nineteenth century on the completion of the system of representative local government. At the time of this settlement doctrines of *laisser-faire* still held sway, at any rate in the political field. It was inevitable, therefore, that very great importance should have been attached to local initiative. The settlement then arranged was, on the political side, extremely reasonable. On the one hand, it was held that local communities, and particularly the large towns, had a right to control their destinies over a wide field. There were (and still are) a number of services which can rationally be treated as of purely local concern, for instance, the development of roads and other amenities used primarily by the local community, and certain police and protection services. On the other hand, parliament was recognized as the supreme authority. There has never been in England a local autonomy comparable to the freedom which, for instance, American and German cities have enjoyed. It is fundamental in the British system that local activities are confined to services specifically allowed, any attempt to extend their functions without specific authorization being *ultra vires*. A considerable amount of control by the centre was thus inherent in the system. In addition there were a number of services which were regarded as national rather than local in character, but which had traditionally been operated by local authorities. Towards the expenses of these it had been customary since the second quarter of the nineteenth century for the central government to make a contribution and to exercise some supervision. The solution aimed at was thus originally one of demarcation of function between the centre and localities rather than of co-operation in the same services.

On the financial side, however, the arrangement was not so happy. Three sources of funds were reserved for local authorities (other than the receipts of trading services and the proceeds of loans). Firstly, the revenue from certain taxes collected centrally was 'assigned' to local expenditure. Secondly, a certain number of specific contributions were made by the central government, ostensibly as an aid towards carrying out national services. Thirdly, to make up the bill, there remained the old Elizabethan property tax, the local rate on the letting value of real estate. As we have seen, however (Chapter III above), an enormous development of the social services began immediately the representative local government system was complete. This had not been fully foreseen, and the tax rights granted to local authorities had not allowed for it. Further, in the course of time the field of expenditure which should objectively be considered national rather than local gradually extended, both through the expansion of old and the establishment of new services. These led, at least after a certain time lag, to an increase in contributions from the exchequer. Finally, the central government gradually developed an extensive although not particularly integrated programme of encouraging specific services by offering new grants in aid. On one ground or another therefore the scope of central grants was so much extended that they came to touch almost the entire field of local activity, except for the commercial trading services. There thus came about an almost complete duality in both administration and finance. In these circumstances it became impossible to solve the dilemma by any sort of demarcation of function. A highly complicated system of mutual co-operation was therefore inevitable.

The peculiarity of the British long-period problem of local finance arises thus from the enormous supplements it has been found necessary to make from the exchequer to assist the local revenue system inherited from an earlier age. As far as short-period cyclical policy is concerned, however, it is to be found in the wide powers of spending wielded by the local authorities taken together. We have seen that the volume of public investment depends more on local than on central activity. In the wider field of general finance local administration, if not of equal weight to that of the national government, is nevertheless of comparable importance. The volume of revenue disposed of through the local budgets taken together is as large as that flowing into the exchequer, neglecting the (transfer) finance of the national debt. Moreover, although the national budget has shown a certain tendency to expand during our period, local budgets have grown at a still faster rate. In other words, the 'weight' of local government activity is on the upgrade. This is reflected in the growth of the proportion of the population dependent on local administration for their livelihood. In 1920 the insured local civil service was twice as large as the national, by 1930 it had become three times as large. Sir E. D. Simon estimated in 1926 that 10 per cent. of the population of Manchester were dependent on wages and salaries paid by the city council. Since that date it is probable that the number has considerably increased.[1] Taking the country as a whole, if the insured workers engaged in public works contracting[2] and housing and their families are counted in, and also those in receipt of public assistance, in 1930 not far short of 20 per cent. of the whole population owed their livelihood to the activity of local government.

Local administrative and financial policy is thus now influential over a wide field. Many of the economic effects of public policy—for instance, on wage-rates—depend on local rather than on national practice. How councils manage their finances matters much more than it used to do, not only to their own citizens, but through their powers of disposal of grants in aid, to the whole body of taxpayers. And as far as cyclical policy is concerned, local action is of first importance.

The post-war position of local finance differed from the pre-war in two fundamental aspects. In the first place, the general level of rates was very much higher. In 1914 rates averaged 6s. 8¾d. in the £ or £1 18s. 11d. per head of the population. By 1921 they had risen to £4 0s. 11d. per head, and remained more or less at that level for the rest of our period. (In 1928 immediately before

---

[1] The number of insured workers in local government service (excluding public works contracting) increased between 1926 and 1936 from 260,620 to 368,110.

[2] The figures for public works contracting are notoriously misleading, since they include a large volume of workers temporarily transferred from other occupations.

derating they reached a maximum of £4 4s. 10d. per head, and in 1933 a post-war minimum of £3 12s. 9¼d., but by 1936 they once more exceeded the £4 mark.) Secondly, and even more important, a very great divergence between rates in different localities had appeared. Total rates varied at one time from about 5s. to 35s. in the £, and public assistance rates (which form the most divergent element) showed a dispersion of from under 6d. to over 11s. In this situation it became evident that drastic steps for the reform of the system of local finance would have to be taken if a widespread break-down was to be avoided.

The changes in the rate-grant system which took place during the period were consequently in two directions. In the first place, the volume of exchequer contributions increased enormously, both absolutely and in relation to expenditure met from rates. This change, as has been noted, was a continuation of a process which had been going on steadily over a long period. The progress of the change is revealed by the following figures:

	Sums (£ m.) provided from		Percentages of rate+grant expenditure met by	
Financial year	Rates	Grants	Rates	Grants
1884 . . .	25·7	3·6	87·6	12·4
1904 . . .	56·0	19·6	74·1	25·9
1924 . . .	146·3	120·5	54·8	45·2

Secondly, the first important attempt was made to counteract the tendency for rate dispersion to increase. In both of these changes, but particularly in the second, the formula grant based on needs and adjusted every five years which accompanied the derating provisions of the Local Government Act of 1929 played a leading role.[1] Prior to 1929 not more than 20 per cent. of grants had been directed to the equalization of resources. As a result of the act the proportion was increased to about 70 per cent. An important although less conspicuous part was played by the Rating and Valuation Act of 1925. This was the first attempt to secure uniformity and regularity of valuation throughout the country. As a result of the two acts both administrative and valuation areas were considerably enlarged and adjusted.

[1] The formula is based on 'weighted population', i.e. estimated population with allowances for (1) large number of children under five, (2) low rateable value, (3) heavy unemployment, (4) sparsity of population in relation to road mileage. For details cf. H. of C. Paper 42 (1937).

Ad hoc committees were appointed to assist in securing uniformity
of valuation practice. The quinquennial valuation which had
hitherto been confined to London was extended to the whole
country. Besides these two measures other changes also attacked
the fundamental problems of high rates and rate dispersion.
Among the most important of these was the transfer of responsibility for the able-bodied poor to the central government under
the Unemployment Act of 1934. We have to examine how far
these reforms were successful in touching the fundamental causes,
and hence of arresting the alarming post-war tendencies of local
finance.

The first cause of the general rise in rates was the steady rise
in prices, and hence in the cost of local government, which took
place owing to the war. But as prices fell services expanded, so that
expenditure continued steadily to rise. The additional weight of
this, as far as rates were concerned, was mainly concentrated in five
lines, as the following figures illustrate:

Increase in rate-borne expenditure in certain services
(England and Wales)

(£ m.)

	1913	1928	1933	Increase in 20 years	
				£ m.	%
Elem. Education	14·1	27·6	31·8	17·7	125
Public Assistance	10·7	29·9	31·5	20·8	194
Roads and Bridges	15·5	33·9	35·4	19·9	128
Public Health	12·1	28·2	40·8	28·7	237
Police	4·4	10·3	10·6	6·2	146

The first four are obviously the most important, and in fact the
expansion in police expenditure mainly reflects the additional
police services required by the roads. In the case of both education
and public health the extension of services had been stimulated
by percentage grants. But the greatest increase in public health
expenditure took place after 1929, and reflected the transfer of the
powers and duties of the guardians to the local authorities. The
rise in public assistance expenditure reflects mainly the high unemployment of the twenties and the inadequacy of the insurance
scheme. The timing of the most rapid expansion of these two
services shows that cyclical forces were also important. Thus on

grounds of increased rate-borne expenditure alone a substantial rise in rates was inevitable.

Since local expenditure was directly stimulated by grants the central government was thus partly responsible for the rise in rates. This is clearly an inevitable and not undesirable pheno-menon of long-period development. But there is some reason to think that the burden of the expansion thrown on rates was actually heavier than might be supposed from the expansion of central aid, and in fact heavier than the circumstances allowed. The action of the central government tends to be somewhat Janus-headed. On the one hand, grants are offered as a bait to secure the development of services, on the other, every means of limiting the financial responsibility of the national budget is employed. It is only natural considering the many unknowns with which the chancellor is faced that he should endeavour as much as possible to throw the uncertainty on local funds and to conserve for the centre a large share of the natural increase of tax receipts. A well-known pre-war example of this practice was the 'stereotyping' of the revenues 'assigned' to local authorities in 1908 in order to keep in central hands for the future the expanding revenue of the taxes concerned. In the post-war period, when the strain on the central budget was much greater, the same sort of thing seems to have occurred in several ways. We have seen that there are strong arguments for supposing that the central government did not shoulder its share of responsibility in the case of road expenditure.[1] The effect of substituting a block grant (of a definite sum or sums for a term of years, budgeted for in advance) for a percentage grant (of approved expenditure, however fast it may expand) is similar. At the beginning of the period the main part of both the multifarious public health and the education grants were on a percentage basis (in some cases the central share was as high as 75 per cent.). During the period, however, they were succes-sively changed on to the block system.[2] In addition, the standing arrangement whereby a minimum grant of 50 per cent. was guaran-teed for elementary education expenditure was abolished as an economy measure in 1931. As a result the proportion of educa-tion costs met by grant fell from 56·8 per cent. in 1929–30 to 48 per cent. in 1932–3.

[1] Cf. Chap. VIII, p. 142.
[2] For details cf. H. Finer, *English Local Government*.

The most important case, however, in which it was argued that the central government was by administrative change throwing an undue burden on the local authorities, was that of the support of the unemployed. The expansion of public assistance expenditure was of quite special significance to the local authorities, both because of its large amount and sudden increase in depression and because it was regarded as specially onerous.[1] In the post-war period chancellors were in a particularly difficult position with regard to the unemployed. Successive acts repeatedly increased budgetary liability both in respect of relief and in the scope of insurance and pensions. This was aggravated by the automatic increase in the relative share of the state in unemployment pay (compared with that of the contributors) as the average period of unemployment lengthened.[2] In the twenties, moreover, the unemployment figures acquired a peculiar political significance. Governments came to be judged mainly on their ability to reduce the unemployment 'Live Register'. Hence there were very powerful incentives for the central government to limit its responsibilities as much as possible.

One method of doing this was to confine the definition of unemployment as closely as possible to the regular industrial army. Sir Wm. Beveridge has drawn attention to the fact[3] that the effect of the 'Genuinely seeking work' clause which was only abolished in 1930 was to make unemployment statistics in the twenties considerably less inclusive than they afterwards became. A full investigation of the effects of administrative changes in unemployment figures would no doubt reveal further cases of the same type.[4]

---

[1] The liability of the central government to compensate local authorities for extra expenditure in depression hardly seems so clear as its liability in the case of additional services centrally imposed, such as police or air-raid protection—even if it could be proved that central policy was in some way responsible for depression.

[2] Thus a sample taken by the Ministry of Labour in 1929 showed that the exchequer share increased from 48 per cent. for a period of unemployment of twenty-five days to 99 per cent. for a year's unemployment. On the other hand, the exhaustion of the savings of the unemployed made their families an increasing burden on public assistance.

[3] Beveridge, 'An Analysis of Unemployment', *Economica*, 1936–7.

[4] The alteration in the 'waiting period' before benefit was payable to the newly unemployed provides one such example. In 1924 the waiting period was reduced from six to three days and the share of the central government increased. The next year the process was reversed. In 1937 the period was once more reduced to three days. The additional cost to central funds of the

It is suggestive that before 1929 changes appear to have been mainly in favour of the exchequer. But it seems that the government then became convinced of the inadvisability of adding further to the rate burden. There has, with the exception of the education economy measure already mentioned, been less evidence of changes unfavourable to the local authorities since. Nevertheless, the desire of the central government to safeguard itself inevitably constitutes a certain danger to rates in the short run. An instance of this which may become important in the future is concerned with the assumption of responsibility for the able-bodied poor by the central government under the Unemployment Act of 1934. The change gave at the time substantial relief to the local authorities. They were, however, compelled to make a grant to the central government, stereotyped at 60 per cent. of their expenditure on the service in 1932–3. Since this was a particularly heavy year for public assistance it is not impossible that the central government may eventually gain on the transaction.

While the general increase in expenditure necessarily put a certain strain on rates, which was probably further increased by administrative changes, the enormous rise in rate poundages was partly the reflection of the inability of a tax with the peculiar limitations of rates to stand up to an increased burden. Valuations are not easily varied in the short run. Hence for rapidly expanding outlay rates are too inelastic a source of revenue. As their responsibilities increased therefore local authorities had two possible alternatives: either to attempt to expand assessments or to raise the poundage on existing valuations.

The history of the relation between central and local finance has very largely been a series of attempts on the part of local authorities to make rating valuations more inclusive,[1] and, as these were successively turned down by the courts, a series of

latter change is estimated at £9·7 m. (over an eight-year period). This change is clearly a reflection of the improved condition of the unemployment fund.

[1] It was undoubtedly the intention of the Elizabethan legislators to establish a general property tax. Failure was due, on the one hand, to the difficulty of assessing movables and, on the other, to the inefficiency of the (unpaid) officials. At that time, however—and even much later—the omission was not serious since it was possible to regard real property as an adequate measure of wealth. But the failure was important as the first round of the struggle to widen the basis of local taxation. The second round—over the inclusion of traders' stock—was fought out in the 1830's. It likewise ended in failure. Cf. Finer, loc. cit.

reluctant concessions in the form of new grants in aid by the central government. We need not go into the detailed history of these. The derating as to three-quarters of its value of 'productive industry' which was the most important part of the 1929 Derating Provisions, was a sequel to one such attempt, in some ways the most important of all—to include machinery and tools in rent valuation. The significance for local finance of the industrial aspect of derating is not really evident unless the stages in this last struggle are observed. Clearly machinery, especially that which is attached to a building, can with some justification be included in the rent for the purposes of a fixed property tax such as rates. Attempts were indeed made to include it in valuations at least as far back as the nineties, when the needs of the newly established local councils were first rapidly expanding. Since, however, there was then next to no co-ordination between different rating authorities, the movement proceeded piecemeal. A Royal Commission reported in 1901 that grave disparities of practice were by then evident. But the greater the needs of local authorities, the more anxious were they to include machinery. In the attempt they were usually supported by the courts. After the war the difficulties of the heavy industries drew the attention of politicians to the burden of rates, and in particular to this new liability of which it was considered they were especially the victims. The idea arose that just as agriculture had (gradually since 1896) been relieved of part of its local obligations, the special burden which was said to lie on the 'heavies' might be lightened by partial derating. A departmental committee in 1923 recommended a compromise which would have dealt satisfactorily with the machinery dispute— namely, that structural machinery should be fully rated, process machinery rated as to one-quarter of its value, and loose tools totally exempted. The Rating and Valuation Act of 1925 went one step farther, and entirely excluded machinery from rates. This, however, did nothing to relieve the structural industries of their previous rating burdens.[1] After the industrial troubles of 1926 both they and the local authorities in whose areas they were concentrated were in urgent, although in part temporary, need of rescue; hence the final step (of derating all industrial undertakings as to 75 per cent. of their assessment) was taken. The

[1] Cf. Chap. IV, p. 78. Most of the arguments used in the controversy were fallacious.

agricultural concession of total derating which accompanied the
measure seems to have been due more to a sense of completeness
than to any special urgency. The new system of railway valuations
introduced shortly afterwards gave an opportunity for what may
perhaps be interpreted as a last flutter in the struggle to widen the
basis of rating. Under it the assessments of the railways were
substantially increased. But as the railways succeeded in convincing the courts of their inability to pay even the rates to which they
were liable under the old system, the outcome of this struggle was
similar to that of its predecessors.

The residential element in rates has always been important.
Since 1929 it has very decidedly increased. The economic and
social effects of this tax on a single type of personal property have
thus become increasingly significant.[1] But it is not so much the
absolute height of rates which is their chief disadvantage as the
extraordinary disparity between one locality and another.

The Rating and Valuation Act of 1925 struck at one cause of
the disparity of rates. Differences in valuation practice had
become increasingly important during the period of rapidly
changing prices. But the cause of the disparity of rates goes far
deeper than the basis of valuation, or any differences in valuation
practice. Local authorities of the same class are expected to maintain not only the same services but more or less the same standard
in them, while areas differ immensely, not only in population and
wealth, but in size, and hence in their suitability for economical
administration. It seems clear that these variations are so great
that it is impossible for some authorities to provide from local
resources even for purely local services at modern standards of
expenditure.[2] To take an illustration. The commissioner for the
N.E. Depressed Area showed in 1934 that the thirteen Tyneside
authorities together had an acreage about equal to that of Birmingham and a population about equal to Liverpool, yet their combined rateable value was hardly two-thirds of these more favoured
districts.[3] Apart from considerations as to the optimum sized unit
of administration for different services, it is hard to believe that
administration of what is essentially a single urban area can ever

[1] Cf. Chap. XVI, p. 268.
[2] Cf. Gibbon, 'The Expenditure and Revenue of Local Authorities', *J.R.S.S.*
1936.
[3] *Report of Investigation into the Industrial Conditions in Certain Depressed
Areas*, 1934, II Durham and Tyneside, p. 120.

be so economical when divided among a number of (frequently antagonistic) small councils as when under the control of a centralized body.

This disparity between the financial resources of districts has the disadvantage that since rates can be interlocally shifted, it tends to be cumulative. The amount by which poundages can be raised with impunity is therefore strictly limited. Rates may be shifted by residential removal, by industrial removal, or finally by a whole district contriving, by means of changing its administrative status, to leave a certain rating area. When it occurs industrial shifting or the removal of factories to lower-rated areas is probably the most serious. Although since the introduction of industrial derating the initial loss of rates is not severe, it carries in its train a heavy burden of residential shifting. This tends, moreover, to be concentrated on the better-paid workers, who can afford to move elsewhere and who are the most useful ratepayers. Those who remain are too often changed from an asset to a liability. In the meantime the high rates, or the fear of them, act as a deterrent to other entrepreneurs, more especially since the modern diffusion of transport and power have substantially widened the choice of location for industry. This is an important aspect of the depressed-area problem.[1] Over the country as a whole, however, it is probable that residential shifting unaccompanied by industrial shifting is responsible for a greater strain on local finances. When the urban population takes to living in low-rated country districts, towns are faced with the necessity of maintaining many services for their day-time citizens who are no longer ratepayers within the area. At the same time, their rateable value falls, and losses on rates from empty property increase. To raise rate poundages risks intensifying the movement which it is wished to arrest. Hence arises the desire to extend the town boundaries to include the new homes of erstwhile ratepayers. This move, however, is opposed not merely by the new residential districts themselves, but by the county councils, who see in the new residential development a lucrative source of future rates. For the counties are troubled not merely by an increasing number of new responsibilities, but by the fear of what we have called area shifting. When towns attain a certain size they naturally desire the greater freedom to control their own destinies which county borough status con-

---

[1] Cf. Chap. XIII, pp. 209, 217.

fers, but a very powerful additional incentive is the knowledge
that they will no longer be required to contribute to the expansion
of services outside their area which are only enjoyed by their own
citizens to a very limited extent.[1]

The attempt to raise rate poundages may thus recoil upon itself
and produce little permanent increase in revenue. There is thus
a tendency to set up a vicious circle. In any case, an uncertainty
and friction is introduced into local administration which must be
prejudicial to good financial administration. These inherent weaknesses of rates are no novelty of the post-war period. It is only
that they become conspicuous when the contribution required rises
to a point at which ratepayers become sensitive. And it does seem
ratepayers are more sensitive to increased burdens than income-tax
payers, either because they feel they have more power of influencing local administration than national, or because the increase
sounds more than an equivalent increase in income tax, especially
if it occurs in the form of an increase of poundage rather than of
valuation.

While residential shifting to the country has been responsible
for a part of the rate losses on empty property, a much greater
cause has been the southward drift of population depending on
the development of the southern industries and the depression
of those in the north. This movement started in the early twenties,
but appears to have been somewhat arrested by 1935. It has thus,
however, been important practically throughout our period, so
that towns in the north and west have been continually exposed
to losses from both. A further influence on the income side has
been the loss of revenue from trading undertakings—the only
other source of funds which local authorities have under their
control. This change was probably in part at least a matter of
deliberate policy.[2] In the north and west overhead expenses of
trading services have also tended to rise with falling population.
Both these sources of strain were secular, or at any rate relatively
long period.[3] A further cause of declining receipts in the depres-

---

[1] This point was particularly emphasized by town representatives in their
evidence before the Royal Commission on Local Government.
[2] Cf. Chap. VIII, p. 142.
[3] There is, however, some cyclical movement in losses from empty property,
thus the L.C.C. rating losses in 1935 were: empties 4·98 per cent. (of receipts),
defaults 5·43 per cent., and in 1936 empties 4·79 per cent. and defaults 5·21
per cent. Cf. *LCC. Annual Statement of Rate Leakages.*

sion years 1929–33 was, however, due to defaults.[1] The relative importance of these last three factors may be illustrated from the case of Manchester.[2] (Net contributions to rates from trading services were not of great importance.)

Income losses in Manchester

	1930			1931			1932		
	£	s.	d.	£	s.	d.	£	s.	d.
Empty property . .	178,636	14	8	231,422	7	7	278,851	3	7
Poverty and irrecoverable	16,618	16	4	16,119	16	4	22,130	15	3
Reduced assessments .	235,523	0	8	182,964	19	0	149,602	3	1
Total . . .	430,778	11	8	430,507	2	11	450,584	1	11

Just as on the income side, so in the case of expenditure, the strain on rates tended to become cumulative. As a result, poor areas which were suspected of being predominantly 'red' politically were frequently accused of extravagance, mostly on the ground of their high rates. Whereas in many cases the will to spend was strong enough, and no doubt things tended to get out of hand to some extent wherever scales of benefit in public assistance were substituted for case inquiry, usually in such areas resources did not allow of much extravagance. Indeed, there is evidence that strenuous steps were taken to reduce expenditure—for instance on public health services so that the standard fell definitely below that of other parts of the country.[3] An illustration of the lack of genuine extravagance among hard-pressed local authorities may perhaps be seen in the very varying success in reducing expenditure of the commissioners who, in the middle twenties, took the place of certain boards of guardians. For instance, within a short period of their appointment an economy of 2s. 2d. in poor rates (from 4s. 6d. to 2s. 4d.) was effected in West Ham, but in the same period the saving in Chester-le-Street was only 9d. (from 4s. 6d. to 3s. 9d.).

It must now be examined how far the reforms carried out in our period, and particularly the formula grant of 1929 have improved the position of local finance. In the first place average rates fell steadily from 12s. 10½d. in the £ in 1928 to 10s. 10d. in 1933,

---

[1] It has been suggested that the easier conditions as to the recovery of debts since the Money Payments (Justices' Procedure) Act 1935 encourages default; cf. Collins, *The Ratepayer's Money*.

[2] Cf. Page, *Co-ordination in Local Government*, pp. 42–3.

[3] Cf. especially *Report on Depressed Areas*, 1934 (cit.), South Wales.

notwithstanding the depression. Part of the decline was due to economy, but part at least must be set down to the additional exchequer assistance afforded and to the effect of area adjustment in spreading both needs and resources. But in 1934 urban rates still ranged from 5s. to 27s. 6d. in the £, and rural from 3s. 4d. to 25s. 3d. Rate dispersion had certainly not disappeared. Nevertheless, if dispersion before and after the reform is compared it is clear that a greater degree of equalization was achieved. It has been calculated that the standard deviation of rates fell from 3·43 in 1928 to 2·95 in 1932.[1]

The effect of the reforms of 1925–9 can be seen in a longer period background if we examine the dispersion of poor rates from 1922 to 1932 (Table 1, p. 166), since it is in this service that the greatest disparity occurs. Excess of public assistance charges is partially masked by economies in other services if the total rate figure is taken. (Poor rates vary from an average of about 16 per cent. of total rates to over 50 per cent. in depressed areas.) While 1923 and 1924 showed some recovery from the effects of the post-war depression, by 1925 the position was already deteriorating. The industrial troubles of the following year greatly aggravated the situation. At that time certain authorities began to run seriously into debt on current public assistance account. By 1930, after the reorganization of areas consequent on the abolition of the guardians and the receipt of increased grants, the general situation had considerably improved. Only two areas had poor rates in excess of 7s. in the £. In 1931 and 1932 there was a slight deterioration due to the depression: in the former year four and in the latter five areas had poor rates in excess of 7s., but in 1927 there had been twenty-three such areas. This improvement reflected also a very great alleviation of the debt position. At the end of 1927–8 it stood at nearly £1 m. By the end of 1930–1 it had already been reduced below £500,000.

In view of the strain on rates which the depression caused the general effectiveness of the reforms would seem to be fairly established. At the same time little or no improvement was achieved in the worst areas. This appears more clearly if we examine the dispersion of poor rates in relation to the population (Table 2, p. 167). Although the range was much reduced by the amalgamation of areas, dispersion within the range showed little improvement.

[1] Cf. Newcomer, *Central and Local Finance in Germany and England*, p. 279.

This suggests that either the reforms were not sufficiently drastic, or that the composition of the basic formula somehow passed by the worst areas. An examination of the areas receiving the highest percentage grants during the second grant period (1932–7) bears this out.

Five urban and five rural areas receiving the highest grants, 1933–4

Area	Grants as a % of rates and grants	Rateable value per head	Rate Poundage
		£	s. d.
South Shields . . .	57·7	4·3	12 1
St. Helen's	55·5	3·8	17 0
Middlesbrough . . .	53·9	4·5	13 11
Dudley	53·3	3·7	16 7
West Bromwich . . .	53·1	3·8	15 6
Huntingdon . . .	77·0	3·5	8 0
Isle of Ely . . .	73·6	3·3	10 1
Montgomery . . .	72·7	3·4	10 0
Rutland	71·9	4·5	9 10
Cumberland. . . .	69·5	3·8	12 6

It is particularly noticeable that none of the five county boroughs with the highest rates[1] are among those receiving the highest grants. Of them only Merthyr received a 50 per cent. grant. The counties similarly which received the highest grants were not those burdened with semi-derelict urban areas, but primarily those which are most purely rural or whose area is small relative to other counties. All the heavily assisted councils are, however, in areas with low rateable value—prosperous urban areas have a rateable value of some £11 per head, and rural of some £9. There was thus on the whole a high degree of inverse correlation between size of grant and rateable value, but a low direct correlation between height of rates and size of grant. But scanty population and derated property, while they make for poor local authorities, do not necessarily spell a needy population. The farmers of Huntingdon and the Isle of Ely are twice blessed in that they receive assistance towards their most important crops, such as sugar beet and potatoes, and also enjoy the benefits of derating.[2]

[1] Merthyr, Norwich, Hull, West Ham, and Salford.

[2] Fen districts are, however, subject to an additional drainage rate, varying from 1s. 2d. to 20s. in the £, with an average of 6s. 2d. Cf. *The Times*, 22 March 1937.

If the smaller county areas—municipal boroughs, urban and rural districts—are examined[1] similar but even more striking misfits are revealed. Although bad areas have all improved substantially, there are individual cases where good areas became conspicuously better off, and others where they became conspicuously worse off, for reasons that are not apparent at a first glance. Notable examples of well-off areas which have benefited still further are small towns such as Godmanchester in Huntingdon and Okehampton in Devon. Their grant income now exceeds total rate and grant expenditure, and in addition, the former at least makes a profit on its housing scheme. In these cases, as in the larger areas which have specially benefited, so far as the formula grant is responsible, the main cause appears to be the effect of the guarantee against loss due to derating. In the case of counties and county boroughs there is no specific term to this guarantee, so that the present state of things will, in the absence of amending legislation, presumably endure. In the case of the smaller areas it will, however, progressively disappear, since in each grant period a larger proportion of the whole grant will be distributed according to the differential formula and a smaller proportion on the basis of derating loss.

In some cases rates have risen sharply in prosperous districts of the smaller county areas. This seems to be mainly due to the rigidity of the grant period in conjunction with the special system of distribution of the county allotment. For the counties themselves and for county boroughs the grant is distributed on the weighted formula on which it is composed. For the smaller areas, however, it is distributed on a flat capitation basis. While population is a satisfactory rough guide to the cost of government, it makes no allowance for differences of income between similar populations in different areas. And what is still more relevant in this connexion, there is no provision for change in population within a grant period. Thus a rural area, which receives in any case only a small capitation grant from the county for its own purposes, may find itself in a very difficult position if population expands rapidly during the grant period. Expensive services such as drainage, water supply, and refuse collection have to be provided, and no additional grant is available. A partial solution to

[1] No complete examination of these has been made, but the result of an investigation into a sample of 40 is published in Newcomer, op. cit., ch. xi.

this difficulty might be found if population could be weighted for trend—at least when population is expanding.

Some of the misfits of the formula grant appear, on the other hand, to be due to the weighting of the various components. The largest weight is allotted to population. Except for the above reservations, this appears to be a satisfactory arrangement. The remaining weights are for low rateable value, number of children under five, proportion of the insured population unemployed, and sparsity of population in relation to road mileage. In a formula designed to be apportioned to needs these are obviously of very different importance. Low rateable value is a good measure of poverty if it can be assumed that valuation practice is reasonably uniform. The position in this respect is steadily improving,[1] but complete uniformity is as yet far from being obtained. Hence undervalued areas tend to gain at the expense of those where valuation has been brought up to date. Experience suggests that in modern conditions the number of children under five is an increasingly poor measure of needs, and in any case the expenditure which is relevant to children is mainly provided under grants which are not included in the formula. The remaining two factors are, however, of great importance. Unemployment provides the most direct measure of needs which it seems possible to get. But it is normally such a fluctuating factor that to give it great weight in a five-year grant is to run the risk of making the formula seriously out of gear for some part at least of the period. A weight which took into account the average length of unemployment would be a more reliable indicator of real need. Highway expenditure continues to be a heavy burden on rates and is clearly related in a general way to sparsity of population. If a national road plan existed it would no doubt be a simple matter to apportion this factor with more direct relevance to needs. So great is the importance of these last two weighting factors that a miscalculation of their effects would be quite sufficient to explain a large part of the misfit of the formula. It is significant that the weights for both are to be increased for the third grant period.

But the failure of the formula grant to achieve a greater degree of rate reduction and equalization appears to be ultimately due more to the very cause which gave it birth than to any single factor

[1] Thus the number of separate rating authorities has already been reduced from 14,330 to 1,770 under the Act of 1925.

—namely, to derating. The loss of income from industrial de-rating has tended to be heaviest in the poorest districts because the factories were the largest ratepayers. The resources of residential areas have been little affected. The long-period working of the narrowed taxation base must be to throw the weight of expanding needs on the remaining ratepayers. Part of the equalizing tendency of the formula grant has thus been wasted in compensation for the tendency towards dispersion inherent in derating.

In addition to the differential aid given under the formula grant there has been a tendency since 1931 for other grants to be distributed with greater attention to needs than formerly. Thus the abolition of the 50 per cent. minimum guarantee for education in 1931 opened the door for a more considerable differentiation of education grants than had hitherto been attempted. There also appears to be an increasing tendency to distribute percentage grants with some attention to needs through the device of dividing local authorities into three or four classes, each of which receives a different percentage of approved expenditure. This has for some years been the custom for road grants. It has also been adopted for expenditure in connexion with air-raid precautions.

On the present system of grant allocation there is thus an increasing amount of differentiation. By equalizing the rate burden it is hoped to prevent a recurrence of such a strain on rates as that which necessitated the reforms of 1929. The full effect of this increased differentiation has not yet had time to make itself felt. And the formula grant will not be in complete working before 1947. At the same time it is at least questionable whether this method of solving—or shelving—the problem of local finance can profitably and safely be carried much farther. Even the large differentiation in grants which is now in force makes comparatively little inroad into rate disparity because it has only partially overcome the inherent tendency of inequalities to grow. The high grant percentages which this degree of equalization necessitates already raise the problem of control in an acute form. It would clearly be desirable to find some alternative solution to the fundamental dilemma of local government.

TABLE I

Movements in the dispersion of poor rates. Range of amounts per £ of assessable value, of rates required for poor relief.

(1) *Poor Law Unions*

Amount			Year							
			1922	1923	1924	1925	1926	1927	1928	1929
under 6d.			3	11	9	4	6	10	5	13
6d.	,,	1s.	47	69	66	65	57	45	55	124
1s.	,,	2s.	271	314	327	326	309	271	307	306
2s.	,,	3s.	172	141	157	154	136	161	137	114
3s.	,,	4s.	69	60	52	54	64	65	68	28
4s.	,,	5s.	33	22	15	12	25	39	20	19
5s.	,,	6s.	21	8	7	8	14	9	11	6
6s.	,,	7s.	7	6	2	4	6	9	8	5
7s.	,,	8s.	6	3	..	2	4	7	6	3
8s.	,,	9s.	2	3	..	..	3	4	6	4
9s.	,,	10s.	5	2	2	2	2	6	3	1
10s.	,,	11s.	2	2	..	..	4	4	3	1
11s.	,,	12s.	..	..	..	..	1	1	..	..

(2) *County areas*

Amount			Year		
			1930	1931	1932
under 1s.			3	2	2
1s.	,,	2s.	26	30	28
2s.	,,	3s.	47	46	40
3s.	,,	4s.	36	33	37
4s.	,,	5s.	15	13	13
5s.	,,	6s.	12	14	12
6s.	,,	7s.	4	3	8
7s.	,,	8s.	1	3	1
8s.	,,	9s.	1	..	3
..		..	..	..	..
13s.	,,	14s.	..	1	..
14s.	,,	15s.	..	..	1

(From *Local Taxation Returns*.)

TABLE 2

Range of average amounts per head of estimated population of expenditure of guardians (and the successor councils) on poor relief.

			Year			
Amount			1926	1927	1928	1929
under 5s.			..	1	1	..
5s.	,,	10s.	78	99	96	95
10s.	,,	15s.	299	306	322	304
15s.	,,	20s.	137	146	134	153
20s.	,,	25s.	33	37	41	34
25s.	,,	30s.	27	18	15	20
30s.	,,	35s.	16	10	9	10
35s.	,,	40s.	7	5	4	5
40s.	,,	45s.	5	1	1	1
45s.	,,	50s.	6	..	..	..
50s.	,,	55s.	2	1	3	2
55s.	,,	60s.	5	2	..	3
60s.	,,	65s.	3	..	..	..
65s.	,,	70s.	1	..	2	..
70s.	,,	75s.	1	1	..	1
75s.	,,	80s.	3	..	..	..
80s.	,,	85s.	2	1	..	1
85s.	,,	90s.	2	..	2	..
90s.	,,	95s.	2	1	..	1
95s.	,,	100s.	..	..	..	..
100s.	,,	105s.	..	1	..	1
105s.	,,	110s.	2	..	..	..
110s.	,,	115s.	1	..	..	1
115s.	,,	120s.	..	1	..	..
120s.	,,	125s.	..	1	1	..

			Year		
Amount			1930	1931	1932
5s. 0d. under 7s. 6d.			1	2	..
7s. 6d.	,,	10s.	16	17	15
10s. 0d.	,,	12s. 6d.	40	41	33
12s. 6d.	,,	15s.	29	28	31
15s. 0d.	,,	17s. 6d.	24	19	22
17s. 6d.	,,	20s.	9	11	10
20s. 0d.	,,	22s. 6d.	7	9	12
22s. 6d.	,,	25s.	10	5	5
25s. 0d.	,,	27s. 6d.	4	6	5
27s. 6d.	,,	30s.	..	3	3
30s. 0d.	,,	32s. 6d.	4	..	3
32s. 6d.	,,	35s.	..	..	2
35s. 0d.	,,	37s. 6d.	..	4	1
37s. 6d.	,,	40s.	1	..	3

(From *Local Taxation Returns*.)

O

X

FINANCIAL CONTROL OF LOCAL POLICY

METHODS of control of local finance by the central government fall into two broad classes: (i) those which emerge as effects of supervision which is primarily political, and (ii) more direct financial control. The elective councils which were set up in the last quarter of the nineteenth century were modelled on the town corporations whose traditional independence had been confirmed by the legislation of 1834–5. Moreover, economic *laisser-faire* was in the eighties and nineties generally accepted without question. The intention was that local finances should be as nearly independent as possible, although the inevitability of grants in aid of certain lines was recognized. Hence control over the expenditure of the assigned revenues was practically nil, except in so far as certain taxes were ear-marked for particular purposes. Of these the devotion of 'whiskey money', or the proceeds of certain liquor duties, to the service of higher education was the most famous. In accordance with the same policy the general accounts of municipal corporations (county and other boroughs) were exempted from audit by the central government—or, indeed, from any compulsory professional audit of any kind. Remnants of this early independence still hang about local finance, especially in the field of audit. The plan of assigned revenues was, however, gradually abandoned in favour of other methods of contribution because of the insuperable difficulty of securing that tax receipts would expand *pari passu* with expenditure requirements. But although traces of the original framework remain, the subsequent development of new services with closer financial control has entirely altered the quality of central control over local finance.

The freedom of local development, and hence of local finance, which was the aim of Goschen and his contemporaries, was in any case impossible of full attainment while parliament held the power of initiation implicit in the doctrine of *ultra vires*. Before the war this was partly concealed by the high proportion of legislation which was only permissive, and which in the absence of stimulating grant remained largely inoperative. Its influence on local budgets was therefore very small. Since the war, by far the greatest changes in the *tempo* and direction of local expenditure are traceable directly to changes in local responsibilities depending on legislation. This new legislation has been either compulsory or heavily grant aided. Permissive unassisted legislation has almost entirely disappeared. The most striking examples of the effect of legislation in securing expansion are to be found in the field of housing,[1] while the economy provisions of 1931 illustrate the reverse course. Changes such as these are by themselves of sufficient magnitude to alter the whole lay-out of local budgets.

How immediate and powerful the effect of legislative enactment is depends partly on technical considerations and partly on the type of financial inducement offered as a bait. It is not easy for the central government to foresee the precise working of these factors. For instance, the main cause of the slowness of the response to housing legislation, especially between 1919 and 1921, was no doubt the time required to build up municipal housing departments. For the great majority of local authorities it represented an entirely new undertaking. But the Addison legislation, although it offered exceptionally favourable terms to local authorities (that their liabilities should not exceed the proceeds of a penny rate), for that very reason required very detailed and lengthy supervision by the central authorities. This considerably delayed action. In contrast to the housing legislation of the twenties, the 'slum clearance act' of 1933 was niggardly in its inducements and stringent in its requirements. It was possible to make it so, and for it yet to be immediately effective because municipal housing departments were in full working order. But it was much assisted by the great fall in building costs which had occurred. In other circumstances the conditions offered might well have caused opposition—or been less effective. The economy provisions secured a fairly rapid reaction, although the maximum contraction appears to have occurred about eighteen months after the beginning of the campaign. It is natural that contraction should take less time than expansion, but the greater speed at which it might be expected to occur on technical grounds is partly offset by the difficulty of holding up investment already started, and the unwillingness of local councils to reverse decisions already made.

[1] It will be recalled that housing expenditure trebled between 1920 and 1921, and more than doubled between 1921 and 1922; cf. Chap. III, p. 41. For the dominating role played by housing in loan finance, cf. Chap. VI, p. 107.

Two other methods of financial control by mainly political means have considerably increased since the war; first, parliament's right of determining the political (and hence financial) status of individual local authorities, and secondly the use by government departments of explanatory 'Orders' and persuasive circulars. The influence of government policy has been clearly discernible in a number of these. The role of the central government in determining status has never been entirely passive. A number of stages of detailed inquiry by the central authority have always been necessary for an urban district to obtain a borough charter. In pre-war days this control had little or no financial significance, but it is by no means certain that it has not to-day. In general a tightening of the regulations for a rise in status (either from urban district to borough or from borough to county borough) has taken place *pari passu* with the increase in urbanization. Since urban districts are controlled more strictly than boroughs[1] this means that larger units of population than formerly find themselves under the more stringent control. On the other hand, reluctance in granting county-borough status to large towns has kept them partly under the control of the county councils, which under the Act of 1929 assumed a new importance in the structure of local government.

More significant is the power which the central government possesses of changing the administrative status, and hence the duties and financial responsibilities, of local authorities. So far the most striking use actually made of this power has been the supersession of certain defaulting boards of guardians by paid officials. Compulsory change of status was, however, recommended by royal commissions as a remedy in two depressed areas (Merthyr and Tyneside). So far the government appear to regard extensive compulsory changes—which might be contrary to the wishes of the inhabitants—as a measure only to be adopted in cases of real crisis. Whether a change of attitude in this respect might not be useful is a matter which must be discussed at a later stage. Considerable changes in the status of particular districts have been brought about as a result of the financial reorganization introduced by the Acts of 1925 and 1929.

Explanatory orders and advisory circulars have long been in use —for instance by the Board of Education in attempting to screw up the standard of the service to a uniform level. In the post-war

---

[1] For instance in the matter of audit.

period the wealth of new legislation has greatly extended the scope
of such orders, especially by the Ministry of Health. This is indeed
a natural corollary of the abandonment of permissive legislation.
But 'government by order' does in practice considerably increase
legislative control, by making it more explicit and detailed than is
possible in the acts themselves. Circulars have little direct mandatory authority. It is even doubtful how effective they would be
if they proved to be in conflict with local policy. There is nevertheless a strong tradition in British financial policy of the power
of moral suasion by a superior authority.[1] When central policy
runs on the same lines as local, circulars act as a strong reinforce-
ment of legislation. The rapid spread of the spirit of economy in
1931 is a good illustration of this.

The extent of financial control which may be exercised indirectly
by political means is thus very considerable. While nominally the
lay-out of local budgets is not affected, given the inelasticity of
local taxation, it is in fact largely determined by the centre. Legislative control is an effective tool for long-period development, but
is naturally too unwieldy to be of much use in the trade cycle. The
experience of the Economy Act of 1931 suggests, nevertheless,
that if backed up by other political measures it may also secure
important short-period changes in activity. This depends mainly
on its financial aspect.

Purely financial control over local activity is exercised in three
ways: (i) by right of audit and by accompanying statutory requirements of certain statistical returns, (ii) by variation of the terms of
grant in aid, and (iii) by control over long-term borrowing. The
relevant central authority for (i) and (iii) is the Ministry of Health.
As regards (ii), the grants contributed by the Board of Education,
the Home Office, and the Ministry of Transport[2] are also of considerable importance. The high degree of flexibility of road grants
—which are of the nature of individual bargains—gives Ministry
of Transport policy a special significance in local finance. Since
departments work in conjunction, and all ultimately under Treasury
supervision, the prospects of steady progress are probably not much
diminished by the insertion of these extra links in the financial

[1] Cf. the influence of the government over the Bank of England, and of the
latter over the joint-stock banks.
[2] In addition to road grants the Ministry of Transport supervises electrical
development.

chain. But they must tend to some extent to weaken the chance of a quick response to cyclical changes.

As a method of directing expenditure neither audit nor statistical return is of much importance.[1] In the absence of detailed information on a number of points (which is impossible to obtain as there is no uniform system of cost accounting), the district auditors can hardly perform any more useful economic function than disallowing obviously illegal excesses. There is much more scope for control by grant than by audit. Grant variations are indeed the most important tool available for the control of current expenditure, and indirectly they also affect the volume of borrowing undertaken.

In practice certain difficulties beset the path of controlling expenditure by grant in aid. In the first place the effect of a grant is not uniform over time. The stimulating effect of a new grant is very considerable, while an old grant is accepted with indifference as part of the established scheme. Just as in the case of legislation, however, time is required for planning, &c., and expenditure can frequently be extended only very gradually. It is difficult for the central government, therefore, to estimate whether the grant has been effective. If the local authorities think the ministry is dissatisfied with the result they may even hold back, hoping for a larger grant. The effects of the threatened withdrawal of a grant are more immediate. If sufficient notice is given so that all plans in hand may be accelerated, it may be a very powerful tool for increasing expenditure. An unexpected illustration of this was the municipal housing boom of 1928, due to the reduction of subsidy.

A greater difficulty is concerned with the type of grant to be offered. The most stimulating of all is ultimately that which limits local responsibility to a definite sum, such as the Addison housing subsidy. But apart from its awkwardness this method throws the onus on central funds to such an extent that the experiment is unlikely to be repeated.[2] The percentage grant, properly adjusted, undoubtedly gives a very great stimulus to local effort. But if the local authorities are unwilling partners, the percentage offered may have to be so high that the increasing weight on the budget, even for quite a small service, cannot be neglected. The necessity for very heavy grants may arise either where resources are very limited

---

[1] Cf. J. H. Burton, *The Finance of Local Authorities*, p. 45.

[2] It is significant that local authorities demanded such a limitation in respect of their liabilities in connexion with air-raid precautions.

(such as the depressed areas and certain Scottish road grants), or where the execution of the policy of the central government is regarded as particularly onerous. This may be either because local authorities are indifferent to the service (as in the case of venereal diseases, where a 75 per cent. grant was barely effective), or where they consider it a purely national matter (for instance, air-raid precautions). Under the block grant system, on the other hand, the government feels free to press expansion on the local authorities, but they in their turn, knowing that the unforeseeable burden of expansion will fall upon rates—at least within each grant period —become wary of accepting the bait. The general change over from the percentage to the block grant system at the end of the post-war decade was no doubt mainly prompted by the desire to limit the budgetary uncertainty of the percentage grant system, although the greater freedom of local planning which it would permit was naturally emphasized. It must be noticed that in whatever form the grant is given the inequality of local resources make it essential that it should be distributed on a differential basis if uniformity of development is to be secured. This is the chief merit of the block grant, but recent developments also show that differentiation can be introduced into the percentage method.[1]

In spite of the practical difficulties of the grant-in-aid system the great expansion of local activity since 1914 suggests that as a method of securing steady expansion, combined with reasonable safeguards, the British system provides a workable solution. Its usefulness for trade-cycle policy is not so apparent, but with this it is not primarily concerned, since public investment is mainly a question of loan finance.

We have already seen[2] that the central government supervises the long-term borrowing of local authorities, but that there is little evidence of the use of its power to achieve any particular economic policy. The methods of control available do not indeed facilitate such an aim. Permission to borrow requires three stages (except for a very small proportion of loans raised under the Local Government Act of 1888 which are exempt from supervision). Firstly, a preliminary sanction must be obtained from the Ministry. This depends mainly on the volume of outstanding debt, relative to rateable value. Next, a local inquiry may be held. Finally, a detailed return of the purposes for which the loan is required must be

[1] Cf. above, p. 165.   [2] Cf. Chap. VII.

furnished. The whole process is therefore lengthy and tiresome, although recent legislation has somewhat shortened the preliminary procedure. Since 1931 a fourth stage has apparently been introduced in the form of an unofficial Treasury control[1] of the date and terms of stock exchange flotations of local stock. It is argued that this is justified on grounds of general monetary policy, but the effect appears to have been to hold up local borrowing, at least in the short run.

The regulations governing local borrowing were codified in the Local Government Act of 1933. It would appear from this and from the Stock Regulations of 1934 that the purposes for which borrowing might be undertaken, and the ways in which sinking funds should be managed, were to be more strictly controlled than formerly. The interpretation of this legislation is, however, somewhat uncertain.[2] In so far as there is an increasing tendency for local authorities to finance capital investment from internal funds any increase in central control can only be partially effective. In general, however, it appears that the effect of control is to lengthen the period between the original decision to embark on a project and its realization. In the relatively short period it almost certainly limits the amount of borrowing undertaken. In the long run the nature of control does not appear to exert any considerable check on the volume of investment. It has certainly been successful in preventing over-borrowing.

It appears that it would be a desirable adjunct to borrowing control if means could be devised which would speed up reaction in the short period. One method of rapidly increasing local investment would be for the central government to increase its grants for capital expenditure. So far this method has been used very sparingly. In 1934–5, for instance, direct grants for capital works were less than £4 m.[3] while total grants amounted to more than £125 m. Another method, which can be useful in the long, as well as in the short, period is for the exchequer to assume responsibility for part of the interest charge. The rapid expansion of housing owes much to this factor. From the budget point of view there is the disadvantage that the general tax-payer may be burdened for a long term of years with a fixed charge not directly of his own choosing, but the special conditions of the capital market in the

---

[1] Cf. Chap. XXIII. [2] Cf. Long and Maxwell, loc. cit.
[3] Excluding road grants.

post-war decade no doubt exaggerated this danger. Finally, how-ever, the only method by which the *tempo* of investment can be fully regulated is by some form of control of expenditure. If loan finance ceases to be important this may become desirable.

It does not appear that the present methods of control over local finances are capable of carrying through a very effective cyclical policy. While over-borrowing is amply guarded against, and long-period expansion probably not hindered by loan regula-tions, sudden changes such as are necessary for a public works policy to be effective are not easy to bring about. Sudden expansion means that local plans must already be worked out, and this is difficult to secure when the number of authorities is large. Sudden contraction can be somewhat more easily secured, but it is difficult to avoid waste when planning is uncentralized and investment vicarious. The chief necessity for successful cyclical policy is an adequate planning department. This is a subject to which we must return later.[1] But it must be noticed here that Great Britain ap-pears to be deficient in co-ordinating machinery relative to those countries which have so far most successfully worked a cyclical expenditure policy. In Australia a seemingly successful device was evolved in the formation of a Loans Council representing the different states, and whose recommendations they bound themselves to follow. A similar body might be attempted in this country. But the large number of independent local authorities whose co-operation would be necessary must add considerably to the difficulty of its smooth working. Nevertheless, it is plainly very desirable to have some sort of co-ordinating mechanism. At present decisions to proceed with or to hold up local schemes go before a select committee of the House of Commons. Not only does this method provide no means of long-period consultation and planning, but the decisions made appear to be influenced rather by the availability of tax surpluses than by economic considerations.

At the same time it is not clear that the present method of solving the fundamental dilemma of the local government problem is finally satisfactory. It must be borne in mind that both the scope and degree of control are steadily increasing as the share of the central government in local finance expands. The process is a slow one, depending mainly on the development of new services where control is stricter than in those which have long been estabished.

[1] Cf. below, p. 229.

But it is a process which will not readily be reversed. There is considerable evidence to indicate that control has already reached a point where it is seriously embarrassing to the planning of local budgets. This does not mean that there is any prospect that the local authorities are likely to cease clamouring for larger grants, for the rate burden is still not much below its maximum. But when grant receipts more than equal rate receipts, a position is reached in which services which are not grant aided tend to be neglected by the local authorities, and hence the rate of progress in different lines becomes uneven.[1] New legislation, such as the 'slum clearance act', again puts on local authorities an unexpected burden of replanning, without offering proportionate assistance.[2] Sir E. D. Simon asserted in 1926 that the increase in central interference in planning, especially under the percentage grant system, was having a seriously deleterious effect on the type of candidate seeking election to the Manchester City Council.[3] If this experience should prove to be general, it would be very unfortunate both in view of the traditional importance of local government as a training-ground for national administration, and from the point of view of the ratepayers. The squabble between the L.C.C. and the central government over Waterloo Bridge is a specific example of the trouble which the grant system may cause. Control of borrowing may also be resented. An instance of this was the refusal of Glasgow to accept the terms suggested for its issue of long-term stock in 1934. One of the advantages claimed for the substitution of block for percentage grants was that since the block grant was non-specific, it would allow the local authorities greater freedom of planning. It is not clear, however, that there has been any real improvement in this respect since 1929. Not only is the percentage system still retained for a number of grants, but the general tendency for control to increase is likely to compensate any movement in the opposite direction due to the administrative change.

In comparison with this problem, the opposite danger—that the interests of central taxpayers may be prejudiced when the greater part of grant-rate expenditure is provided out of grants—seems up to the present not to have caused very serious trouble. It is signifi-

---

[1] Cf. E. D. Simon, *A City Council from Within*, chap. viii, and the rush to obtain grants from the Unemployment Grants Committee for such unaided services as sewerage, Chap. XII, p. 201.

[2] Cf. Page, loc. cit.   [3] Simon, loc. cit.

cant, however, that the government decided to provide Merthyr with a special 'adviser', and to bring its municipal accounts under the jurisdiction of the district auditor, as a condition of receiving further exchequer assistance. This does not appear to be a precedent which could safely be carried very far. It would certainly be preferable to attempt a more fundamental adjustment of the resources of local authorities or of their responsibilities.

There are at least three avenues which might be explored in the search for a general solution of the problem of local finance. Firstly, the taxing rights of local authorities might be extended, by empowering them to levy other contributions in their own areas. A local income tax has frequently been suggested, and many other types of local taxation have been tried in Germany and America. A solution along these lines would entail a fundamental alteration in the British tax system, and would be likely considerably to upset the national budget. It would, on the other hand, very much alleviate the difficulties of some local authorities. But since incomes in any area are closely correlated with rateable value it would do little towards equalizing resources, which appears to be a necessary part of any complete solution. Alternatively other forms of property might be included in rates. This would be an improvement, although open to some extent to the same absence of equalizing tendencies as an income tax. The rate is a considerably less elastic and more regressive tax than it used to be. A tax on almost any other form of property would bear less heavily on the poorer members of the community.

A more hopeful line of attack would seem to be to transfer additional services *en bloc* to the central government, as has been partially done for trunk roads and public assistance. This plan appears to have definite attractions, since it is probably true that even the normal size of the existing units of local government is too small for the optimum administration of a number of services. The objections are on the one hand the expense of setting up elaborate and often overlapping machinery, responsible only to the central government, and on the other the loss of the local personal touch in administration. As far as can be judged from the early experience of the Unemployment Assistance Board the first is the more serious. This objection appears to be much less important in the case of roads. An extension of central responsibility for highways would not merely be a considerable relief to the rates of rural areas, but would also promote a very desirable increase in uniformity of road service.

Thirdly, as suggested at the beginning of the chapter, a much more drastic and fundamental use might be made of the government's powers of area amalgamation and boundary reorganization (implying alteration in political status). This has already been found beneficial in the transfer of the duties of poor law unions to the wider bounds of the counties and county boroughs. While small areas are not necessarily uneconomic, amalgamation could be applied with great advantage to areas which are poor mainly because they are abnormally small, such as are the Isle of Ely and the Soke of Peterborough. Small counties such as Rutland, Huntingdon, and Cambridge could hardly fail to benefit if they joined together for administrative purposes. Amalgamation with the county (or abolition of county borough status) was also suggested for Merthyr. When an area has no apparent future it would seem better frankly to recognize the situation, and to relieve it of the responsibilities which are no longer appropriate to its population and rateable value. But the most important application of such a reform is in relation to the growing number of 'conurbations' or continuous urban areas where local government functions become hopelessly entangled and over-lapping.

Neither of the recent royal commissions on local government was given a general reference to investigate the possibilities of area reorganization. But the Tyneside commission[1] did nevertheless examine them with reference to the special amalgamation problems of Tyneside. Two schemes were suggested—by the majority and minority reports respectively. The former consisted essentially of dividing the services of the whole area between a regional county council embracing the whole of Northumberland and a not inconsiderable part of Durham, on the one hand, and on the other, an enlarged county borough of Newcastle, containing the thirteen Tyneside authorities and parts of two other towns. The minority report was less ambitious and aimed merely at unifying the smaller authorities under an enlarged 'Newcastle-on-Tyneside'.

The problem of finding a suitable form of local government for the complex conurbations of the present day is of such general urgency that it deserves very careful consideration. Several possible methods of amalgamation suggest themselves. Probably any

[1] Cmd. 5402, 1937.

of them would promote economy and co-operation in administration, and so react favourably on the problem of high and divergent rates. There are objections, however, to the method which is apparently the simplest—straightforward amalgamation under the most powerful authority of the group. It is highly repugnant to local politics and patriotism for one town to be put under the jurisdiction of another. This is not an imaginary difficulty. The smaller authorities would probably find it almost impossible to reorient the interest of the council of their large neighbour so as to ensure the dispassionate consideration of the interests of the entire new area. The solution of the Tyneside majority report was also open to another objection which is perhaps more fundamental. The evil of divided administration which has already done much to retard progress and economy on Tyneside would be perpetuated in the dual control of the new regional county council and the enlarged county borough. Further, while the additional resources of the county council would no doubt improve the quality of the services transferred to it, the advantages to be derived from a county borough council with less wide powers than formerly are not so obvious. And the new county authority would find its task of caring equally for the interests of its very heterogeneous community by no means simple. It has generally been found in practice that where a single authority is responsible for both urban and rural administration, the latter tends to suffer.

A solution which is of the nature of a compromise between the two suggested by the commission would be to create a new self-contained authority for Tyneside on the lines already tried out with reasonable success for the largest conurbation of all. Such a Tyneside County Council could function exactly as the L.C.C. does at present, and would naturally work in close co-operation with the Tyne Improvement Commission, just as the L.C.C. does with the Port of London Authority. The Tyneside boroughs would indeed (and rightly) lose some of their independence. Room might still be found, however, for treasured civic distinctions. They are not unknown among the London boroughs. In compensation, the area in whose administration they were concerned would be of increased importance and autonomy. While no doubt the former county boroughs would exert a predominating influence in the new T.C.C., the smaller towns would be spared the humiliation of being directly absorbed into Newcastle. There would naturally (following the London practice) be a considerable equalization of rates. A united urban authority of this kind would be able to devote itself to urban problems with a single mind.

There is, however, one serious objection to this suggestion. The effect on the county finances of Northumberland and Durham might well be disastrous. The writers of the majority report were evidently somewhat nervous of the effect of their solution on Durham. But the adoption of the compromise plan would be even more serious. And it is clearly undesirable in any case to add to the number of poor counties who have to be given 70+ per cent. grants in order to keep them floating. But the problem of county borough contributions to county expenses is one of such pressing importance and generality that it would be worth attempting to find a permanent solution of it at the same time as the more general problem was attacked. Would it not be possible for all urban areas to pay a contribution to the counties in which they were situated— fixed perhaps on a population basis—in compensation for the county services they enjoyed—such for instance as road connexions brought to their gates from all sides. Under the present system it is usual for a borough which attains county borough status to make some contribution to the county as a condition of its emancipation. While this arrangement is no doubt an improvement on that ruling in the post-war decade when all resources were lost to the county, it makes no provision whatever for expanding needs. And it gives the county no compensation for the services supplied to towns which have long held county borough status.

If a solution of the area problem of British local government could be found along some such lines as these it would have advantages far wider than the mere equalization of rates, however desirable that may be in itself. It would probably be possible to allow larger authorities considerably more freedom in controlling their own destinies and would thus contribute to raising the status of local councillors and local government officers. The progress of public investment and the economical operation of trading services would also be facilitated by the wider jurisdiction and greater borrowing powers of semi-regional councils. And for cyclical policy the possibility of securing the co-operation of a few large areas might well make all the difference in the speed and unanimity of changes in the *tempo* of investment.

XI

UNEMPLOYMENT

IN previous chapters we have repeatedly referred to the problem of unemployment. For instance we have seen how in some years nearly half of social expenditure was aimed, more or less directly, at relieving the unemployment situation; how again virtually every item of economic expenditure had one eye on this most intractable of post-war problems. We have remarked that the distribution of expenditure which might have been planned, or so it may be supposed, with a view to mitigating fluctuations in employment does not in fact seem to have been so planned. It is now time to place the treatment of unemployment in the centre of our inquiry. This is indeed the inevitable finish to the examination of expenditure, although the problem of employment and its relation to output embraces in fact the whole economic problem.

Unemployment has had a quite exceptional significance in the British post-war economy, both in relation to other contemporary social problems and to its significance at other periods. It has been the British post-war problem *par excellence*, epitomizing for England the social and economic strain which was the aftermath of the war, and which in other countries showed itself in such ways as social revolution and violent currency inflation or deflation. In England, not infrequently, unemployment was a kind of substitute for these disturbances, the channel into which they were, more or less unconsciously, directed. For instance the burden of the war debt was eased in some countries by a currency inflation which wiped out its value in real terms. Here, however, there was no hesitation in imposing sufficient taxation to meet the debt service. Thus the integrity of long-term contracts was preserved, but at the cost of high interest rates, the limitation of investment, and consequently of unemployment. Again, the overvalued pound was kept on an even keel for five years without the consequences normally to be expected, of either excessive deflation or a collapse of the exchanges—but at the cost of the substitution of a growing amount of foreign goods and employment for home services. Finally, social unrest, which had already showed itself in the early twenties in formidable labour troubles, was later partly at least dissolved by the strict maintenance of wages,[1] coupled with a (relatively) generous system of relief for the unemployed. Under this arrangement the wage-earning classes as a whole were better off in 1928–30 than they had been for instance in 1923–5—but the unemployment figures were higher.

Both foreign observers and the British public thus rightly, if often without full understanding of the situation, came to regard the unemployment figures as a measure of what was wrong with the British economy. Foreign money fled from the country in 1931 because the debt of the unemployment fund was thought to be undermining England's financial stability. The electorate weighed governments in the balance against changes in the Live Register of the Employment Exchanges, and found one after another wanting. Unemployment in fact became a political ramp, and it was not strange that this should have been so. Throughout the post-war period the army of the unemployed was never less than a million, or about 8 per cent. of insured workers. From February 1931 to July 1935 it was consistently over two million, rising to a maximum in August 1932, when 23 per cent. of all insured workers were unemployed. Even in July 1936, after three years of recovery, the percentage had not fallen below 12·6. In the twenties the aspect of the problem which appeared to be the most disturbing was the sheer weight of numbers of the unemployed. In the thirties the centre of apprehension shifted to the depressed (or special) areas. This was very natural. While in London and the south-east the percentage of unemployment in 1936 was less than half what it had been in 1932, in the north the improvement was very much less. Above all, in Wales things were actually worse than they had been in 1930—30·1 per cent. of all insured workers were unemployed, as compared with 26·6 per cent. in the earlier year.

This carrying of the sorrows of the country by unemployment has had strange and somewhat unfortunate results. From the point of view of policy it led, not to a systematic and fundamental probing of the situation, which might have revealed its true causes, but to the adoption of simple explanations and hand-to-mouth remedies, such as might be expected to have a quick reaction and

[1] This broad statement is naturally open to criticism in detail on the movements of post-war wages. See Ramsbottom, 'The course of Wage Rates in the U.K. 1921–34', *J.R.S.S.* iv. 1935.

hence be politically useful. In the field of economic analysis, while it has inspired much new and useful work on the economics of depression, there has been noticeable a tendency to regard depression conditions as chronic. One result has been a crop of theories postulating a long run or natural insufficiency of spending, for which there is little basis in normal times. Another has been the tendency to analyse problems concerned primarily with the theory of money or of capital, via the volume of employment rather than via the more fundamental approach of price.[1] It is not impossible that this relative neglect of prices has led to an underestimation of the difficulties of remedies which if unsuccessful might have a profoundly disturbing effect on the economy.

Yet the notoriety of unemployment in post-war Britain has had to some extent a fictitious basis. The habit grew up of identifying unemployment with the numbers on the Live Register. Many of the changes in this have, however, primarily an administrative rather than an economic significance. Until recently the unemployment figures came out earlier and had a larger circulation than the corresponding figures for employment. The latter, however, would have made more cheerful reading, since they showed a steady absorption into employment of an increasing industrial population.[2] Moreover, British unemployment statistics, well known to be the most accurate figures in the world (just because their significance is administrative rather than economic), were compared unfavourably both with less accurate foreign statistics and with the less comprehensive pre-war trade union figures. Even when full allowance is made for these mitigating factors, however, unemployment remained a problem of first-class importance. In November 1936, coexisting with symptoms normally associated with a boom, there were still 1·6 million unemployed. More serious still, areas existed in which literally half the population were without work and without hope.

In the modern world unemployment may be due to a number of causes. It is a necessary preliminary to the examination of the problem to make some broad distinction between them according to their economic significance. For our purposes it will be convenient to split up the problem into four different parts.

---

[1] See discussion in the Multiplier argument in Chap. XIII.
[2] They also showed the striking—and unforeseeable—effect of the cessation of emigration after 1929.

(i) *Cyclical unemployment*—depending on (more or less inter-national) trade fluctuations. This is the most devastating cause, because its effect is both very large and very sudden. In compensation, however, there is little doubt that state action can considerably mitigate its violence. On the other hand, in so far as depression is international, even the most successful national policy can only restore partial prosperity. The characteristics of cyclical unemployment are well known from nineteenth-century experience, and they do not appear to have changed in the post-war period in spite of advances in technique, and the presence at the same time of other forms of unemployment. Its incidence is overwhelmingly on the heavy constructional industries, and in so far as it is international, on the export industries. Since the 'heavies' also rank as important British export industries they are exposed to a double danger. In the post-war years cyclical unemployment has been particularly heavy at two periods—1922–3 and 1931–2.

(ii) *Monetary unemployment* seems the most convenient name for unemployment of various types attributable more or less directly to monetary institutions and practices—such as international currency relations on the one hand, and the usages of internal financial institutions on the other. In one aspect monetary unemployment, whether internal or external in cause, is basic to all industries, and frequently appears as an addition to strictly cyclical unemployment, through the effects on the financial system of the curtailing of spending and investment which smaller incomes and heightened uncertainty counsel. There is a further incidence of external monetary unemployment on international trade industries, since with an over-valued currency home goods are relatively dear to foreigners, and foreign goods relatively attractive in the home market. The latter effect can be partly offset by tariffs, but only at the cost of some reduction of real home incomes. The events of 1925–31 made these phenomena of external monetary unemployment very familiar in England. The effects of internal monetary unemployment are more subtle. We shall be concerned with them again in Chapter XXII, when we come to examine monetary policy in the gold standard period. On the whole, however, the effects of internal monetary unemployment seem to have been less devastating than for instance they were in America during the depression. This relative immunity can be partly explained by the rapid improvement in the debt situation in

Great Britain after 1932, and by the greater flexibility of British financial institutions. On the whole, monetary unemployment must be treated by monetary measures, and so will fall outside the scope of our discussion in the present section.

(iii) *Secular unemployment* arises from the need to make gradual and long-period adjustments, for instance on account of international changes in competitive conditions depending on technical factors, or for changes in social habits, or in the trend of population growth. It is not surprising that this cause should have been important in the post-war period relatively to the nineteenth century, or even the first decade of the twentieth. Apart from other influences, the war caused very considerable changes in all these factors. Unfortunately the incidence has been particularly heavy on the staple British exports of coal and cotton, but they are by no means the only victims.

(iv) *Reserve unemployment* may be defined as unemployment existing at any particular moment, which no amount of improvement in the demand for labour would be able to reabsorb within a short period. It can be regarded as mainly 'frictional', or, in the pre-war phrase, as 'the irreducible minimum', but it is necessary to recognize that it arises from a number of different causes. Part is due to technical conditions existing in different industries, part to the amount of transfer required to keep up with changing conditions, and to the ease with which it can be made. Just how large the reserve will be at any moment depends as much or more on the residue from the preceding industrial situation and the expected demand for labour in the near future as on the current situation. Throughout the post-war period, and even up to 1936, a number of causes contributed to make the reserve very much higher than it was in the steady conditions of the nineteenth century.

We must now examine the unemployment figures themselves in order to see the effect of these causes. First, to present the dimensions of the problem—for this it is clearly desirable to take as long a period as possible. The extraordinary increase in the demand for labour in 1936, however, does not make it a very suitable end-point any more than the disturbed conditions in the early twenties make them a good starting-point. Taking, therefore, the twelve years from July 1923 to July 1935, the number of insured workers increased by 17 per cent., but the numbers of those in employment by only 12 per cent., so that unemployment increased by 5 per cent.[1] Within the average increase of 12 per cent. (or more precisely 11·7 per cent.), industries fall into two groups, of *progressing industries*, where the increase in employment exceeded, and *declining industries* where it was below the average. The relative sizes of the two groups is shown in Table 1, p. 190. Over the period the progressing industries absorbed labour to the extent of 2·1 million workers (or 40 per cent.), while the declining part of the economy lost 1·2 million (or 30 per cent.). Whereas in 1923 the declining industries employed 74 per cent. as many workers as the progressing, by 1935 the proportion was under 40 per cent. This large movement illustrates the heaviness of the process of readjustment which was going on. Even without other causes of unemployment a large amount of frictional unemployment due to reorientation must have been present, and consequently heavy calls on insurance benefit were inevitable.

The two groups of industries are, however, of very different composition. Even the most important progressing industries are relatively small, unless we group related industries together, such as the various branches of the distributive trades, with a labour force in 1935 of nearly 2 million; building and brick and tile making, nearly 1 million; and the various branches of the paper, printing, and publishing trades, nearly 400,000. All the others are very much smaller. In the declining part of the economy, on the other hand, the situation is dominated by a few large industries— coal, with a labour force in 1923 of 1·2 million, and even in 1935 of over 900,000; heavy engineering employing nearly a million, and the main textiles over 850,000. That is to say, the influence of bad conditions was highly concentrated, and that of improved prospects widely but thinly spread. On the other hand, if we look, not at the increase of employment, but at the size of the unemployed labour force attached to the progressing and declining industries, there is surprisingly little difference between the groups, except for the class of rapidly declining industries. The post-war reserve of labour was not only very high but very widely spread.

Table 2, p. 191, examines the position of the worst declining industries more closely. In the first place all have suffered, as

[1] Employment and unemployment figures are given monthly in the *Labour Gazette*, and annually in the *Abstract of Labour Statistics*. The unemployment figures are also given annually in the *Statistical Abstract*. The tables in this chapter are based on Beveridge, 'An Analysis of Unemployment', *Economica*, Nov. 1936 and Feb. 1937.

exporting industries, from the decline of international trade—absolute in the early post-war years and again during the depression of the thirties, and relative to other countries during the gold standard period. Iron and steel and engineering, however, which have a very strong cyclical movement have normally an extensive power of expansion in the home market in time of boom. In 1929 the absence of a tariff (given the exchange disequilibrium) prevented them from taking full advantage of this, but in 1935, while the percentage unemployed was still higher than in 1929, their position improved relatively to other industries. Cotton and coal, where imports of finished goods are relatively unimportant, have less chance of expanding by a concentration on the home market. Cotton, which has not a very strong cyclical movement, profited to some extent by devaluation in spite of the depression. Later the position of the British cotton industry in world trade was partially stabilized by the imposition of tariffs in those overseas possessions whose fiscal policy is controlled by England[1]—politically and socially, it may be noted, a very doubtful expedient. Neither of these mitigating forces, however, serves to conceal the seriousness of the secular decline in cotton. The case of coal is worse. The secular decline became apparent after the termination of the occupation of the Ruhr, and its pace if anything increased as the years passed. Its normal cyclical expansion was, owing to monetary conditions, only partially effective in 1929, and the depression broke on the industry with full force, preventing any benefit from devaluation.

We must now examine the consequences of the fact that the large declining industries are strongly localized in adjacent districts of the north and west, while the progressing industries are widely scattered without any strong localization. Table 3 (a), p. 192, shows the percentage of unemployment for all industries, by districts, at the top of the boom (1929), at the bottom of the slump (1932), and in 1936. The great difference between the south-east and the rest of the country persists throughout, indeed it is actually increased in the later figures. Even if we eliminate the effect of the large declining industries, the same distribution remains. Table 3 (b) shows the incidence of unemployment by districts in a group of generally prosperous and expanding industries. In London and the south-east the percentages unemployed are of the order of four or five, as we proceed north and west they

[1] Cf. *Economist*, 5 Dec. 1936.

climb steadily, even reaching the twenties. This illustrates the pervasive effect of unemployment. Where incomes are generally low because large numbers of workers belonging to one or two highly localized industries primary to the district are out of work, the secondary industries necessarily also show high unemployment—both because their market is reduced and because they serve as a reservoir to which workers in other industries transfer in the hope of employment. The reserve is thus higher in these districts. But it also tends to be higher in the prosperous districts than in more favourable periods, on account of interlocal market connexions. These influences on the reserve are independent of the industrial readjustment forces referred to above.[1]

We may say broadly then that up to 1935 the incidence of unemployment had been of two types: (i) general but relatively light over the whole country, due overwhelmingly to cyclical causes, and hence of relatively short duration, and (ii) of a much heavier variety concentrated in certain districts of the north, and above all in Wales, where all the causes were operating at once. In so far as unemployment had a cyclical basis it was also of greater severity because of its industrial incidence. But the main problem in these areas was the unemployment caused by the much longer period forces of secular change. The average duration of unemployment per worker was therefore much longer in the bad districts than in the good.

The year 1936 saw a greater improvement in the unemployment situation than any previous single year since the war. The increase in insured workers employed over the whole country during the year (Nov. to Nov.) was over 500,000.[2] But the distribution of the improvement was very uneven. Durham and Tyneside showed a reduction of 20 per cent. in the unemployed, while for the country as a whole it was 13·1 per cent. In south Wales the improvement was of the negligible amount of 0·6 per cent. The great increase of employment in the north and east suggests that the recovery of 1936 was of a typical cyclical nature. In fact cyclical unemployment may be said to have steadily dissolved in 1936, being negligible by the end of the year. The secular forces in south Wales

---

[1] This phenomenon is of course only a special case of the contagious effect of depression. See discussion in Chap. XIII.

[2] November 1936 is the last month in which employment figures are unencumbered with the addition of the newly insured agricultural workers.

were, however, almost entirely unaffected.[1] Thus the plight of the depressed areas, while it has become more circumscribed, stood out more clearly as the major unsolved problem. There was some reason to fear on this account that the many-headed character of the main unemployment problem might sink into the background. On the one hand the depressed areas were in danger of becoming a political question, just as the Live Register had done in the twenties. It is essential if their problem is really to be solved, that the government should not let itself be hustled out of a policy of careful long-period planning.[2] On the other hand it is equally important that the need for cyclical control, which is no less necessary in boom than in depression, should not be overlooked. Further, the problem of the abnormally large reserve still remains. Unless the tools available can deal with all these problems there can be no permanent reduction of unemployment. The way in which expenditure has hitherto been directed should afford some guide as to the appropriateness and sufficiency of existing expenditure policy.

[1] But Sir George Gillet's first report (Cmd. 5595, Nov. 1937) showed that during 1937 the fall of unemployment in south Wales exceeded that in the rest of the special areas, being 30 per cent. as compared with an average of 25 per cent. for the areas.

[2] See discussion of the work of the Commissioner in Chap. XIII.

TABLE I

Industrial distribution of unemployment (Great Britain and Northern Ireland)

	Numbers in the Group (total insured) July 1935		Numbers in employment Thousands		% Unemployed		
	Thousands	% of 1923	1923	1935	1929 calendar year	1935 financial year	(1st half) 1936 financial year
Progressing Industries							
I Very progressive (38)	4296·7	142·9	2828·2	3867·5	8·1	10·8	8·7
II Industries subject to special conditions¹ (7)	3446·6	167·2	1941·7	2931·8	8·5	16·2	14·3
III Relatively stationary (14)	1335·4	107·2	1051·2	1130·9	10·0	11·6	9·9
Totals . . .	9078·7		5821·1	7930·2			
Declining Industries							
I Very declining (12)	2079·6	76·4	2432·0	1501·4	11·7	23·0	20·1
II Industries subject to special influences (2)	260·8	72·8	338·6	234·8	8·0	11·1	9·6
III Relatively stationary (27)	1638·7	89·5	1595·4	1387·6	12·7	12·9	10·6
Totals . . .	3979·1		4366·0	3123·8			

¹ The percentages unemployed in Group II refer to manufacturing industries only, since special conditions of high unemployment obtain in both the progressive and declining industries in this class.

(Based on Beveridge, 'An Analysis of Unemployment', I, *Economica*, Nov. 1936.)

TABLE 2

Industrial distribution of unemployment. Per cent. unemployed in certain industries, January and July of each year

	1923¹	1924	1925	1926	1927	1928	1929
All . .	11·6	11·9 9·8	11·2 11·2	11·0 14·4	12·0 9·2	10·7 11·6	12·2 9·7
Coal mining	3·0	4·7 6·9	8·0 15·0	11·2 8·8	16·4 21·5	18·1 29·1	19·1 18·9
Iron and steel	21·2	23·6 20·4	23·8 26·2	22·3 58·5	20·5 18·2	20·4 24·4	20·2 19·9
Engineering	20·5	19·3 14·5	14·0 12·5	12·6 17·6	14·3 9·2	9·8 9·7	10·9 8·9
Shipbuilding	43·6	32·2 28·3	31·8 37·3	37·3 41·7	37·1 22·3	20·6 28·3	27·6 23·0
Cotton .	27·6	15·4 15·9	6·1 11·4	8·3 28·3	11·4 9·4	9·7 15·2	11·2 14·4

	1930	1931	1932	1933	1934	1935
All . . .	12·4 16·7	21·1 21·9	22·2 22·8	23·0 19·5	18·6 16·7	17·6 15·3
Coal mining .	12·9 28·3	19·5 37·2	27·2 41·3	28·2 38·7	25·6 33·8	23·0 31·3
Iron and steel	23·7 32·6	45·2 45·7	46·9 48·9	44·9 38·1	29·7 24·9	34·3 22·7
Engineering .	11·7 16·7	24·9 29·1	28·1 30·1	30·1 24·6	20·2 14·5	14·6 12·5
Shipbuilding	23·4 31·7	46·6 57·1	69·1 63·8	63·3 60·1	54·7 17·7	46·1 42·6
Cotton .	20·0 44·7	43·9 42·5	28·2 33·0	25·9 26·3	21·8 25·6	22·0 22·6

(From *Statistical Abstract*.)

¹ July.

TABLE 3 (a)

Unemployment by divisions. All insured 16–64. Per cent. unemployed in July of each year

Division	1929	1932	1936
London . .	4·7	13·1	6·5
SE. . . .	3·8	13·1	5·6
SW. . .	6·8	16·4	7·8
Midlands . .	9·5	21·6	9·4
NE. . . .	12·6	30·6	16·6
NW. . .	12·7	26·3	16·2
Scotland . .	11·2	29·0	18·0
Wales . .	18·8	38·1	28·5

TABLE 3 (b)

In a group of progressive industries

	1929				1935			
	Building	Gen. Engineering	Elec. Engineering	Motors	Building	Gen. Engineering	Elec. Engineering	Motors
London	10·4	4·1	2·8	3·9	14·8	6·0	4·5	5·1
SE. .	7·2	3·8	2·2	4·7	8·7	5·4	3·9	4·3
SW. .	9·9	4·5	3·7	4·5	13·0	5·4	6·2	6·7
Midlands	12·7	6·6	3·6	9·3	13·3	6·7	4·2	10·0
NE. .	19·4	13·5	8·1	7·3	21·9	16·7	10·6	10·4
NW. .	17·9	14·3	5·8	8·1	22·1	19·4	9·2	14·2
Scotland	15·0	11·2	8·6	9·3	22·1	19·1	11·3	12·5
Wales .	26·8	14·1	8·0	9·8	33·9	27·4	20·8	20·6

(Based on Beveridge, loc. cit.)

XII

UNEMPLOYMENT EXPENDITURE

B ROADLY, unemployment expenditure is likely to conform to one of three types. It may be merely passive, satisfied if physical and psychological deterioration among the unemployed is prevented by straightforward relief in money and kind granted more or less unconditionally. At the other extreme it may take the form of an active stimulation of investment. Finally, as a middle policy, it may combine relief with occupation in a variety of ways, some approximating to a purely passive policy, others almost indistinguishable in practice from normal public investment. Expenditure in this country has taken all three forms, and indeed it is difficult to imagine any depression policy which did not make use of them all. Their aim, however, is logically distinct, and their economic results somewhat different. They are not equally useful at all times and occasions; the problem is to determine the appropriate moment and proportions for their application. This is not a matter on which it is safe to reason *in vacuo*, and in this country at least there is very considerable difference of opinion as to the respective merits of active and passive policy. In this chapter it will be our task to examine the distribution of actual expenditure in the period.[1] If thereby we can throw any light on questions of policy in the setting of contemporary British institutions, the somewhat thankless task will be well rewarded.

Table 1 (p. 194) attempts to bring together the different items of expenditure directly concerned with unemployment policy. The table does not pretend to a very high degree of accuracy, except in the case of purely passive policy. As far as the rest of the figures are concerned the only guides to special unemployment expenditure are specific parliamentary decisions. These mature after a longer or shorter interval in the 'votes' and 'sub-heads' of the Appropriation Accounts, but it is not always possible to identify the original measures accurately. Almost without exception in British experience, the time-lag between vote and expenditure is very considerable, so that new parliamentary allocations become entangled with unexpended portions of former votes, and in fact

[1] Excluding Special Area expenditure for which cf. Chap. XIII.

TABLE I

UNEMPLOYMENT EXPENDITURE

Actual expenditure relevant to unemployment policy, Great Britain

(£ m.)

	1920	1921	1922	1923	1924	1925	1926	1927	1928	1929	1930	1931	1932	1933	1934	1935	1936
I. DIRECT RELIEF.*																	
(1) Unemployment insurance, &c. and public assistance	46·4	118·1	96·2	90·0	91·0	93·8	111·3	88·3	97·7	98·4	144·1	164·0	161·8	147·6	148·3	150·8	137·9
(2) Civil pensions	20·7	23·0	22·4	23·0	25·7	29·6	38·4	45·1	57·7	62·2	72·1	78·3	81·2	83·9	85·6	88·4	89·2
Total of I.	67·1	141·1	118·6	113·0	116·7	123·4	149·7	133·4	155·4	160·6	216·2	242·3	243·0	231·5	233·9	239·2	226·1
II. GRANTS FOR PUBLIC WORKS SCHEMES, ETC.†																	
(1) Employment schemes	not comparable			0·6	0·7	0·5	0·2	1·4	0·5	1·7	2·2	3·0	3·5	4·0	4·2	4·2	4·1
(2) Relief grants to local authorities‡		1·3	1·5	1·8	2·0	1·8	4·5	0·2	..	..	..	..	..	..	..	..	..
(3) Public works by central departments			0·04	0·26	0·25	0·1	0·002	..	..	0·037	0·1	0·02	..	..	..	..	..
(4) Miscellaneous relief and public works		..	0·14	0·5	1·1	1·6	0·1	0·26	1·0	..	..	..	..	0·01	..	..	..
(5) Relief to particular areas									0·1	0·02	0·3	0·15	..	0·5	0·45	0·7	2·0
Total of II	..	3·1	2·18	3·16	4·05	4·0	4·802	1·86	2·6	1·757	2·6	3·17	3·5	4·51	4·65	4·9	6·1
III. GRANTS FOR TRANSFER AND TRAINING.†																	
(1) Transfer and resettlement§	not comparable			..	0·01	0·01	0·01	0·01	0·2	0·2	0·1	0·05	0·03	0·03	0·5	0·2	0·4
(2) Training the unemployed‖				2·7	1·7	0·8	0·5	0·3	1·0	0·8	0·8	0·7	0·6	0·7	0·9	1·2	1·7
Total of III	..			2·7	1·71	0·81	0·51	0·31	1·2	1·0	0·9	0·75	0·63	0·73	1·4	1·4	2·1
IV. ROAD WORKS TO RELIEVE UNEMPLOYMENT.																	
(1) Annual grants made¶		4·53	3·53	5·64	6·41	4·89	4·12	3·87	2·29	4·27	16·21	6·97	2·38	0·92	0·61	0·27	0·22
(2) Estimated cost of schemes (at 31/3/1937) to central government	2·76	3·95	5·02	7·47	14·83						16·6						
V. ORIGINAL ESTIMATES OF WORKS PASSED BEFORE 1932.**																	
(1) Unemployment grants committee schemes	..	26·6	15·9	24·2	20·6	17·6	0·8	0·3	6·2	43·5	35·2	0·2	..	..	..	..	..
(2) Road works	..	13·5	10·8	5·1	4·7	3·7	3·7	2·7	2·9	12·9	51·3	2·3	..	..	..	..	..

* From the *Return of Social Services*, 1936 figures estimates. † Appropriation Accounts, net issues.
† Administrative assistance to local authorities, and minor public works of a relief nature. § Omitting land settlement transfers aided by the Special
Areas Fund included in II (5). ‖ Ex-service training, 1923–7. ¶ From *Annual Reports of the Administration of the Road Fund*.
** (i) From U.G.C. Final Report. The Road Fund schemes were later heavily scaled down, as shown in IV (2). The exchequer share of U.G.C. schemes was
finally estimated at 35 per cent, and the central share of road schemes at 65 per cent.

considerable sums which have been allocated never get spent. Again, in expenditure the original sums may be divided between several different ministries and among several different departments in them, and eventually be spent by a still larger number of local authorities. Nor in expenditure is the line between 'special' and 'normal' clearly drawn. The local authorities keep no separate record of public works expenditure. Administratively it is merely an addition to their normal programmes, organized by their permanent staffs and differing only in the special labour conditions and financial assistance attached. Further, government departments were urged from time to time—for instance in 1924 as a result of the Report on the Provision of Work for Relieving Unemployment—to concentrate on creating work within their usual programmes. Probably only a part of this effort is reflected in any of the sub-headings of the Appropriation Accounts. Again, the normal course of capital expenditure of such departments as the Post Office and the Ministry of Education was influenced by repeated requests to accelerate their building programmes.

Owing to these difficulties it is only possible to make a rough estimate of total expenditure on public works. The amounts shown in Table 1 (II) are the sums allotted in the appropriation votes. Those which were dispensed by the Unemployment Grants Committee were given in the form of percentage grants of an average of about 30 per cent. of approved expenditure. Some, at least, of the rest was given in the form of grants for definite purposes so that they led to specific expenditure by local authorities. If we assume that all except the direct expenditure by the central government departments led to expenditure on a similar scale to the U.G.C. grants, the total expenditure of a sort which might reasonably be called public works[1] would be about £14 m. or £15 m. in the years of maximum expansion. In most years, however, it was undoubtedly much less, especially since an uncertain amount was a substitute for normal investment. This would exclude relatively large sums devoted in the early post-war years to the training of ex-service men for civilian life.

[1] This is exclusive of 'Road Works to relieve Unemployment' (Table 1 (IV)). In view of the fact that highway expenditure was kept roughly constant (cf. Chap. VIII, Table 1, p. 145) it is extremely doubtful how much, if any, of this expenditure should properly be classed as 'public works' in the sense of additional expenditure. The works were distinguishable from the normal programme mainly by the greater emphasis put on new construction.

Under V in the table the estimated total expenditure to completion, for grants of the U.G.C. and for road relief works is shown. As explained later, only a small proportion of this was actually spent before 1932. Expenditure on the road works was not completed by 1936,[1] and it is quite possible that some of the U.G.C. schemes held up in the economy campaign will never be completed, at least in the form originally contemplated.

A similar difficulty besets the classification of public works. It is difficult to estimate the economic significance of even such limited influence as the total expenditure may have had, because of lack of information as to the type of works undertaken, or relief given, except in the case of direct relief on the one hand, and the grants of the U.G.C. on the other. Precise information on this and other aspects of public works policy awaits the detailed analysis of the outlay of the individual local authorities.[2]

The table as a whole exhibits one or two points of interest. Passive policy (unemployment insurance, transitional payments, public assistance, and civil pensions) evidently played by far the most important part. Even if we deduct pensions this is true. This may partly be ascribed to the fact that it is by far the cheapest method of dealing with the unemployed, the cost of maintenance of a single man being of the order of £60 a year, as compared with a minimum of about £250 to provide him with work. A government which is in budgetary difficulties may very well not be able to afford less direct but ultimately more effective ways of treating the unemployment problem. Partly, however, there is no doubt that it reflects a want of confidence in the effectiveness of active policy. It will be observed that the two types of policy have been to some extent alternatives. U.G.C. grants, for instance, were pretty well shut down in 1926–7 when the new pensions services were introduced. Indeed, there is at any time little sign of co-ordination or self-confidence in policy, although it may be true that 'no stone was left unturned'. Another point worth noticing is that while the time distribution of passive policy is necessarily closely correlated with changes in the numbers of the unemployed, none of the other figures in the table shows any such correlation. The heaviest public works expenditure synchronized with the top of the quasi-boom of 1929. Political reasons were of course responsible.

[1] Cf. *Report on the Administration of the Road Fund*, 1935–6.
[2] Such as that undertaken by the Oxford Institute of Statistics.

When we consider the table in detail the first question that presents itself is the lay-out of the large sums comprising passive unemployment policy. Where the amounts to be found are so heavy this policy throws a considerable current burden on the exchequer, even if some proportion of the payments are covered by accumulated contributions. We have seen that the inelasticity of local taxation in England necessitates the exchequer taking the lion's share of the burden, although during the twenties this was only tardily recognized. Now while it is generally agreed that direct relief must form part of unemployment policy, there seem to be two possible sound ways of administering such expenditure. Either payments may be confined to small sums which can be covered by accumulated funds, and which are regarded as supplementary to savings rather than as capable of satisfying needs; or relatively high rates may be paid for short periods to meet special depression conditions. (A case might also be made out for high rates paid over a longer period to special cases in particularly afflicted districts.) But to maintain a considerable part of the population at relatively high rates of relief for long periods is demoralizing for the recipients, a heavy tax burden on industry, and tends further seriously to disturb the lower end of the structure of wage-rates, since payments cannot be much below unskilled wages.[1] Moreover, if unemployment is widespread and obstinate (due to other than cyclical causes) payments must gradually be scaled up. They can no longer be regarded as supplementary to savings.

This is exactly what happened in the twenties. Between 1920 and 1930 basic insurance payments were raised from 22s. to 30s. (and supplementary payments still further). The rise in real relief was still greater, since no reduction in money rates was made until 1931 in spite of the fall in the cost of living. Thus, although unemployment was fairly steady until the onset of depression, and consequently there was no reason why the insurance fund should not have been made to balance actuarially, it was in fact continually out of pocket.

The most effective effort to restore the position of the fund before 1931 was the Insurance Act of 1928.[2] Even this, however,

---

[1] On this aspect of the problem cf. Chap. III, p. 50.

[2] Cf. Beveridge, *Unemployment: a Problem of Industry*, 1930, chap. xii, for a concise account of the history of unemployment insurance in the twenties.

was based on a somewhat optimistic estimate of the number employed, and it was in any case immediately upset by the swift increase of unemployment at the end of the following year. Thus there was no alternative to borrowing in the early years of the depression. While economically there may be arguments in favour of an occasional resort to borrowing even for current purposes for short periods,[1] to rely on loans for large current obligations is obviously both bad finance and an invitation to administrative laxity. The subsequent reaction from such practices has, however, not been entirely fortunate from the economic point of view. Under the economy provisions of 1931 and the Unemployment Act of 1934 it was laid down that not only must contributions cover 2·5 million unemployed on benefit—this time an overestimate—but they must be sufficient to start repaying the debt of the fund, even in depression. This imposed an additional tax on industry in the early stage of recovery, just at the moment when it was most desirable to lighten its fiscal obligations.

The moral to be drawn from the experience of the unemployment insurance fund appears to be that for long periods of widespread depression it is not appropriate to place main reliance on passive policy. More active measures to remove the cause of unemployment must be taken.[2] The difficulties into which both the insurance fund and local finances were drifting were realized some years before the crash of 1931. It is therefore pertinent to inquire why so little reliance was placed on more active expenditure policy.

The largest item of identifiable public works expenditure is the series of grants made by the U.G.C. over the period 1920 to 1932. It is worth examining the history of the U.G.C. grants in some detail, although the amounts concerned were relatively small and could not in themselves have made much difference either to the employment situation or to the prospects of investment. The committee did its work with remarkable thoroughness and conscientiousness. Consequently, if we find them coming up against the same difficulties and repeating the same observations again and again, the figures may assume a greater significance than the actual amounts would suggest.

---

[1] Cf. discussion in Chap. XVIII.

[2] Above all, expenditure policy by itself is not sufficient. Unemployment of this type can probably only be countered by monetary measures.

The cost of the schemes approved by the U.G.C. and their distribution through time is shown below:[1]

Period	Estimated total cost (£ m.)
Dec. 1920–Mar. 1922	26·6
Mar. 1922–June 1923	15·9
July 1923– ,, 1924	24·2
,, 1924– ,, 1925	20·6
,, 1925– ,, 1926	17·6
,, 1926– ,, 1927	0·8
,, 1927– ,, 1928	0·3
,, 1928– ,, 1929	6·2
11 June 1929–Aug. 1929 . . .	1·7
Sept. 1929–Aug. 1930	41·8
,, 1930–Dec. 1931	35·2
Dec. 1931–June 1932	0·2
Total	191·1

The exchequer share of the cost of these schemes was estimated at £60 m. As appears from Table 1 (II), however, the actual issues for such purposes during the period must have been considerably short of this figure. The Committee estimated in fact that by 1932 not more than £24 m. of central funds had been disbursed. On this basis the total spent during the period would be of the order of £60 m.,[2] not a very impressive effort.

Even, however, had the whole £191 m. been spent, the volume of employment provided by schemes of the type chosen could not have been large. The Committee estimated that on the average the expenditure of £1 m. provided 2,500 'man-years' of direct primary employment on the spot,[3] plus a varying amount of indirect employment (which it is convenient also to classify as primary) on raw materials, &c., required for the works. In addition some allowance must be made for secondary employment due to the expenditure of the newly employed, in so far as the employment was actually additional and not merely substitute. It is probable, however, in view of the smallness of the annual expenditure and

[1] *Final Report of the Unemployment Grants Committee* (1935), p. 22.

[2] Allowing for the fact that in the early years the grant conditions were considerably less favourable than in 1929–30.

[3] Loc. cit., p. 24. The U.G.C. steadfastly refused to make any estimate of the amount of indirect employment.

the length of the period over which it was spread, that the importance of secondary employment was not very great. On the other hand, the direct primary employment given by the schemes seems to have been quite up to what is usually expected. It agrees closely with the estimate given in the liberal programme.[1] From the nature of the schemes, however, it would appear that the indirect employment was not likely to have been very large, since planning, lawyers' fees, and expenses in connexion with the acquisition of land must have been considerable. If we follow the liberal estimate (although it is not unlikely that it is somewhat optimistic), and assume indirect primary employment to have been equal to direct, the expenditure of the whole £191 m. would have produced some 950,000 man-years of employment—not a very encouraging amount to put against the 20 million or so of man-years which would have been worked by the unemployed if they had been in jobs. The actual expenditure cannot have provided more than two or three hundred thousand man-years. Nor is it probable that the whole was new employment. All the evidence suggests that much of it would in any case have been carried out, actually within the period, by the local authorities in the normal performance of their duties.

The work of the U.G.C. may be regarded as disappointing both in respect of the number of schemes and of the time-lag in carrying them out once they had been submitted. One explanation of the small number of schemes is to be found in the strict terms on which grants were given. In the first place, the field was limited to 'durable works normally undertaken by eligible authorities [for the greater part of the period this was synonymous with local councils], except those grant aided by the exchequer'.[2] Remembering the ubiquity of the grant-in-aid system, it is clear that the field was a very narrow one. Secondly, it was required that the works should be a substantial acceleration of normal programmes. The definition of this was by no means clear. At first it was held to be sufficient if the engagement of a quota of men from the employment exchanges was shown, but later it became necessary to indicate an antedating of a definite period—for instance three or five years before the works would normally have been undertaken.

---

[1] Cf. *Can Lloyd George do it?* (1929).

[2] Official recommendations that the schemes passed by the Committee should have high public utility or economic value limited the activities of the Committee still further.

This was an effective check to the submission of schemes. Thirdly, the rate of grant was unattractive. While 35 per cent. of capital expenditure was estimated to be the average,[1] the precise percentage differed considerably from one scheme to another. It is clear from the reports of the Committee, however, that there was a steady upward trend, 70+ per cent. being not unknown in the later years. Within the trend the rates fluctuated in a two- or three-year cycle. Each relaxation in the definition of eligibility tended to bring forth a large amount of new applications, but after a year or two the supply began to dry up unless stimulated by very much more favourable grants. In general the rates offered were beyond the means of poor areas. In the early years, however, they alone were eligible for assistance, since a certain percentage of local unemployed was a condition. There were thus very few areas which both found the terms sufficiently attractive, and were themselves eligible. Under the labour government the Development Act of 1929 and the Public Works Facilities Act of 1930 considerably relaxed the terms of eligibility and increased the rates of grant. The result was the submission of a much greater volume of schemes than at any previous period. (Since, however, grants had been almost shut down from 1926 there had been time for an accumulation of schemes on the old terms to appear.) Nevertheless, after the impact effect of the new terms had worn off a shortage was again becoming evident.

In their final report the U.G.C. gave an estimate[2] of the proportion of each kind of work for which they had approved schemes. This is given below, together with the estimated relative cost of

Service	% of all schemes passed	Average expenditure for one man-year of direct employment
		£
Sewerage	24·4	504
Roads and paths . . .	21·5	440
Docks and harbours . .	10·9	470
Water supply	10·7	390
Electricity supply . . .	12·8	840
Amenities	6·6	255
Municipal offices . . .	2·1	605
Sea defence	1·3	590
Miscellaneous. . . .	9·7	585
	100·0	

[1] U.G.C. final report, p. 35.   [2] Ibid., p. 33.

the different types of work, in terms of the cost of employing one man for a year.

These may be broadly grouped: local government normal services 70 per cent., aid to industry 21 per cent., miscellaneous 9 per cent.[1] All the schemes showed a very high cost per worker employed, which is generally synonymous with a small amount of direct labour, expenditure being swallowed up in negotiations for and purchase of land, materials, &c. On the other hand, only a few were likely directly to improve prospects for industry, and these were the poorest of all in labour provision for a given expenditure. Further, there were special reasons why grants for sewerage and for by-roads and foot-paths should be welcomed by the local authorities, since they had hitherto been passed over by the grants-in-aid system. But there can be no doubt whatever that the schemes were in themselves admirable. In detail none of the money seems to have been wasted, and in every case some useful durable work remained as a memento.

This experience seems definitely to point to the conclusion that the machinery for putting a public works policy into operation is slow and cumbrous. Moreover, as long as public works are confined within the customary British definition and considerable expenditure has to be met from local resources, the opinion that there is a genuine shortage of schemes seems to be well founded. The inherent difficulties of antedating wants, the small field of eligibility as long as commercial services are not widely under direct public ownership, and the chronically strained condition of local finances in areas with high unemployment are all contributory factors in the impasse. Probably only an exhaustive analysis of individual experience would enable a reliable estimate of their relative importance to be made. Hence, so long as conditions are what they are—and given the vicarious nature of expenditure, many of them appear to be necessary precautions to preserve administrative and financial control—what is commonly known as 'The Treasury View'[2] (of the uselessness of public works) seems to be justified. General want of confidence in public works as a method of fighting unemployment is therefore understandable. It must be remembered, however, that public works, like special direct relief, are primarily a cyclical tool. If they are carried on year

[1] Cf. the very similar distribution of Special Area commitments up to 1936. Chap. XIII, pp. 210 ff.   [2] Cf. Chap. XIII, p. 218.

after year it is inevitable that they should become a semi-permanent additional subsidy to local authorities. The only conditions on which it seems that a case could be made out for continuous schemes is as part of a long-period policy for rehabilitating areas threatened with secular decay.

If public works in the narrow sense are not to be pushed with more vigour than they have been in England, it would at least seem desirable, both on humanitarian and on economic grounds, to give considerable weight to a middle policy of relief *cum* occupation. A great variety of this sort of policy has indeed been tried—so various indeed that it is extremely difficult to get any idea of its total dimensions.[1] Table 1, however, shows that it cannot have been very large in money terms. Since even amenity public works are expensive relative to pure maintenance, this suggests that the relief afforded cannot have been very extensive. The various schemes may be grouped under three heads, although the demarcation is by no means clear: (i) provision of transfer facilities and training; (ii) provision of occupation, including physical exercise; (iii) public works whose primary aim is relief.

The first specific expenditure for the transfer of workers from depressed areas was in 1929—not, in fact, until after its urgent necessity had been pressed by the report of the Industrial Transfer Board (1928). In view of the large volume of unemployment prior to that date this appears remarkably tardy, especially as the depressed areas already showed up very distinctly. The explanation, though hardly the justification, is probably that prior to the depression periods of unemployment for any individual were relatively short, so that the necessity for measures supplementary to direct relief was not realized. But from 1929 onwards considerable efforts were made to accelerate the redistribution of labour which was taking place through the gradual operation of economic forces.[2] Apart from the group scheme subsequently used in the special areas, three different types of transfer were attempted: first, the removal of single men from districts with high unemployment

---

[1] For details cf. Hill and Lubin, *The British Attack on Unemployment* (Brookings Institute, 1934), and R. C. Davison, *British Unemployment Policy, The Modern Phase, since 1930*.

[2] The extent of migration may be realized from the fact that the insured population of the south-eastern area into which the migration mainly took place rose between 1923 and 1931 from 24·9 per cent. to 27·1 per cent. of the total of Great Britain. Cf. Brinley Thomas, *Economica*, May 1934.

(mainly colliery areas); secondly, the transfer of entire families; and thirdly, the settling of boys and girls in expanding districts. The experience of all three methods was closely parallel, and was moreover strikingly reminiscent of the type of difficulties encountered by the U.G.C.

Whenever a new scheme was started, a certain accumulation of suitable labour, ready and willing to be transferred, was found to be available, but after a short period the supply was apparently exhausted. Transferees could not be found, or else they returned home. The figures for single men and for families, 1929–33, illustrate the phenomenon.

Transfer from depressed areas

Year	Single men	Families
1929	32,000	2,850
1930	30,000	2,100
1931	19,000	1,680
1932	12,000	890
1933	8,000	605

But as soon as recovery began there was no difficulty whatever in securing the removal of the most able workers.[1] The main factor determining transfer appears to be the general demand for labour. Even if there are expanding areas, as long as demand for labour in general is slack the task of transfer in excess of the gradual unassisted leakage which is always taking place appears to be almost impossible.

It did not take long to discover that one obstacle to transfer was that workers who had been unemployed for considerable periods were unfit for work without reconditioning—physical, technical, and psychological. Training centres had been established in the immediate post-war years for ex-service men, but they were not revived and opened to workers from depressed areas until 1927. After some experience of transfer difficulties a more comprehensive system was inaugurated, providing three different types of training which together catered for the different classes of the insured unemployed more or less completely.[2] In addition, local

[1] Cf. figures for 1935 and 1936, Chap. XIII, p. 211.

[2] (1) The Government training centre, aiming at reproducing factory conditions and discipline and giving an intensive course of 23 weeks; (2) the transfer industrial centre, more purely concerned with reconditioning, and having at first at any rate some element of compulsion; (3) the home training centre providing three months' courses in domestic service for women and girls. In

authorities were required (originally under an order of 1930) to provide occupation, amenity public works, or physical training, as a condition of public assistance. The aim of these was to make provision for the non-insured unemployed. Further, occupational courses and physical training were occasionally provided for the youthful unemployed. Under the Unemployment Act of 1934 it was intended that these should be universal and compulsory.

On paper the main difficulties about this programme, as it is about the transfer schemes, was that it was not started much earlier. Most of the schemes were hardly going before recovery began. It has been estimated that not more than 17 per cent.[1] of paupers came under the public assistance occupational schemes. The others were either personally unsuitable for such schemes as could be devised, or the local authorities had not the funds or facilities for organizing a service which is after all entirely outside their province. Evidence of the inadequacy of the provision both of training and occupation is to be found in the reports of the Commissioner for the Special Areas.[2] And even as late as the end of 1936 the position was still reported to be unsatisfactory. This is the more disturbing since a large amount of voluntary effort was also being expended in parallel directions.

Our examination of the more active side of unemployment policy tends to confirm the initial impression given by the distribution of expenditure. Chief reliance has always been placed on straightforward maintenance. The largest concentration of public works schemes was launched at the top of the boom. When prosperity was on a fair way to returning, training courses and the provision of occupation for the unemployed was tardily accelerated. It is questionable whether it is wise to rely so heavily on a mainly passive policy. It is also pertinent to ask whether some more effective weapons for fighting unemployment cannot be found, as well as some means of applying them more precisely when they are most wanted.

certain depressed areas local centres were also opened where the unemployed were given occupation and training without having to live away from home.

[1] Cf. Hill and Lubin, op. cit.

[2] One reason for the unsatisfactory experience of reconditioning policy is clearly the reluctance of the long unemployed to attend centres. It may or may not be possible to find a solution of this difficulty without compulsion, but as long as it remains it is clear that a middle policy can only be partially effective.

XIII

PUBLIC EXPENDITURE AS A CURE FOR
UNEMPLOYMENT

FOR considerations of expenditure policy unemployment may be divided into two classes, cyclical and secular. The basis of cyclical unemployment is general. When prices and incomes fall all industries decline, although some fluctuate much more violently than others. The basis of secular unemployment, on the other hand, is localized in particular industries which are suffering from a permanent decline in their markets. This may be caused by a change of taste. But history suggests that causes on the supply side—changes in relative cost advantages as compared with some other district or country—are more important. Since all industries are to some extent localized, the industrial concentration of secular unemployment is accompanied by a greater or less degree of physical localization also. Hence the problem of the depressed area arises. A particularly awkward special case of this is where the change in costs is due to the exhaustion of a raw material supply. The industry was originally placed in a locality for the purpose of exploiting this natural resource, and there is no reason to suppose that the site will be suitable for other uses. Further, the fact of threatened physical exhaustion implies that there can be little hope of revival from any turn of the wheel of relative prices or technical invention. In addition to the technological forces giving rise to secular decay, other causes may accentuate the unemployment problem. Monetary factors tend to hit exporting districts with particular force. Cyclical factors tend to add their weight to highly fluctuating industries, but these are aggravating forces rather than independent causes as far as depressed areas are concerned.

Both cyclical and secular unemployment can (and hence must) be treated by public expenditure. But it seems probable that fiscal and monetary policy can make a more useful contribution to the cyclical than to the secular problem, if only because they may hasten the advent of the reverse movement which may be confidently expected to appear eventually. Moreover, it is easier to apply expenditure policy to the secular than to the cyclical problem.

There is both more time to plan, and less difficulty in timing out-lay. The secular problem is a long-period affair, the cyclical is only amenable to sudden and swift action. We may therefore start by examining the possibilities of dealing with secular unemploy-ment by public expenditure.

The depressed area problem is, of course, not new. It is at least as old as commerce. Particularly notorious cases in English history have been the abandonment of the Sussex iron industry after the exhaustion of the local timber supply, the intermittent collapse of the Cornish tin-mining industry for long periods, and the ruin of the domestic textile industry in many parts of the country with the advent of the factory system in Lancashire. Nor is there any hope whatever that the depressed area problem will become extinct. Other mineral sources will be exhausted—the condition of the Forest of Dean is already serious. Other localities will suffer changes in demand and the world localization of industry, as Lancashire is already suffering. But the problem has seemed particularly pressing in our period, and mainly for four reasons. On the one hand, the normal forces of secular decline have operated with extraordinary severity over wide areas—largely owing to the arrestation of the normal rate of change during the war years. They have, moreover, been unusually aggravated by cyclical and monetary factors. On the other hand, a new consciousness has arisen of the appalling plight of depressed areas, and a new belief in the possibility of treating them effectively by expenditure policy. But if we consider the depressed area problem in its more funda-mental aspect it becomes obvious that the important thing is not so much to determine how to relieve south Wales or Durham to-day, however pressing their immediate situation may be, as to evolve a general policy which can be applied to depressed areas as and when they appear.

It was not until towards the end of the post-war decade that the depressed area problem began to emerge in the public and political consciousness. It was 1927 before the ex-service training and transfer provision was made available to men from depressed areas. The report on industrial transfer in 1928 was the first public inquiry which gave promise of a more active policy. When this came, however (with the labour government), it took the form of a general loosening of the purse strings for public works rather than of special measures directed at the worst areas. And exchequer generosity came to an abrupt end with the depression. Indeed, it was hardly possible to evolve an *ad hoc* policy for depressed areas before they had been adequately surveyed and defined. A first examination was carried out in 1932 in a series of special reports published by the Board of Trade, but for the preparation of which the provincial universities were mainly responsible. The government reaction to the body of information thus presented to it was somewhat curious. Instead of attempting to formulate any general policy, it was decided to narrow the problem by concentrating on four particular areas, two in England, one in Wales, and one in Scotland. These were submitted to further examination by government investigators. On the basis of their reports the Special Areas (Development and Improvement) Act of 1934 was drafted. Two permanent commissioners were appointed, one for England and Wales, and one for Scotland.

Thus certain of the depressed areas became Special Areas, the particular objects of public solicitude, and all others were henceforth without the rubric, being left very much to their own devices. The chosen four were: (1) the coal-field area of south-west Scotland, (2) a small district in west Cumberland, (3) Tyneside with a hard core in the exhausted Durham coal-field, and (4) south Wales. The last was both the largest and the most serious case. (Following our previous practice we shall not attempt to deal with Scotland.) Although the boundaries of the south Wales area were drawn fairly wide, the really depressed area was the steam coal district lying between the anthracite district (which extends as far east as Neath) and the small domestic coal-field in east Glamorgan and Monmouth.

All of the areas were burdened with highly fluctuating industries which were heavily depressed, and with districts where mineral resources were nearing exhaustion. Nevertheless, while the special areas were no doubt the most conspicuous bad districts, there remained outside them areas with unemployment at least as high as many of the included districts. For instance, large tracts of agricultural Scotland appear to have strong claims for the favour of a special policy, and a very plausible case has been made for the inclusion of the weaving and coal-mining districts of Lancashire.[1] Even apart from possible omissions the boundaries of the special areas themselves appear to have been chosen in a somewhat hasty

---

[1] Cf. *Readjustment in Lancashire* (Manchester University Press), chap. vi.

and haphazard manner,[1] with more than a suspicion of a desire to 'reduce the field of survey to the smallest dimensions which considerations of homogeneity would permit'. No attempt has been made to readjust them, and until 1937 there appears to have been no relaxation as regards benefits[2] of the hard line drawn between included and excluded areas.

There was nothing very startling in the new act. The Commissioners were empowered to grant financial aid[3] to local authorities and non-profit-earning companies for services for which they were not already receiving a grant from some government department, and for small-holdings and allotments even when such a grant was already being received. It is difficult to see what advance this represented on the policy which had already been tried out by the Unemployment Grants Committee—without very encouraging results. Nevertheless, the Special Areas Act was a landmark in depressed area policy, since, in addition to his more specific powers, the commissioner was given an open mandate to make suggestions and recommendations which might lead to a more constructive policy.

The English Commissioner at once began work with great activity. He held from the first that equilibrium could only be restored to the areas by a dual policy of population and industrial adjustment. Surplus labour must be transferred elsewhere, and new industry attracted. In his first report, issued in July 1935, the Commissioner announced the result of a questionnaire to entrepreneurs as to the possibility of their establishing works in the areas. Seventy-five per cent. had made no reply, 75 per cent. of the rest gave a flat negative to all suggestions. It appeared from the remaining 250 replies that the obstacles were of three types: economic (inaccessibility), psychological (unpleasantness and fear of labour trouble), and financial (high rates and want of starting capital). This was not encouraging, but undaunted the Commissioner set himself systematically to remove the obstacles in turn. In the meantime the appointment of Royal Commissions on the local government of Tyneside and Merthyr Tydfil in 1935 gave some hope of disentangling the confusion of local finance and administration. In the second report (of Feb. 1936) the establish-

---

[1] Ibid., chap. vii.

[2] With the exception of a concession as to the charge for the maintenance of the able-bodied unemployed, see below, p. 217.

[3] A sum of £2 m. was provisionally allotted, with power to exceed.

ment of a trading estate for the north-east coast area was announced by the Commissioner. The most important innovation of 1936, however, was the establishment of a Treasury company (The Special Areas Reconstruction Association) to make grants and advances to new industries. This started operations in the autumn of 1936, and was reinforced in the last days of the year by the Nuffield Trust of £2 m. for the same purpose. In his third and final report (Nov. 1936) the first Commissioner advocated the granting of additional financial inducements by way of fiscal concession to new firms. He further drew up an imposing list of specific suggestions for new industries which might be established within the areas with a reasonable hope of success.

In contrast to all this activity and planning the results of special area administration down to the end of 1936 were meagre. By the time of the second report (Feb. 1936) grants amounting to £3 m. had been approved, but expenditure was said to be considerably in arrears. The position at 1 January 1937 showed that total commitments (including Scotland) were between £10 and £11 m.; but that actual expenditure was no more than £2·8 m. Trading estates had been established both on the north-east coast and in Wales, but of the 551 new factories started in 1936 only 8 were in the special areas. It later appeared that it had not been found possible to place much above 50 per cent. of the new armament provision in the areas.[1] A plan for a short length of new road on the north-east coast had been passed, and a Cumberland coast road was being planned. But the Commissioner's important scheme for an arterial road in south Wales had been opposed by some local interests and rejected by the government. During 1935 the north-east coast began to share in general recovery, but down to the end of 1936 little or no improvement was to be seen in Wales. The recommendations of the commissions on local government were not accepted by the central government, and a makeshift arrangement was adopted for Merthyr.[2] Practically no improvement in the rate position of the worst areas had taken place.

It was to be expected that in the first few years the greater part of the fruits of the Commissioner's activities would be found in those parts of depressed area policy which had been tried out previously under the administration of the Unemployments Grants

---

[1] Cf. Debate on Second Reading of Special Areas Amendment Bill (*The Times*, 7 May 1937).　　　　　　[2] Cf. Chap. IX, p. 177.

Committee. Thus there continued to be a marked preponderance of grants for local government purposes, particularly for health and welfare services. Since there had been a few years for these to accumulate there was no doubt a large collection of eligible schemes. The distribution of commitments at the end of our period (actually 1 Jan. 1937) illustrates·this bias towards public rather than industrial investment. £5·18 m. had been allotted for health and welfare, £3·85 m. for land settlement and forestry, and only £0·93 m.[1] for industrial purposes. Sewerage schemes were still a leading feature as they had been in the days of the U.G.C. Similarly, the process of labour transfer had been actively continued, and from 1935 had begun to meet with almost embarrassing success. Whereas in the decade 1921–31 only 242,000 had left the four Welsh counties in all, during the four years 1931–5 72,000 had left the small industrial area alone.[2] During 1935 21,620 workers had left the areas, of whom 9,494 were men.[3] The programme of land settlement also showed promise, although it was naturally slower to get going. Two thousand families had been planned for by the end of 1936, and by the summer of 1937 nearly 800 of these were in occupation.

It is disturbing to observe, however, that in his last two reports the first Commissioner found it necessary to criticize the arrangements made for the occupation and training of the unemployed as seriously deficient. The training centres for young workers, which under the Unemployment Act of 1934 were to be universal and compulsory, had largely failed to come into existence. It was common knowledge that current health services were progressively falling behind the standard of the rest of the community. Both in respect of these and in the failure to develop road communications are apparent the disadvantages of a policy which prevented the Commissioner from giving help where another authority had a prior responsibility, whether or no it was in fact backing up his policy. It appears that so far from a solution to the depressed area problem having been found, the unfortunate communities were not even receiving very reliable maintenance assistance up to the end of 1936.

[1] Cf. White Paper on the Special Areas (Cmd. 5386, 1937).
[2] Cf. *Second Industrial Survey of South Wales*, 1937.
[3] According to the Third Report of the Commissioner the numbers were: 1935, 21,713 (+ an unknown amount of 'unassisted'); 1936 (first eight months), 21,620 (+ about 9,000 unassisted).

It is a matter of common sense that the restoration of equilibrium to a depressed area depends on a dual policy of population and industrial adjustment. It is in the nature of the case that both require a considerable amount of financial aid from the rest of the community. The first problem is to determine at what point the social and economic advantages of bringing the industry to the workers is offset by the cost of doing so, taking into account the alternative costs involved in taking the labour to the places where the industry would otherwise be. The second problem is to determine the amount and distribution of expenditure which will bring about the equilibrium thus shown to be most desirable—remembering that the total sum available for depressed areas ultimately depends on the continued willingness of the rest of the community to help their more unfortunate brethren. In a dynamic world, and especially one subject to violent alterations of good and bad times, the correct equilibrium of transfer and attraction is exceedingly difficult to determine. Thus it was calculated in 1936[1] that there were some 80,000 redundant workers in south Wales, but that on the 1935–6 scale of migration this surplus would have disappeared completely by 1943. It is clear that the estimate could only be made on the basis of two very big unknowns—the further extension of the boom and rearmament expenditure on the one hand, and the feasibility of establishing new industries in the area on the other. These two factors were only exerting a small part of their expected influence by 1936.

It is socially very desirable to restore equilibrium at as high a level of population as possible in the depressed areas. The break up of communities and families involves hardship and social loss which we should surely be prepared to pay much to avoid. Loss of population means a fall in receipts without a corresponding fall in the cost of government. Indeed, some services may actually be more expensive to run for a small than for a large community. The burden of fixed interest charges also bears with particular weight on a reduced and impoverished community.[2] Many of these difficulties are merely an aggravation of those which the advent of a stationary population are forcing on the notice of the

---

[1] Cf. *Second Industrial Survey*, op. cit.

[2] Additional local causes of financial difficulty are (i) the high cost of salaries when the proportion of the relatively old is high, and (ii) extensive borrowing during the fortuitous prosperity of the early post-war years.

whole community. The special problems of selective migration which confront a depressed area are, however, more intense than those of a natural decline in the population. The removal of the younger and more active members of the community proceeds at a faster rate than a mere change in the relative weight of different age groups due to natural decline. There is a real danger of physical and moral deterioration in the population which remains. It is also more likely to be in need of the social services, and hence more expensive than a normal population. Moreover, the losing areas have already invested capital in the rearing and education of workers on whom they will receive no return as income makers and spenders. Selective migration thus inflicts a heavy social and economic burden on the areas which are left with an expensive population and with equipment and administrative machinery in excess of requirements. It is true that if we consider the community as a whole there is some offsetting gain in the areas receiving new immigrants who are already equipped for industry. But in the short period the expense of providing new houses, roads, &c., which are only partially self-supporting, has in turn to be set off against this.

In contrast to the community loss caused by migration it is argued that the corresponding social loss on the transfer of industries to areas with excess population is negligible. Location is stated to be increasingly less important as a factor in industrial cost. Cases are cited where location has apparently been determined on quite other than economic grounds. It is also argued that there are direct social disutilities in the development of immense urban agglomerations,[1] and that these being of the nature of external diseconomies are not perceived by any individual. Tightly packed urban communities are also particularly vulnerable in case of war. Finally, since the state already determines changes in industrial location through its distribution of quotas, tariffs, and other forms of differential subsidy, it has already assumed some degree of responsibility for industrial location in general.[2]

There is undoubtedly great force in many of these arguments. The enormous improvement in communications, and particularly in road transport, have probably considerably diminished the location factor in costs. The wide distribution of power through the

[1] Cf. Third Report, op. cit.
[2] Cf. First Report of Second Commissioner, Nov. 1937.

electric grid has also tended to lessen the advantages of industrial concentration. And if large urban agglomerations are exposed to health and military dangers, there is certainly a field for directed location which did not exist before. But the duty of the state is surely to consult the advantage of the community as a whole, and to preserve the balance between particular interests. Permanently to subsidize firms in the depressed areas is ultimately little better policy than any other form of differential treatment. It is therefore essential to examine just what part location does still play in industrial costs, and to frame industrial policy for the areas accordingly. It is to be hoped that much light will be thrown on the matter when the report of the royal commission is available. It would seem, however, in view of the difficulties already experienced in attracting industries to and in placing armament factories in special areas, that the location factor cannot be negligible. In a number of cases where non-economic grounds are alleged it is easy to see that important economic inducements were also present.[1] Notorious cases have also occurred where a location chosen primarily on non-economic grounds has proved untenable.[2] It may well be that there are now fewer occasions on which location is uniquely determined, and that the position is rather that there are a number of sites of nearly equal eligibility. Choice between these would be relatively indifferent on economic grounds and might well be determined by non-economic considerations. This does not mean that the economic factor in location is negligible. But it does perhaps increase the possibility of getting a site in a depressed area on to 'the short list' of eligible locations. It is also certainly the case that location is of very different degrees of importance for different industries. It would seem, therefore, that there is room for very considerable skill, both in choosing the industries to attract and in preparing the ground to meet them.

It cannot be denied that the special areas offer few natural attractions. As a tourist centre west Cumberland has possibilities and perhaps also certain parts of south Wales. It is significant, however, that the Commissioner experienced great difficulty in finding suitable land for afforestation in or near these somewhat

[1] Obviously favourable factors in the Morris location at Oxford are (i) abundant cheap local labour, (ii) availability of skilled labour and parts for assembling (from the Coventry district), and (iii) proximity to consumption markets.

[2] For instance, the relative failure of the Ford location at Cork, chosen primarily on personal grounds.

bleak and inhospitable regions. On account of their natural features, of the shortage of local funds, and of the fact that their former products were mainly exported by sea, the areas are even more inaccessible than they need be. Road development has seriously lagged behind the standard of the rest of the country. When we consider these factors and the unattractive appearance of abandoned industrial sites and rows of obsolete houses, it is easy to understand the emphasis which entrepreneurs placed on inaccessibility and unattractiveness as deterrents to industrial transfer. Nevertheless, there are very considerable possibilities of improvements in these respects in all the areas. Tyneside, for instance, is adjacent to the large and reasonably diversified market of Newcastle. Improvement of local road and cross-river communication would greatly enhance accessibility. Even south Wales has a large and expanding consumers' market within a short distance—were it not for the intervention of the Severn estuary between Bristol and Monmouth.

The types of industry which it is most feasible and desirable to attract are obviously those for which the areas still show some natural advantages—those which are either subsidiary to the materials used in or the labour skill required for the old basic industries. The reports insist that there is some scope for these in the form of coal hydrogenation, carbide manufacture, and the various applications of tin plate, &c. But all the evidence suggests that chief reliance must be placed on the introduction of new consumers' goods industries. Light industries are undoubtedly less dependent on particular locations than others. The abundance of female labour in the special areas also creates an *a priori* case in their favour. Relative immunity from fluctuations makes them a particularly desirable addition to these highly cyclical areas. But good road communication is a vital necessity for light industries. Accessibility on the one hand to raw materials and on the other to markets appears in fact to be the only consideration of importance in determining their location. Even apart from the question of accessibility of raw materials it cannot be supposed that the areas themselves are at present either sufficiently large or sufficiently prosperous to provide in themselves an adequate outlet. The new industries must therefore be enabled to take full advantage of adjacent markets. This suggests that perhaps the most urgent requirement of all is a south Wales arterial road with a low crossing of the Severn leading directly to Bristol. Without it the only alternative to sea or rail transit is a fifty-mile detour through Gloucester. None of these approaches provide suitable communications for either light industries or tourist traffic. An important subsidiary to such a road would be an adequate secondary road connecting the upper ends of the parallel valleys which constitute the depressed area. This would provide a new link with the outside world for just those districts which are most isolated on the present system of road and rail communication.

Leaving aside the financial aspect for the moment, the depressed area problem appears to resolve itself into one of pressing on with the attraction of new industries as fast as possible. But this in turn requires the rapid development of good road communication. Until the areas are made accessible it is not possible to predict their real scope for industrial development. It is essential to proceed rapidly with this side of the problem since in the meantime useful labour is leaving the areas and the problems created by selective migration are in danger of being seriously aggravated. It is clearly undesirable to allow labour transfer to proceed too far. At the same time, it cannot be hoped to avoid a considerable decline of population, particularly in districts suffering from exhausted mineral resources. Even the most favourable equilibrium, for instance, would hardly require more than one-half or one-quarter of the former inhabitants of Merthyr in its future industries. There is, however, some scope in population policy for lessening the effects of selective migration. Family transfer to land settlement colonies has clear advantages over other forms of adjustment. It does not materially increase the want of balance in the population left behind, and it throws the burden of education on the receiving areas where it can more easily be borne. Of great importance also is the development of areas adjacent to the most depressed districts, and the encouragement of interlocal migration. This is considerably less disturbing to community life than distant settlement. The unspoilt rural parts of Monmouthshire appear to offer a particularly suitable field for such development, since they lie directly between the depressed districts and the Bristol market. This provides an additional argument for road development.

For any solution of the depressed area problem very considerable financial aid is clearly required. The local authorities in depressed areas have received some differential treatment since 1933.[1] In 1934 they received a further small special allowance under the Unemployment Act.[2] The modification of the block grant since its establishment has also worked in their favour. But since rates have remained conspicuously above the rest of the country this is clearly insufficient either to give the local authorities equal opportunities compared with other areas, or to make them equally attractive to would-be entrepreneurs. Industry received only very slight encouragement under the Special Area Act of 1934. S.A.R.A. offered more direct advantages. But its policy has been persistently criticized for undue caution,[3] and it appears that the rates offered on loans are indistinguishable from those which commercial enterprise is prepared to grant. The prospects both of loans and grants were, however, considerably improved by the establishment of the Nuffield Trust.[4] But the impoverishment of local authorities remains a serious obstacle to improvement. A more fundamental reorganization of areas and administrative duties, taking account of the new distribution of wealth and population, would no doubt enable considerable economies in local administration to be carried out. Some further assistance can also be looked for from the modification of the block grant. But the indefinite enlargement of the share of the central government in the financing of general local services is clearly undesirable. It would appear preferable for the exchequer to assume complete responsibility—financial and administrative—for additional services. Thus local resources in depressed areas are clearly insufficient for the necessary road development. A transfer of part of the local debt burden to the shoulders of taxpayers elsewhere would do much to set local

---

[1] Early in 1933 highly rated areas appealed for the transfer of the proceeds of a ½d. rate from prosperous districts. On the refusal of the latter the government distributed £500,000 (annually) to counties and county boroughs in depressed areas, on the basis of the cost of out relief.

[2] This subsidy was allowed as a deduction from the quota due to the exchequer under the Unemployment Act, 1934.

[3] In the first four months of its existence loans totalling £287,400 were made.

[4] By the end of June the amounts 'provided or agreed in principle' were:

	South Wales	Durham	W. Cumberland
S.A.R.A.	£155,150	£170,800	£66,650
Nuffield	£527,750	£416,350	£263,350

The increased bias towards industry is reflected in the distribution of commitments at 30 Sept. 1937, viz. Industry £3·8 m.; Land settlement, £3·3 m.; Public Health £4·9 m.; Other £0·8 m.

finances on their feet without providing any additional incentive for unwise expansion.

The depressed area problem is a long-period one which can only be solved by long-period methods. If we expect quick results we shall certainly be disappointed. But it has a cyclical aspect also which should not be neglected. Adjustments of all kinds are easier to make during prosperity. Tax surpluses are available, and entrepreneurs are in a mood to embrace new possibilities. Past experience shows that it is almost impossible to move labour unless there are very promising prospects of its profitable employment elsewhere. It is therefore essential to push on secular unemployment policy during prosperity. Eventually the present depressed area problem will no doubt get settled somehow as its predecessors have done. But it seems clear that a well-directed government policy can greatly assist, both by accelerating the process and by establishing the new equilibrium for the areas on a higher plane than would otherwise have been possible.

Cyclical expenditure policy presents an entirely different aspect. Whatever can be done is necessarily concerned with short-period action. But to be effective it must be swift and decisive. This implies both unified control and long-period planning. If for the moment we neglect the difficulties concerned with these it still remains to consider what precisely may be expected—or hoped— from the expenditure side of cyclical policy.

On few points of practical economics are more divergent views held than on the possibility of reviving prosperity in the midst of depression by means of public expenditure. While it is obviously outside our field to attempt any general discussion of the controversy, it is clearly our duty to make some attempt to relate current British opinion to our study of institutional data and recent British experience. At one extreme of British opinion stands what is known as 'The Treasury View', stoutly denying that public works can effect any improvement in the employment situation. The following may be quoted as a typical expression of this opinion:

'The Municipal relief works encouraged by Mr. (Joseph) Chamberlain's circular of 1886, have been in operation for twenty years, and we think must be pronounced a complete failure—a failure accentuated by the attempt to organize them by the Unemployed Workmen Act of 1905. The evidence we have collected seems conclusive that relief works are economically useless. Either ordinary work is undertaken, in which case it is merely forestalled, and later throws out of employment men who are in more or less regular employ of the councils, or else it is sham work, which we believe to be even more demoralising than direct relief.'

It comes from the majority report of the Poor Law Commission of 1909, and is obviously not fully applicable to modern conditions —for instance, the type of public works organized by the U.G.C. But its terms are practically identical with those of a memorandum sent to the League of Nations in 1932 in reply to a questionnaire addressed to all member countries for information on the types of public works which had been found most useful in depression. The fact that this is and remains the official view, in spite of small temporary deviations in a more expansionist direction, is a datum in the British situation which it is important to bear in mind.

The Treasury View assumes that at the best expenditure on public works puts a number of additional workers into direct employment on the spot, and indirect employment in preparing raw materials, &c., elsewhere, but that there the matter ends. Increased demand for consumers' goods or for materials will presumably be met out of stocks. Owing, it must be supposed, to depression psychology, their depletion will not provide a sufficient incentive to stimulate new investment, either directly or through the increased demand for consumers' goods. At the worst the public expenditure will entail no net new employment and so will be a direct burden on the taxpayers. The new workers will be substituted for regular employees, so that there will be no reduction in the cost of unemployment. The newly disbursed money will find its way into the bank accounts of local authorities, or of the lawyers, where presumably it will be hoarded until better times.

The boldest claim for the practicability of public works in this country put forward by responsible opinion in our period was that which figured in the liberal programme of 1929.[1] The scheme, which had already been elaborated in detail in the *Liberal Yellow Book*,[2] was for a large-scale programme of national development involving expenditure of the order of £100 m. a year for three years. The argument that suitable schemes for such a vast

[1] Cf. *Can Lloyd George do it?* (1929).
[2] *Britain's Industrial Future* (1928).

programme would not be forthcoming was met by pointing out the enormous scope for the development of such national services as roads, housing, telephones, and electric power. The successful financing of the programme was to be secured in the first instance by an extension of bank credit, but it was implied that the subsequent expansion of tax receipts and the saving of unemployment expenditure would prevent the debt from weighing upon the community. The international effect presented some difficulty owing to the existence of a rigid gold standard, and to the fact that the condition of the exchanges was in 1929 somewhat precarious.[1] It was, however, claimed that the necessary funds for financing the increase in imports which reviving prosperity would entail, could be obtained by the cessation of foreign lending. The extent to which these funds might alternatively be required to make good a deficit in exports does not appear to have been examined.

The liberal programme emphasized particularly the importance of indirect employment. It was implied that neglect of this factor had quite unjustly predisposed opinion unfavourably towards public works. (We have seen that the U.G.C. refused to commit themselves on this point although acknowledging an average of direct employment which was fully up to the liberal estimate.) But the analysis of secondary employment was carried to a much higher pitch of refinement two years later by Mr. R. F. Kahn in what subsequently became famous as the 'Multiplier' argument.[2] Briefly it was pointed out that public expenditure in depression may be expected to increase total spending not merely by the primary (direct and indirect) outlay occasioned by the public works themselves, but also by secondary expenditure due to the higher incomes of the recipients of the primary expenditure. Thus higher incomes will generate higher incomes, and new employment new employment in a continuous chain. If it is assumed, as seems reasonable, that only a proportion of the new incomes in each turnover is actually spent, the chain becomes not an expanding, but a convergent series. This implies that it can be summed. The relation of this to the original expenditure will give a figure (or multiplier), whereby the total new spending (or *mutatis mutandis* the total new employment) for a given initial expenditure can be calculated. On the assumptions made a guess was hazarded

[1] Cf. Chap. XXII.
[2] 'Home Investment and Unemployment', *E.J.* 1931.

that the value of the multiplier in Great Britain was of the order of 2 or $2\frac{1}{2}$. The important point to notice about the argument is that it claims that the activity thus generated does not go on accelerating until it reaches a crisis. (It is naturally assumed that the banks do not cause a crisis at an early stage by refusing to lend.) On the contrary, owing to the leakage into hoards and cash balances at each turnover, it is asserted that the movement eventually settles down on a higher plane of employment and income. Thus it has been argued, any desired degree of re-employment can be achieved by means of public works.

It must be observed that at any rate in its original form[1] the series which is to be summed to find the multiplier was confined to the history of the single new investment. The possible stimulus to further investment was expressly excluded from the calculation by its first author. Assuming a fair elasticity of supply of the goods which will be newly demanded (which includes also an elastic supply of the labour required to make them), it seems reasonable to suppose that costs and prices will remain fairly steady. Thus the relation between them will remain more or less constant, and the expansion will proceed at an even pace. It is important to realize, however, that it is assumed that no incentive for investment to spread arises. For a small movement this is probably realistic enough. It is possible also to conceive a condition in which the incentive to invest depends on the movement of retail prices. If these remain constant the incentive for fresh investment is lacking. Alternatively it might be assumed that unemployed resources (labour and materials) exist more or less in the proportions in which they will be wanted (and as regards labour in the places in which it will be wanted). But it is clear that none of these assumptions is necessarily valid. If decided 'bottle-necks' develop—as they may do even at an early stage—some prices cannot fail to rise rapidly. In this case we cannot safely limit attention to the original public works investment. Rising prices are very likely to stimulate investment in other parts of the economic field. The movement can then no longer be regarded as a small one, and the initial assumption of price steadiness becomes decidedly suspect. In this case the series will not continue at a steady pace, and we can no longer calculate the multiplier by summing it.

[1] For a more developed version of the Multiplier argument, see Keynes, *General Theory of Employment.*

It all depends on the policy of the monetary authorities, what view is taken of government action—or ultimately on what incentives to invest entrepreneurs are given.

On reflection it appears that the Treasury View and the multiplier argument are not alternative and contradictory analyses of general application, but descriptions of particular special cases—both it must be admitted very considerably over-simplified.[1] The first tells us what will happen when the effect of the new spending is either negatived by the cessation of old spending, or else is exhausted within the first turnover; the second where secondary expenditure continues at an even pace but does not stimulate secondary new investment or substantially raise prices. We owe some respect to the Treasury View since it is built up of past experience of public works in this country. It is a description of what in fact has been found often to happen. In contrast the multiplier has never been allowed to try its wings (at any rate in the form envisaged by its first author). But in its more general form it is merely a rather elaborate analysis of normal experience in the upswing—only we must be prepared for the possibility of prices rising a good deal more than the particular assumptions made in the development of the analysis would suggest.

How are we to know which path history is most likely to follow in any given situation? The place which psychology, and especially entrepreneur psychology, plays in booms and depressions is now universally recognized. But one of the difficulties in controlling fluctuations is that reactions appear to be largely irrational. In some circumstances the most favourable omens will fail to generate any expansion. In others the clearest sign of recession will fail to restrain over-investment. But even in our present state of knowledge psychological reactions cannot be regarded as wholly irrational. We may be sure that they depend to a very important degree on deductions from current events. Hence the sequence of development, and the speed with which outlay can be proceeded with, are of vital importance for the success of a public works programme. It is not a very simple matter to orient these matters in the desired direction.

In the first place in practice it appears to be difficult to avoid a deflationary movement intervening before the expansion has had

---

[1] Cf. J. R. Hicks, 'Mr. Keynes and the Classics', *Econometrica*, 1937.

time to get under way. Eventually if the public works are a success, the national income will increase and tax receipts expand. But the government must first raise the money to finance expenditure. Assuming that the more deflationary path of financing expenditure out of increases in taxation is avoided, the simplest method of acquiring funds is presumably by ways and means advances or by expanding the floating debt. But either of these methods is generally regarded with suspicion[1] except in times of political crisis. The country must be very well convinced of the necessity for and the good result of the outlay for the movement to be received with equanimity. Eventually a long-term loan has to be floated, and this may also entail some psychological upset. But there is a more fundamental difficulty. The central government has only extremely limited powers of borrowing for capital expenditure. For new types of investment fresh legislation would have to be introduced. This is both upsetting and time-consuming. If on the contrary the central government continues to invest vicariously, through the local authorities or such bodies as the Central Electricity Board, formidable problems of co-ordination at once begin to arise.

If as at present the local authorities continue to be the chief spenders for public works purposes, the first expansion of outlay would no doubt be financed out of bank advances with little or no preliminary deflation. But eventually the councils would have to raise long-term loans, a notoriously time-consuming process. Even supposing that the outlay itself is accepted as desirable, there is then the further possibility of a saturation of the market for local stock. It is an undoubted fact, however irrational its foundation, that the debt of local authorities and public boards is not so readily accepted as the debt of the central government. Similarly in respect of the foreign balance, the natural sequence of events is not directly favourable to expansion. There is a grave danger that unless special steps are taken to control the export of capital, the reduction of foreign lending will not take place in time to relieve the strain on the exchanges due to the increase in imports. The degree of strain depends primarily on the extent to which home prices rise, and the consequent stimulus to imports and restriction of exports. If exchange restrictions are imposed at an early

[1] Cf. discussion of the effects of borrowing, Chap. XX.

stage the difficulty about the foreign balance can be avoided. But the action of imposing restrictions will itself be deflationary, and will tend to restrict exports still further. These difficulties do not imply that a public works campaign is foredoomed to failure, but it must be acknowledged that the omens are not altogether encouraging. There is a not inconsiderable danger that the campaign may have to be launched in an atmosphere less favourable than that existing when it is planned.

This awkward tendency of the sequence of events would be of small importance if there were a prospect that the time lag would in any case be short. But on this point British experience is not very reassuring. In addition to the time spent in land purchase negotiations, months are normally consumed in negotiations between the local authorities and the central departments before plans are approved. Further, even when the works are started there appears to be a technical lag of probably something like two years before expenditure reaches its peak, and hence its maximum effectiveness. Thirdly, although incomes may be expected to increase steadily from the point where outlay begins, the exchequer only benefits very gradually. The saving on unemployment expenditure may begin to accrue at an early stage, but this is an extra-budgetary relief. Income-tax receipts will not rise until at least a year, and surtax receipts until two years, have elapsed from the beginning of rising incomes. There is a similar lag in the movement of commodity tax receipts.[1]

The existence of these time lags greatly complicates the task of a cyclical public works policy. The difficulty of synchronizing peak expenditure with the desired point of the depression is manifest. But it must be noted that neither the U.G.C. nor the liberal scheme was put forward as a strictly cyclical measure. The time factor would therefore appear to be less important for their success. Nevertheless, the length of time which must elapse between the adoption of the programme and the beginning of outlay makes the ultimate success of the programme considerably less certain. As soon as the money is voted it tends to be regarded as spent, and when no apparent result is forthcoming it is naturally assumed that the public works have been a failure. It requires considerable faith in the ultimate effectiveness of expansionary policy to plan new investment on the basis of rising national debt and stationary

[1] On the timing of tax receipts cf. Chap. XVIII, pp. 302–3.

or falling price indices. Just what importance the debt factor will have depends to an important extent on the size of the current bill for the service of the debt. During the twenties this was so large that even an expansion which was regarded as temporary was viewed with apprehension.

It is by no means certain, however, that the expansion of the debt will be temporary. Of the public works suggested in the liberal programme, telephones and electricity investment might reasonably be expected to pay for themselves eventually. Road expenditure (if within the commercial road plan)[1] should raise the national income by at least an amount equal to the expenditure, but it is by no means certain if and when the exchequer could fully recoup itself. A large housing campaign, however desirable socially, will certainly not pay for itself, and it does not seem likely that it will provide an increase of tax receipts sufficient to cover the gap in interest and amortization quotas. The relation between the rise in the national income and the rise in tax receipts must differ to some extent according to the type of public works chosen. On the other hand there is indeed some reason to believe that a certain expansion of public debt may be a lesser evil for a country suffering from the ills of a stationary population.[2] But the relevant point here is that the psychological and economic effects of such an increase must be allowed for in calculating the expected advantages of the public works programme.

These considerations serve to bring out the somewhat melancholy fact of the immense economic superiority of a rearmament campaign over other forms of public works available in Great Britain. When armaments are desired at all, they are regarded as of much more vital importance than doubtfully paying schemes of national development. There is hence relatively little difficulty in securing the necessary legislation for central government borrowing.[3] The fact that the central government has undivided responsibility for planning and expenditure helps to shorten the period before the works can become effective. The increased ease of planning in advance when land is not an important item is another favourable factor. Even the technical lag between initial outlay and peak

[1] Cf. Chap. VIII.
[2] Cf. Chap. XVII, pp. 284 ff.
[3] Nevertheless, the launching of the first defence loan in the spring of 1937 was a considerable shock to the market.

expenditure is probably less important than in other forms of public works. In the case of armaments the community tends to concentrate attention not so much on the rising tide of expenditure as on the ultimate objective—an adequate insurance against international danger. If it is apparently obtaining this at a smaller rate of expenditure than was anticipated, it may actually be a bull point in the initial stages, just where it is most badly needed.

But, perhaps fortunately, an armament campaign cannot be conjured up to meet every depression. Even large housing and road schemes cannot be fully repeated at intervals of eight or ten years. We cannot therefore neglect the narrower but more general problem of adapting expenditure policy to relieve depression on the assumption that no such special remedies are available. Even if they are present a general orientation of expenditure policy is also likely to be necessary. The first task is obviously to prevent depression getting out of hand. If this can be done it will probably prevent the extensive development of internal monetary unemployment which is the worst menace to recovery. A factor of vital importance in such a policy is to provide a means which will mitigate the shrinkage of expenditure. Thus what we have called passive unemployment policy has in fact an active significance, and an important economic function to perform. Relief public works do the same thing in rather more intensive form, since income can then be distributed at wage and not merely at maintenance rates.

It is important to realize that from the point of view of distributing consumer income the economic significance of the works chosen is a matter of indifference. Digging holes and filling them up again is as good as any other method. The less money that is spent on planning and equipment the more quickly can the works be started, and the smaller the danger of the expenditure failing to accrue as final income. But relief works have also an important social function to perform, and this effectively determines the most desirable types. Public amenities near the homes of the unemployed, such as sports-grounds and lidos, are excellent examples of works which will help to restore the workers' self-confidence by the realization that they are engaged on a project which will be of real benefit to themselves and their friends, and at the same time be a convenient medium for the distribution of consumer incomes. Since, however, the scope for such works is somewhat limited it is probably wiser to keep them strictly as a depression resource and abandon them immediately on the revival of prosperity.[1]

This type of public works is closely akin to that particularly emphasized in the liberal programme and the multiplier analysis. It concentrates on employment and pins its faith to the increased expenditure thus generated as a recovery measure. Possible difficulties if it is attempted to apply it on a large scale have already been pointed out. On a more limited programme, however, it appears to be a necessary item in any cyclical expenditure policy. There is, however, another type of public works which if properly carried out has a much more direct effect on investment. It aims first at stimulating industry and trusts that increased activity will expand employment.

The crux of the matter is, that after the crash the demand for the constructional industries in the lines which they have been supplying is for the time being as good as dead. It seems very unlikely that any reasonable moderate monetary stimulus can rapidly revive a satiated demand of this type. But all lines of capital equipment have not been expanding with equal force in the boom. It should not be impossible to find some for whom the pace has been too hot during the period of high costs and interest rates, but who are ready for new investment as soon as these fall. The role of the government is to make conditions secure and attractive for all such candidates. If the central government itself controls large resources the task is so much the easier. Thus the Swedish government was able to put into operation in the 1931 depression the electrification of its important line from Göteborg to Stockholm. The government can also use the investment opportunities of local authorities. But even if the scope of these is also somewhat limited, it still has a third channel open. It can directly stimulate private investment—for instance, by guaranteed loans—the Railway Finance Corporation is an excellent example. It can also by monetary, fiscal, and publicity policy expand the home market in a number of less direct ways.

This, however, brings us to the first fundamental difficulty in the way of what may be called an ideal programme of trade-cycle expenditure. Such prevention and cure of depression inevitably relies on home-market policy. It is very little use attempting to

[1] Apparently Sweden employs a system of centrally aided relief works as part of regular cyclical policy, cf. Childs, *Sweden, The Middle Way.*

stimulate international trade during depression. Owing to the fact that depression occurs at different moments in different parts of the world, it may even seem advisable temporarily to offer some protection to the home market, even if this reduces what little volume of international trade remains. Both the monetary policy which is a necessary accompaniment to expenditure policy, and the increase in activity which is a measure of its success, will put some strain on the exchanges, and they may also need to be protected by fiscal policy. Difficult as it may be to avoid such measures it is important to realize that they are a definite evil. Development of the home market implies some degree of economic isolation. For a country like England, whose economy is founded on international trade, this probably means that complete recovery by even the most skilful manipulation of the home market is impossible. This is the reason for hoping that conditions will arise in which it will be possible to remove from international trade and foreign lending whatever shackles have been imposed. Such action would tend to prolong the period of prosperity in two ways: by mitigating the rise in home prices it would make the pace of the upswing less hot, and by widening the market it would extend the opportunities for investment as the home market becomes satiated.

The time factor presents the second fundamental difficulty of an ideal cyclical expenditure policy. It is much easier to get public works going in the upswing than in depression—there is more money to start them with, and they are encouragingly effective. More money is available both because tax receipts are higher and because an effective policy stands a much better chance of being continued by parliament. It therefore inspires more confidence at the outset. Now government action may be ineffective because an inappropriate fiscal or monetary policy is being followed. Care must naturally be taken to see that there are no obstacles on these accounts. But in a bad depression it cannot be hoped that visible results will soon be forthcoming. At the bottom of the downswing the Treasury View is probably more nearly a universal truth than at any other time. It does not follow that because public investment is apparently ineffective an active government policy at an early stage is the less necessary. The business of preventing collapse and preparing the field for new investment may have to go on underground for some time, but if it is self-confident it will almost certainly be effective in the end.

Here, however, we meet the final difficulty. Successful public works policy calls on the one hand for long-period continuous planning, and on the other for swift and decisive action. It does appear that in this country at any rate the machinery for either is very inadequate. Is it conceivable, however, that it might be developed? So far indeed no country[1] has succeeded in carrying out a theoretically ideal public works policy on a large scale, so that it is not possible to make up the correct prescription from past history. Nevertheless, on the experience of the last depression some points seem definitely to be established. If the government clearly announces the objectives of its own expenditure (as well as of its monetary policy), and obviously plans public investment with these in view, it can hardly fail to influence the tone of entrepreneurs. As things are here at present, a guaranteed loan to the railways is probably more effective than direct government action. Past experience has led entrepreneurs to believe that direct government expenditure policy will be short-lived and vacillating. Consequently they are not prepared to risk much. Again, if local authorities had on the one hand a clear lead from the centre, and on the other full liberty to borrow for new investment when interest rates were low, it is probable that the timing of public investment would become somewhat more appropriate. Just how much improvement might be expected demands a detailed analysis of past experience, and of the relative effectiveness of the different methods of stimulus available.

The question remains, however, whether some more drastic development of the available tools should not be attempted. We have already mentioned the possibility of a body after the model of the Australian Loan Council to ensure a rapid and effective borrowing policy. Even more essential is the development of a long-period planning service. Here the Ministry of Transport might play an important part without much extension of function. But roads are not the only possible form of depression development. It is probable that the local authorities on whom the task of execution would presumably fall, would have neither the time nor the personnel for such work. But they could make valuable suggestions. The experience of the Commissioner for Special

[1] It is worth noting, on the one hand, that a very wide definition of Public Works was adopted in the American New Deal, and on the other, that the big Swedish £8 m. programme was never put into operation. Cf. Childs, op. cit.

Areas, however, suggests a possible method—a permanent government public works planning office. Centrally it would have to work in conjunction with the Ministry of Health, the Treasury, and other relevant departments. Locally it would have to keep in close touch with the work of counties and county boroughs. Without some such extensions as these there seems little hope that the timing of public investment in future booms and depressions will be any more appropriate than it has been in the past.

But we are brought up in the end against the consideration with which we started. Expenditure policy can only hope to cover part of the field in any case. The difficulties of carrying it out successfully in this country appear to be somewhat formidable. There is the more need that fiscal and monetary policy should also be appropriate.

PART II

TAXATION

'Then better sure it charity becomes
To tax directors, who (thank God) have plums.'

POPE.

XIV

THE TAX STRUCTURE

THE examination of social and economic expenditure tends to give the impression of a period of easy and popular expansion rather than one of abnormal strain. The weight of unemployment expenditure alone suggests the budgetary troubles that were going on beneath the surface. As we move to the other side of the balance sheet, however, the exceptional character of the period becomes very noticeable. Indeed, so abnormal were fiscal and monetary conditions in the first decade after the war that it might appear that their study would be lacking in permanent interest. This would be too hasty a conclusion. They afford an exceptionally interesting illustration of the difficulty of preventing the different parts of social and financial policy from frustrating and neutralizing each other. Further, the fiscal effect of the war was even in 1936 far from being fully worked out. Income tax at 4s. 9d. was clearly related to the war-time 6s. rather than to the pre-war 1s. 2d. The main war-time increases in indirect taxation had never been seriously modified. The fiscal change back to pre-war relations was thus very much less than for instance the recovery that had taken place in prices and interest rates.

The obvious cause of the failure to return to a more normal tax structure was the recurrent difficulty which chancellors experienced in making the budget balance. This difficulty is apparent, not only in the occasional deficits recorded, but in the small amount of debt repayment accomplished, and the devious methods used to effect a nominal balance. It is possible that when incomes are fluctuating violently an unnecessarily heavy burden may be imposed by too great insistence on an annual balance. This is a question which we shall have to investigate at a later stage.[1] But it may be assumed

[1] Cf. Chap. XVII.

S

that in the longer period the budget *must* balance. Uncontrolled recourse to borrowing is obviously contrary to any principles of sound finance.

As far as balancing the budget is made difficult by causes on the revenue side there seem to be two possibilities: either the tax structure is not adjusted to take advantage of the distribution of wealth, or something like the limits of taxable capacity are being approached. Cases have not been wanting in the history of this and other countries in which recurrent budget difficulties appear to have been mainly due to the failure to establish for instance a general enforcable income tax. But it is extremely difficult to give any precise meaning to the concept of the limit of taxable[1] capacity, except in the sense that powerful classes in the community may be unwilling to have particular taxes raised beyond a certain point and consequently withdraw factors of production under their control. It might perhaps be conceded that the limit has been over-reached if it could be shown that the national income had been damaged as a result of revenue demands. Well-authenticated long-period examples of this are not unknown to history. But except in the final stages it would be very difficult to identify them at the time. It is somewhat less difficult to detect when individual taxes have been pushed to a point where they are depressing to spending or investing, or where they are frankly wasteful. If it can be shown that equally remunerative alternatives were not available to the taxing authority, this provides measure of a relative limit of taxable capacity, although it may depend principally on psychological reaction rather than on a shortage of funds in any real sense.

Broadly the tax structure of a country is fixed. If revolutionary change is to be avoided it takes years to switch over from being a commodity-tax state, or from relying mainly on monopoly revenues, to being an income-tax economy. But in our period there have been two minor movements of considerable importance —a swing away from commodity taxes and back again. It has to be investigated whether the cause of the change was predominantly political, or whether it was closely related to the difficulty of balancing the budget.

The broad movements in the yields of the different parts of the

---

[1] Difficulties of identifying the limits of taxable capacity do not of course apply to the concept of changes in the *relative* taxable capacity of different economic groups in the community. Cf. Chap. XVIII.

tax structure are shown on Diagram I. Hitherto we have followed
traditional usage and spoken of direct and indirect taxes, or, as
occasion demanded, of commodity taxes. These distinctions are
completely satisfactory neither for economic nor distributional
analysis. It seems desirable therefore to adopt at this stage a more
convenient classification. Accordingly the tax structure is divided
into (i) income and capital taxes, (ii) consumption taxes, and
(iii) miscellaneous levies, mainly extra-budgetary, classed together
for convenience. This division is useful from the economic point
of view. For distributional analysis it is necessary to make the
further distinction in group (ii) between taxes on commodities
and services which are purchased roughly in proportion to income, from those where revenue is mainly raised from buyers with
small incomes. It is not possible to make the classification completely watertight without dividing the receipts of certain taxes,
where levies of differing economic significance are classed together.
For instance, stamp duties is a sales tax on a variety of transactions.
But a very large part of the receipts (and in years of prosperity a
quite predominant part) are due to capital transactions. The affini-
ties of the tax are therefore mainly with the income and capital
group. Although the data for dividing up the receipts of levies
with a multiple economic significance are usually available, it has
not seemed worth while to carry through the operation in detail.

The first two groups are divided by a real economic difference.
Income and capital taxes are those whose yields react strongly to
changes in business sentiment and activity, and where the rates
levied in turn react on the business situation. The importance of
short-period variations of yield is apparent from the diagram, even
without correction for changes in rates of levy. The second group
comprises taxes on the consumption of commodities (including
periodic licences on durable commodities) and of services. It
covers consumption in a broad sense, not necessarily by the final
consumer. As argued below there is not much distinction of
analytical importance between taxes on consumers' goods and
taxes on producers' goods; there is therefore no reason for classing
them separately at this stage.[1] The particular effects of the various
taxes in group (iii) are discussed elsewhere. They are brought
together here for convenience in viewing the tax structure as
a whole. Except for local rates their pre-war counterpart was

[1] But see below, p. 262, for a discussion of the difference.

THE TAX STRUCTURE

negligible. Such social insurance as was in force in 1913 required a levy of less than £20 m.

The first step in evaluating the effect of taxes is to observe what changes in rates lie behind variations in yields. In group (i) if we neglect miscellaneous inland revenue receipts, swollen in the early twenties by experimental profits taxes which were not retained, it is clear that the main differences between the pre- and post-war situation are the larger part played since the war by the income taxes, especially surtax,[1] and to a less extent by stamp duties. The post-war income and capital-tax structure was in fact largely determined by the fiscal expedients used in the war.

Before the war the standard rate of income tax was 1s. 2d. in the £. Since the war, except for a few years during Mr. Churchill's chancellorship, it has never been below 4s. 6d.[2] The standard rate, however, is in itself less important than the graduation of effective rates when income tax and surtax are considered jointly. The standard rate is actually only paid by companies on their undistributed profits, and by a group of surtax payers (numbering about 15,000 in 1935) at the point where allowances and progressive rates cancel out at the standard level. The company contribution has been estimated at a rough 10 per cent. of total receipts. The general plan of progression has not been essentially altered since the war. Effective rates increase sharply at about the surtax minimum, but flatten out slightly at about £5,000–£10,000. The effective differential in favour of earned income and the allowances for dependants, which are of great importance for small incomes, gradually disappear as the taxpayer moves up the scale. Although the main upward movement in rates had already taken place by 1920, there has been a considerable stiffening in the upper ranges since:[3]

| Income group | Additional charge per £ in excess of lower range | | | | |
	1920–1 to 1924–5	1925–6 to 1928–9	1928–9	1929–30	1930–1
	s. d.	s. d.	s. d.	s. d.	s. d.
£2,000 to £2,500 ·	1 6	0 9	0 9	1 0	1 0
£30,000 to £40,000 ·	6 0	6 0	6 0	6 6	7 1
£50,000 and over ·	6 0	6 0	7 6	7 6	8 3

[1] For convenience I shall speak throughout of surtax when super or surtax is in question.　　[2] Changes in standard rates are shown on p. 246 (n.).

[3] Rates shown are standard, not effective rates. The rates given for 1930–1

In the death duties, on the other hand, the more important movement came after 1920. Receipts at the end of the war were lower relatively to the rest of the group than they had been in 1913. Before the war the maximum rate of estate duty was 15 per cent., payable on estates of £1 m. By the end of the war the percentage had been increased to 20. In the post-war decade, however, this levy was extended downwards to estates of £110,000. On the larger estates it was made to increase rapidly, reaching 35 per cent. at £1·5 m., and above that 40 per cent. In 1930 a still higher progression was introduced, reaching 50 per cent. at £2·5 m. The revenue now relies on the death duties to bring in some £80 m. In 1920 the receipt was £8·5 m. less than super tax, in 1935 it was £30 m. more. No tax except the motor duties has shown such a large increase, either absolutely or proportionately.

Consumption taxes were also made to bear their part in financing the war. The most important change was the heavy increase in the rates on the two most important items in the group—the liquor and tobacco duties. In 1913 these two had brought in under £60 m. In 1920 the yield had risen to £260 m. A few additional customs and excise duties had also been imposed, including increased levies on common articles of food. Of these the worst sufferer was sugar, which was made to yield three times as much in 1920 as it had done in 1913. The only new consumption tax of any importance was the duty on entertainments which yielded nearly £12 m. in 1920. Post-war chancellors continued to make the fullest use of the more important war-time expansions. The tobacco taxes, which had been given a final increase in 1920, were left at war levels. Both in 1927 and 1931, the two years when the needs of the exchequer were greatest, they were further raised. A still greater strain was put on the alcohol duties. In 1920 taxes on spirits, beer, and wine were all raised to an extent estimated to yield an additional £57 m. This followed increases calculated to bring in £27 m. and £52 m. respectively in the two preceding years. In 1923 the beer duty was slightly reduced, but even then it was thirteen times above the pre-war level. Ominously, however, receipts were only seven times as great. There were further increases in liquor duties in 1927, 1930, and 1931 (the latter a rise of 30 per cent.). Receipts were £75·7 m. in 1930, but only £73·7 m.

are as fixed by the Finance Act 1931. They were subsequently increased by 10 per cent. (retrospectively) by the Economy (Finance No. 2) Act of that year.

in 1932. Diminishing returns had clearly set in. In 1933 there was a moderate remission of the beer duty, estimated to cost £14 m. Actually it cost rather more than the estimate the first year, but receipts recovered in the following year. Industrial recovery had revealed some resiliency in the tax, but it was clear that its former position as a pillar of the revenue was not being regained.

The relative failure of the alcohol duties was not the only gap in the revenue that chancellors had to face. Contemporary social philosophy clearly marked out a path of tax remission in order to lighten the burdens on small incomes. Snowden naturally proceeded farthest in this direction, but Mr. Baldwin and other chancellors also subscribed to the policy. Mr. Churchill's zeal was almost a match for Snowden's.

Concessions on common articles of diet and working-class luxuries began immediately after the war. In 1919 the duty on cheap seats at entertainments was relaxed. In 1922 the tea, coffee, and cocoa duties were reduced by a third. The following year the table-waters tax was halved. In spite of its abnormal war increase, however, the sugar duty was not relaxed until Snowden brought it down with a crash in 1924 (from 25s. 8d. to 11s. 8d. per cwt. basic rate). His other concessions included halving the remaining duties on tea, coffee, and cocoa, other remissions of food duties, and further important relaxations of the entertainments tax. The process of concession was continued in 1928 and 1929. Another concession which was introduced soon after the war[1] and proved of considerable economic and financial, although not of social, importance, was the abolition of the tax on motor spirit. The taxation of motoring was not reduced *pari passu* since at the same time vehicle licence duties were revised upwards.

Income-tax concessions were no less important than those on the consumption group. It is hardly too much to say that the changes introduced as a result of the report of the Royal Commission on the Income Tax in 1920 revolutionized the relative weight of the tax on small incomes. Some alleviation of the burden had already been introduced in 1919. The upward tendency of allowances continued unbroken until 1931, and was resumed in 1935. Owing to the fall in prices the reduction of allowances in 1931 still left them of greater value than they had been in 1920, so that ground was lost in a relative rather than in an

---

[1] In 1920. For discussion of this point, see below p. 257.

absolute sense. The concessions were of three types: (i) the fixing of personal allowances (or the exemption limit) at a relatively high figure, and leaving it unaltered when prices fell; (ii) increasing differentiation in favour of earned income; and (iii) increased allowances for dependants. The actual changes are summarized in Table 1 (p. 246). Several of the details are noteworthy. The most valuable item in the list is the earned income allowance. The combined effect of this and the allowances for dependants puts the family man in a materially better position than the rentier bachelor or spinster. The increase in the children's allowances in 1928 and their equalization for all children in 1935, together with the increase in the married persons' allowance in 1935, are some small encouragement to families. They can hardly be very effective, however, as long as the practice of counting husband's and wife's income as one makes it cheaper to remain single. Another point of interest is Snowden's increase of the reduced rate allowance in 1930 and of the earned income differential in 1931, both designed to mitigate the effects of the heavier standard rate imposed in those years.

It is not possible to give more than a rough estimate of the effect of these various concessions. The income-tax changes of 1919 and 1920 were estimated to cause a loss of some £35 m. The only other important revenue reductions in this group were those of 1925, estimated to cost £7 m. and of 1928 £4·5 m. Over the period the proportion of small incomes which were above the exemption limit but which were in fact exempted, increased from about 50 to 56 per cent. The loss to the revenue by the consumption-tax concessions was perhaps slightly less, allowing for those income-tax allowances for which it is impossible to give any reliable estimate. The annual yield of the entertainments tax was reduced by about £10 m. as a result of the changes. The repeal of the inhabited house duty by Snowden cost about £3 m. and the table-water tax about £1 m. At the end of the period the food taxes brought in some £39 m. less than they had done in 1920. Altogether it seems probable that the total loss of revenue by remissions was rather less than the yield of death duties at the end of the period, and rather more than that of surtax. There was a substantial and growing hiatus in the revenue to be filled.

In view of the growing volume of tax remissions and the relative failure of the alcohol duties, chancellors were naturally anxious to

open up new sources of revenue. Unfortunately they were not
very successful in this quest, at least during the post-war decade.
The first experiments were concerned with the attempt to continue
the war-time taxation of profits. The rates of excess profits duty,
which had been halved in 1919, were raised again in 1920, although
as a temporary measure. At the same time a new corporation
profits duty was imposed. The results were not very encouraging.
E.P.D. was expected to bring in an extra £10 m. in 1920 and
an extra £100 m. in a full year. Actual receipts for 1920 were,
however, not above, but more than £70 m. below those of 1919,
in spite of boom conditions. Nevertheless, since the duty brought
in £218 m. and was chiefly responsible for the budget surplus of
the year, it can hardly be counted a failure from the exchequer
point of view. Its industrial effects were less auspicious. The duty
was abolished in 1921, but arrears continued to be slowly and
painfully extracted at the rate of about £2 m. a year, over the
next ten years—a source of expense and irritation both to industry
and to the Inland Revenue. The results of C.P.D. were even more
disappointing. In the first year it brought in £0·7 m., in place of
the (written down) estimate of £2·9 m. The next year it produced
£17·7 m., but this was more than £7 m. less than the (twice written
down) estimate. In 1923 the rate was halved, and the tax was
finally repealed by Snowden in 1924.

In spite of their failure to come up to expectations these attempts
to tax the boom were important, both as a precedent and as a
pioneer excursion into a field which holds decided promise for the
future. Apart from the special needs of the exchequer in the early
twenties and from general considerations of cyclical policy—
which had not at that time been made explicit—there were strong
arguments for attempting to tax profits in 1920. The degree of
prosperity, if not the expansion in itself, was clearly based on government expenditure and monetary policy. During the war the taxation
of excess profits had been both fairly easy and unobjectionable.
Since normal economic activity was at a standstill, large profits,
in whatever industry they were made, were primarily due to the
special conditions created by government expenditure. E.P.D. did
useful work, both in bringing material assistance to the exchequer,
and indirectly by helping to check inflationary tendencies in the
final stages of the war. Had rates been raised at an earlier date
it might have been still more effective. But once the war was over,

conditions altered completely. Profit opportunities began to change with alarming suddenness. The very firms which had been doing best as long as government contracts lasted now frequently found themselves the most high and dry. The exchequer gains were therefore seriously diminished by compensation for losses. With profit changes came capital changes and transfers. It was increasingly difficult to attribute particular profits to particular firms. They were frequently found to have been lost or transferred to other hands before they could be taxed. Moreover, as soon as normal economic differences as to risks and profits began to re-establish themselves, the equal treatment of different industries became more dubious. At the same time the pre-war base normally used for the calculation of excess profits became increasingly inappropriate. It was considerations such as these, no less than the probable expense of refunds where profits were shown to have fallen below pre-war rates, which led to the abandonment of the tax. It is clear that some, but not all, of these difficulties were of a temporary nature due to the peculiarly chaotic conditions of the time.

C.P.D. was designed to side-step some of the difficulties of E.P.D. in peace time. It was a flat-rate tax on all corporation profits (after paying interest on debentures and preference shares). Profits were calculated on the same method as for schedule D of income tax, thus getting round the necessity for either a base date or capital valuations. The first £500 was exempt, and some allowance was made for accidental differences in the capital structure of companies by limiting the duty to 10 per cent. of the balance of profits, thus protecting the high-geared equity share. The duty did not, however, extend to private firms, and this was a fertile source of complaint and inequity. In spite of its specious air of simplicity C.P.D. proved complicated in operation. This may be gauged from the fact that in the first two years there was a difference of £8 m. and £4 m. respectively between assessments and payments, due to the difficulty of collecting arrears and to numerous appeals. A number of accounts were still open in 1929, five years after the final abolition of the duty. C.P.D. was apparently designed as a permanent addition to the tax structure. Public utilities working under a statutory limitation of profits were to be exempted up to 1925, but would have been included thereafter had the tax survived. It was not in operation long enough for any regular policy of cyclical variation of rate to be developed. A profit tax of the C.P.D. form differs only from company income tax in being levied before profits are distributed, and it is pertinent to ask what advantages it possesses over an extension of the accustomed levy. This is a question to which we must return later.[1]

The chancellorship of Mr. Churchill was rich in fiscal experiments. The most original new tax which he sought to impose was the betting duty. It was a dismal failure. Introduced in 1926 with an estimated yield of £6 m., it proved so easy to evade that receipts were only £2·7 m. After a few years the only possible step was taken and it was repealed. The most successful new tax, if it can be called so, was the revival of the petrol duty in the form of the hydrocarbon oils tax. It arouses surprise rather by the tardiness of its adoption than by its success, which might have been deduced from the course of motor-licence duties. Other Churchillian experiments were concerned with the methods of paying taxes rather than with opening up new resources. Thus the period of brewers' rebates was twice reduced, and—a much more serious burden— the dates at which income-tax instalments became payable were altered so as to secure an antedating of receipts to the exchequer. During the year of change particularly, this entailed a considerably greater hardship than a sixpenny rise in rates would have done. This unfortunate device also formed a precedent for Snowden. It would appear from Mr. Churchill's failure to tap any important new sources of revenue, at least until the imposition of the hydrocarbon oils duty, that even the most ingenious of chancellors was conscious of the limits of taxable capacity pressing upon him.

There remained, however, one avenue down which Mr. Churchill never ventured to stray far, but which even in a relatively depressed year has since been made to yield over £40 m. to the exchequer— namely, the device of a protective tariff. The startling reversal in 1931 of the free-trade policy of the nineteenth century is the chief fiscal surprise of the post-war period. It is worth observing just how a tariff revenue became available. It is indeed a fact that from the time of the introduction of the McKenna duties in the war, British import taxes have never been wholly for revenue purposes. It will be recalled that immediately after the war there was a move

[1] Cf. Chap. XVIII, pp. 306 ff.

in favour of a general tariff (cf. Austen Chamberlain's budget speech of 1920). The only result had been a crop of stillborn 'safeguarding duties'. But the idea of imparting relief to industry through a new method of increasing consumption taxes remained. It appealed especially to entrepreneurs on whom the high rates of income tax bore heavily after the collapse of the post-war boom. Mr. Neville Chamberlain brought forward the proposal again more formally in 1923, in connexion with the imperial conference, but this time it was turned down if anything more decisively, and the labour party returned to office on a specifically free-trade vote. With the establishment of Mr. Churchill at the exchequer, how-ever, the scene changed. Year by year, from 1925 onwards, he proceeded to introduce a series of little independent import duties. It was not a general tariff policy; in so far as there was a long-period policy about it at all it was intended to be a cure for parti-cular pools of unemployment.[1] Only on one occasion did he admit a duty to be frankly protective. Mr. Lloyd George not unjustly stigmatized the duties as a 'kind of kangaroo protection, jumping here and there, making little advances here and there'. From the fiscal point of view the total receipts of the new duties were not very significant, but psychologically there can be no doubt that they helped to pave the way for a general tariff as soon as the opportunity occurred.

The breaking of the 1929 boom provided the occasion. Once again high income-tax rates were felt as an intolerable burden. Talk of a moderate (10 per cent.) tariff began to crystallize. But even then it required many strands before the fabric was complete. Besides the desire to ease the direct tax schedule, it was ingeniously argued by some economists that since the reduction of wage rates was impossible on political grounds, and was in any case a defla-tionary measure which must recoil upon itself, a simple method of securing the same end of a reduction in labour costs was to raise prices by a tariff, and so improve profit prospects at the other end. Although this argument was too subtle to make a wide ap-peal, its support strengthened the hands of the protectionists. In the summer of 1930 it was common knowledge[2] that even among

[1] For instance the button duty imposed in 1928 was intended to bring relief to a small industry (employing some 3,600 workers, of whom the greater part were unemployed). The troubles of the industry were subsequently found to be due to a change in fashion, not to an increase in imports.

[2] Cf. Snowden's *Memoirs*.

the labour party leading members were in favour of a 10 per cent. tariff, both in the hopes that it would help the unemployment situation and in the suspicion that it would prove a useful election plank. Public opinion was thus steadily moving away from free trade. All that was needed was to show that the volume of imports was a pressing danger.

During 1930 and 1931 there was an increase in imports of some magnitude. For this there were at least three good reasons: the earlier collapse of the boom in some countries, bringing their prices down before British prices had fallen, the increasing instability of the sterling exchange, and intelligent anticipation of a restriction of imports. But all three of these were of a temporary nature, and afforded no permanent argument for tariffs. Nevertheless, the fear of the adverse trade balance, which of all the arguments advanced in favour of protection was probably the weakest, alone proved of sufficient publicity appeal to convert the country. In the end this momentous fiscal change was carried through in the course of a few months, and excited practically no comment. Although England was from 1932 a highly protected country the aggregate exchequer receipts from protective duties did not at first make a very impressive showing, relatively to other sources of revenue. Even in 1935 with recovery in full swing they brought in about £6 m. less than the breakfast-table duties had done on the average from 1920 to 1923. One cause of this is the extent to which home interests were enjoying protection in the form of import quotas which were not reflected in the budget. Another cause was the fall in prices of British imports, due mainly to general depression factors, but occurring after the imposition of the tariff. Exchequer receipts declined more than proportionately to the volume of imports. The result of these factors tended to make tariffs appear unduly innocuous from the distributional standpoint. It cannot be denied that the possibility of increasing consumption taxes in this manner opened up a much-needed new resource to chancellors. But it may be questioned if it was the best or the only source available.

During the post-war decade there was a noticeable tendency for tax receipts to lag behind estimates. This happened too often to be attributed merely to over-optimistic budgeting. There were, however, three important groups of consumption taxes where receipts always proved unexpectedly resilient—the breakfast-table duties, the motor taxes, and the stamp duties. On purely fiscal grounds it would appear that more use might have been made of them. It is therefore pertinent to inquire whether economic and social objections were sufficient to outweigh the needs of the exchequer.

The most unexpectedly resilient part of the tax structure was the breakfast-table duties. The case of sugar illustrates this particularly well. It was argued in 1923 that the revenue could not afford to sacrifice the war-time expansion, and demand for sugar was said to be so inelastic that receipts would fall off *pari passu* with remissions. This proved to be a complete misapprehension. After two reductions of rate demand was still rising. In 1935 consumption was 5 m. cwt. above the boom year 1929. But the exchequer was only partially benefiting from this, since with the extension of imperial preferences a considerable proportion of demand had been transferred to Empire sources. As might be expected from the increasing age of the population, consumption of tea expanded even faster. The duty had been reduced in 1922 and 1924, and finally repealed in 1929. It was reimposed by the national government in 1932. In 1935 the tax was bringing in £4·1 m. and consumption was 15 per cent. above the boom year 1928, when the duty was negligible. In 1936 rates were again raised and once more estimates were exceeded. The history of the reduction of the coffee and cocoa duties was similar. Reduction in tax rates in 1924 was followed by less than proportionate reduction of commodity consumption, and in every case receipts exceeded estimates. The history of the entertainments tax was similar. Reduction of the duty on cheap tickets in 1924 was estimated to cost £5 m. Actually the decline was only £0·5 m. While there are naturally distributional objections to heavy taxes on common articles of diet, there is little objection to moderate duties. It would appear from the extraordinary resiliency of receipts that rather smaller reduction of rates would have afforded desirable relief to the taxpayer, while at the same time safeguarding a steady source of revenue.

The yield of motor-vehicle licences rose from £10 m. to £16 m. between 1920 and 1925, rates of duty remaining substantially the same. In 1926 the taxation of commercial vehicles was heavily increased. The increases were expected to bring in £1·5 m. the first year and £2·4 m. in a full year. The realized gains were £3 m. and £6 m. respectively. The tax on hydrocarbon oils[1] was imposed

---

[1] Including of course motor-spirit. Petrol is estimated to be responsible for about three-fourths of the receipts of the Oil Tax.

in 1928. It immediately brought in more than £1 m. above its estimate. In 1931 the rate was twice raised with an estimated total gain to the exchequer of £15·8 m. But the realized gain was £20 m., in spite of deepening depression. The reduction of motor-vehicle licence duties in 1934 was expected to cost £4 m. Actually the fall in receipts was less than £1 m. There are no distributional objections to taxing motors, and it does not appear that chancellors were—or need have been—greatly swayed by economic objections.[1] Probably the main reason why this fertile source of revenue was relatively neglected during the twenties was the feeling that motor-tax receipts were in a sense reserved for road development, and were not available for general exchequer purposes. In the end, however, no notice was taken of this understanding, private motors were taxed as a luxury, and the petrol duty was reimposed to finance derating. It might just as well never have been removed.

The modern importance of stamp duties is due to the change in the method of financing long-term investment,[2] and to the growth of the limited liability company. Both movements have been very much accelerated since the war. If we include stamps on the issue of new securities, transfer of shares, and on bills, cheques, receipts, &c., over 60 per cent. of the receipts is normally collected on financial transactions. It is possible that the greatly increased importance of security business as a source of revenue was not taken account of before the stock-exchange boom of 1928–9. Receipts commonly exceeded estimates. It is significant that the duties received somewhat scanty discussion from the Colwyn Committee.[3] The stamp duties are now, however, by no means a negligible part of the revenue. In a reasonably good year they bring in at least £30 m. There seems little reason why more use should not be made of them. There are no distributional objections to raising the rates, and the economic arguments[4] are probably favourable rather than the reverse.

But finally it must be admitted that the expenditure bill set chancellors a very difficult problem. The revenue raised in taxes was large relatively to the national income, both in contrast to the pre-war relation and in view of its somewhat stationary condi-

---

[1] Cf. discussion of the effect of motor taxation, Chapter XV, p. 257.
[2] Cf. Chap. XVI, p. 259.
[3] *Report of Committee on National Debt and Taxation*, pp. 199 ff.
[4] Cf. Chap. XVIII, p. 306.

tion. Had it not been for the possibility of maintaining high standard rates of income tax, and of continually raising surtax rates without fear of serious opposition; had it not been above all for the existence of a comparatively untapped resource in the death duties, it is conceivable that a revenue crisis of some magnitude might have arisen. Broadly speaking the revenue was maintained by imposing heavy rates on a small number of proved sources. There is therefore a strong case for supposing that whatever economic effects these taxes normally have must have been considerably increased. It is therefore pertinent to inquire into their probable effects in some detail.

TABLE I

Principal income-tax deductions in force, 1920–36[1]

	1920-1 to 1922-3	1923-4	1924-5	1925-6 to 1927-8	1928-9 to 1929-31	1930-1	1931-2 to 1933-4	1934-5	1935-6	1936-7
(1) Earned income allowance maximum allowance	1/10th £200	1/10th £200	1/10th £200	1/6th £250	1/6th £250;	1/6th £250	1/5th £300	1/5th £300	1/5th £300	1/5th £300
(2) Age allowance (65+ if income below £500)	..	..	..	1/6th	1/6th	1/6th	1/5th	1/5th	1/5th	1/5th
(3) Personal allowance:										
Married	£225	£225	£225	£225	£225	£225	£150	£150	£170	£180
Single	£135	£135	£135	£135.	£135	£135	£100	£100	£100	£100
(4) Incr. for wife's earnings	£45	£45	£45	£45	£45	£45	£45	£45	£45	£45
(5) Dependant's allowance:										
(a) Housekeeper (before 1925 if looking after children) . (c) Unmarried persons' female relative in charge of children	£45	£45	£60	£60	£60	£60	£50	£50	£50	£50
(d) Children, first	£45	£45	£60	£60	£60	£60	£50	£50	£50	£50
others	£36	£36	£36	£36	£60	£60	£50	£50	£50	£60
(under 16, or as long as being educated)	£27	£27	£27	£27	£50	£50	£40	£40	£50	£60
(e) Aged dependent relatives	£25	£25	£25	£25	£25	£25	£25	£25	£25	£25
(6) Reduced rate on first part of income	2s. 6d. on £225	2s. 3d. on £225	2s. 3d. on £225	2s. 0d. on £225	2s. 0d. on £225	2s. 0d. on £250	2s. 6d. on £175	2s. 3d. on £175	1s. 6d. on £135	1s. 7d. on £135

[1] In addition to allowances for Life Insurance payments and compulsory State Pension contributions. Standard rates of Income Tax were: 1920–1, 6s.; 1922, 5s.; 1923–4, 4s. 6d.; 1925 to 1929, 4s.; 1930, 4s.; 1931 to 1933, 5s.; 1934–5, 4s. 6d.; 1936, 4s. 9d.; (1937, 5s.).

XV

THE ECONOMIC EFFECTS OF TAXES

TAXATION of the order to which we have grown accustomed in post-war Britain inevitably has important economic effects. Some of these are by-products of social policy, and can only be regarded as undesirable if they tend to frustrate such policy. Others may be condoned as the least cost method of raising the necessary revenue, although their effects may not be altogether desirable. Others may have effects which are not recognized at all because they are indirect. Just on this account they require the most careful watching. It is the duty of the economist to draw attention to all such possible effects. To do this fully requires a complicated statistical technique, and would in any case be inappropriate here. But to make some inquiry into economic effects is perhaps the most important part of our task on the revenue side. This involves considering both the effects of particular taxes considered separately, and their cumulative effect when set in the background of the tax structure. It would be hardly necessary to say, if the matter had not often been neglected, that—especially in the case of taxes such as income tax and death duties—the analysis of tax effects makes very little sense unless some assumption is also made as to the manner in which the government spends the revenue. At this stage, however, we are primarily concerned with tax effects in so far as they can be isolated.

The merits of particular taxes have been extensively, it might be held exhaustively, discussed. But the successive recognition of new phenomena as economic analysis progresses, on one side, and the steady enlargement of the field of taxation on the other, necessitates periodic revision. Adam Smith's four canons—of *ability* to pay, *certainty* of levy, *convenience* of time and manner of levy, and *economy* in burden and collection—must still form the basis of judgement. Indeed, they have acquired a deeper meaning with the growing complexity of the tax structure. Other outstanding contributions of nineteenth-century theory were Ricardo's demonstration of the innocuousness of taxes on economic rent, and Marshall's of the relative advantage of taxing commodities of inelastic demand. On the whole, however, nineteenth-century economists tended either to regard tax theory as a convenient tool for illus-trating the working of propositions in pure economic theory, or to concentrate on the distributional, as distinct from the economic, effects of taxes. Since the social effect in which these writers were primarily interested depends ultimately on economic movements arising from the fiscal system, this was to neglect an important aspect of their subject.

Income tax formed an exception to the general lack of interest in economic effects. An extensive literature on the double taxation of savings grew up, based on the work of Professor Einaudi[1] and Irving Fisher. The Colwyn Committee[2] also made a bold if not very profound attempt to analyse in general terms the economic effects of a number of income and capital taxes. Professor Pigou had drawn attention to the need for distinguishing tax effects according to period.[3] Thus for the analysis of some problems we may have to take into account (1) the initial psychological reactions to the imposition of the tax (or change in rate or tax); (2) the short period effects of paying the tax before substantial shifting of the tax burden or adjustment of production can take place; and (3) long period working out. But both Professor Pigou's analysis and the Colwyn discussion were mainly in terms of what may be called a normal reaction. There was no discussion of the fact that the same tax may have very different effects in times of moderately good trade when no violent movements either of expansion or contrac-tion are taking place, from those when a strong cyclical movement is present. In Chapter XVIII we shall be particularly concerned with tax effects and fiscal manipulation as a part of general cyclical policy. It is necessary to bear in mind from the beginning, how-ever, that particularly in the case of income and capital taxes, initial and short period effects may be completely different, for the same tax, according to the state of trade.

It is significant that all modern tax structures are mixed. What-ever the theoretical attractions of a single-tax system, its practical application has not found supporters. The British structure is indeed relatively simple. It makes very little use of two types of tax much in vogue abroad. Stamp duties are the only sales tax

[1] Cf. especially Einaudi, *Contributa alla ricerca dell' ottima imposta*. Further references are given in Guillebaud, 'Income Tax and the Double Taxation of Saving', *E.J.* 1935.
[2] *Report of the Committee on National Debt and Taxation*, pp. 106 ff.
[3] Pigou, *A Study in Public Finance*.

of any importance, and rates the only property tax—unless we wish to include death duties in this category. But even the British structure contains a variety of income, and a very large number of consumption taxes. It differs from others in two respects—in placing chief reliance on a few lines only, and even more decidedly in the great weight given to income tax (including surtax) and death duties. It will therefore be convenient to start by examining the effects of these two levies.

On the score of convenience, and ability to pay, a graduated income tax gets very high marks indeed. Especially when tax is deducted at the source both the Inland Revenue and the taxpayer are relieved of trouble, and evasion is minimized. From the distributional point of view it has the further advantage that its incidence can be calculated with fair accuracy and fitted naturally into the scheme of social policy. But the overwhelming arguments in its favour are economic. Provided that economic conditions are normal, and that the burden does not transcend a certain point, it is probably possible to raise a larger amount of revenue without disturbance in this way than in any other. This is due in the first place to the fact that income tax is paid only on positive earnings, and thus differs from a property tax such as rates, where a fixed amount must be paid whatever income may be. Secondly, income as it accrues is not normally earmarked as between its several uses—consumption, investment, and cash holding. Normally therefore the burden will be spread among these uses, so that there need be no shift in their proportions, and no considerable reduction in any one. To these advantages must now be added the practical absence of initial effects. There was a time in the nineteenth century when a rise in income tax—even the very existence of the tax—produced the very worst psychological reaction. Having survived a 6s. levy in the war period with relatively little damage, it hardly seems possible to frighten the British capitalist with any lesser obligation.

When, however, rates are high in relation to income, the innocuous effects of income tax become very much more doubtful. Normally the effect of taxing income must be somewhat deflationary, since it will cause some curtailment of investment or consumption or of both. When tax rates are high the net return on investment is appreciably diminished, and the relative advantages of holding cash increased. The nearer the rates on deposit (or other safe and liquid forms of holding cash) to the expected return to investment, the greater the incentive to refrain from taking the risks of investment. Such a convergence between the rate of return on investment and on more liquid holdings may occur for a number of reasons, as was evidenced in England in the late twenties. It is, however, a usual accompaniment of depression, and it is then that high income tax rates become most dangerous. A particular manifestation of the reluctance to undertake investment is the curtailment of replacement for depreciation and obsolescence. In theory it should be possible to allow adequate rebates to avoid this difficulty. In practice, however, accounting difficulties have proved insurmountable.

Note. The effect of income tax on investment was discussed at length in the Colwyn Committee literature. In so far as the discussion got beyond the effects on saving (a concept which was used in a manner which fails to distinguish between investment and cash holding and is mainly of very long-period relevance), the emphasis was laid on the effect of income tax on risky investments rather than on the risk of investment (cf. D. H. Robertson, 'The Colwyn Committee, the Income Tax and the Price Level', *E.J.* 1927) (i.e. the attractiveness of the chance of a high gain is disproportionately reduced by the prospect of losing a large part of it in taxation). The general proposition, of which this is a particular case, seems to me even more important. Mr. Robertson's argument applies with particular force to cyclical conditions, although he appears to have had in mind mainly normal conditions.

As a result of the deflationary effects of income tax the funds available for investment are reduced. This must tend to raise the rate of interest. It does not follow, however, that in practice there will be any visible movement in official rates. What is reduced is rather the effectiveness of the rate—the amount of investment that will be undertaken, given the rate. Indeed, there may be in this a force tending to offset the rise in rates. The actual movement depends mainly on the state of the trade cycle—at least if we neglect the possible effects of monetary policy.

It has been argued that income tax tends to increase consumption relatively to 'saving' (which must here be understood to include investment and cash holding), since spending evades double taxation—on profits and on their fruits when reinvested. When this reaction occurs the first effect would naturally be a tendency to increase employment as a result of the change in the rate of expenditure. Subsequently the national income in real terms would tend to be lower than it would otherwise have been, owing to the curtailment of investment. If the movement persisted, interest rates might tend to move permanently on to a higher plane. This argument appears to be mainly of long-period or normal relevance. There can be little expectation—or hope—in depression at any rate, that a rise in income tax will stimulate consumer spending. Nor does it seem very likely that it will have this effect to any important degree during the boom when the incentive to invest is strong.

It thus appears that generally speaking the contention that income tax is the most innocuous of levies is well founded. There is, however, evidently a limit above which it may become dangerous even in normal times (assuming that it is combined with a highly progressive surtax). In depression it may have seriously deflationary effects. On the other hand, it may exert some restraining influence in a boom. There is, therefore, a strong case for giving income tax an important weight in the tax structure, with the proviso that it may be wise to vary it to meet cyclical conditions.

Apart from an incentive to curtail investment which may arise on psychological grounds, there is little in income or surtax which hinders the realization of big incomes. This conclusion, however, does not necessarily hold good in the case of death duties. Not only are accumulated savings confiscated, but the steep progression of the levy tends to equalize income distribution. This implies a reduction in the number of those incomes where a high proportion is saved, and hence a decline in the proportion of the national income which is saved by individuals. Hence it is probable that in the long period death duties have a considerably greater tendency to check investment and raise the rate of interest than income tax. Nevertheless, death duties have certain economic advantages apart from their obvious distributional attractions. Initial and all psychological effects are as low as they are likely to be for any tax bringing in a comparable revenue, since no taxpayer finds his own immediate prospects adversely affected. On the other hand they may lead to reinvestment losses where the capital has to find a new investor. There may also be considerable loss in withdrawing funds already invested to pay the duty, particularly if they are in a form such as real estate which is not easily realizable. Death duties thus do not get very high marks on grounds of economy.

The ultimate effect of taxation, and particularly of income and capital taxes, depends, however, on the use the government makes of the revenue. If receipts are not used to bring in as large a return as they would have done in the hands of the taxpayers, then the real national income will suffer, although it may of course be more evenly distributed. It has sometimes been contended that 'community capital decumulation' will occur if the state does not reinvest an amount equal to total death duties.[1] This may be true, but the whole situation must be considered: (i) the net return on the capital before the death occurred, (ii) any loss in earning power arising from liquidation caused by the tax, (iii) the net return from the government's use of the funds it receives, and (iv) the net return on the remainder as reinvested by the successors. The last two may equal the first two in some cases if the government invests more and in others less than the tax receipts. Similarly, in the case of income tax the correct comparison is between the use made of the funds by the state and the opportunities available and likely to be taken by the taxpayers. Our investigations into public investment suggest that the British government has not had either much opportunity for or shown much activity in normal investment. It is thus not unlikely that, as things are, the combined effects of death duties and public expenditure has so far been unfavourable to total investment. On the other hand, the expenditure of revenue from direct taxes in depression will probably be at the expense of cash holding only, and is much more likely to increase investment, whatever the rate of return. The success of the British government in this field has, however, also been very limited up to the present.

There appear thus to be definite limits to the availability of the income and capital tax group, if the real national income is not to be seriously diminished in the future. It is therefore desirable, at any rate from the long-period point of view, to include some proportion of consumption taxes in the structure. Two questions then arise to be answered, first, how can consumption taxes be most innocuously imposed, and, secondly, are there any indications as to the optimum distribution of the tax structure between the two groups?

When we come to the respective merits of different consumption taxes we are on the familiar ground of nineteenth-century public finance discussion. Taxes are usually divided into those on consumers' and those on producers' goods, the latter being universally

[1] Cf. for instance Lindahl, *Die Gerechtigkeit der Besteurung.*

condemned. Since, however, the effect of a tax is normally to check consumption to some extent, both of the taxed and of associated goods, it follows that production cannot be unaffected. Hence every tax is ultimately a tax on production, irrespective of whether the full amount of the tax can be charged in the selling price of the commodity or not. In a closed system there appears to be no essential analytical difference between the two types of tax, hence we may for the moment continue to treat the two forms of taxes together.[1] Is it then more or less a matter of indifference from the economic point of view what commodities are taxed?

Marshall showed conclusively that there were decided advantages in concentrating commodity taxes on goods of inelastic demand. Since, however, his analysis is tied up with the somewhat obscure doctrine of consumer's surplus, it may be clearer if set out in somewhat different terms. We must assume to begin with that the state wishes to collect a certain sum from each taxpayer, but to do so in a manner that will injure him as little as possible. Let us suppose that, initially, a tax is in operation on a certain commodity *a* the demand for which is inelastic. Now let us suppose that in the hope of lightening the real tax burden the state decides to switch over to another commodity *b* also of inelastic demand. What will be the effect on the consumer's budget? A moment's reflection shows that there will be no effect whatever. Since his demand for *b* is inelastic, the consumer will continue to buy the same amount of it as before. For the same reason he will not want to buy any more *a* although its price has fallen. Nothing has occurred to affect the remainder of his outlay.[2] Where a commodity is in absolutely inelastic demand a tax upon it is equivalent to an income tax of the same amount. (It may be noted that, strictly speaking, demand must be inelastic both against price and income, but the elasticity which is directly related to the effect of the tax is naturally that in respect of price.[3])

Now let us suppose that the state instead of choosing *b* decides to tax *c*, a commodity for which demand is elastic. Our consumer will now buy less of *c*. Since by definition he must still make the same contribution, we must assume either that he pays the full tax on his reduced consumption of *c* or that he buys further quantities

---

[1] Cf. discussion on international effects of the tax structure, below.
[2] A tax of this type is akin to the Ricardian tax on rent.
[3] Cf. Allen and Bowley, op. cit., and below, p. 298.

of other taxed commodities, d, e, and f. It is immaterial in which way he chooses to fulfil his tax liability since in any case it is plain that his lay-out of expenditure is altered, and he must now be content with another combination of goods. But it was within his power to purchase this new combination during the time when the tax on a was in operation. Since he did not do so, we must conclude that the new combination represents an inferior choice. The consumer thus suffers a loss over and above the actual money income given up when the tax falls on a commodity of elastic demand.

It can hardly be supposed that sufficient commodities of absolutely inelastic demand can be found to satisfy the tax structure, but the nearer taxed goods approximate to this ideal condition the less will consumers be injured. Demand is more likely to be—and to remain—inelastic if only a narrow range of each consumer's demand is affected, that is if the price of the commodity+tax still represents only a small proportion of total outlay. To bring in sufficiently large receipts to justify the levy therefore it is desirable to choose a commodity of widespread consumption so that only a very low rate of tax will be necessary. This is the justification for taxing common articles of diet and similar goods. Unless commodities can be found the consumption of which is at least proportional to income, it is also essential on distributional grounds to keep rates low if the tax is not to be seriously regressive.

The advantage to producers of taxes on commodities of inelastic demand follows even more directly. Where consumption is not seriously cut down as a result of the tax the total sales of the industry will be only lightly diminished, and the loss to individual producers small. Any readjustments in the purchase of other goods which consumers make will be spread over such a large number of lines that the effect will be negligible. When, however, the demand for the taxed commodity is heavily reduced production must be cut down considerably. The extent of loss to individual firms cannot, however, be stated generally. It depends on such factors as cost conditions, and the possibility of transfer to untaxed lines of production. It is by no means impossible that the elimination of marginal producers on the one hand, and the narrowing of the market on the other, will enable infra-marginal producers to obtain a better control of the market, and actually increase their net profits. The possibility of increasing concentration of production[1] through commodity taxation is one which should not be over-looked, particularly if no method of price control exists to prevent monopolistic exploitation of consumers.

Finally it must be asked whether the exchequer is indifferent to the source from which its revenue comes. There is evidently some advantage for it also in choosing commodities of inelastic demand. The possibility of making close estimates of revenue is convenient and economical. Suppose the chancellor is hesitating between taxes on b and c (commodities with whose demand functions we are already familiar), and that it is estimated that the value of con-sumption is initially the same for both articles. He can calculate at once what rate of tax to impose on b in order to bring in the desired revenue. Unless he makes the mistake of imposing such a heavy tax as actually to alter the character of demand, he can go on im-posing the tax with impunity, year after year. To raise the same revenue by the taxation of c, however, an allowance, difficult to calculate, must be made for the decline in demand after the imposition of the tax.

The primary interest of the state in any particular tax is to obtain a steady or increasing revenue year after year. It is therefore important to have resilient taxes. Resiliency is not, however, a clear indication of inelasticity of individual demand. A case may easily arise in which individual demand has a fairly constant elasticity, but where the number of consumers is steadily increasing. Such a condition will produce resilient revenue, and will obviously be attractive to the state. It is less certain that it offers any real advantage to consumers or producers. It is indeed arguable that consumption and production are less injured where taxation falls on a new want and an expanding industry than where existing consumer budgets or invested capital are disturbed. On the other hand, taxation of new wants may cause the nation to fall behind in the exploitation of a new resource. This may entail a serious loss of satisfaction, and may also become an international drawback.

In the light of these general considerations, is it possible to appraise the relative merits or demerits of the taxes and tax rates composing the post-war British tax structure? The subject urgently calls for the application of modern statistical technique, particularly in order to evaluate the relative importance of price and income factors in determining, on the one hand, reactions to

[1] Cf. for instance the recent history of the brewing trade.

the income and capital taxes, and, on the other, variations in the consumption of taxed commodities. In the absence of such investigation it is only safe to venture a very general application of theoretical argument based on common observation.

It is clear in the first place that the present rates of alcohol duties stand condemned on any but moral grounds. Not only is there evidence of a steady secular decline in demand, but there is a strong probability that individual demand is highly elastic. The initial effect of increased rates supports this view. Further there are obviously a large number of close substitutes for alcoholic consumption. This would tend to make demand elastic even in the absence of a secular trend, indicating that the goods are on the margin of consumption for a large part of the market. There can be no reasonable doubt that the continued exploitation of the duties has hastened the trend and increased the elasticity. Nevertheless, the effect of such small concessions as have been made from time to time indicate that there remains some resiliency in the tax, no doubt a small income elasticity, depending on trade conditions. The reliance of the revenue on the receipts of the alcohol duties is still so great that it can hardly be expected that considerable remission could be contemplated, even if it were shown that it would postpone the extinction of a source of revenue. It does appear, however, that rather larger concessions than have been granted since the war would be beneficial to the revenue both in the short and long period. The moral issue involved in the duties probably makes objective treatment difficult. As it is, however, the alcohol duties provide an excellent illustration of the abuse of a consumption tax. It also provides further evidence of the tendency for long run interests to be sacrificed to the needs of the current budget.

When we turn to consider the other consumption taxes we are at once held up by the absence of reliable statistics of the consumption of taxed commodities by different income groups. The position is further complicated by want of knowledge of the degree to which tax changes are passed on to the consumer—in price changes or variations of the product. Where at least the former is ascertainable—for instance in respect of petrol—there have evidently been considerable differences as between one increase of rate and another.[1] Broadly speaking, the motoring taxes, the new

---

[1] It seems evident that producers are strongly influenced by the state of trade. A unified price policy implies a monopolized market.

protective duties, and the entertainments tax represent commodities which have a number of close substitutes, and hence are likely to have individual demands of fairly high elasticity. As far as the motoring taxes (including the industrial use of hydrocarbon oil) and some of the protective duties are concerned this is true not merely in the consumers' goods market, but in production also. Where these taxes have proved resilient, therefore, secular expansion of demand is likely to have been a more important factor than the condition of individual elasticity of demand. The case of tobacco is rather less clear, since some individuals vary their consumption very considerably—certainly with income and probably also with price. It is likely, however, that they are in the minority. There is good evidence of a strong expansion of the market during the period, due to the growth of smoking among women. This would probably be quite sufficient to account for the resiliency of receipts in face of successive increases of rates.

The effects of the group of motoring and allied taxes present in themselves a situation of great complexity. The hydrocarbon oils tax has at least three types of economic significance—as a tax on petrol, as a tax on heavy-oil using vehicles, and finally on the industrial use of oil for power. Although the secular trend for all these and equally for motor licences is roughly similar—all represent rapidly expanding uses—there are important differences of detail, and a high degree of substitutability between differentially taxed articles. Thus the high taxation of horse-power led to the development of small vehicles. Since small cars have naturally a light petrol consumption this must have made receipts from the petrol duty, when it was reimposed, smaller than they would otherwise have been. The reduction of the horse-power tax in turn led to the substitution of heavier, higher-powered vehicles. The petrol duty was at that time higher than it had been formerly, but nevertheless appeared as a relatively less important factor. Other changes, such as the early improvement of road surfaces and the later congestion of roads, calling for greater powers of acceleration, have also played a part in determining types of road vehicles manufactured in this country. But it seems probable that tax changes have been the most important factor. Similar substitution is evident between heavy-oil and petrol vehicles, and in the commercial use of oil. Any change of rates requires to be considered in relation to this high degree of substitutability, and to possible secondary effects such as road congestion, as well as to more direct effects such as on the introduction of different types of vehicle.

In so far as modern consumption taxes are levied on commodities of elastic demand they have less to recommend them than the old breakfast-table duties. They must be classed as convenient rather than ideal. The change over has mainly been made on distributional grounds. It is probable as a result that the poorest classes make an appreciably smaller contribution to the revenue under the new system than under the old. The relative improvement in their position, which is no doubt very desirable—slight as it is—could, however, have been brought about more directly by expenditure policy. It is at least questionable whether the improvement secured by the change in taxation has been worth the extra loss imposed on other classes of taxpayers by taxing commodities of elastic demand.

Except for the fairly clear case of the alcohol duties and except for a noticeable buoyancy of receipts in certain parts of the field there is little unambiguous evidence to show whether consumption taxes have been levied at the most desirable rates, or whether this part of the tax structure has been over- or under-used in relation to income taxes. It must therefore be asked what indications there are that income and capital taxes have been unduly exploited—in the sense that present rates cannot be maintained with impunity. Here a new difficulty of interpretation arises. Not only is it necessary to distinguish between price and income factors, but also between the effects of monetary and fiscal policy. Income and capital taxes show their effects in the monetary field—in changes in the rates of spending, investing, and holding cash balances, and hence in the rate of interest, in exactly the same way as other monetary phenomena. But the magnitude of their effects is likely to be smaller than changes brought about by direct monetary policy. The smaller effect may be swamped by the larger. To determine the relative weight of these complex factors in any given situation is probably not beyond the powers of statistical technique. There is, however, one difficulty in attempting an analysis at present. The period available for study in which tax rates have been sufficiently drastic to exert an independent influence is still very short. In these circumstances it seems possible to do little more than recall the main points which urgently call for investigation.

The first point to determine is in what sense taxation can be said to have been a cause of the limitation of funds available for investment. Complaints of the difficulty of procuring intermediate loans —funds of medium size for small and new businesses and for medium-term requirements—have been so frequent that it would appear that here at any rate a real shortage has been experienced. It is obvious that there has taken place since the war a change amounting almost to a revolution in the methods of financing industry. The stock exchange has taken the place of the direct private lender. This is of course bound up with the growing use of the company form of industrial organization. Neither the banks nor the stock exchange are, however, very suitable media for providing loans of this medium variety. It is not unnatural therefore that some hiatus in their provision should have been noticeable. But it appears from the reports of such specific public organizations as have been created to deal with the situation (such as Credit for Industry) that a large number of requests have to be turned down owing to the risks involved. Are not these just the investment opportunities which might be undertaken by private individuals in direct contact with the borrowers, but which an organization with public responsibilities could not entertain? It is undeniable, on the one hand, that surtax has limited the accumulation of individual surpluses, and, on the other, that death duties provide a powerful incentive to keep funds in a liquid form where they can be realized at short notice without loss. It is hard to believe that high taxation has not been partly responsible for the shortage of funds. On the other hand, the increased valuation of the risk factor in general and especially in depression, seems likely to have been a more important cause of the substitution of cash holding for general investment.

Another point which has received wide publicity, but to which it is not possible to give any certain answer, is the extent to which heavy taxation of industrial profits has tended to delay the process of modernization of British plant beyond that of her international rivals. This question was only very lightly touched by the Colwyn Committee. Their discussion turned mainly on two points: first, whether high income tax rates in general led to the dissipation of reserves in dividends; and, second, whether the reserves of British companies remaining after the payment of standard income tax could be shown to be inadequate for the needs of industry.

Although the evidence does not appear to have been very exhaustive they concluded that companies were well supplied with liquid reserves in spite of high taxation. They did not discuss, however, whether the reserves were in fact adequately used to replace obsolete and outworn equipment—in other words the possible effects of taxation in encouraging the accumulation of liquid holdings rather than the reorganization of plant. Recent examination of the distribution of company earnings suggests that the proportion of profits distributed differs materially according to the state of the trade cycle,[1] depending on such factors as the rate of expansion of profits and the expected need for borrowing. It seems likely that the state of trade is a much more important factor in determining dividend policy than British income tax which does not aim at discrimination against undistributed profits as such.[2]

There is, however, an *a priori* case for supposing that when tax rates are high they will—given the notorious difficulty of determining adequate rebates for obsolescence—weigh with particular severity on depreciation and renewal funds. In spite of the Colwyn Committee's dictum the complaints of British industrialists on this score were frequent and insistent. The most important debate on the subject took place in 1930 over the increase in the standard rate of income tax. Two propositions were then put forward: first, that reserves applied to plant and machinery should be charged at a rate sixpence below the standard; or alternatively that there should be a reduction on schedule D for sums so expended. The first concession was stated to be likely to cost no more than £2 m., and was very narrowly defeated. The second was estimated to cost £5–6 m. It seems probable that the cost of such changes would be considerably higher when allowance is made for the inevitable delay and litigation, not to mention the incentive created to evade taxation by increasing expenditure. When in 1931 tax rates were once again raised some attempt was made to mitigate the industrial effects by increasing the wear and tear allowance by 10 per cent. and by making more liberal concessions for obsolescence. It was claimed that the value of these remittances was fully equal to 6d. off the standard rate. It is not clear that they did much to meet the main contentions of industrialists.

On the question of industrial reorganization it must be borne

[1] Cf. frequent articles in the *Economist*.
[2] In contrast to American policy under the New Deal.

in mind that during the twenties at one time America and at another Germany experienced conditions considerably more favourable to rationalization than was the lot of British industry. British taxation may have been a hindrance but it was not the only or even the most important cause of the difficulty of modernizing plant. But in the thirties the position has to some extent been reversed, and it is noticeable that the chorus of complaint of this effect of income tax has considerably died down. Nevertheless, the various cost-raising tendencies of a tax on industrial profits cannot safely be ignored in a country which has an important place in world trade to maintain.

The relation between high tax rates and evasion must also be considered. The possibility of evasion spells a limit to taxable capacity which a chancellor cannot afford to neglect, for all that its basis is almost wholly psychological. There is, however, some difficulty in distinguishing cause and effect. When tax receipts lag behind estimates it is natural to suspect evasion, although reduced incomes may be the real culprit. But the success of occasional drives for the payment of arrears—particularly in the early post-war years—suggests that delayed payments were not infrequently a species of evasion. Legislation against evasion has been endemic throughout our period. It has been aimed at such different devices as fictitious companies and insurance premiums, personal trusts and revocable gifts to children, removal of residence or of company registration abroad, and the sale of securities carrying the receipt of tax-liable interest payments. There are grounds for surmising, however, that chancellors have been fighting a losing battle against the ingenuity of taxpayers who believe themselves to be hardly treated—and the ingenuity of their legal advisers.[1]

It is worth noting that certain of these types of evasion may have important economic effects, in so far as they lead to a substitution of corporate for individual saving. When funds are left in the form of company reserves (whether of genuine or fictitious companies) primarily in order to escape surtax there is no particular reason to suppose that they will be used to the best economic advantage. Since they are invested in a particular form it is probable that they will be less generally available than if they had been transferred to the private accounts of the shareholders.

A further aspect of tax evasion which has not yet received

[1] There are no figures on which to base an estimate of the change in evasion.

legislative attention is the practice of making extensive gifts for charitable and educational purposes. While the donor stands to gain little or nothing in money terms, there can be little doubt that the personal satisfaction and prestige accruing are powerful inducements. An allied practice is the bequeathing of residual rights in estates to colleges and other perpetual corporate bodies. The effect of this is to deprive the revenue not merely of surtax on all future investments, but also of death duties in the future. The fall in the birth-rate and the consequent scarcity of successors of near kin makes this practice a matter of growing importance.

It remains to consider more generally the international aspect of British taxation. International comparisons of tax burdens can never be very satisfactory, since apart from the initial difficulty of comparing international standards of living and prices, it is impossible to allow adequately for evasion. Such estimates as have been made, even when compiled with the greatest care and accuracy, still reveal considerable differences of opinion.[1] Broadly, however, it appears that while Great Britain was highly taxed relatively to the United States as late as 1925, the differential had practically disappeared ten years later. On the other hand, there seems to have been little difference in the proportion which the revenue bore to the national income between Britain and her principal trade rivals, either before or after the war.

It is possible, however, to point to particular items in the British tax structure which are definitely disadvantageous to her as a competitor in world markets. These fall into three groups: (i) taxes reducing funds available to industry, (ii) taxes on consumption goods which limit their availability as exports, and (iii) taxes on the factors of production. The first has already been discussed. The insuperable difficulty of combining flexibility of obsolescence rebates with a high levy on undistributed profits is probably the most serious item, at least in the short run. An instance of the second is afforded by the limited export value of British cars as a result of the combined effect of petrol taxes, licence duties, and the particular form which road development has taken. There is a strong British tradition against taxing the factors of production, which is recognized to be a most reprehensible method of raising revenue for a country relying extensively on her income from

---

[1] Estimates made by Bowley and by Lindahl (*Undersökningar rörande det Samlade Skattetrycket i Sverige och Utlandet*) are given at the end of the chapter.

exports. Nevertheless, several taxes of this type have crept into the structure. Employers' contributions to social insurance constitutes a poll tax per worker employed. Taxes on oil, and to some extent on petrol, tend to raise industrial costs and the cost of transport. The more general taxation of raw materials was already noticeable during Mr. Churchill's chancellorship.[1] But the process was considerably extended on the imposition of the general tariff. Duties imposed at the request of the iron and steel interests call for particular comment in this respect. The indirect effects of a general tariff in raising internal prices and costs must also be taken into account. Many of these drawbacks are common to all high tariff countries.[2] The taxation of motor spirit has also become very general.[3] But Britain is definitely at a disadvantage in respect of the importance of the social insurance levy. She has also had higher income taxes more stringently levied and higher death duties for a longer period than other countries.

Examination of the effects of various taxes composing the post-war tax structure suggest that the three most doubtful aspects of recent changes from the economic point of view are, first, the shift in favour of taxes on articles of elastic rather than of inelastic demand, secondly, the increase in the taxes on the factors of production, and, thirdly, the continued exploitation of the income and capital taxes. The maximum relative weight of the income and capital group was realized in the structure of 1930, but the absolute weight was subsequently increased. While the post-war relation between income and capital and consumption taxes is no doubt an improvement on the pre-war norm of 50 : 50, both on distributional and personal grounds, it would appear somewhat dangerous to revert to the 1930 proportion, at least as long as no means exist of tempering the burden to take account of economic change, and the absolute burden remains at its post-1930 height. This judgement, however, depends largely on inference, since the period available for observation is extremely short. Before a more definite conclusion can be reached it is necessary to examine the distributional effects of the tax structure, since these afford some guide as to the trend of long-period effects.

---

[1] For instance the wrapping paper duty, imposed in 1926.
[2] High tariffs are, however, frequently offset by bounties on leading exports.
[3] It is worth noting that a petrol duty is more purely a consumption goods tax in countries where commercial road transport is unimportant than in Britain.

THE ECONOMIC EFFECTS OF TAXES

A Note on the International Tax Burden

Estimated total tax burden as a percentage of the National Income

	1913	1925	1933
Sweden . .	9·5	12·8	15·2
Denmark . .	..	19·6	20·1
Germany . .	8·1	17·8	23·0
France . .	..	21·1	26·3
Italy . . .	..	17·5	30·6
U.S.A. . .	(6½)	11·0	23·4
U.K. . .	(11½)	22·6	25·2

(From Lindahl, loc. cit. Figures in brackets from Bowley, *Economic Conse-quences*, cit. Where they overlap the two estimates are sufficiently close for these figures to be consistent.)

XVI

TAXATION AND DISTRIBUTION

REDISTRIBUTION of income is an end of social policy. Very considerable progress has been made in this as a result of post-war changes in taxes. We have examined the probable economic effects of the taxes by which it is accomplished. We must now turn to the other side and examine the resulting distribution itself. It must be remembered that this in its turn will influence the national income of the future and should properly be considered as part of the long-period effects of the tax structure.

To arrive at a reliable estimate of the distribution of the tax structure—that is of the proportion of revenue raised from different levels of income—it is clearly necessary to have a considerable amount of information as to the distribution of incomes and the habits of particular classes. In the first place we want to know the numbers in each income group, secondly, their consumption of taxed commodities and services, and, thirdly, the final incidence of taxes, after allowing for price changes whereby the real burden of the tax is shifted. In the absence of complete information the gaps must be filled by assumptions based on such information as the data afford. A number of private estimates of the tax structure have been made from time to time, but it is to be regretted that nothing more official than the Colwyn Committee's discussion exists. Before examining these estimates in detail it will be advisable to review the information available and the assumptions on which they are based.

The inland revenue reports contain complete information as to the distribution of super(sur)tax payers in different groups. The only limitation to the use of the figures is that they do not become complete until seven years after the first assessment. After the first year, however, the additional annual assessments are of moderate amount, so that they can be adjusted with reasonable confidence for years in which the early assessments are known.[1] The only regular information as to the number in income groups below

---

[1] Cf. Stamp, 'The Influence of the Price Level on the Higher Incomes', *J.R.S.S.*, 1936, and Clark, *National Income and Outlay*.

the surtax level is the number at the exemption limit. The Royal Commission on the Income Tax in 1920 attempted an estimate of the lower income groups. No adequate check, however, to this exists, and it cannot be assumed that the 1920 distribution was either normal or representative of conditions ten or fifteen years later. But if we accept the view that income is distributed according to the 'Pareto law' it is possible to make a rough estimate of the numbers in each income group by plotting the income and surtax information on a double ratio scale.[1] The gap from £150 to £2,000, however, is obviously too great to hope that the calculation will be very accurate.

In order to ascertain the distribution of the consumption of taxed commodities of final consumption, budget studies for various income groups are necessary. Until the new survey of working-class expenditure is complete the only existing official estimates are based on a modernization of investigations made in 1904. It does not need emphasizing that tastes in respect of certain highly taxed commodities have altered very considerably in the interval. It is clear that estimates of consumption even by working-class families at the present time are largely guesswork. There have been several small private inquiries as to the layout of middle-class incomes,[2] but in no case have the data been very extensive or reliable. There is no information as to the consumption of taxed articles by the wealthy. This gap is not so serious as it might be, since, on the one hand, the middle and upper classes make the bulk of their contribution in the form of income and capital taxes; and, on the other, the largest amount of consumption tax revenue is still raised on articles where it is working-class consumption which is of prime importance. The proportion of revenue raised from articles largely consumed by the middle and upper income ranges is, however, of growing importance—for instance the silk and similar import duties, and a considerable part of the motoring duties. For these taxes only guesses as to the distribution of consumption can be made. It is clear that information is far from being adequate. As we shall see, this is a very important matter. The incidence of

[1] Cf. Clark, op. cit. An estimate of income distribution is graphed in Appendix 11. From this and the calculations of the tax burden it is possible to make a rough estimate of the numbers subject to each particular tax burden. The fact that the incomes shown are gross exaggerates inequality.

[2] Cf. Allen and Bowley, *Family Expenditure*, and sources quoted in O'Brien, 'A Middle Class Budget Enquiry', *Review of Economic Studies*, vol. iv.

considerable stretches of the tax structure may be completely altered, according to the estimates of consumption used.

The final incidence of the income and capital taxes is a simple matter, since there can be no question of shifting in the sense in which the term is used of consumption taxes. For all practical purposes the incidence of these taxes is on the *de jure* payer, whatever after-effects the community may subsequently experience as a result of alterations in his propensity to consume or invest. Consumption taxes are another matter. Where demand for a commodity of final consumption is obviously inelastic it is fairly safe to assume that the incidence is on the consumer. Where receipts increase, at least *pari passu* with increased rates of levy, it is probably also justifiable to assume that the tax is mainly shifted on to consumers. These conditions cover a very considerable part, but by no means the whole, of the consumption tax field. Because of the difficulty of making any other assumption all calculations have attributed the incidence of consumption taxes wholly to the final consumers.

Greater complications arise in the case of such levies as employers' insurance contributions, part of the motoring taxes, and the stamp duties. It may be that in certain cases the eagerness of labour for employment is so great that workers consent to pay the employers' contributions in the form of lower wages. More normally it should probably be attributed to the consumers of the final product—or to the owners of the business. Hence it is very difficult to allot this tax at all. The taxes on commercial motors and hydrocarbon oils must probably be attributed to consumers of the final product.[1] (With these should be included taxes paid by vehicles taxed on horse-power but used for business purposes.) There is little evidence to show, however, whether the distribution should be proportionate to income, progressive or regressive. Because of the difficulties involved most of these taxes have generally been omitted from calculations. This was a perfectly legitimate step even as late as 1925, but by 1935 it constituted a serious drawback.

The incidence of local rates present still more formidable difficulties. Those on business premises might reasonably be distributed in a manner similar to the levies on commercial motors. But especially since the derating of industrial premises the

---

[1] See below, p. 271, for the principles adopted in the various estimates of the tax burden.

non-residential part of the rate contribution is relatively unimportant. We have seen that local variation is characteristic of rates, and it is by no means certain that it is fully allowed for by rent adjustments. Thus to take an average for the whole country is not very satisfactory. Information as to the proportion of income spent on rent at different income levels is little better than for the consumption of other commodities, and we have also to determine a relation between rent and rates which will be typical for the country as a whole. It is clear that a considerable amount of guesswork is involved. There is, moreover, in the case of rates a weaker basis for assuming that the incidence of taxation falls on the final consumer (the occupier) than for most consumption taxes. It is generally considered that ultimately the burden falls on the owner as rents are in the long period completely adjusted. This may often be the case even in the short period when rates are paid in the first instance by the landlord, and rates may alter faster than rents can be adjusted. Further, if the demand for house room is very elastic, a rise in rates may quickly lead to a fall in rents. Elastic demand may be experienced by owners of old-fashioned property even when there is a considerable housing shortage. On the whole, however, the supply of house room since the war has been so notoriously inadequate that it seems reasonable to assume, for this period at any rate, that the incidence of rates was on the occupier. A different assumption would, however, as we shall see, make a considerable change in the form of the tax structure.

The only remaining levy of any importance which might be fitted in are the estate duties. In order to compare the death duties with taxes currently paid it is necessary to resort to some artifice by which the lump sum payment can be expressed as an annual levy. The method that has been adopted[1] is to calculate the insurance policy necessary to leave the estate intact, and express this as a proportion of income—determined by the size of the estate. This is obviously not a satisfactory method. It is not likely that taxpayers commonly attempt to cover the whole of their liability by insurance. To do so would leave them but a very modest income during life. Moreover, differences in the rate of interest at which the premium is calculated, or in the age at which the estate owner is supposed to start insuring, impart such large variations to the results that their final value is extremely doubtful. Nevertheless,

[1] Cf. *Committee on National Debt and Taxation*, p. 82.

just as in the case of rates, the omission of the tax tends to give a misleading appearance to the tax structure, so that the attempt to include it seems to be justified.

In view of the difficulties of interpretation and the nature of the assumptions which have to be made, it may well be asked whether the attempt to estimate the incidence of the tax structure is worth while. Mr. Clark[1] is of the opinion that it is not. But it is not apparent that his attempt to assess the total burden on the working classes and the well-to-do respectively is in an appreciably better position as to evidence than a more detailed analysis. For economic purposes, as distinct from social or political, it is certainly quite as desirable to attempt to estimate the change and extent of regression and progression, as to know the burdens on the population conceived as divided into two classes.

Diagram I (p. 270) shows in graphic form the most important calculations of the incidence of the tax structure. They illustrate the position at six points of time—1903, 1913, 1918, 1925, 1930, and 1934. None is wholly complete, but it is not difficult to make allowance for the most considerable omissions, particularly as on the whole the same basic assumptions about consumption have been adopted. We shall have to examine these later. The broad movements are, however, obviously both clear and consistent over the period. Since pre-war days the tax structure has changed from an approximately proportional incidence to one that has become highly and increasingly progressive in the upper ranges, and at the same time definitely regressive over a gradually extending range of the lower incomes. At the beginning of the century there was an almost complete absence of progression. Indeed, there is some evidence of regression at the upper as well as at the lower end of the structure. But by the pre-war decade progression had definitely set in. A slight flattening tendency at the upper end is almost inevitable if confiscatory levies on the largest incomes are to be avoided. It is most noticeable in 1918, before the post-war rise in surtax had taken place, but has become much less conspicuous since. The fact that the upper end of the 1925 structure is substantially below, and the lower end above, the war curve is explained by the remission of income tax on the one hand and the maintenance of high rates on tobacco and alcohol on the other. These two taxes (on the estimates of consumption used) quite

[1] Cf. Clark, op. cit., p. 142.

DIAGRAM I. CALCULATIONS OF THE INCIDENCE OF THE TAX STRUCTURE

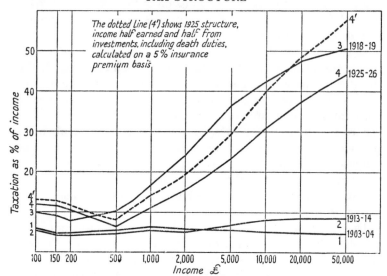

The dotted Line (4') shows 1925 structure, income half earned and half from investments, including death duties, calculated on a 5% insurance premium basis.

(A) COLWYN COMMITTEE CALCULATIONS
(Income all earned, married man with three children)
(Ratio Scale)

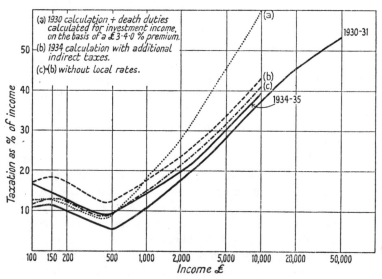

(a) 1930 calculation + death duties calculated for investment income, on the basis of a £3·4·0 % premium.
(b) 1934 calculation with additional indirect taxes.
(c)-(b) without local rates.

(B) LATER CALCULATIONS
(Income all earned, married man with three children)
(Ratio Scale)

outweigh the very considerable remissions which had taken place in other consumption taxes. The small progressive turn at the extreme lower end of the 1930 calculation is due to the reduction of food taxes in the twenties on the one hand, and to the inclusion of additional non-food taxes on the other. In the 1934 calculation this is concealed by the inclusion of rates (cf. Diag. I B, line *b*), but appears again when rates are deducted (line *c*). The points which call for examination are obviously the effect of progression of this order on the sources of revenue, and the cause and probable effects of the regressive tail on the one hand and the middle-class dip on the other. In the first place, however, it will be as well to observe and allow for the variations in the field covered by the different calculations.

The first four calculations are those made by the Colwyn Committee, incorporating the earlier ones of Lord Samuel.[1] They cover all food taxes (including drink and tobacco), but omit motor, stamp, miscellaneous import duties, and rates. Death duties are calculated on a 5 per cent. insurance premium starting at 45, one-tenth the value of estates being reckoned as an equivalent income. If these results are added to the burden of income and supertax, taxation becomes confiscatory at a relatively early stage in the case of unearned incomes. This illustrates the weakness of the method of getting over the death-duty difficulty. In order to avoid absurd results the calculations were therefore shown only for wholly earned income, and for income half earned and half from investments. For comparison with other estimates only the earned-income curve is shown except for 1925. Except for rates, which is a serious item, the omissions are not important, particularly as far as 1918 is concerned. Even in 1925, since the motor-fuel tax had not been reimposed, the exclusion of motoring duties, stamps, and insurance contributions do not leave more than about £100 m. unaccounted for. Of this about £40 m. should probably be allocated on the lower end—presumably in proportion to income, and the remainder on the upper ranges.

The calculation for 1930 was intended as an extension of the Colwyn Committee researches, but is somewhat more comprehensive.[2] It also includes new taxes imposed between 1925 and

---

[1] Cf. Samuel, *J.R.S.S.*, 1919, and Colwyn Committee.

[2] Cf. Sandral, *J.R.S.S.*, 1931. The death duty premium is calculated at £3 4s. per cent.

1930. Food duties were apportioned on the basis of the Colwyn Committee's estimate of the consumption of alcohol and tobacco—which probably gives a better approximation than in the case of the commodities to which it is supposed to apply. Sugar taxation was calculated on the higher non-imperial rates of duty which, as we know, slightly exaggerates its burden. All other import duties, as well as stamps and motoring levies, were apportioned proportionately to income among the income-tax paying classes. Once again rates were omitted, but this appears to be the only important gap in the estimate. The calculation of 1934 made for the information of the Swedish government[1] is on a somewhat different basis from the others. Broadly it represents the emergency tax structure of 1931, but without death duties and others included in the 1930 calculation. If the latter are included and the tariff of 1932, the curve has to be raised substantially (cf. Diag. I B, lines *b* and *c*). The most important difference between this and other estimates is, however, the inclusion of rates. These are calculated on the relation between rent and rates in London, Southampton, and Sheffield. It is assumed that incidence is wholly on the occupier. In 1925, 1930, and 1934 rates amounted to roughly £170 m. By comparing the course of the 1934 curve with and without rates (*b* and *c*, Diag. I B), it is thus possible to judge by inspection the adjustment necessary to make allowance for this tax in the earlier estimates.

At first sight it is probably the regressive tail of the structure which appears to be its most serious drawback for socio-economic policy. This phenomenon is a peculiarity of British finance. In Sweden, for instance, where the general lay-out of revenue and expenditure is closely similar, the tax structure is progressive throughout its range.[2] The British situation suggests that the increase of social expenditure is being largely negatived by taxation—more especially when we remember that there is no element of progressiveness towards the lower incomes in expenditure.[3] If we examine the details of the 1934 calculation, however (Table 1, p. 277), it is evident that regression depends on three groups of taxes—rates, alcohol, and tobacco. In the case of the first two, particularly the second, we have seen that the assumption that the consumer bears the whole tax is not very well founded. This is some consolation. But the regressive nature of high rates is sufficiently well

[1] Cf. Lindahl, *Samlade Skattetrycket*, cit., p. 115.   [2] Cf. ibid.
[3] Cf. Chap. III, p. 47.

established to present a serious problem. It is a further demonstration of the desirability of the reform of local finance. It is notable that the weight of rates[1] remains a serious item further up the income scale than any consumption tax. It is still appreciable on incomes of £2,500.

There are further consolations in the case of the tobacco and alcohol duties. In the first place the estimates of consumption adopted by the Colwyn Committee and used by all subsequent investigators depended ultimately on a not very well informed guess.[2] There is no real evidence that the working classes ever spent this proportion of income on these two commodities, much less that they do so to-day. This is a question which it is much to be hoped will be solved by the new budget investigation. Secondly, there is no evidence that—as is assumed—consumption of these commodities is spread evenly among people with similar incomes. Common observation would suggest that this was far from being the case, especially in regard to alcohol. The effect of altering the assumption of uniform consumption, while retaining that as to total lower-class consumption, is shown in Diagram II (p. 275).[3] The lower end of the tax structures of 1913 and 1925 are redrawn for the two possible extremes (which may be called abstainers and indulgers). In 1913 the difference was already important, but by 1925 it had increased enormously. For the later curves the divergence would be still more substantial. There is therefore little reason to assume either that the tail of the tax structure is necessarily so regressive as the curves suggest, or that such regression is normal for the incomes indicated.

Nevertheless, it is clear that a distressing amount of regression remains. But with the substitution of the new import duties for the breakfast-table duties it becomes increasingly difficult to estimate its extent. It seems probable that since the newly taxed commodities are of more elastic demand than the old, there is more 'tax evasion'—by refraining from purchasing—by the poorer classes in 1936 than in the early post-war years. This is probably undesirable from the point of view of the optimum lay-out of their

[1] The weight of local rates on some small incomes is probably less than on lower-middle-class ones since there is a discontinuity in the tendency of expenditure on rent to fall proportionately as income increases; cf. Singer, *Review of Economic Studies*, iv.
[2] Cf. Bowley, review of Clark (op. cit.), *Economica*, 1937.
[3] Based on Caradog Jones, *J.R.S.S.* 1927.

expenditure, but is a factor formally mitigating the increase in regression since 1931.

On the other hand, it appears that lower-middle-class income receivers have increasingly been made (relatively) better off by the evolution of the tax structure. The dip has become progressively deeper. It has also tended to move up the income scale. In so far as it is not fictitious (depending on the extent of regression), it arises from the very light rates of income tax on the lower ranges of income-tax payers, due to the increasing importance of allowances. Income tax does not become an appreciable burden until some way further up the income scale than the point where the main consumption taxes cease to be burdensome. The dip is most noticeable in the range from £300 to £600. According to the 'Pareto line' there are about 1·35 million taxpayers in this range. The number naturally varies slightly with the national income, although the data of income distribution do not allow this to be estimated very precisely. But it seems probable that incomes in this range are considerably steadier than those either above or below. It is, of course, possible to exaggerate the social and economic importance of the dip in the tax structure. But if it is remembered that the relatively lightly taxed elements in the community comprise the top grades of wage earners, a large number of salary earners and small entrepreneurs—including probably an abnormal number of young people—it does appear that the effect must be both beneficial and stabilizing. The combined economic effect of the enviable position of this class, and of such decrease of regression as has taken place since the war, is perhaps to be discerned in the generally favourable experience of the industries catering for the support and entertainment of such income receivers.

It remains to consider the effect of progression in surtax and death duties. Here it is possible to speak with more assurance, since the actual numbers in each income and property group are recorded. Table 2 (p. 278) shows the total number of surtax payers corrected to allow for the completion of assessments up to 1934. (The numbers in the smaller groups are not adjusted because the margin of error in attempting to make the adjustment would be considerably greater.) All the figures show a very strong cyclical sensitivity for which allowance must be made. If we concentrate on those from 1922 to 1930, however, there is not much need to take this into account. It appears that the total numbers have increased

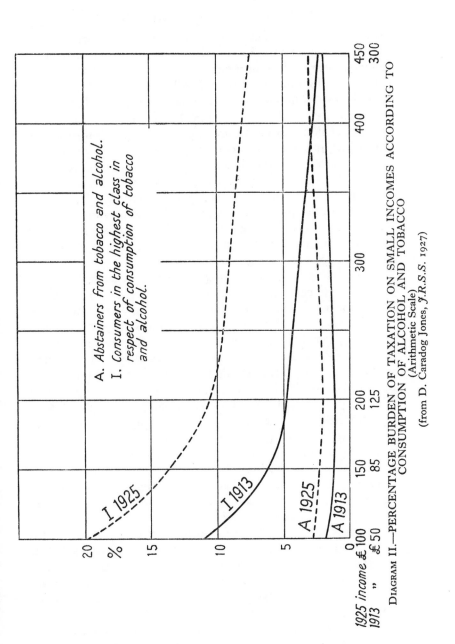

A. Abstainers from tobacco and alcohol.

I. Consumers in the highest class in respect of consumption of tobacco and alcohol.

DIAGRAM II.—PERCENTAGE BURDEN OF TAXATION ON SMALL INCOMES ACCORDING TO CONSUMPTION OF ALCOHOL AND TOBACCO
(Arithmetic Scale)
(from D. Caradog Jones, *J.R.S.S.* 1927)

steadily, if not very rapidly. The increase in the higher incomes has, however, been much less rapid. Those over £5,000 were practically stationary, while the figure for those over £100,000 for 1930 (a boom year for this purpose) was hardly above the average for the whole period. The numbers in the table are gross. If they are calculated after taxation has been paid a very striking decrease in large personal incomes is apparent, particularly if a comparison is made with 1913. For instance in 1913 there were 5,310 individuals with income over £10,000, in 1924 9,760, and in 1932 6,155. After taxation these numbers were reduced to 4,260, 4,280, and 2,345 respectively. The numbers in the higher tax-paying classes were thus reduced by one-half as compared with the pre-war situation.

The effect of death duties is shown in Table 3. Experience here has been roughly similar to that in the case of surtax. In the smaller estates a satisfactory increase of wealth has been apparent. The number of estates between £10,001 and £100,000 increased by over 83 per cent. In the next higher group, however (£100,001 to £1,000,000), the increase fell to 70 per cent. The figures in the highest group are so few that no general conclusion as to trend can be made, beyond the fact that there is no evidence of any increase at all. In spite of the declining rate of increase in the larger estates, it must be admitted that the figures do not suggest that up to the present the inroads of death duties into the national wealth have been very serious. It may be that in our period compensating factors were present. It is possible, for instance, that the decline in the size of families has had a tendency to keep estates from becoming dissipated by division among heirs. It must be remembered that during the whole of the period the exchequer was continuing to receive taxation on wealth accumulated during the period of high prices. Comparable opportunities for amassing fortunes were not present during the twenties. These less favourable estates will shortly be in the majority of those liable to death duties. Further, since death duties only gradually attained their present height over the period, the disruptive effect of really heavy rates cannot yet have become apparent. There is thus some reason to fear that there may be a considerable fall off in yields at no distant date.

The examination of the distributional effects of income and capital taxes suggests that there is little in the long-period effect of income and surtax at present rates which tends to reduce the number of large gross incomes or the opportunities for making them. There is, however, some support for the contention that while death duties provide a more effective path towards the eventual equalization of wealth, they do so only at the cost of declining revenue.

TABLE I

Tax incidence as a percentage of income in various income groups 1934–5. Income all earned. Married person with three children

Income (£)	65	100	150	225	335	500	750	1,125	1,675	2,500	10,000
I. Direct taxes (income and surtax) . .	..	..	..	..	..	1·2	5·7	9·8	13·0	17·2	36·1
II. Indirect taxes:											
Alcohol .	4·2	4·4	4·7	3·8	2·6	1·8	1·5	1·3	1·2	1·1	1·0
Tobacco .	3·4	3·5	3·3	2·7	1·8	1·3	0·9	0·7	0·5	0·4	0·1
Tea . .	0·5	0·4	0·3	0·2	0·1	0·1	0·1	..	..	..	..
Miscellaneous food . .	0·3	0·3	0·2	0·1	0·1	0·1	..	..	..	..	..
Sugar . .	1·5	1·2	0·9	0·6	0·4	0·3	0·2	0·1	0·1	0·1	..
Entertainments	0·2	0·2	0·1	0·1	0·1	0·1	0·1	0·1	0·1	0·1	..
Total indirect	9·9	9·8	9·5	7·6	5·2	3·6	2·8	2·3	1·9	1·7	1·2
III. Local taxes (rates) . .	7·2	6·8	5·3	4·4	4·5	4·3	3·9	3·3	2·8	2·5	1·8
IV. Total burden of taxes shown .	17·1	16·6	14·8	12·0	9·7	9·1	12·4	15·4	17·7	21·4	39·1

(Source: *Undersökningar rörande det samlade skattetrycket i Sverige och utlandet.*)

The following additions have been made for the purpose of series *c*, Diagram I *b*.

Income (£)	50	100	150	200	500	1,000	2,000	5,000	10,000
Non-food duties . .	..	..	3·0	3·5	3·5	3·5	3·5	3·5	3·5
Food	1·0	0·9	0·8	0·8	0·5	0·3	0·3	0·25	0·2
	1·0	0·9	3·8	4·3	4·0	3·8	3·8	5·75	3·7

TABLE 2

Surtax payers

Year super tax	Numbers assessed		Numbers with incomes over	
	Recorded	Adjusted	£5,000	£100,000
1921	93,099	..	28,803	206
1922	91,156	..	26,114	139
1923	94,378	..	27,067	133
1924	96,573	..	27,428	144
1925	98,868	..	28,229	144
1926	100,470	..	28,304	150
1927	101,183	..	28,120	135
1928	103,715	..	28,879	135
1929*	108,272	..	29,846	166
1930*	109,749	..	29,856	141
1931* (0·8)	104,321	105,156	27,302	111
1932* (1·6)	93,797	94,367	22,953	95
1933* (2·0)	86,712	88,446	20,531	84
1934* (3·0)	83,419	85,921	19,713	65

Last complete year 1930, adjustments made for remainder, by adding the percentages shown in brackets in column 1.
* = surtax years for the year preceding.

TABLE 3

Numbers of estates of different sizes liable to death duty

	£101 to £10,000	£10,001 to £100,000	£100,001 to £1,000,000	Over £1,000,000
1920	47,051	4,845	309	11
1921	51,404	4,998	325	11
1922	52,944	5,482	348	15
1923	53,753	5,720	378	9
1924	57,330	6,022	418	13
1925	58,065	6,087	397	7
1926	60,257	6,636	463	10
1927	67,251	7,269	477	15
1928	64,547	7,553	515	20
1929	71,395	8,129	566	15
1930	68,490	7,676	475	22
1931	71,648	7,354	425	9
1932	75,918	8,003	437	3
1933	73,782	7,876	446	12
1934	74,718	8,435	488	14
1935	78,804	8,967	532	14

XVII

BALANCING THE BUDGET

A NECESSARY preliminary to a discussion of whether—or when
—balancing the budget is essential, is to determine how far
it represents an account that is economically significant. The
budget which the chancellor presents every April, amidst much
flourish and excitement, is an estimate of foreseeable outlay by the
central government for the ensuing year, and a proposal as to how
it shall be met. The greater part is concerned with expenditure
on current account, and it is intended to be mainly, perhaps almost
wholly, financed out of tax receipts. The budget is thus purely an
income and expenditure, not a profit and loss, account, and in no
sense a balance sheet of even a part of the national accounts. It
represents a definitive opening and closing of the accounts for a
particular annual period. Any surplus from the previous year has
normally been applied to writing off debt. No credit is taken for
fixed assets, no account is included of sums or balances of independent funds in the hands of the Treasury, and no provision is
normally made for liabilities which may fall within the accounting
period, but the amount of which cannot be definitely foreseen.
While, however, it is thus apparently concerned with income
account only and with a single period, the budget is in reality far
from having such a simple financial character. Sums standing
over from previous years are not infrequently brought in to make
up the balance, whether they belong properly to income or to
capital account. On the other hand, a not inconsiderable proportion of receipts is destined to be devoted to investment of a capital
nature—in durable assets—either by the central departments
themselves or as contributions to local revenues.

These considerations suggest that the *Chancellor's Budget* as it
stands cannot be an account of primary economic significance, that
is to say, that it does not clearly reveal the true economic position
of the whole, or indeed of any part, of the public finances. The
exact components of the two sides of the account in any year are
to some extent at least a matter partly of chance and partly even
of choice. In any case they are always an amalgam of current and
capital accounts, the proportions of which, on either side, may vary

from year to year. On the other hand, the budget does not cover the whole of even the central income and expenditure account. This would require the inclusion, for instance, of the social insurance funds. It is also far from including the whole of the central capital account, the main part of which is financed by borrowing under specific Acts of Parliament. It interlocks to a considerable extent with the finances of local authorities,[1] both on income and capital account. Ultimately, indeed, the budget is responsible for all subsidiary accounts, in the sense that if any one in particular becomes bankrupt it must be financed by the general body of tax-payers (via short-term borrowing and a supplementary estimate or both), at least until some method of restoring its solvency has been devised. Thus the debit balance of the Unemployment Insurance Fund (which it must be remembered reached at its maximum in 1931 the not inconsiderable amount of £115 m.) is a net addition to the deadweight debt. Since, however, it has been funded on a separate account (and in contrast to the rest of the debt is actually being repaid), it is generally disregarded in calculations of the national debt. The budget has also an ultimate responsibility for the finances of local authorities, although normally their financial plans are virtually independent. If any area becomes unable to cover its obligations from existing resources, it must be supported by the Treasury until means have been devised of restoring its independence.[2]

From the economic point of view the information which it is desirable that the national accounts should furnish is of two types. In the first place it should be possible to see clearly what the position of public activities as a whole is, and, secondly, it is highly desirable to be able to distinguish at a glance income from capital transactions. Would it not be possible to present the national accounts in a manner which would reveal this information? The first point is considerably complicated in this country by the small volume of central investment and the interlocking of central and local finances. In spite of the great amount of published information on the subject it is not possible to do more than make a rough estimate of the aggregate position, and that several years in retard.

---

[1] The extent of central contributions is not easy to ascertain from the national accounts. The most complete list is that given in the Financial Statement.

[2] As was done in the case of certain boards of guardians in the post-war decade.

The second point would be largely met if the budget were divided
into a current and capital account. Such a reform is highly desirable on financial as well as on economic grounds. Something of
this nature has been widely adopted or discussed abroad,[1] and
appears to be perfectly feasible. It must be noted, however, that
if the current budget is regarded as the ordinary account, and the
capital budget as an extraordinary account, a certain danger of
financial laxity is introduced, which it is necessary to guard against.
It was not uncommon during the depression for governments to
relieve themselves of their too-pressing financial obligations by
transferring items for which they could not find the revenue to the
extraordinary budget, where they were only met by free recourse
to new borrowing. Budget reform was thus turned into a device
for concealing rather than revealing a deficit. A true division into
income and capital accounts would of course be of a functional
nature, and should be adopted as a permanent and not as an
emergency measure.

The exact method of reshuffling the accounts which might be
adopted in order to separate capital and income items is naturally
a technical matter, and it would be out of place to discuss it at
length here.[2] There are a number of possible alternatives, the
adoption of any one of which would no doubt be an improvement
on the present arrangement. The essential point is that the ordinary budget should contain all current expenditure (such as normal
government expenses, contributions to local revenues, statutory
sinking funds, &c.). Capital expenditure, that is to say funds intended for the purchase of durable assets, either directly by the
central government or through the medium of grants to local
authorities, debt repayment and appropriations to capital funds,
&c., should either be relegated to the capital budget, or, if long-
term policy includes a programme of progressive public investment
and debt amortization, capital items to this extent should also be
included in the current budget, to be covered by current revenue
(taxes, trading receipts, &c.). If this principle is adopted, the
extent of balance or deficit can be ascertained from the current

[1] For instance in Sweden. In this section I have drawn largely on the plans
of Prof. Lindahl ('Arbetslöshet och Finanspolitik', *Ekon. Tidskrift*, 1935), and
of the experts called in to advise the Swedish government in 1936.
[2] But cf. *Balancing the Budget* (mainly a translation of the Tidskrift article,
in Lindahl, *Studies in the Theory of Money and Capital*), to be published by
Allen & Unwin.

budget. If true current revenue exactly equals the expenditure total of the current budget, the budget is exactly balanced. If one side exceeds the other, the difference shows the true surplus or deficit. A deficit will be met by a transfer from the expenditure side of the capital budget to the receipts side of the current budget, and a surplus will be dealt with in the opposite manner.

It would be natural on this plan to include at least the aggregates of independent funds, since if they show a deficit, this will fall eventually on the budget. But the reform could be carried through with a minimum change of accounting methods. Nevertheless, it would be very desirable at the same time to take the opportunity of introducing a greater degree of comprehensiveness into the accounts. As far as the position of local authorities is concerned, this could be achieved by drawing up alongside the central budget a national account of local activities, showing clearly by identical items the interlocking of the two accounts, and similarly divided into current and capital sections. Since local authorities already have to do part of their planning in advance, it would not seem an incredibly long step to the preparation of a complete national budget. In the first place it might perhaps be drawn up in the form of a completed account, rather than of a budget plan—so long as the time lag in bringing it out was not considerable. In view of the importance of local investment, and the growing scope for independent financing by the local authorities, unified information of this sort could not fail to be of great assistance, both in directing the long-run policy of the community as a whole and in assisting the development of a unified short-period policy.

But once the problem of local accounting is considered, it becomes evident that a true picture of the economic state of the body public requires the inclusion of a valuation of public assets and a calculation of the interest and depreciation necessary to maintain them. The inclusion of these items would make it possible to estimate changes in the public wealth and the extent of new investment. It would then probably be most convenient to show total new investment together in the capital budget, distinguishing only between that which was expected to be self liquidating and that which was expected to add to the national wealth only in real terms. Total public investment would be covered either by transfers from the current budget (derived from taxes and sinking funds), by payments from capital funds, such as investment

equalization funds, or by borrowing. Such an extension of accounting methods would be specially desirable as a record of the
local investment position, but it would be no less desirable in
respect of capital funds and such central investment as armaments.
Once the most desirable method of exhibiting the accounts has
been determined, the question of balancing policy requires discussion. It is clear that economically it is only the balance of the
total account which is significant. (There is thus no particular
economic sanctity in balancing the chancellor's budget as it stands.)
The definition of a balance for a current budget is a comparatively straightforward matter. Receipts of a revenue nature must
be available fully to cover anticipated expenditure. This is the
recognized criterion for the central budget. The use of receipts of
a non-recurrent nature is not generally regarded as an adequate
balance, although condoned in emergency. The criterion, however, properly applies only to a pure income budget. It then constitutes an adequate financial balance but not necessarily a true
long-run economic one. For this it is surely necessary to take a
longer view, both on account of the accidental time incidence of
many items in respect of any particular accounting period and of
the related nature of expenditure occurring in different periods.
For instance, it is clearly not a true economic balance if expenditure
proper to the accounting period is held over, or debts on current
account are not paid when they fall due. The same effect occurs,
however, if expenditure already contracted for tends automatically
to expand and revenue is stationary, or again if expenditure is
stationary but the present balance is obtained only with the help
of declining taxes, or finally if there is an undeclared liability outstanding. These considerations suggest the necessity for an additional condition—that in respect of a 'planning period'—of, say,
five years—the budget will remain balanced in the sense that it
will not be necessary to raise fresh taxation to meet normal expenditure already contracted for.

The desirable balance of a capital budget is, on the other hand, a
matter of policy. We are here concerned with the accumulation
of debt on one side and the gradual acquisition of different sorts
of assets on the other. In what sense can the two be regarded as
balancing in any real sense? It is clearly necessary to distinguish
according to the purpose of the borrowing and the type of assets
acquired with the loan funds.

Firstly, borrowing may have been undertaken by the trading services. In this case the budget is clearly balanced as long as interest charges are met and fixed assets are written off in a period roughly corresponding to their economic life. We may term debt of this type *active*. An increasingly large part of public borrowing is, however, in respect of non-earning or not fully self-liquidating durable assets, such as houses, government buildings, hospitals, and schools. The inapplicability of the price calculus to the output of many of such assets precludes an exact economic evaluation of the addition to the national income due to borrowing, but that there is normally an important net addition in real terms is evident. Debt of this type may be termed *inactive*. By far the largest part of the British public debt is, however, what is usually termed *deadweight*, that is to say either there are no tangible assets remaining over to the present, to set against it, or they are of such an ephemeral nature that they cannot be reckoned in a long-period calculus. In this country deadweight debt is roughly seven times as large as the active and inactive debts of the government and the local authorities. While it has mainly been incurred in respect of armaments—and this is probably always likely to be the main cause—borrowing for current civil needs or failing to balance the current budget have been contributory causes.

Since the problem of borrowing is thus primarily one of deadweight debt, it will be more convenient to postpone discussion of its effects until we are ready to deal with the national debt in relation to monetary policy.[1] Here we need only be concerned with the general relation of borrowing to the budget. In the case of borrowing for self-liquidating assets no true budgetary problem arises. Nor are the economic arguments against the extension of public activity in such directions very convincing. Although, naturally, sectional private interests may be injured, as long as public production is conducted on the maximum output least cost basis, and a restrictive price policy is avoided, these investments will accrue to the benefit of the community as a whole, since they will contribute to maximizing the national income in real terms.

From the opposite point of view it has been argued that a programme of gradual extension of public investment should be included in a long-period budget policy.[2] This is held to be desirable

---

[1] Cf. Chap. XX.
[2] Cf. Chap. VI. This argument is a favourite with Mr. Keynes and his

on general economic grounds, as an offset to a possible decline in private investment as population becomes stationary. It has also been urged as a fiscal measure.[1] A larger volume of trading receipts would allow of a reduction of the tax burden, and hence of a lightening of both its economic and social drawbacks. But whether the tax burden would actually be reduced depends on the management and the price policy of the public utilities from which the alternative revenue would be derived. It is no less possible for quasi- than for explicit taxes to be economically harmful and socially regressive. To these long-period arguments must be added the cyclical advantages of an extensive public control of investment. There is thus a fairly strong case for the inclusion of a definite programme of debt amortization and extension of public investment in a long-period budgetary policy.

These arguments point also to a possible desirability of a certain extension of inactive debt, particularly of the quasi-active type represented by such services as housing and highways. Well-chosen borrowing of this nature tends not merely to enlarge the capital equipment of the community (and hence the real national income), but will also help to raise the national income (in money terms)—or mitigate its decline—by outlay on present goods and services. There may even on occasion be economic arguments in favour of deadweight borrowing. Circumstances may conceivably arise in which the consequent expansion of the national income in money terms in the present is not likely to be offset by corresponding contraction in real terms—either in the present if the borrowing is not undertaken, or in the future if it is. Nevertheless, inactive and deadweight debt lead inevitably to a budgetary problem of interest and repayment which presents a deflationary danger. In the case of inactive or quasi-active debt this is likely to be partially offset by some long-period extension of taxable capacity in real as well as in monetary terms. But this is much less likely to occur in the case of deadweight borrowing. The budget cannot be regarded as adequately balanced in any period where there has occurred an extension of deadweight debt—or more precisely in the cost of its service. Indeed, it is obviously advisable

followers. Its importance depends upon the extent to which we can trust in new inventions stimulating investment in the future as they have done in the past.

[1] This argument is widely advanced in Sweden, cf. Myrdal, discussed in Lindahl, *Balancing the Budget*.

to be extremely chary of acquiring new obligations of this sort, as much on budgetary as on psychological grounds. The arguments for repaying deadweight debt are on the whole stronger than those for extending it.[1]

The conditions for the balance of actual budgets, since (whether central or local) they are a hybrid of current and capital accounts, naturally do not exactly conform to those of our theoretical accounts. The orthodox criterion for the chancellor's budget is illustrated in Table 1 (I) (p. 289) for the depression years 1930–4. The budget surplus or deficit represents the nominal balance. A more precise calculation, however, would take into account the amount of nominal debt redemption (the net budget surplus). On this basis the budget only failed to show a balance in 1932. If, however, we calculate the true amount of debt repayment the matter is somewhat different. In 1930 it is necessary to make deductions for borrowing both on behalf of the Unemployment Fund and for interest payments on saving certificates. This reduces the favourable balance to very small proportions. In 1931 similar (but larger) deductions must be made, and in addition the sum of £8·75 m. (the dollar reserve) transferred from capital account must be subtracted. There was thus in reality a large deficit. In 1932 the nominal deficit was again increased by borrowing, but only very slightly. There was, however, a large payment to America (£19·9 m.) for what proved to be a non-recurrent obligation.[2] On internal account there was therefore a substantial surplus. In 1933 the budget was balanced with the aid of a capital account (the War Loan Depreciation Fund), but this was almost offset by excess of repayments on the unemployment insurance account. From that date to the end of our period the budget was balanced by a handsome margin. If, however, a definite programme of debt redemption is considered to be necessary to a complete balance, it cannot be said that much progress was made in any year.

The different interpretations of the term 'balanced budget', which it is possible to put forth, serve to illustrate the shortcomings of a hybrid account. A situation in which one section of the press can acclaim a surplus while another laments a deficit[3] is desirable neither on economic nor on financial grounds.

---

[1] Cf. Chap. XXI, pp. 325 ff.   [2] For the time being at any rate.
[3] As occurred in 1937.

We may now inquire what modification in our conclusions as to the degree of balancing actually achieved would be necessary, if changes in funds and in outstanding debt held against assets had been included in the account year by year. These are shown in II and III (Table 1). It appears that the deficit on the Unemployment Fund in 1930 and 1931 was partly offset by increases in the other social funds. But in 1932, although the Unemployment Fund was made to balance by drastic increases in the rates of contribution, and the cutting of benefits, the decline in the National Health Insurance and Pensions Funds left a small deficit on this part of the accounts. In the early years of the depression both the government and the local authorities added substantially to their stock of capital equipment. The greater part of this gave rise to active rather than to inactive debt. Hence it cannot properly be classed as an addition to the deficit. In addition, although comparatively small amounts of deadweight debt were written off, very extensive savings in the cost of service were achieved as a result of the conversion operation of 1932. If all these items are included it seems only reasonable to conclude that, economically, the complete national accounts were quite adequately balanced year by year in the depression, with the sole exception of 1931.

Returning to the central budget, as the only account of which we have complete details, if we add up the debt redemption balances and deficits over the six years, it is clear that there was a considerable excess balance. Is it possible that if the period is considered as a whole this was an overbalance? On general grounds it is clear that an overbalance in years when the national income is low, and which is not urgently required for debt redemption, may be economically harmful. The national income is decreased by the taxation necessary for the effort, and there is no assurance that the funds released by the repayment of debt will be invested in ways which will cause it to increase again to the former figure. Indeed, in depression, whatever the distribution of holdings of the national debt, there is good reason for fearing that they will not be so invested. Before welcoming a balanced budget we must therefore count the cost of enjoying it. If the decrease in the national income is greater than the subsequent increase, or more precisely if the national income in real terms is smaller than it would have been without the imposition of taxation necessary to achieve the balance, we must conclude that economically there has been an overbalance.

Some indication of the cost of achieving such a degree of balance as was secured during the depression in the thirties may be gathered from the amount of additional taxation which had to be imposed. According to the estimates of yields the cumulative net additional revenue (from tax changes remaining in force) was as follows:

	1930	1931	1932	1933	1934
(£ m.)	33·4	97·1	136·0	140·2	124·6

It was inevitable in 1931 that tax rates should be substantially raised if a large and immediate increase in deadweight debt was to be avoided. Indeed, 1934 was the first year in which it was thought possible to reverse the process by reducing taxation to any substantial extent. The problem of balancing the budget is thus intimately related to the behaviour of the tax structure in the trade cycle, and hence to the whole question of cyclical revenue policy.

But the cost of balancing the budget in depression cannot be measured merely by taking account of the additional money burden imposed in taxation. Depression implies a heavy fall in incomes. The poor naturally suffer most from this since they have little or no reserves, and the incidence of unemployment is much heavier on wage than on salary earners. But a heavy decline also takes place in the incomes of the well-to-do which are derived from industrial profits. An investigation[1] into the relation between large incomes and prices shows that, broadly speaking, the larger the income the closer the correlation with price movements. Chart I (p. 290) illustrates this by showing movements in the 1,000th and the 25,000th incomes from the top, in relation to the wholesale price index and the national income, over the period 1910 to 1934. The difference of sensitivity is of course due to the larger number of entrepreneurs among the very rich, and to the greater holding of equity stocks—since the movement in personal incomes is only the reflection of the change in industrial profits. While we need not shed tears over the relative poverty of the captains of industry, the chart does suggest the check to the spirit of enterprise which depression may cause. The loss of entrepreneurial income is dangerous just because it may lead to a community loss more than proportionate to the increased burden falling on the higher incomes, in so far as the entrepreneurial class is thereby led to cease to

[1] Cf. Stamp, 'The Influence of the Price Level', cit.

exercise its function. (If we like to put it so, the danger is that social net loss will be greater than private.)

We have to inquire what changes in the tax burden and in relative taxable capacity these changes in income distribution imply, and what is the most intelligent method, not merely of allowing for them, but of adjusting the tax structure to mitigate their effects.

TABLE 1

The Balance of the Budget

I. *The chancellor's budget*

(£ m.)

	1930	1931	1932	1933	1934
Nominal budget					
Surplus (+) or deficit (−)	−23·28	+ 0·36	−32·28	+31·15	+ 7·66
Nominal Sinking Fund	+66·83	+32·50	+26·33	+ 7·75	+12·34
Net budget surplus	+43·55	+32·86	− 5·95	+38·90	+20·00
Deduct (−)					
(1) Borrowing (−) or repayment (+) for Unemployment Fund	−36·44	−39·61	..	+ 8·31	+ 0·91
(2) Borrowing (−) for savings certificate repayment	− 3·50	− 8·43	− 2·66	..	..
(3) Capital funds used as revenue	..	8·75	..	10·00	..
Total Deductions	−39·94	−56·79	− 2·66	− 1·69	+ 0·91
True Debt Redemption	+ 3·60	−23·91	− 7·60	+37·21	+20·80

II. *Social insurance funds*

	1930	1931	1932	1933	1934
Social Insurance Funds Excess of payments into (+) . Of payments out of (−)	−31·9	−39·1	− 4·8	+ 3·7	+ 6·9

III. *Changes in active and inactive debt*

	1930	1931	1932	1933	1934
Excess of redemption (−) Excess of new borrowing (+)					
A. Active					
(a) central	+ 6·96	+ 5·39	+ 4·53	+ 0·83	+ 1·41
(b) local (E. and W.)	+17·61	+ 9·68	+ 5·46	− 4·05	+ 3·07
B. Inactive (including housing)					
(a) central	− 0·96	− 0·57	− 0·50	− 0·57	− 0·77
(b) local (E. and W.)	+60·56	+42·73	+30·87	+14·19	+13·30
Total change	+84·17	+57·23	+40·36	+10·40	+17·01

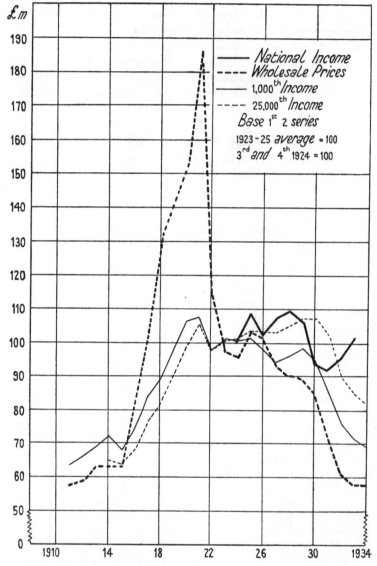

£m

190

180

170

160

150

140

130

120

110

100

90

80

70

60

50

0

—————— *National Income*
- - - - - - *Wholesale Prices*
———— 1,000th *Income*
- - - - - 25,000th *Income*
Base 1st 2 *series*
1923-25 *average* = 100
3rd *and* 4th 1924 = 100

1910   14   18   22   26   30   1934

CHART I.—THE PRICE SENSITIVITY OF LARGE INCOMES
The Relation between the 1,000th and the 25,000th Incomes, the Price Level
and the National Income
Based on Stamp, *J.R.S.S.* 1936
and C. G. Clark, *National Income*

XVIII

TAXATION AND THE TRADE CYCLE

THE effect of depression is to divide the community into three groups. First come those whose incomes are fixed in money terms—a group comprising the fixed interest rentiers, most salary earners, and a large proportion of the skilled and upper-grade wage earners. (Rentiers may of course suffer at a later stage from conversions, but the extent of this in the 1931 depression was quite abnormal and depended on very special causes.) All these classes experience an increase in real incomes, and hence of taxable capacity. Secondly, there is a small group for whom the fall in prices is more or less exactly balanced by the fall in money incomes. Some entrepreneurs, and probably a considerable number of wage-earners, fall into this class. Their taxable capacity is unaltered. The remainder of the community experience a fall in incomes more than proportionate to the fall in prices, and a consequent reduction in taxable capacity. This group includes not only the unemployed but most entrepreneurs and equity stockholders.

The incidence of the existing tax structure is naturally altered by the fall in prices and incomes, but the effect differs as between consumption duties (distinguishing as to whether they are *ad valorem* or specific), and income and capital taxes. As regards consumption taxes those in group 1 find themselves better off, in the sense that even if they spend the same amounts as before on taxed commodities (and hence get more of them) they are left with a greater real income than before, owing to the fall in price of other commodities. If, further, the duties happen to be *ad valorem*,[1] the tax paid will be lowered as prices fall, and they will actually make a smaller contribution to revenue than before. Those in group 2 will also benefit from the lightening of *ad valorem* duties, but not otherwise. Those in group 3 also derive some benefit from this source, but it can hardly afford much compensation for their

[1] *Ad valorem* duties play a fairly important part in British import duties. In 1936 taxed imports were divided as follows: Food, Drink, and Tobacco £314 m., Raw Materials £74 m., Mainly manufactured goods £182 m. The last two classes were almost entirely *ad valorem*, and there was some trace of this method in the first, cf. Leak, *J.R.S.S.* 1937.

other losses. For those members of the community which make their main contribution in the form of consumption taxes, therefore, the depression brings some alleviation of normal tax incidence. On the other hand, their contribution to local rates is only lightened in the sense that they have more real income available after paying the tax than under the old system of prices. Similarly in the case of income tax, those whose money incomes are unaltered derive some advantage from the fact that a constant money contribution leaves over a greater value of income. On the other hand, since tax liability falls (for the most part more than proportionately) with contracting income, tax contributions are reduced, and taxpayers are made better off—except in so far as the lag between assessment and payment works to their disadvantage in the downswing. Depression causes a rapid fall in the value of estates, particularly those which depend mainly on stock exchange equity values. The money liability to death duties is thereby reduced. (Since progression is much less continuous than with the income taxes, owing to the absence of allowances, this is not certain to happen.) On the other hand, the loss sustained in realizing securities to pay the duty may be considerably increased.

The broad effect of the existing tax structure in depression is thus to enhance the favourable experience of fixed income receivers, particularly in so far as *ad valorem* duties or surtax are important to them, and somewhat to mitigate the evil plight of those whose incomes are reduced.

The chancellor's position in depression is almost as unpleasant as that of the entrepreneurs. Wages and salaries are notoriously sticky. He can hope for only trifling economies on the expenditure side. Meanwhile the local authorities are clamouring for additional assistance, and the unemployed require continually greater attention. The bill to be met will probably be larger than usual, however much he may economize. On the revenue side, in addition to a fall in income tax more than proportionate to the contraction in incomes, and other incidental reductions, the sharp decline in stamp and death duties leaves a substantial gap to fill. The chancellor's problem is to determine the manner of preserving financial integrity which will not merely impose the smallest additional burden, having regard to the depression alinement of incomes and the incidence of the tax structure, but also, if he can, to use the tax structure to stimulate revival.

The movements which occur in depression are of course only half of the total cyclical movement. When prices rise the real income and hence the taxable capacity of fixed interest receivers are reduced, while those of entrepreneurs and some salary and wage earners increase. The task of the chancellor, however, appears relatively easy since tax receipts tend to rise faster than liabilities. Nevertheless, it is equally desirable that the movements of the boom should be taken into account when framing fiscal policy. For instance, if the receipts of certain consumption taxes do not show an anticipated resiliency it is an indication either that real incomes of consumers of the commodities have fallen too much to allow of increased purchases, or that there is little elasticity of demand against income for these products. The first would suggest that a relaxation of the rates charged should be made, in the interests of the taxpayers, the second that a relaxation might be in the long-run interest of the exchequer. A much more important consideration is that if the state undertakes to temper the wind to the shorn lamb in depression it has surely the right to demand an increased contribution in prosperity from those whose money incomes are rising faster than prices—on the assumption that it can turn the tax receipts to good account. Properly understood this does not mean seizing the opportunity to start new services with an election appeal, but rather forging a suit of armour against depression and the violence of fluctuations.

There is an *a priori* case against tax changes if they can be avoided, particularly during abnormal periods when psychological reactions are magnified, and the course of tax receipts is hard to foresee. Before discussing the possibilities of cyclical tax manipulation therefore it will be well to examine the scope for meeting the situation by other methods.

The adoption of a plan of long-period budget balancing or of increasing investment is not inconsistent with the introduction of short-period deviations designed to mitigate the intensity of trade fluctuations. If this policy were in practice the long-period criterion would be satisfied only over a considerable period—say of eight or ten years. Within this period depression budgets would be underbalanced and boom budgets overbalanced to a compensatory degree. Economically such a policy would have many advantages, and financially it would be unimpeachable if carried out conscientiously. It demands, however, a high degree of financial integrity, and is not entirely free from other difficulties. In the first place abandoning the policy of annual balance means running counter both to the universal practice of industry and to a natural rhythm which is fundamental over a large part of the economic field. There would no doubt be a danger of postponing commitments in the hope of more favourable conditions later. It would therefore be essential to keep the long-period plan well in the forefront. This might be achieved by including in each annual budget a scheme which would satisfy the long-run criterion for the next eight or ten years[1] (according to the period chosen). Alternatively the budget might be balanced on a series of five- or ten-year plans. This would perhaps provide a greater safeguard against laxity, as modifications in the plan could less easily be introduced. Experience suggests that there is a certain periodicity in trade cycles of which it should be possible to take some advantage. Unfortunately this periodicity is hardly regular enough to form the basis of a budget-planning period, although it is strong enough to wreck a plan if it once got 'out of step'. A fairly long planning period—eight or ten years rather than five— would probably have some advantages in allowing a greater opportunity for balancing out good and bad years. The success of a long-period plan with cyclical deviations depends ultimately not so much on its technical details as on the manner in which it is carried out. It would undoubtedly be more successful as part of a comprehensive policy than as an isolated measure.

Whether or not a definite balancing period has been adopted, if once the budget has been unbalanced, deliberate steps must be taken to restore financial equilibrium at a later stage. The most desirable method of doing this depends partly on what means have been used to ease the fiscal burden in depression. For instance, it may be that the profits of government trading services will be sufficient to repay the debts incurred in depression. In this case budgetary equilibrium is restored automatically, and the policy of periodic rather than of annual balance justifies itself. If new public investment, which will eventually become an earning asset, has been undertaken in depression, the same result will be achieved, although only in a longer period. Where such oppor-

[1] This method has been adopted in Sweden, with a ten-year plan, cf. Lindahl, *Balancing the Budget*, cit. An eight-year plan has apparently been adopted in the British Unemployment Fund.

tunities for investment are hard to find, debts will no doubt have to be incurred in depression which can only be repaid out of taxation in the boom. It may be, however, that it has been possible, with the help of accumulated funds, to avoid new borrowing in depression, although not balancing the budget out of current tax receipts, or, less reputably, by the use of accidental capital reserves. In this case the depleted reserves must naturally be restored. It is obvious that these methods are of very varied applicability to British conditions.

The large provision for social insurance in this country suggests that the method of deliberately accumulating funds would be particularly suitable. So far, however, there has been little attempt to make use of it. When the depression of 1931 occurred the Unemployment Fund was already in debt, mainly owing to the rates of contribution having been set too low in the twenties. There was thus no reserve available. It was then attempted to build one up, starting immediately in 1931 when depression was at its worst. However desirable to restore the solvency of a fund, it is clear that to attempt to do so during depression can only serve to postpone recovery by taxing enterprise and spending during the early stages. Then, as eventually prosperity began to return and reserves to mount up, instead of investing them, it was proposed to extend benefits. In the case of the other funds, in which there were considerable reserves, not only was disbursement policy extremely conservative throughout the depression, but the rates of health insurance contributions were raised, in addition to those for unemployment insurance.

The movement of autonomous funds over the depression and recovery was thus contrary to what economic reasoning would suggest as desirable, but this does not appear to be inevitable. In practice the use of such funds as a tool of cyclical policy may be limited by the method of separate accounting, which necessitates the maintenance of larger balances than if the funds were pooled. In the case of National Health Insurance it is probable that administrative reform in respect of the approved societies might promote a more economical reserve policy.[1] There is also the consideration that large reserves are a convenience for monetary policy.[2] This, however, is a secondary use which should hardly be allowed to stand in the way of a more vital function.

[1] Cf. Chap. III, pp. 53 ff.   [2] Cf. Chap. XXIII.

These, presumably, are matters which could be remedied fairly early.

There is, however, one general difficulty in the policy of accumulated funds which has frequently been advanced. How are the funds to be invested and disinvested without causing disturbance in the market? It has been suggested that selling long-term government stock in depression would have such an unfortunate effect, and would tend to involve the funds in such serious capital losses, that it should strenuously be avoided. One method of avoiding it would be for the Treasury to borrow on short term for the additional expenditure of the funds, taking over their reserves in exchange. But it can hardly be hoped that fresh borrowing in the money market, even when backed up by reserves, would not have an even more unfortunate effect than the disturbance to the long-term market caused by selling stock. An alternative would be for the funds as they accumulate to buy gold[1] rather than gilt-edged. There would certainly be no difficulty in liquidating this—on the assumption that there is no danger of an alteration of the relation of the national currency to gold. Such a course would, however, deprive the funds of all opportunity of investing in earning assets. But it is questionable if the disinvestment difficulty is really so serious as has been suggested. Expenditure would tend to be gradual and continuous rather than in sudden large amounts. There seems to be little ground for supposing that during depression, when the advantages of holding gilt-edged stock rather than industrial securities are great, there will not be considerable periods when stock can be safely unloaded without the slightest fear of raising the long-term rate of interest. The matter is primarily one of confidence and of alternative investment opportunities. The realization by the market that official sales are part of deliberate long-term policy would further tend to limit their disturbing effect.

Investment in new earning assets is the most direct method of fighting depression. It naturally covers both normal development timed to take place in depression, and specially planned works. Whether or not the assets acquired do actually become remunerative within the period of the depression in which they are constructed is largely immaterial. Since such investment entails no permanent increase in the national debt, any increase in the cost of

[1] Cf. Robbins, *Lloyds Bank Monthly*, May 1937.

its service will only be temporary. If a net profit policy is followed some accumulation of receipts will accrue which will be available either to pay off debt in the boom or to be accumulated to ease the next depression. There is, however, a considerable difference in effect between the different types of investment. The more commercial in nature they are, the more fluctuating are their receipts likely to be. To rely on the profits of state investment as an important source of normal revenue is unsatisfactory. For cyclical purposes, however, it is ideal. Since this country with its strong tradition of private enterprise is relatively poor in opportunities for such investment, it is particularly desirable that the budgetary path for their expansion should be made as smooth as possible. A most important first step in this direction is the general recognition that the creation of debt against assets does not hinder, but assists, the balancing of the budget. This is one of the chief arguments for showing the capital budget separately.

It has no doubt been partly the small opportunities for the use of reputable methods for easing the burden of depression which has encouraged the use of capital reserves to balance the budget. Although financially this policy is extremely reprehensible, in practice deficits of this type are generally condoned during depression. Mr. Churchill adopted the device more than once— though not, it must be noted, with the justification of a major depression. It is interesting to reflect that Snowden in spite of his invincible orthodoxy did not disdain it in 1931. Capital reserves are inevitably built up from time to time—as a precaution against an international contingency, or perhaps as a result of a currency change.[1] The transfer of such funds to balance the budget can be used with great advantage at times when it is psychologically important to preserve a nominal balance. The present method of accounting both simplifies and increases the necessity for such a form of window dressing. It is necessary to bear in mind that in the present state of economic understanding there is a psychological danger in deliberately unbalancing the budget. This danger is not confined to the internal effects. Indeed, the events of 1931 suggest that the external effect of a suspected decline of British financial integrity may be more serious than the

[1] Road Fund reserves do not fall under this heading. They should be earmarked to increase the national income, not to provide window dressing for the chancellor.

internal reactions.[1] It would surely be better policy from both points of view to adopt a system of accounting which revealed the true state of balance at a glance, but which at the same time allowed for cyclical deviation. Even if unorthodox methods were still occasionally used, the existence of a period plan and the publicity of the account would both provide some guarantee against the situation getting out of hand. This would probably be sufficient to satisfy the suspicious.

But in addition to such methods of lightening the fiscal burden in depression there is an obvious *a priori* case for supposing that a more active part might be played by the tax structure itself than is at present the case. For instance, such considerable weight might be given to taxes whose yields decline relatively little in depression, that the need for taking other measures to balance the budget would be minimized. If the 'spread' of taxes is carefully arranged with a view to cyclical reactions it should be possible also to allow for some measure of relief of the fiscal burden in depression by giving a considerable weight to taxes whose burden declines when prices fall.

The feasibility of a crisis-proof tax structure depends on the difference in sensitivity of taxes, that is to say, on the extent to which receipts may be expected to vary in relation to variations in the national income. This is no more than the consideration from the chancellor's point of view of changes in income and tax burden on different classes of consumers. As far as consumption taxes are concerned the most important item in this is the elasticity of demand in respect of income[2] of the various taxed commodities. This is a matter which calls for further statistical investigation. Income and capital tax receipts vary directly with the size of the relevant income groups, although administrative details may introduce certain modifications. There are three aspects of sensitivity which require separate attention: (i) the rate of change in the downswing, (ii) the rate of change in the upswing, and (iii) the timing or the extent to which changes in tax receipts are in advance or retard of changes in the national income. This last reflects two different movements—a *real* time difference depending on the order in which different incomes are affected by a change in

---

[1] In this respect it is probable that small nations whose currency changes do not upset world markets have more liberty of action than large creditor nations.　　　　　　　　　　　　[2] Cf. Allen and Bowley, op. cit.

industrial conditions, and a *nominal* time difference depending on institutional causes. Thus, on the one hand, incomes depending on the stock exchange react first, entrepreneurial incomes next, while wage incomes tend to lag behind both on the down- and on the upswing. On the other hand, income and surtax receipts have nominal time lags of one and two years respectively, depending on the relation between the year of assessment and the year of payment. The main part of the burden, however, probably falls in the year in which the payment is made, so that this administrative detail slightly accentuates the tax burden on the higher incomes in the downswing and lightens it on the upswing, a movement therefore contrary to what is desirable. It is obviously good policy to take the fullest advantage of real time differences, but to endeavour to ease nominal ones.

The measurement of tax sensitivity has unfortunately received scanty attention from economists or statisticians.[1] There are indeed very real difficulties in assessing its importance in any particular situation. In the first place the reactions of individual taxes depend on the rest of the tax structure—changes in prices lead to changes in the goods which are adopted as substitutes. Secondly, it is usually not safe to assume that sensitivity will be the same at different rates of tax. Hence arguments drawn from one set of data are not necessarily consistent with those from another time and place. Further, when tax rates are changed, it does not seem possible to estimate with any precision what the true sensitivity is. To assume that it remains constant over the different phases of the trade cycle appears to side-step a most important part of the problem we particularly want to isolate. This is perhaps the most serious difficulty. It therefore seems safer, although the results are naturally rather limited, to confine our examination on the one hand to post-war experience, and on the other to taxes the rates of which were not changed during the sub-periods of either the down- or the upswing.

From general observation, which is fully confirmed by such special studies as have been made, it is possible to arrange the most usual taxes roughly in an order of (ascending) sensitivity, as follows: poll taxes, taxes on necessities, particularly working-class

---

[1] But cf. Colm, *Social Research*, 1934, pp. 319 ff., D'Albergo, *Riforma Sociale*, 1934, pp. 152 ff., and Bretherton, *Econometrica*, 1937, p. 171, and sources therein mentioned.

necessities, taxes on luxuries, property taxes, sales taxes, income taxes. The sensitivity of any particular tax differs according to the technical details of its levy. Thus *ad valorem* consumption taxes are more sensitive than specific. British death duties are considerably more sensitive than is usual with property taxes both because of their steep progression and because of the important part that stock-exchange securities play in estates. Since the war British income tax has been made more sensitive by the change-over from the three-year to the annual system of assessment. This has also slightly reduced its nominal time difference. The growth in progression in surtax has also increased sensitivity. On the other hand, the British income taxes are less sensitive than their counter-parts abroad which allow of the offsetting of capital gains and losses.

Table 1 illustrates the sensitivity of taxes available for examination on this method in the downswings of 1920-3 and 1930-2, and the upswings 1927-9 and 1932-5. The exclusion of the Irish Free State territory after 1921 to some extent hinders the comparison of the depressions, but it seems nevertheless worth including the earlier figures for such comparability as they afford. The two booms are also not entirely on a par, since prosperity in 1929 was very unevenly distributed over the economy. Further, owing to the great number of changes in tax rates, and particularly to the large number of increases in 1931, it is only possible to find a small number of duties which ran through even a sub-period with unaltered rates. Nevertheless, enough remains to be fairly representative, since there are examples of income and capital taxes, and consumption taxes both of elastic and inelastic demand, and with expanding and contracting markets. Although it can hardly ever be hoped to include income tax directly on this method —since it is the levy above all others which is varied to meet short-run emergencies—it is possible to deduce its true sensitivity from changes in 'actual income-tax income' so long as the exemption limit has not been altered during a sub-period. The sensitivity of surtax may be indirectly deduced from the variation of large incomes in relation to the national income (Chart I, Chapter XVII). The want of a steady rate of mortality of millionaires renders it impossible to draw very definite conclusions from death-duty receipts. Working with average receipts per estate does something to even out variations, but even so since the number of very large estates is very small, the results are only approximate.

TABLE I

Income and tax sensitivity in boom and depression††

Year	Sub-period	National income (£ m.)	Actual I.T. income§	Sur-tax	Estate Duties‖ (£s.)	Stamp Duties	Tax Receipts (£ m.)						
							Tobacco	Beer	Spirits	Sugar	Entertainments	Silk	Motor Licences
1920	Down-swing	5,600*	2,661·2	..	484	26·5¶	55·5	123·4	71·0	30·4	11·7	..	7·8**
1921		3,900*	2,462·5	..	400	19·6	55·2	121·9	62·8	36·8	10·3	..	11·1
1922		3,500**	2,353·2‡	..	571	21·9	53·4	92·3	53·6	40·2	9·6	..	12·6
‡1923		3,800*	2,303·3	..	576	21·6	51·9	81·7	54·0	38·1	9·3	..	14·6
1927	Upswing	4,719†	2,416·2	60·1	661	26·9	58·1	83·3	47·4	..	6·1	5·9	24·7
1928		4,710†	2,494·4	56·2	688	30·1	59·1	75·8	45·7	..	6·0	6·1	25·5
1929		4,765†	2,530·8	56·6	609	25·3	62·8	77·2	42·6	..	6·7	6·2	26·6
1930	Down-swing	4,698†	2,497·0	..	687	20·3	..	..	40·6	..	..	..	27·8
1931		4,264†	2,725·1	..	497	17·1	..	..	34·9	..	..	..	27·3
1932		4,210†	2,553·7	..	553	19·1	..	..	34·5	..	..	..	28·0
1933	Upswing	4,334†	2,505·1	52·6	635	22·7	67·5	..	33·5	..	9·2	..	..
1934		4,624†	2,615·6	51·2	604	24·1	70·7	..	32·4	..	9·7	..	..
1935		4,926†	2,709·9	51·0	540	25·3	75·0	..	34·9	..	..	..	..

* Layton's estimate to Colwyn Committee.   † C. G. Clark, gross estimate.

† Figures prior to 1922 include territory now in I.F.S.

§ The exemption limit was lowered during sub-periods in 1921 and 1931.   ‖ Average receipts per estate.

¶ Increased duties came into operation 20 Sept. 1920.   ** Increased duties came into operation 1 Jan. 1921.

†† A blank indicates either that rates were changed during a sub-period, or that 1935 figures are not available. 1923 is included although it is a recovery year, in order to give a basis of comparison with 1922 on the altered territorial arrangement.

It is evident that all consumption taxes have a very low degree of sensitivity, with the exception of the declining alcohol duties. These represent an extreme case of a tax on what has become a luxury (a commodity of elastic demand). Tobacco and motor duties both show a greater sensitivity in the upswing than in the down, indicating no doubt that variations in receipts depend more on an expanding market than on the elasticity of demand of existing consumers. The same movement can be observed, though to a less degree, in the case of the entertainments duty. Exactly the opposite is true of beer, which is more sensitive in the downswing than in the up. It is significant that the slight recession in the national income in 1928 was reflected in an absolute recession in beer and entertainments duty receipts, but not in tobacco, silk, or motoring taxes. Although not typical of any other tax, the spirits duty is particularly illuminating since rates of duty ran through the whole period unaltered. Sensitivity in the downswing is more marked than in the case of beer, but the most significant fact is that there was no absolute increase in receipts in an upswing except in 1935.

Income and capital taxes, on the other hand, show a marked degree of sensitivity.[1] This is especially noticeable in the case of stamp and death duties, which depend mainly on the violent fluctuations of the stock exchange. While there is no doubt of the sensitivity of income and surtax part of the variation is due to acceleration and laxity in collection. People tend to get behind with payments in depression. It is sometimes but not always possible to track down the presence of this factor.

The timing of the different types of taxes varies quite as significantly as their sensitivity. The turning-point in consumption

---

[1] In order to side-step the difficulty of changes in tax rates, Mr. Bretherton calculated a hypothetical tax yield, based on official estimates of the effect of changes. Apart from official fallibility, this leads to difficulties where rates are changed at shorter intervals than tax effects require to work out. Nevertheless, the device enabled Mr. Bretherton to construct an index of sensitivity. According to this the change from highest to lowest in the 1931 depression was:

Tax	Income tax	Surtax	Sugar	Tobacco	Entertainments
Highest .	101·6	120·6	108	114·8	123
Lowest .	74·6	74·5	94	113	119

tax receipts is invariably after that of the national income. For articles of food (conventional necessities) the lag appears to be roughly two years, for the expanding service group rather less, and for the elastic demand commodities roughly one year. This is just what we should expect, having regard to the lag in changes in working-class incomes, and to the normal lay-out of expenditure on these commodities. This delay represents a real time difference, and hence one which the chancellor can take advantage of without inflicting hardship. On the other hand, stamp and death duties move roughly a year in advance of the national income. This is also a true time difference, which consequently should be fully exploited. Income tax receipts would naturally move very closely with changes in the national income, were it not that the delay between earning and assessment interposes a nominal time lag of a year. Surtax receipts similarly have a nominal time lag of two years, but, in fact, surtax incomes must tend to move in advance of others.

The variations in sensitivity of the different parts of the tax structure is thus quite sufficient—without undertaking a more elaborate analysis—to show where the shoe pinches, and where advantage can safely be taken of differences. It is evident, however, that fiscal policy in the past has paid little attention to such considerations. So far indeed as changes in rates have been made during cyclical conditions they have invariably run counter to those which economic considerations would suggest, thus tending to accentuate fluctuations. There have no doubt been weighty reasons for this, above all the relatively stationary condition of the national income. Chancellors have not been unaware of the burden they were inflicting, but tax receipts at their minimum were insufficient to cover routine expenditure. On the other hand, in better times tax rates have already seemed so high that a fall in burden was insistently demanded. It cannot be denied that the legacy of the exceptional effort of 1931 inflicted a burden which any chancellor had to be very chary of increasing. Further, owing to the failure to time expenditure in such a way as to mitigate fluctuations, the decline in tax receipts has been greater and the task of balancing the budget more difficult than it might have been. At the same time, the method of presenting the accounts has tended to make it appear a more formidable task than it actually was.

Granted that these hindrances exist—and from the fiscal side they are more or less part of the data—it must still be asked whether the tax structure might not with some adjustment have been a better instrument of cyclical policy. For instance, the drastic reduction of the breakfast-table duties removed a source of revenue which both on account of its low sensitivity and delayed timing is a particularly useful tool for the purpose. We have seen that there are some arguments in favour of a small increase in these taxes from their present low levels, even in normal times. They are to be preferred on both fiscal and nutritional grounds to duties on such foodstuffs as meat, fresh vegetables, and dairy produce. Moreover, the change in relative taxable capacity which occurs in depression tends to lighten the weight of taxes of this class. The increase in rates need only be very moderate since the commodities concerned are known to have a very low price elasticity. In addition a greater permanent rate on stamps and the motor duties would tend, in present conditions, to diminish fluctuations in tax revenue. A corresponding relaxation of the more sensitive taxes would be a natural corollary.

While a more stable tax structure would obviously be a great convenience to the chancellor, measures to attain it cannot of course be pushed so far that any danger of social injustice arises. A moderate adjustment, based on relative changes in real incomes and on real time differences of tax receipts, should actually impose a lighter burden than a similar total of revenue raised from a haphazard tax structure. It is naturally assumed that revenue policy will be backed up by an active expenditure policy for the unemployed.

But since in fact tax rates are frequently increased in the middle of depression, it seems only reasonable to go one step further and deliberately plan to introduce such short-period changes in the tax structure as would enable it to become an active contributor to cyclical policy. Without going deeply into the matter, certain broad lines of attack immediately suggest themselves. In depression it is clearly in the public interest to revive the entrepreneurial function and consequently the demand for labour at as early a moment as possible. This is the essential step to turn stagnation into recovery. While expenditure policy naturally has the more important role to play here, there is some scope for stimulating investment from the revenue side also. The most direct method would probably be drastically to reduce the tax liability of funds applied to reconstruction and replacement during depression. This has frequently been urged by business men. While the uncertainty of the future course of demand might prevent very extensive or specific works being undertaken, the pause in normal production and the fall in costs which accompany depression suggest that it is a particularly suitable time for catching up with the march of progress.

An alternative method of stimulating investment would be to increase the attractions of employing labour by making it cheap relatively to other commodities. This might be achieved by a general forcing down of wage rates. Even if it were practicable, however, such a policy would tend to restrict consumption, and so negative its expansionary effects. From the entrepreneurs' point of view the same change in the price of labour can be brought about by removing the poll tax on employment (the employers' contribution to social insurance).[1] On the expenditure side the effect of this would be wholly expansionary. If it was feared that the mere removal of a liability would not in itself provide sufficient inducement to expand, the concession could be supplemented by a small direct subsidy per worker employed. If the subsidy is made applicable to all workers, and not merely to the newly employed, there can be no disturbance to the natural distribution of labour between different industries. The administrative cost of the additional subsidy would be negligible, since it could be administered through the normal social insurance channels.

Both the cost and the benefit of a wage subsidy of this type depend, on the one side, on the extent to which additional labour would be employed with a slight increase in apparent profitability (the elasticity of demand for labour), and, on the other, on the rates of contribution and expenditure for social insurance. As long as some additional labour is taken on, there must be some saving on unemployment expenditure. The higher the employers' contribution the greater the inducement offered by its removal. The higher the allowances of the unemployed the greater the saving on their re-employment. This suggests that in England the opportunities for such a policy are particularly favourable. But the manner in which the subsidy should be financed remains to be considered. It is not, of course, necessary that the whole of the

---

[1] For an elaboration of this proposal cf. Kaldor, *J.P.E.* 1936.

cost should be met from current tax receipts. The reserve of the social insurance funds themselves should be able to sustain part of the burden, even if there are no other funds which can be drawn upon. But even if the subsidy has to be wholly financed out of income tax, it may still be preferable to offering no inducements to entrepreneurs. In general to raise income tax in depression runs the danger of being seriously deflationary. But to raise the contribution of fixed interest receivers need be no more than an adjustment to allow for their increased real incomes and taxable capacity. If, therefore, a small increase in income tax were imposed, but the proceeds were passed back to entrepreneurs in the form of a subsidy on employment, it would tend both to equalize the real tax burden of rentiers over the trade cycle and to revive the incentive of entrepreneurs.

The depression problem is mainly one of applying help where it is most needed. But an increase of taxation in prosperity may be desirable, not merely for the purpose of building up reserves, but as a method of controlling the boom. If so, what form should this flexibility take? An increase in stamp duties could perhaps be made to bring in some £5 m., and would almost certainly be useful in checking excessive stock exchange speculation. But for larger amounts it would be necessary to look elsewhere among the income taxes.

As we have seen, two varieties of boom taxation were experimented with in the post-war boom—E.P.D. and C.P.D. The justification for taxing *excess* profits rather than all profits during the war was that profits were due to public expenditure, and not to normal economic factors, and that they were consequently very unevenly distributed. The same argument would apply to some extent whenever a boom was due to public expenditure.[1] The war-time E.P.D. was a flat rate, but if the tax were possible at all there seems no reason why it should not be graduated. This would certainly increase its usefulness and productivity. But it must be noted that the feasability of taxing the increment of profits depended on special war-time conditions. Besides being themselves the cause of the profits made they provided an unequivocal point from which to measure the excess. Although the war occurred in a period of boom, ordinary conditions of productivity had ceased some time before the duty was imposed. In

---

[1] As for instance a rearmament boom.

the absence of a base point some method of capital valuation is inevitable. Technical difficulties make the expense of this almost prohibitive, while the economic difficulties are probably well nigh insurmountable. In any lesser catastrophe also, ordinary boom profits might continue to be made alongside those due specifically to government expenditure. It would thus be impossible to distinguish either the excess, or the extent to which profits were attributable to public expenditure.

There thus seems to be no justification for attempting to single out profits specially due to the public expenditure. Once a boom has been started profits will expand in all lines. There are also further difficulties in taxing the increment of profits in non-war conditions. In the first place there is normally a very considerable difference in the fluctuations of profits between one industry and another, depending on vulnerability to cyclical conditions and on the importance of the risk factor. Secondly, there is a marked difference between the rate of profit expansion in a new and in a well-established business. Allowance could possibly be made for these differences, but only at the cost of still greater complication in calculating the excess. A more general drawback is that so long as it is merely the increment of profits which is liable to the tax it is to the advantage of a firm to show stable rather than expanding profits. Thus the incentive to economical management is weakened, and may be replaced by one to increase equipment and labour force, thus intensifying the boom. Hence it does not seem that a tax of the E.P.D. type is a practical proposition in a boom with any pretence at normality.

The C.P.D. variety of boom tax side-steps the difficulty of equitably calculating the increment by taxing all profits (before distribution). The post-war edition caused a great deal of trouble and inequality by applying only to corporate incomes. Since it is easy to fix a minimum exemption limit there seems no difficulty in abolishing this anomaly. On the other hand, when all profits are to be taxed the definition of 'profits' becomes of first-rate importance. It is by no means easy to make equitable allowance for the differences in the capital structure of firms. These are frequently purely accidental in origin, with no economic significance whatever. The treatment of investments presents another ticklish problem. It is by no means simple to estimate the difference in allowance which should be made for the different function of security holdings between one 'industry' and another when financial businesses have also to be taken into consideration. The C.P.D. variety, however, has the great advantage that it requires no *ad hoc* capital valuation or tax, but can use the schedule D valuations as a base. This does not constitute it a simple tax, however.[1]

But both forms of tax smack very much of being crisis levies. While boom taxation must no doubt have some restraining effect, to overdo this aspect risks turning boom into recession. It cannot be said that entrepreneurs view any type of boom taxation with equanimity, hence there are obvious arguments for making it as little alarming as possible. Above all, if such emergency taxes are imposed they will do least harm if they are withdrawn the moment profits begin to sag. It must be noted that this is contrary to what was anticipated in 1920. C.P.D. was apparently intended to be a permanent part of the tax structure.

There are evidently objections to boom taxation of either the E.P.D. or C.P.D. variety. This being so it must be asked whether an intelligent manipulation of the income taxes might not be sufficient both to restrain the boom and to build up such reserves as were desired. Three effects of a rise in income and surtax in a boom require to be distinguished. An increase in the standard rate would increase the liability on undistributed profits, and on the incomes of a large number of middle-range income receivers whose money incomes are fixed, and whose taxable capacity would consequently already be reduced. A rise in surtax would further increase the liability of the larger incomes. The great majority of taxpayers in this class would no doubt already be enjoying boom profits, whether entrepreneurial or professional. The increased duty on undistributed profits might induce a slight tendency to raise the proportion distributed. This would presumably have an expansionary tendency. Since, however, companies commonly plan to build up reserves in prosperity, there would be no very great incentive for them to part more easily with the non-taxed remainder. In this respect, however, the income tax method must be judged inferior to a method of boom taxation which taxes all

[1] In the original C.P.D. estimates were repeatedly scaled down because of litigation and delayed payments. It is significant that within a few months of the adoption of this form of N.D.C. a guide of several hundred pages to its intricacies appeared.

profits before distribution. The increase in the burden of fixed income taxpayers is certainly undesirable. But for the most part it could be easily allowed for. Snowden's skilful manipulation of allowances in order to negative the 1930 rise in income tax as far as the small incomes were concerned pointed the way. The incidence of income tax can be adjusted by means of allowances and by alterations in the surtax exemption limit to fit any desired scheme of progression. The increased liability of large incomes is as necessary a part of taxing boom profits as the direct levy on companies. It appears that there is considerable scope for the taxing of a boom of any variety without venturing beyond the well-tried paths and methods of the income taxes. The advantages of this method on grounds of flexibility, certainty, and economy are too obvious to require comment.

It is probable that by a skilful application of active fiscal policy the task of balancing the budget would be very much lightened. It must nevertheless remain somewhat doubtful whether, even allowing for other types of assistance such as have been discussed, the British budget can be balanced in depression without some increase in tax rates, at least if we continue to have an increasingly stationary population and a relatively stationary national income. It may prove impossible to solve the dilemma between increasing the wrong taxes and forcing down the national income, on the one hand, and maintaining the national income at the moment but increasing debt, on the other. In this case the gradual accumulation of debt (preferably against assets, but not necessarily active) is probably the lesser evil. For this to be possible without serious danger of financial laxity, however, it is highly desirable, if not absolutely essential, both to separate current and capital items in the national accounts, and to widen their scope so that they may be of real economic, and not merely financial, significance.

PART III

MONETARY POLICY AND THE DEBT

So burdensome, still paying, still to owe.

MILTON.

XIX

THE MONETARY SETTING

BEFORE the war it would generally have been considered unnecessary, if not actually out of order, to include a section on monetary policy in a work on public finance. For this there were two good reasons. In the first place such monetary management as was necessary was held to be the business of the Bank of England rather than of the government. If a question were asked in the House, for instance, as to why Bank Rate had been raised, the chancellor of the exchequer was wont to reply that the bank was a private institution, managed in the interest of its shareholders and depositors, and that hence its actions were none of his concern. Much more important than such an attitude—which it may be suspected was sometimes no more than an excuse for the cloak of secrecy regarded as becoming in monetary affairs—was the limitation of the field of pre-war monetary policy. With a national debt whose weight was scarcely felt, under an international gold standard, and with an established price system, monetary management, if not always smooth and automatic, at least worked along narrow and well-defined paths.

Even, however, when monetary management is confined to the protection of the reserve and the maintenance of the international value of the currency, it already influences the internal economic situation. Changes in Bank Rate bring about changes in all other interest rates and rates of yield. Open-market policy, even if it is designed solely to make Bank Rate effective, alters the volume of bank cash, and is therefore a highly important factor in determining the credit situation. In the post-war period, however, monetary policy has perforce been of much wider scope. Important decisions have had to be taken on the relation of the national currency to other currencies, and to gold. These have reacted on the internal situation by affecting both the foreign balance and foreign lending. Owing to the war debt and its management the government has become the controlling operator both in the money market and the bond market. Public policy necessarily therefore exerts an important influence on the national income, both directly, and indirectly through the level of interest rates.

There is, indeed, a considerable part of monetary policy which is obviously outside the direct concern of public finance. The international aspect which covered practically the whole field before the war is still of great importance, but with the relative growth of home investment its interest for public finance has steadily decreased. Similarly, the relations of monetary policy to the banking system and to the organization of industry only impinge on public finance in so far as they determine broad movements in the national income. With their technical details it is not concerned. Our task, therefore, in this part will be mainly to draw attention to the relation between monetary policy and public finance. We shall make no attempt to examine monetary policy in detail or first hand. The limitations of our field and the extensive literature on the subject alike make such a task unnecessary.

There is, however, one part of monetary policy which, since it enters into the budget, is so closely related to public finance that it might reasonably be considered to form an integral part of it, namely, borrowing policy and debt management. During our period this has been of quite unique importance. The whole of the post-war period, at any rate until 1933, was dominated by the shadow of the war debt. Scarcely had this been lightened than its place was taken by the prospect of a fresh accumulation of deadweight debt on rearmament account. In 1927 the Colwyn Committee published their investigation of the effects of the war debt on the economy. Between that date and the conversion operation of 1932—which permitted the first substantial reduction in the burden of the debt—new dangers attaching to deadweight debt came into prominence. On the one hand, during the gold-standard period the debt proved an additional embarrassment to the exchanges and to the control of interest rates. On the other, the persistent fall in prices after 1927 heavily increased the real burden of the debt. The course of subsequent events has made it clear that the Colwyn conclusions only covered a part of the story.

The magnitude of the disturbance due to war borrowing can

be seen by comparing the relation between debt service and total revenue on the one hand, and the level of interest rates on the other, before and after the war. The first can be seen at a glance from Diagram I, Chapter II. Debt interest required 12·3 per cent. of the revenue in 1914. By 1919 the proportion had risen to 29·8 per cent. As expenditure and taxation were gradually reduced from war levels it came to occupy a still larger place, reaching 38·7 per cent. in 1925, nor was there any considerable reduction before 1933. Chart I illustrates the monetary side of the picture by comparing the long-term interest rate (represented by the yield on consols) in the twenty years 1914–34 with its movement in two similar periods in the recent past—periods which were by nineteenth-century standards relatively disturbed. The greater height and far greater fluctuations of the post-war curve is at once obvious. Hardly less striking is the long period of rigidity (except for a brief rise in 1931–2 covering the abandonment of the gold standard), followed by a sudden fall. By 1934 the yield had receded to a point which was low, but not exceptionally so, on nineteenth-century standards.

Although the debt problem has been stated in terms of the internal deadweight debt of the central government, its significance is considerably wider. England has by no means always resorted to foreign borrowing to finance her major wars. Whenever she has done so the result has inevitably been a subsequent period of budgetary stringency.[1] Although there is no clear evidence that the external debt contracted in the Great War was smaller relative to the national income than it had been, for instance, in the eighteenth century, on the whole it proved a lighter burden. Firstly, the volume of pre-war foreign lending was sufficient to bear the brunt of adjustment. Secondly, strenuous efforts were made to reduce external liabilities in the early post-war years. Thirdly, the debt settlements with the allies secured an inflow of funds which approximately balanced the service of the external debt. England, therefore, almost entirely escaped both the Scylla of making net transfers abroad and the Charybdis of the embarrassment of receiving reparations in kind. Finally, less than thirteen years after the war international

---

[1] Two striking instances in which foreign borrowing led to budgetary stringency appear to have been (i) Flemish loans in the first part of the Hundred Years War, and (ii) Dutch loans in the American War of Independence. Foreign borrowing was also an aggravation of Elizabethan budgetary troubles.

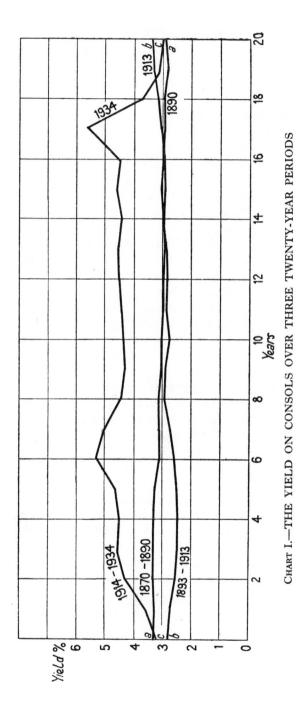

CHART I.—THE YIELD ON CONSOLS OVER THREE TWENTY-YEAR PERIODS

payments were suspended. We can therefore legitimately restrict our field by neglecting the effects of external debt except in so far as they impinged directly on the internal situation—for instance as an aggravation of budgetary stringency in the early twenties, and in connexion with monetary policy.

On the other side deadweight debt is only a part of the problem of internal borrowing. For the investor it is usually a matter of indifference whether his gilt-edged stock represents deadweight, active, or passive debt. The problem of war borrowing cannot therefore be strictly separated from other types of loan finance by the central government. Indeed, since municipal stocks are very close substitutes for war loan, for many purposes total public borrowing must be included, and deadweight debt owes its relative importance merely to its enormous volume. Nevertheless, this is so great that the *milieu* created by deadweight borrowing is that in which the other types are forced to operate.

The war debt has gone through three quite distinct phases. The period of new borrowing lasted from 1914 to 1919. There followed twelve years when the interest charge remained practically unaltered in money terms, in spite of every effort to reduce it. Finally, from 1932 there was a progressive return towards normal,[1] if we can so designate a situation in which debt service though large presents no conspicuous budgetary problem. Something like these three phases is no doubt a common experience in the accumulation of deadweight debt, and each phase presents a problem peculiar to itself. The prime necessity in the first is cheap borrowing, in the second the rapid alleviation of the real burden, while the third gives some opportunity for wiping the slate clean again. The peculiar and difficult feature of the British war debt consisted in the length, and hence the intensity, of the second phase. It may be said therefore that the particular British problem is the consideration of means for shortening this stage. It is obvious that the real burden might have been prevented from rising if it had been possible to avoid a fall in prices when the borrowing

---

[1] If the pre-war relation between funded, unfunded, and floating debt is regarded as normal the goal was still distant. The relevant percentages were:

						1914	1936
Floating .	.	.	.	.	.	2	7
Unfunded	.	.	.	.	.	8	41
Funded .	.	.	.	.	.	90	52
						100	100

period had come to an end. A moderate inflation such as took place in France would even have reduced the real burden. The same end might have been achieved via a reduction in the nominal burden, secured either by cancellation or conversion. None of these methods was adopted in the nineteen-twenties, but it is not necessary to suppose that they would not be available in the future.

Only the second and third phases of the debt fall within our period and hence these must be our main concern. It will be desirable, however, to make a brief preliminary examination of the manner in which the war debt was acquired, both on account of its relevancy to the problem of rearmament borrowing and because the management of the debt was largely dictated by the terms of war borrowing.

XX

WAR BORROWING

SINCE new borrowing continued throughout 1919, March 1920 is the first convenient occasion at which we can observe the completed debt. It stood then at £6,226·7 m., and as regards maturity was divided into three large blocks:

	£ m.
I. Relatively long loans	2,884·8
(8–10 years from date of issue)	
II. Short-term debt	2,089·5
(Less than the above, and more than a year, including £273·5 m. War Savings Certificates of five-year nominal duration)	
III. Floating debt	1,252·4
(A year or less, mainly in Treasury bills)	
	6,226·7

(From *Statistical Abstract*)

While stock of one maturity naturally shades into another, or changes into it with the passage of years—and, indeed, this constituted one of the most difficult problems in the management of the war debt[1]—these three types of borrowing each raised particular problems.

When interest rates are fairly low but rising, with no immediate prospect of a fall, as was the case for a great part of the actual war period, short-term rates tend to rise sooner and farther than long-term. Hence it is more economical to float a long-term loan than to pile up floating debt. It is somewhat surprising, therefore, that the proportion of long-term debt was not larger relatively to the other two blocks. Let us see what light the history of the war loans throws on the question. Table 1a (p. 334) shows how the long-term debt came into being.[2] The progressive deterioration of government credit is evident in the rise in the (real) yields offered on successive loans. Although the first war loan was popular, and was subscribed above expectation, when in less than a year a loan was issued with a yield nearly a point higher, the banks had to take up at least a third of it. The 1917 borrowing represented a further and most

---

[1] Cf. Chap. XXII.

[2] The account here given is founded mainly on Hargreaves, *The National Debt*, chap. xiii.

significant rise. The 5 per cent. loan gave an approximate running
yield of 5⁵⁄₁₆ per cent. Although the 4 per cent. loan was intended
to contain equivalent attractions, it was an almost complete failure.
The scarcely lower yields offered in 1919 were counterbalanced by
a longer run to maturity. Yet although the government was inevitably forced into offering progressively more favourable terms, at
the time of issue a number of loans—in particular the 4½ per cent. of
1915 and those of 1919—were criticized as being quite unnecessarily
generous. It would appear that with more forethought, or better
preparation, long-term financing might have been more economical.

The rise in the yield offered on long-term loans does not, however, fully represent the increase in the cost of this type of borrowing which actually took place. Expensive privileges were included
in the terms of offer in all the later loans, with the object of making
them more attractive. The most important of these were conversion rights on the one hand, and tax concessions on the other. In
particular Mr. McKenna's loan of 1915 created both a backward-
and a forward-looking conversion right (covenanted benefit). Under
the former, existing government stock could—under certain conditions as to the purchase of the new loan—be 'converted' upwards
to its rates. Under the latter the right of switching over (at a rate
which represented a substantial premium) into subsequent war
loans was introduced. The right of subsequent conversion was
also included in certain short-term issues, notably the American
Dollar Bonds. The extent of the exercise of this privilege in the
war period is shown by the last column (Table 1 a). The greater
part of the later long-term loans did not in fact represent new
funds for the government, but only a transfer of those previously
lent—for the most part on terms which had been considerably
less favourable to the lenders. Conversions were chiefly made into
the 5 per cent. War Loan of 1917, which all things considered
offered the most attractive terms. Even during the post-war
decade this particular security continued to swell, reaching a
maximum of £2,184·5 m. in 1929. This privilege, mainly due, it
would appear, to an over-optimistic view of the probable duration
of the war, had thus two unfortunate effects. On the one hand, a
high rate of interest had to be paid on a larger proportion of the
debt than would otherwise have been the case. On the other, holdings tended to be canalized into one gigantic security (the 5 per
cent. War Loan) with a single maturity date.

The tax concessions[1] offered varied from total exemption, or exemption from deduction at the source, to the right of tendering stock in payment of death duties at a premium above its current price. Besides offering an additional inducement to investors, these privileges may have been intended to allow of borrowing at a lower rate than would otherwise have been possible. It is doubtful, however, whether such concessions are ever worth their price. It stands to reason that to make them attractive the government must offer more favourable terms for a privilege the value of which depends on an estimate of the course of future events, than for one the effect of which can be calculated with certainty. At the time the loans were issued it was generally considered that tax rates would soon fall sharply, so that the concessions were probably not very highly valued. As things turned out, however, the government gratuitously threw away considerable sums in tax receipts. There seems to be no means of measuring the loss, but the evasion of taxation on the 5 per cent. loan due to the absence of deduction at the source was undoubtedly very heavy. Tax receipts from abroad in particular were necessarily almost entirely lost.

The ultimate cost of long-term borrowing was further raised by the issue of loans at a substantial discount.[2] This practice offers a speculative benefit—depending on the course of interest rates—which may attract a certain type of investor. Since it is on the nominal interest, and not on the real yield to the investor, that tax is paid, when the price of the security rises he will have a lower tax to pay than if the loan had been issued at the same real, but at a higher nominal, yield. The offer of this privilege is open to the same objections as others which depend on estimates of the future. As far as later purchasers are concerned the tax benefit will tend to be partly, at least, allowed for in the price of the stock. The issue of loans at a low nominal rate of interest, however, has the advantage for the government that it offers a small saving on the debt charge. Accordingly it was chiefly practised in 1919 when budgetary stringency was first becoming evident, and in the post-war decade (for instance in 1925 £129·6 m. of 3½ per cent. Conversion Loan was issued by tender at an average price of 77½). The somewhat doubtful short-run advantages of borrowing below par are, however, far more than offset by the obstacle it places in the path

[1] Cf. *Colwyn Report*, pp. 56 ff.   [2] Cf. ibid., pp. 51 ff.

of future conversion. This has been amply demonstrated in the period of very low interest rates following the 1932 conversions, by the failure to convert any of the government 3½ per cent. stock (including over £400 m. Local Loans stock, much of which was issued at a substantial discount).

The terms of long-period war borrowing thus suggest that in several respects the government did not use its resources to the best economic advantage, hence the burden on this part of the debt turned out higher than it need have been. Perhaps the most serious consideration, however, is that the privileges included in the loans prevented a full use of the long-term market, through the fear of increasing their unfortunate effects still farther. An extra weight was therefore thrown on short-term borrowing and on the floating debt. This bar to long-term borrowing was particularly unfortunate in the early years of the war when long-term rates were still comparatively low.

At the other end of the scale to the long-term loans, all of which were inconvertible before 1925 at the earliest, was £1,252·4 m. of floating debt, requiring constant renewal. This sum compares with an average of £13 m. in the last pre-war year. The justification of floating debt is, of course, as a highly convenient method of financing current expenditure in advance of the receipt of revenue. Normally the debt created is cancelled out as revenue is received. When, however, large amounts of expenditure are financed by floating borrowing, it becomes impossible to cancel the new debt created. Its increase therefore continually expands the basis of credit. There are thus two main objections to an uncontrolled expansion of floating debt—the inflationary tendency inherent, and the recurring cost of renewal. When borrowing is taking place and interest rates are rising (by 1916 short-term rates had already reached 6 per cent.), this cost is a continuously expanding one. Since the Nemesis of acquiring a large amount of floating debt is evident, and unlike that of longer-term borrowing begins to appear almost at once, it is necessary to seek for an explanation of this extraordinary increase.

The need for a continuous supply of funds to finance a much greater rate of public expenditure than the normal implied in the first place that throughout the war the volume of floating debt was immensely larger than in peace time. In this respect, however, it is clear that Treasury bills were mainly being employed for what was merely an extension of their normal use. From time to time, however, the floating debt expanded to an extent that even in such days of easy financing was regarded as excessive. The most notable occasions on which this occurred were: first, in the early months of the war, before the floating of the first long-term loan; secondly, in 1916 between the McKenna and the Bonar Law Loans; thirdly, in the autumn of 1917; and, finally, just after the cessation of hostilities. It appears that expenditure which should properly and more economically have been financed from long-term borrowing was being met by floating debt. On the first occasion a misapprehension as to the probable duration of the war was no doubt to blame. Later on the difficulties connected with the long-term loans must have been at least partly responsible.

The greater part of the floating debt was in the form of Treasury bills, of which there was £1,068 m. outstanding in March 1920. The exploitation of this form of borrowing was a continuation of a movement which had already been observed before the war. The legacy of the war in this respect was to constitute one of the most important aspects of post-war finance. The war-time method of Treasury-bill finance differed, however, in one essential from normal practice. Instead of being offered for tender, bills were from April 1915 on sale continuously 'on tap', at fixed prices. The rate fixed by the government's estimate of its necessities thus rendered Bank Rate entirely ineffective. The three months' rate ceased to reflect at all closely conditions in the market. Indeed, the government did not necessarily fix the rate primarily with a view to the home market. For instance it was moved up in 1916 after a rise in New York rates, in the hope of retaining American balances. Thus in the money market, as in the market for long-term securities, the methods of borrowing employed tended to push up rates and to keep them high.

A not inconsiderable part of the floating debt consisted of Ways and Means advances. Normally this type of borrowing only occurs very occasionally when for some unexpected reason the government experiences difficulty in renewing its bills. Used more extensively as it undoubtedly was during the war, it is rightly considered to be a strongly inflationary type of borrowing. The loans from the bank have no other basis than the securities pledged by the Treasury. As the borrowed funds are disbursed bank cash is increased, and the banks have a direct incentive to expand their operations. But by no means all the Ways and Means borrowing of the war period was of this 'normal' type. The government developed the habit of borrowing from the Bank the spare balances of the commercial banks and of foreign depositors, and using them itself. These advances were thus rather through than from the Bank.[1] The government made use in a similar way of balances in the hands of the public departments. This method of financing was also expansionary in so far as that the turnover of funds was made more rapid than it would have been had they been left in the hands of their rightful owners. The banks in particular had little use for the funds until the later stages of the war. In addition fairly high rates of interest were paid on the deposits so used. (At the end of the war these were $4\frac{1}{2}$ per cent. for foreign and 3 per cent. for home deposits.) The rate on home deposits was not out of line with rates for similar purposes, but the paying of any interest on deposits of this class was, of course, an innovation due to the necessities of war finance. The foreign rate, however, was expressly designed to attract foreign lending as a means of securing the foreign exchange so necessary to pay for imports. The dependence of the credit structure on foreign loans, which was to prove such an embarrassment in the post-war decade, thus also had its origin in the necessities of war finance.

The expansion of floating debt is thus very easily explicable in terms of its easy acquisition, the special obstacles in the way of long-term borrowing, and the failure to develop any alternative method of securing a continuous flow of funds until the last year of the war. But at the end of the war both the enormous volume of the floating debt and the methods of borrowing in use greatly added to the difficulty of restoring normal financial conditions.

The short-term debt may justly be considered the most important feature of war borrowing. Except for a very limited use of exchequer bonds—a security introduced by Gladstone to attract the professional money-market type of investor—the short-term debt was wholly the creation of the war. It was only gradually, however, that its full possibilities were realized. Although when it becomes mature, short-term debt is apt to be all too homogeneous, in reality the different types tried out differed considerably in significance. In the early months of the war the use of

[1] Cf. Hargreaves, op. cit., and Grant, *A Study of the Capital Market in Post-war Britain*, p. 73.

exchequer bonds was much extended. When, however, the big loans were floated, they catered more than sufficiently for the market which had hitherto been served by exchequer bonds. These consequently became a kind of supplement to the floating debt, being (from Dec. 1915) like Treasury bills issued on tap at fixed rates. Used thus they were almost as much open to objection as the uncontrolled expansion of the floating debt.

Nevertheless, a demand for short-term securities existed in two directions which had not hitherto been tapped. The introduction of War Savings Certificates[1] in February 1916 and of National War Bonds in October 1917 at last pointed the way to its fuller exploitation. Savings certificates made the strongest appeal yet invented to the small investor. They also served to employ the temporary idle balances of the more wealthy until they had accumulated sufficiently for the normal lines of investment. Although savings certificates were issued on attractive terms which included tax exemption, they were not an expensive form of borrowing in the main. The rates of interest paid fell very sharply after five years, so that if, as frequently happened, the certificates were left in the hands of the government after this maturity, the average rate paid over the whole period probably worked out very reasonably. Nor was the tax concession very expensive since investors were mainly situated in relatively low tax ranges, and individual holdings were limited to £500. The introduction of National War Bonds was due to the necessity for discovering a method of longer borrowing than floating debt, which would be free from the inconvenience of the exercise of covenanted benefit. The bonds were issued for five, seven, and ten years, and besides carrying some tax privileges protected the investor from capital depreciation by offering him a small premium on repayment. Since they were issued only late on in the war, when the price of government stock was falling fast, this was an attractive item. National War Bonds thus catered very adequately for the institutional investor, and were not unattractive to the personal one.

The change-over to short-term borrowing in 1917, in preference to attempting to float another big war loan, was probably the cheapest method then available of continuing to finance the war. It combined the advantages of being considerably more under parlia-

---

[1] The Origin of War Savings Certificates was a recommendation of the Committee on the Utilization of Savings.

mentary control than the floating debt, with the saving in expenses of issuing a longer term security. The short-term methods introduced during the war have played a considerable part in financing the debt since. Treasury bonds took the place of National War Bonds and occupied a similar place as investments. They were used, however, mainly for refinancing rather than new borrowing. Savings certificates have apparently become a permanent part of the national debt. From the government point of view the short-term method did finally, by means of the combination of the continuous sale of savings certificates and the recurrent issues of war bonds, solve (at least for as long as was necessary) the problem of a continuous supply of funds.

The difficulty about short-term debt is, however, just as in the case of floating debt, the question of maturity and renewal. When borrowing has continued for a period of years, then even in respect of short-term debt this becomes a constant rather than a recurring problem. At 31 March 1920 the distribution of the short-term debt as to interest rates and maturity was as follows:

Maturity	Average interest, per cent.	Amount, £ m.
1920	5	28·1
1921	5	71·9
1922	5	239·1
1923	5	376·6
1924	5	53·3
1925	5½	196·9
1927	4¾	314·2
1928	4¾	450·2
1929	4¾	48·0

Total (exclusive of savings certificates) 1,778·2

This table, however, fails to reveal the full complexity of the situation. Each yearly figure represents a collection of different issues, bearing different rates of interest and arrangements as to repayment or conversion. As the years passed, moreover, reborrowing operations were continually altering the distribution of rates and maturities. If we compare the maturities with those of the big loans (Table 1), the final and most important complication becomes apparent. From 1925 at least the distinction between short- and long-term unfunded debt to all intents and purposes disappeared. Thus before the end of the post-war decade some means had to be found of dealing with practically the whole of the war borrowing.

But although the different forms of borrowing thus eventually tended to collide, each particular type presented its own particular problems and difficulties. Some of these at least were mainly due to the new situation created by the necessity for foreign borrowing—for instance, the raising of money market rates in competition with New York. Similarly the high rates offered on foreign deposits were due to the exigencies of war finance. These weaknesses were probably inevitable in war time. But certain other difficulties would seem to have been avoidable. For instance, it is very doubtful whether the tax concessions on the big loans ultimately did anything to enable flotations to be made more cheaply than would otherwise have been possible. Even if some additional attraction was necessary to allure investors, it is hard to believe that it need have been of a type so expensive to the government, nor that it was necessary to broadcast it at such an early stage in the war. Again, the floating debt might well have been kept within more modest dimensions if it had not already been allowed to grow at a very rapid pace in the early months of the war. Still more important, more attention to the spread of maturity dates at the time of borrowing would greatly have facilitated the task of conversion. On more than one occasion the terms offered were criticized by the market as over-generous. Obviously the government could not afford to fail. But the methods used certainly appear crude in contrast to the technique for preparing the market which was subsequently developed. The monetary authorities were only serving their apprenticeship as large borrowers during the war period. But another and more permanent weakness is also apparent here as in other parts of the field of public finance. The incentive to concentrate on the current financial situation is irresistible. Its corollary is neglect of the difficulties which are being heaped up for the future. No mechanism has yet been devised for making governments careful and intelligent long-period planners.

One very important way in which future difficulties might have been lessened would have been to meet a larger proportion of war expenditure from taxation, and so reduce the need for borrowing. It is pertinent therefore to ask whether there was in fact any considerable field for increasing taxation. It can hardly be supposed that a very large proportion of war expenses could have been met from taxation. Politically this would have been impossible. Moreover, the tax structure in use at the beginning of the war was if anything less adapted to changes in incomes and prices than that at the end of our period.[1] Some attempt was made to tax war fortunes by means of E.P.D. But although the duty was imposed at a fairly early stage, the rate was so low that it had little effect either in restraining the profiteers or in supporting the revenue. Effective taxation of war profits only started in 1917 when the rate became 80 per cent. Even more important, however, on at least three occasions before 1920, reasonable opportunities of increasing taxation seem to have been deliberately thrown away.[2] First, in the second budget of 1915, Mr. Lloyd George announced that the government considered it unnecessary to raise tax rates. Britain could afford to finance the war out of savings at a rate of at least £600 m. a year. This betrayed a total disregard of the subsequent repercussions of borrowing. Secondly, in 1917, when it was extremely desirable to check incipient inflation, Bonar Law saw fit to increase no taxes except those on tobacco, entertainments, and excess profits. Thirdly, in 1919 when it was an urgent necessity to bring war methods of finance to a stop, Austen Chamberlain not merely imposed no additional taxation but halved the rate of excess profits duty.

It thus appears that more effort could and should have been made to finance the war from taxation. It is true that the main advantages of so doing would only have accrued in the post-war period, and so their appeal to chancellors was slight. But a larger tax revenue would have contributed immediately to restraining the rise in long-term rates and the expansion of the floating debt. A more conspicuous tax burden would have done something to restrain the course of inflation.

Before proceeding to examine in detail the effect of the vast accumulation of deadweight debt in our period, it will be convenient to consider in more general terms the implications and effects of the process of borrowing. When any borrower indulges in new borrowing, the rate at which he can get loans tends to rise. In other words, the price of his debt tends to fall. This is only natural as there is more of it outstanding. When the government expands its borrowing the fall in the price of its debt becomes a tendency for the rate of interest on the relevant type of borrowing to rise. By arbitrage this is transmitted into a general tendency for

[1] Cf. Chap. XVI.   [2] Cf. Hargreaves, loc. cit.

interest rates to rise. Thus one aspect of government borrowing constitutes a movement in a direction which is normally deflationary. But this is not the end of the story. We have to consider the reaction of the government's new creditors when they have acquired their security.

It has been customary to draw a sharp distinction between cases in which the government borrows directly from the Bank of England, expands the floating debt, or makes an issue to 'the public'. It is recognized that the effect of the first is generally inflationary. Bank cash is directly increased as a result of the Ways and Means advances which are the reflection of the government's resort to the bank. The borrowing in fact is closely akin to the creation of additional currency. But are the reactions so very different if the borrowing has taken the form of an expansion of the floating debt? In order that financial institutions may be able to carry on their business of making advances to borrowers they must be able to preserve a high degree of liquidity. At the same time they cannot afford to keep all their liquid assets in the non-earning form of cash. Nor is it necessary for them to do so since they will not require their whole reserves simultaneously. An increase in the supply of bills—an asset which will automatically become completely liquid within a definite short period—will only reduce their contemporary liquidity to a very small degree. In other respects it may actually put them in a better position to pursue a forward policy. Thus the issue of floating debt is expansionary in the same sort of way as an increase of Ways and Means advances. It may still be regarded as the creation of an additional kind of credit. The difference is one of degree rather than of kind.

It is even possible that the creation of a somewhat longer term security may have a similar effect. It will afford lenders some of the advantages of a Treasury bill, on the assumption that they are reasonably certain that some part of their assets will not be required for a fairly long period. They are probably willing to run certain additional risks[1] for the chance of getting a higher interest yield and for the saving in the cost of reinvestment. The additional risk involved when maturity is some way ahead is that it may be necessary to sell the security at a time when capital depreciation and the cost of the original investment together more than swallow up the income realized from interest payments. The more distant

[1] Such an attitude implies that the risk of total default is negligible.

the maturity the greater this risk. If, however, the risk is considered small it seems that even a longer term government security may have a similar effect to an increase of Ways and Means advances or an expansion of the floating debt. So long as some lenders do not feel their liquidity position seriously damaged as a result of exchanging money for the security, the total demand for cash and bank credit will be diminished by the transaction.

It is clear, however, that for most lenders longer-term securities do not serve a monetary purpose in any sense. The investment is made in order to bring in a fixed annual income, and there is no definite intention of selling the security. This income demand is probably the most important use of long-term government securities, particularly those which have no redemption date, or one so distant as to be ineffective in present calculations.

It thus appears that short-term government borrowing usually has, and long-term may have, an effect which is equivalent to an extension of bank credit, in other words which is expansionary. But before we apply this principle to the interpretation of the effect of British war borrowing it will be advisable to examine in a little more detail the particular characteristics of the situation with which we shall have to deal. It is clear that we must take into account: (i) the type of borrowing and composition of the debt; (ii) the different possible types of lenders; and (iii) the changes in their demands which occur owing to changes in their economic prospects.

Of the effects of different types of borrowing little more need be said. Ways and Means advances are the most directly expansionary form because they are the most nearly related to bank credit. But the short maturity of Treasury bills makes them almost as acceptable. On the other hand, circumstances may arise when both these forms of borrowing have an opposite effect to what might be expected because they are taken as a sign that the government is letting things get out of hand. This is particularly true of Ways and Means advances. Such borrowing may consequently have the effect of causing a sharper rise in interest rates than the issue of a longer term security would have done under similar circumstances.[1] Another type of borrowing which is also normally very expansionary is borrowing abroad.[2] This is natural because no investor

[1] There is little doubt that this factor contributed considerably to the rise in interest rates during the war.
[2] Defining 'borrowing abroad' as raising a loan in a foreign country. Foreign

within the country has had to make himself in any degree more illiquid than before.

The inflation that occurred during the war had, of course, other bases in addition to government borrowing. For instance, the direct expansion of the currency was considerable, although there is little evidence that it ever became a prime cause. (There was no resort to the printing-press to meet current bills.) And on the commodity side the shortage due to the cessation of normal economic activity and imports played an important part in raising prices. It is clear, however, that much of the war borrowing was of a strongly inflationary type. The extent of the inflation which occurred is thus easily explicable.

So far we have been concerned only with the effects of borrowing during the period when debt is expanding. But once the debt has been acquired some, at least, of these effects will continue. The composition of the debt does not remain unaltered as time passes. Some adjustment is taking place almost continuously, partly as a result of particular blocks of debt changing class as they approach maturity, and partly owing to refinancing operations. (The amount of net repayment is always small and we may neglect it at present.) Thus over time the composition of the debt may alter completely from what it was at the time of borrowing. And some of these changes are likely to be of such large dimension that they will exert an influence independent of the general effect of the debt. This may occur both automatically as maturity approaches, and as a result of a planned programme of refinancing operations.

The process of evolution to maturity is one of turning longer debt into shorter. Hence unless special steps are taken to counter-act it, time tends to increase the expansionary effect of outstanding debt. But the reborrowing process appears generally to work in the opposite direction. Save in exceptional circumstances debt does not come up for renewal until it reaches maturity, by which time it already serves many of the purposes for which a money-market security is demanded. It would naturally be considered retrograde and inflationary to replace an issue with one of shorter run—or at any rate to turn an issue for a term of years into floating debt. Hence reborrowing has at the moment the effect of

borrowing in the sense of an influx of funds from abroad may be the reverse of inflationary, if it is accompanied by a reduction of imports by the owners of the funds. But this is a case of hoarding rather than lending by foreigners.

increasing the weight of longer-term securities in the composition of the debt.

The government has further almost an instinctive fear of inflation—partly no doubt because it raises the cost of administration, and partly because it dreads the possibility of being forced to borrow from the Bank. Hence it probably has a natural bias in favour of funding floating debt whenever possible. This is accentuated by apprehension of the element of uncertainty which a large volume of floating debt introduces into the current budget. The cost of service may rise for causes totally unconnected with the public finances, or even with the internal economic situation. To fund debt puts an end to this uncertainty for the current budget, and postpones it so that there is a good chance that it will have to be shouldered by others. The force of these arguments is very considerably influenced by the spread of borrowing rates for different periods. If long-term rates are low there is a natural incentive to borrow for as long a period as possible, and thus minimize the annual cost of service. If short-term rates are low relatively to long term, on the other hand, substantial economies may be derived from keeping a large proportion of the debt in floating form. But from the government's point of view this is only one consideration to set against the other disadvantages of floating debt.

Against the changes in the composition of the debt must be set the different (and changing) demands of possible lenders. One large and probably increasing class of investors is fairly easy to account for since they operate principally with longer term securities, and their holdings are relatively inert. These are the private and institutional rentiers—such as insurance companies, trade unions, &c., and (to some extent) building societies. Their main interest in government debt is on account of its extreme convenience. Only a very decided change in the rate of return would be likely to jerk them into another investment policy.

The class of investors whose reactions it is important to consider are those who use government debt as a basis for more speculative operations. These are, broadly, the banks and other financial institutions which provide finance for industry and commerce, firms engaged in active production or dealers in commodities, and private investors of the more adventurous type. The demands of most of these lenders are fairly simple. Firms may hold gilt-edged or bills, but in any case their main need of government debt is as a deposit for temporary reserves. They will sell the securities and spend the proceeds as soon as they see an opportunity for profitable investment. The position of traders is similar except that their principal needs are for a short security. The private investor, on the other hand, is only interested in the long-term market. Gilt-edged forms a basis for, or an alternative to, equity holdings.

But the demands of the financial institutions are more complicated and more important than those of other investors because they are normally both much larger and very much more varied. It is for them that government debt is in the strictest sense a form of additional credit, and it is their conditions which the government primarily affects by altering the supply of money and its substitutes. This is easily seen if we consider the stock-in-trade of these establishments. The money market has a constant need of cash and of floating debt, or very near substitutes for it. The banks, on the other hand, prefer a wide lay-out of cash and its various substitutes. Besides the well-known 10 per cent. cash ratio there appears to be a definite feeling for something like a 30 to 40 per cent. cash+bills ratio. (If the return on bills is very low the banks may attempt to do without them, either by using a substitute or by restricting their activities.) Long-term debt of various maturities both forms the basis for more active investments and, as in the case of the private investor, provides an alternative earning asset.

The proposition that an extension of government debt implies an expansionary movement may appear at first sight to conflict with the well-known effects of open-market policy on the banks. Is not the sale or purchase of securities by the monetary authority equivalent to an issue or retirement of debt? And yet we know that it has the reverse effect. But the paradox is only apparent. Open-market policy is, like borrowing policy, an operation between cash and a cash substitute. But when it sells securities the government intends to hoard, not to spend, the cash, and so the action is contractionary. (Moreover, the securities sold are often too long-term to be a good substitute for cash.) Similarly, for the government to release cash to the market is expansionary. Fresh borrowing may on occasion have the same effect as open-market sales. For instance, where an issue of Treasury bills is made to 'mop up' cash in the market, its effect is a tightening rather than an incentive to expansion. (To offer any less expansionary form of debt for such a purpose would of course be useless, since it would not provide an acceptable substitute.) But in other circumstances the issue of an increased supply of bills for the market would have the normal effect of government borrowing. Indeed, where the banks are operating on a cash+bills ratio such an issue may be an essential condition for the effectiveness of open-market expansion.

The consideration that the demand for government debt is a demand for additional credit points immediately to the state of trade as the dominating factor in determining this demand. The effect of the same debt will vary with the different phases of the trade cycle. An intelligent borrowing policy must take into account both the total demand and the relative strength of demands for debt of different types. In the absence of information covering total holdings of the different forms of debt, it is not possible to say just what form the cyclical movement in and out of debt will take, more particularly as a slight change in conditions may cause a very considerable shift in relative demands. This is a subject which would well repay investigation in the annals of companies and the less well-known financial institutions. Common-sense observation would suggest, however, that the sequence is somewhat as follows. In the early stage of recovery, firms and dealers tend to substitute cash for their debt holdings in order to spend it on goods. At this point the banks will probably be glad to increase their holdings, at least of bills, in anticipation of coming demands upon them. But during the whole upswing and boom they must preserve sufficient liquidity to be in a position to lend freely. In the next stage, industry will be unable to finance further expansion without new funds—in the first place, no doubt, bank advances, followed perhaps by new issues. Later still they will begin to build up reserves again. Some of these will be in a liquid form suitable for repaying bank advances (particularly as soon as market rates fall). The rest may be invested in longer term gilt-edged. Thus there is a certain tendency for the demands of different lenders to cancel out. But as a whole this is overshadowed by the general move out of government debt in boom, and in again in depression.

It must be remembered, however, that relative demands depend to a great extent on the particular spread of interest rates. Thus if market rates are high it will be just as cheap, and perhaps more convenient, to finance by bank advances transactions for which bills are normally used. On the other hand, if the market rate is abnormally low, the banks, and perhaps also the financial houses, will be forced to substitute longer term securities for part of their bill portfolios. The main determinant of the spread of interest rates is naturally the trade cycle itself. But other forces may also exert an influence. In our period both the condition of the debt and the adventitious working of external events intervened powerfully to affect rates.

The debt transactions of 1919 provide an apt illustration of the relative significance of different forms of debt. They may thus serve both as an object-lesson to the general discussion and a starting-point for discussion of events from 1920.[1]

The pace of the last months of the war and the change-over to peace conditions led to the development of the most inflationary situation which had yet occurred. Payments of high rates on foreign and bank deposits had filled the market with cash. (The amount has been estimated at £170 m. foreign and £30 m. home.) In addition there was an enormous floating debt. (The average for April 1919 totalled over £500 m. in Ways and Means advances, and nearly £1,000 m. Treasury bills.) At the same time government expenditure was still heavily outrunning receipts. Absolutely nothing was wanting to stimulate an enormous boom. The first step was obviously to reduce the volume of cash. This had to be done in two stages, owing to the differential interest paid on foreign deposits. Since the floating debt was already so large it was obviously desirable to force as much as possible into a longer-term security. The Victory Loan was designed for this purpose. In order to reduce the possible substitutes, for the time being the Treasury bill issue was temporarily suspended, the government in the meantime covering its current expenditure by Ways and Means advances. In order to mitigate the inflationary effect of these it took care to use as far as possible the 'through the Bank' rather than the 'by the Bank' method. The terms of the Victory Loan were made as attractive as possible. The rate of yield was high, and there were special privileges designed to allure the rich taxpayer and the adventurous investor,[2] as well as the institutional holder. A week after the Victory Loan lists were closed (and there

---

[1] For this section cf. Grant, op. cit.   [2] Cf. Table I *a*.

was no further hope of attracting funds into it), the issue of Treasury bills was restarted, with a fixed rate of interest equivalent to that paid on home deposits. The latter rate was then dropped. Thus a strong incentive to transfer deposits into bills was created. This successfully dealt with the problem of home deposits. The next step was to make the Treasury bill rate equal to the rate paid on foreign deposits. Their rate was then reduced, and so they, too, were successfully mopped up.

The series of manœuvres succeeded in clearing the market of excess cash, and of bringing to an end the abnormal state of Ways and Means advances. But the Victory Loan had not been a success. Such demand as there was for government debt was all of the boom variety. Industry wanted cash or bills to finance immediate or anticipated expansion. The banks were persuaded to take up some of the new loan, but their real preference was for bills. Hence the volume of Treasury bills, which had slightly contracted with the issue of the loan, soon began to expand again. The monthly average for January 1920 totalled £1,201 m. Thus the debt manœuvres did succeed in removing the most inflationary element in the situation, but left a heritage of Treasury bills only one degree less awkward. In addition, future budgets had been saddled with one more expensive long-term security. But in the meantime expenditure had been taken in hand. The budget was no longer unbalanced, and the situation had ceased to be critical.

Conditions in 1919–20 were abnormal if for no other reason than that it appeared that the market had the government at its mercy. The rate on Treasury bills might be fixed by the authorities, but the market could choose whether or not it would take up sufficient for the government to cover its current maturities. But in reality the apparent powerlessness of the government was due to the fact that it had—in the public interest—undertaken to follow a self-denying ordinance. The situation might have been eased by expanding the currency—but to do so would have contravened the resolution of December 1919. If the authorities were prepared to raise the discount rate sufficiently, they had the power to squeeze all other borrowers out of the market until their own needs were satisfied—but to do so would have raised a fierce outcry from industry. In later years the position was never so critical for the government. At the end of the period, indeed, it would be more plausible to argue that the government held the market in its hand.

In either condition, however, the fundamental paradox of debt management is evident. The government as a monetary authority must serve the public interest, but the public interest may be defined in conflicting terms. An act which pleases taxpayers may upset the money market or curtail investment, and thus finally work to the detriment of taxpayers. There appears to be no simple and unambiguous criterion open to policy. It is largely a matter of weighing imponderables.

TABLE 1. LONG-TERM WAR DEBT

(a) As issued[1]

Date of issue	Chancellor responsible	Nominal interest	Issue price	Approx. running yield offered	Date of maturity	Rights included *	Amount issued	
							Cash	Conversion
							£ m.	£ m.
1915	Ll. George	$3\frac{1}{2}$	95	$3\frac{3}{4}$	1925–8	..	350·0	..
1915	McKenna	$4\frac{1}{2}$	100	$4\frac{1}{2}$	1925–45	Conversion Covenanted Benefit	587·2	313·5
1917	Bonar Law	5	95	$5\frac{1}{16}$	1929–47	tax not deducted + duties SF.	836·5	1,230·8
,,	,,	4	100	4	1929–42	tax free + duties SF.	22·0	30·3
1919	Chamberlain	4	80	5	1960–90 (Funding Loan)	+ duties at 80 SF.	288·9	119·0
,,	,,	4	85	$4\frac{3}{4}$	drawings to 1976 (Victory Bonds)	+ duties at 100 SF.	287·9	71·5

* Notes to Table: tax not deducted = liable to tax but not deducted at the source; + duties = tenderable for death duties (at par or as stated); SF. = special sinking fund attached.

(b) Amounts of Long-term Debt outstanding at 31 March 1920[2]

	Per cent.	£ m.
1915	$3\frac{1}{2}$	62·7
1915	$4\frac{1}{2}$	12·8
1917	5	1,976·8
1917	4	64·1
1919	4 F.L.	408·9
1919	4 V.B.	359·5
		2,884·8

[1] (a) From Hargreaves, op. cit.
[2] (b) From Statistical Abstract.

XXI

DEFLATION AND REPAYMENT (1920-4)

MONETARY history 1920–36 divides itself even more abruptly than other aspects of public finance into three periods. From 1920 to 1924 the authorities were fully occupied in setting the financial house in order and preparing for the return to the gold standard. 1925–32 was dominated by the gold standard. The years 1932–6 were remarkable for extreme monetary ease. Between September 1931 and April 1932 a curious interlude or bridge passage intervened. It marked the transition from easy spending to easy money. If we examine the course of interest rates (Chart I) we find these phases quite clearly indicated. In particular the odd rigidity of the period 1925–31, the frequent crossing of the rates, and the repeated alterations of Bank Rate reflect the difficulties which were encountered in maintaining the exchange. The third period may be considered to have ended early in 1937, when for the first time industry came widely under the influence of the rearmament programme. It appears, however, that the turning-point in the long-term interest rate occurred some two years earlier.

At the beginning of 1920 financial conditions were still extremely chaotic. While the debt operations of 1919 had done something to remove the most inflationary elements from the scene, there had also been tendencies in the opposite direction, so that the public finances were hardly, if at all, in better state at the end of 1919 than they had been at the end of the war. Public expenditure in 1919 had reached the enormous total of £1,665·8 m. Since the embargo on stock exchange issues was not removed until the spring of 1920, the condition of the floating debt favoured an even larger expansion of bank advances than the circumstances would normally have called forth. In December 1919 these totalled £1,018 m. Many of these were naturally for capital purposes, so that they represented fairly long loans. In 1920 the flood of new borrowing was transferred to the stock exchange, where the new issues reached the unprecedented figure of £300 m. Hence in the post-war boom both industry and the government contracted large new debts at very inflated rates.

The first step towards general financial recovery was the re-establishment of budgetary control. The second was to be the restoration of the gold standard. The first movement towards reorganization followed the publication of the Cunliffe Report (on Currency and the Foreign Exchanges after the War) in December 1919. Bank Rate had been raised in November 1919, and although as long as Treasury bills were on sale at fixed rates this could not have its normal effect, it was no doubt useful psychologically. More important, a maximum was imposed on the fiduciary issue from December 1919. These measures reinforced the improvement which had already been made in the money-market position. The first quarter of 1920 was the first in which revenue exceeded expenditure, and it was followed by a budget in which increased taxes and the end of fresh borrowing were announced. Since, however, the stock exchange boom appeared to be continuing unabated, Bank Rate was raised again in April. Thereupon ensued what Mr. Hawtrey[1] has described as 'a period of deflation the intensity of which it would be hard to match from the economic history of the last two centuries'. It will be remembered that when the financial year 1920-1 ended, the surplus was found to amount to £230·6 m.—a significant contrast from the previous year's deficit of £326·2 m. Nor was another (at least nominal) deficit allowed before the restoration of the gold standard. The reduction of expenditure was hastened by the efforts of the Geddes Committee, who presented their final report at the beginning of 1922. In the financial year 1919-20 expenditure fell by over £470 m., and in the following year by a further £116 m.

There is no doubt that the deflationary effect of policy in these years was considerable, although it must be remembered that Mr. Hawtrey was writing before the world had witnessed the lengths to which deflation could be carried, for instance, by the gold bloc nations between 1932 and 1936. It is probable that the potential dangers of deflation were not realized. Falling prices had not been experienced for a generation. The intensifying effect of the slump was certainly not foreseen by the government, since the rate of excess profits duty was raised from 40 to 60 in 1920, and a large increase of revenue was confidently expected. British policy necessarily attached itself to American, both because the dollar was the only important gold currency which had not been

---

[1] Cf. Hawtrey, *Currency and Credit*, 3rd edition, p. 415.

seriously disorganized either by the war or by the post-war inflation, and because every approximation to the pre-war dollar parity
brought nearer the day when the gold standard could be restored.
Nevertheless, the pound did not by any means attempt to follow
the dollar in all its deflationary movements. For instance, in 1923,
when considerable progress had already been made towards the
recovery of the exchange, this was apparently deliberately sacrificed when American rates were raised and the dollar began to
appreciate.[1]

Moreover, there is some reason to believe that policy during
these years was not in fact so deflationary as would appear from
a mere recital of the measures adopted. The rise in prices after the
war had been fed on the expectation of further government inflation. As soon as it was understood that this had come to an end, a
fall was only to be expected. In many respects 1921 represented
no more than a wiping out of the excesses of 1919, leaving things
much as they had been before.[2] Just because general confidence
was restored by the reform of public finance, apparently deflationary actions turned out to be ultimately encouraging to industry.
Further, the reduction of expenditure reflected mainly the termination of war contracts and the fall in prices. These should not have
had the deflationary effect of unexpected economies. After 1920–1,
when the budget surplus principally reflected the windfall profits
of the boom, the only considerable surplus forced was in 1922–3.
All the surpluses of these years, moreover, were largely composed
of capital receipts, sale of war stock, &c., and did not represent an
equivalent tax burden. Indeed, it would be possible to maintain
that fiscal policy at this time was more suitable for depression than
that followed ten years later.

Further, it must not be forgotten that at the same time as the
government was contracting expenditure at the centre, it was
urging—not without success—a policy of rapid expansion on the
local authorities. Expenditure out of loan by local authorities in
England and Wales reached a maximum (not surpassed during our
period) of £128·7 m. in 1921–2. In the same year other expenditure (less loan charges) was over £340 m., a net figure which was
not exceeded until 1929–30. While the wisdom of encouraging
local borrowing at high rates of interest may be questioned, and

---

[1] Cf. Hawtrey, loc. cit., p. 437.
[2] This was also true of most of the wage increases given in 1919–20.

policy was so far undesirable that the boom year 1920 saw the
biggest increase in expenditure, although not the highest aggregate,
the expansion of 1921 was undoubtedly a fortunate circumstance
for the depression.

Monetary movements arising out of the management of the
debt have yet to be considered, however. The two most serious
aspects of the debt problem in 1920 were the enormous amount
of principal outstanding, and hence the large proportion of taxes
which must go to its service; and the awkwardness of the floating
debt. After 1919 the central feature of this was the large volume of
Treasury bills. This had been swollen even beyond its war-time
dimensions by the events of 1919. It was to remain the leading
factor in the money market throughout our period. Fluctuations
in the Treasury bill issue are shown in Chart II. After the issue
of the Victory Loan the volume outstanding immediately shot up,
and did not recede below the £1,050 m. mark until February 1922.
This meant a constant problem of renewal for the government at a
time when money substitutes were emphatically not in demand.
Hence it was not considered safe to abandon the close control of
the market which fixed rates of issue allowed, and to restore the
normal practice of tender offers to the market, until April 1921.
In spite of extraordinary efforts to bully and cajole creditors into
buying bills, renewal could only be guaranteed by pushing rates
to a point which would normally be considered, and eventually
became, highly deflationary.[1] Further, a new complication was
now making its appearance as the short-term war debt began to
mature. Austen Chamberlain drew attention to this in the budget
speech of 1921: 'As these issues reach maturity they become to
all intents and purposes Treasury Bills.' The effect, therefore,
of what was virtually an additional floating debt of from £50 m.
to over £500 m. (varying from year to year) had henceforth to be
taken into account.

From 1921 there were two available methods of dealing with the
money-market position—direct reduction of the Treasury bill
issue, both by economies and by transferring some borrowing to
other channels; and consolidation of the short-term debt by
funding maturing bonds into long-term issues. Both were immediately set going. From July 1921 for about two years the
Treasury bill issue was drastically cut down, month by month.

[1] Cf. Grant, op. cit., p. 74.

An issue of Treasury bonds with lives of from five to ten years was made in partial replacement. In the budget speech of 1921 the first issue was announced of $3\frac{1}{2}$ per cent. Conversion Loan, redeemable at the government's option after 1961. In the following years further issues were made, so that by 1932 this security (at £750 m.) was easily the largest block of new long-term debt after the 5 per cent. war loan.

Such a drastic reduction of Treasury bills, however desirable in the long run, could hardly have been other than deflationary when concentrated in such a short period, and in the downswing of a violent depression. It constituted not merely a reduction in the total volume of debt, but even more important, a heavy swing over from short to longer term securities. Although some of the new Treasury bonds were within the money-market range of five years, they could only be imperfect substitutes for Treasury bills. Nor does it appear that such a rapid reduction was called for at the moment. The problem of the short-term debt was not very serious until after 1925, when it became complicated with the maturity of the big war loans. Reducing the Treasury bill issue in the early twenties could hardly touch this. Moreover, in June 1921 the three months' rate fell below the yield on gilt-edged, and remained below, practically without exception, until 1929. Hence, during that period it was more economical to keep as large a portion of debt in floating form as was compatible with financial stability.

The wisdom of the time and method adopted for funding the short-term debt is also open to some doubt. The issue below par of $3\frac{1}{2}$ per cent. loan made in 1921 constituted a virtual guarantee of 5·6 per cent. for forty years. Altogether this 'Conversion' loan added substantially to the burden of the debt. It also continued the war-time vice of issue at a discount. On the other hand, it did nothing to deal with the most important aspect of the short-term debt—the large block of war loan which would mature in 1929. A more direct effort was made in 1924 to deal with this problem by an issue of $4\frac{1}{2}$ per cent. Conversion Loan (repayable by 1944). The terms, however, did not prove sufficiently attractive. Only £148 m. war loan was exchanged (for £152·9 m. Conversion Loan). All things considered, the 5 per cent. remained the most popular investment, and continued to draw funds to itself by the exercise of covenanted benefit in maturing bonds. The question has been raised whether it would not have been worth making a large-scale effort at this stage to break up the 5 per cent.[1] Any judgement on this naturally depends on what opinion is held as to its precise effect from 1929 to 1932. In any case, however, whatever view is held on this point, the peculiar position of the gold standard was an important aggravation of the trouble, and this could not have been foreseen in 1921. Moreover, there was little scope in the budget in the early twenties for an increase in the debt service. Although taxation was relatively light, compared with ten years later, and might conceivably have been increased (for instance in 1920, 1923, and 1924),[2] there were other, more urgent uses to which additional revenue would probably have been put.

In spite of the reluctance to increase taxation, a genuine effort was made in the early post-war years to reduce the cost of the debt by wiping off part of the principal. The first concern was the external debt. The Colwyn Committee commented[3] favourably on the 'energetic measures taken immediately after the war to deal with the position'. These included the cancellation (mainly out of the Canadian debt) of £87 m. of American debt in 1919, the repayment of over £262 m. gross in 1920 and the following years, and the funding of the entire American debt into a terminal annuity under the agreement of 1923. By these measures the burden of the external debt was reduced to about one-ninth of the total service, even without the counter arrangements for repayment of debts to Britain. Thus after a few years the external debt ceased to present a serious budgetary problem. The considerable budget surpluses realized in these years were devoted to debt repayment, as well as sundry miscellaneous exchequer funds accruing from the sale of war materials, &c. By the end of the financial year 1924-5 the grand total of £1,463·9 m. of war debt had been paid off, but as £934 m. had in the meantime been raised in cash by new borrowing, the net amount was about £530 m.[4] A year later, when the net amount was £583 m., the Colwyn Committee estimated that the saving in debt service attributable to repayment was £29½ m.[5]

---

[1] Cf. N. F. Hall, *The Exchange Equalization Account*, p. 13.
[2] Cf. Chap. I.   [3] loc. cit., p. 32.
[4] In 1920-1 new borrowing totalled £134 m., of which £104 m. was applied to redemption (in addition to £271 m. from revenue and capital receipts). In the following year £432 m. was raised in cash, and during the next three years a further £364 m. Cf. *Colwyn Report*, pp. 41 ff.
[5] Cf. *Colwyn Report*, p. 61.

How far did these efforts, admirable as they may have been from the point of view of the budget and the taxpayer, merely serve at the time to increase the forces of deflation? Normally the effect of debt repayment is exactly the opposite to that of new borrowing, that is to say, it is deflationary. Debt cancellation swallows up budget surpluses, whereas any alternative use the government makes of them—such as expenditure or tax remission—can hardly fail to be more stimulating to industry. On the other hand, a lower tax burden and a continuation of a safe investment leaves debt holders in a better position to expand than if they are faced with the necessity of reinvesting the repaid funds. Since gilt-edged stock tends to be held as the final basis of security —whether by rentiers or not—the investor has little choice but to seek as similar an investment as possible. As a result of repayment and reinvestment there may be some tendency for interest rates to fall, but it can hardly be more than very slight. In the case of personal holdings there is perhaps some chance that repayment will encourage holders to take up more active investments, but since institutional holdings (such as those of banks and insurance companies) predominate, this hope, again, is very slender. Just as external borrowing is generally more inflationary than internal, so the repayment of external debt is more deflationary. If the repayment is a real net payment, the funds are not reinvested in the country. This aspect of external repayment is necessarily present whatever other complications may arise in connexion with the acquisition of the foreign currency necessary for repayment.

Since the service on external debt is a net burden on the community, the urgency of paying it off is obvious. The desirability of repaying internal debt is by no means so clear. Nevertheless, there can be no doubt that in the long run it is highly desirable to get rid of accretions of deadweight debt, both in order to free the budget from an excessive interest charge and to clear the ground for future borrowing. It is naturally desirable, however, to concentrate repayment (whether of internal or external debt) when the deflationary effect will be relatively light and unimportant, when, in other words, the tax burden is at its lowest. Normally this means repaying debt in the boom, and doing so out of the surpluses on existing taxation rather than imposing extra taxation for the purpose. Besides the tax burden, other factors, such as the effect on confidence, the extent of future budget relief, and changes in the composition of the debt may intervene to make the net effect more, or less, deflationary.

None of the years 1921 to 1925 have any claim to be regarded as boom years. The depression was exceptionally severe in 1921, although by 1923 trade had again became moderately brisk. It was certainly no more than that in 1924. It would seem, therefore, that the time chosen for making a strenuous effort to retire debt was singularly inopportune. There are some reasons for believing, however, that the effect was not so deflationary as might have been expected. In the first place there is no doubt that when it was fully realized, the mere size of the war debt aroused something like consternation. The seriousness with which a capital levy was discussed suggests as much. A reduction of principal, since it improved confidence, probably had a stimulating effect on enterprise. Secondly, although boom profits were not being made, the tax burden imposed was not unduly heavy. In all years a large amount of the revenue applied to debt repayment was on capital account. Thirdly, although the immediate effect of repayment was deflationary, the consequent reduction in the cost of service had increasingly beneficial results as prices fell and the burden of the debt increased. This was particularly true in respect of the annual drain of funds out of the country which would have been required to meet the service on the external debt. Finally, the refinancing which accompanied the repayment of (non-floating) debt was made on terms at least as favourable to lenders as the issues repaid.

While obviously it is not possible to say without a great deal of further research how far monetary financial and debt policy, taken together, were deflationary during the reconstruction period, it looks as if on the whole their effect was fairly mild. It might plausibly be maintained, indeed, that in several respects, for instance the methods and extent of new borrowing and the lightness of the tax burden, current budgets were eased at the expense of budgets five or ten years later. In this connexion the rapid recovery from the depression of 1921 is significant. Unemployment was indeed grave in 1921, but in January 1922 it passed below the 2 million mark, and continued steadily to improve until the middle of 1924. New issues continued to be actively floated in 1921,[1] which suggests that falling prices were expected to be very temporary. In fact the turning-point in ordinary share prices

[1] Cf. *Economist*, 'The Year's New Capital'.

(which is a fair index of industrial prospects) came as early as December 1921.[1] There was thus by 1924 considerable ground for an optimistic view of the prospects of British industry. Nevertheless, such equilibrium as had been reached was at a substantially lower level of prices than that ruling in 1920, when the great re-financing of industry took place. It was clearly desirable to avoid a policy for the future which might risk driving prices to a still lower level.

[1] Cf. London and Cambridge Economic Service, *Index of Security Prices*.

XXII

THE GOLD STANDARD AND THE DEBT, 1925-31

FROM the moment when her internal finances were taken in hand, England's anxiety to have the international gold standard restored at as early a date as possible was manifest to all the world. This does not imply that drastic or even very explicit steps to bring the pound itself back to gold are discernible before 1924. Indeed, as we have seen, the pound did not always follow the dollar slavishly if the latter showed a tendency to rise. The report of the Cunliffe Committee, British pronouncements at international conferences (for instance in 1920 and 1922), and the evident desire to promote international trade and foreign lending,[1] are sufficient indications of the trend of British policy.

In the course of 1924, however, it became apparent that conditions for a return to gold in the very near future were definitely maturing. The recovery from the depression was reasonably good. Statistical evidence suggested that in most directions the direct effects of the war might be considered to have passed over.[2] Exports of coal and steel had increased satisfactorily during 1922-3. This, it was true, was mainly due to the occupation of the Ruhr, and in 1924 there was already some recession. But other exports were showing a moderate increase. British and American prices appeared to be moving in harmony while gradually converging. Hence on the whole the economic outlook appeared favourable for the stabilization of the pound. There were also a number of monetary and technical factors favouring a return to gold. In the summer of 1924 American credit policy once more turned expansionary.[3] This gave grounds for hoping that the pound might be screwed up to the dollar without imposing severe internal contraction. Light restriction was almost immediately applied (by making the existing 4 per cent. Bank Rate effective), and in the following January the rate was moved up to 5 per cent. in order to complete the process of re-establishing the pound. In Europe the air had been considerably cleared by the adoption of the Dawes plan.

---

[1] The embargo on foreign issues on the stock exchange was lifted shortly after that on home issues. [2] Cf. Bowley, *Economic Consequences*, cit.
[3] Cf. Hawtrey, op. cit., p. 437.

Finally, the expiry of the Gold and Silver Export Control Act at the end of 1925, and the expectation that South Africa was about to return to gold, suggested that 1925 was the chosen year.

Although expectations of a coming stabilization were gradually hardening during 1924, the actual decision to return to gold was taken with the element of shock and surprise typical of Mr. Churchill's financial administration. Scarcely had the step been taken than it began to appear that the interpretation of the world financial situation on the one hand, and of British industrial prospects on the other, had been unduly favourable. Unemployment, which had been stationary since the first breath of credit restriction, began to increase from January 1925. Exports were falling off slightly. Much more serious, however, it became apparent that the coal industry could not carry on without substantial assistance. Labour unrest in this and other industries was increasing menacingly.

The failure of international trade to expand, and hence the disappointing experience of the export industries in 1925, was partly explicable by the extent to which European economies and currencies were still in a chaotic condition. It was partly, no doubt, also due to the external influence of British internal restriction. Sterling was still the dominating currency in world finance. The fact that this restriction was required indicated the fundamental inadequacy of the moment chosen for return. True equilibrium had not been restored in the balance of payments. The equilibration of the exchanges could not have been effected without the aid of American balances. Events which occurred even before the end of 1925[1] showed that their presence was only due to the higher interest rates to be obtained in London. It does appear that a little less precipitancy on the part of the chancellor might have enabled the situation to be examined in a somewhat colder light.

In 1931, after the departure from gold, it was commonly said that the mistake of 1925 was to fix the pound at too high a parity. It appears that the possibility of a permanent depreciation was only discussed in the case of belligerent currencies where it was obvious

---

[1] Net imports of gold totalled £9 m. up to August; Bank Rate was then lowered, and again in November, in spite of gold losses of £5·5 m. (to the end of October). By the end of the year losses amounted to £11 m., and Bank Rate was hurriedly raised. Cf. *Economist*, 'Money in 1925'.

that inflation of pre-war standards had been very considerable. In the case of England and the neutrals, where a small depreciation might have been desirable, the question seems hardly to have come up. Nevertheless, from the point of view of financial policy it is extremely relevant to consider the events of 1925-31 in the light of such a possible exchange difference. While the Macmillan Committee emphatically rejected the plan of a 10 per cent. depreciation in 1931, it is clear that they felt that such a course taken in 1925 might have had solid advantages.[1]

It is noticeable that the return to gold was not in its early days considered by British financial interests to have been either a failure or a mistake. At the end of 1925 the *Economist*[2] was ready to declare that 'The Bank of England is now solidly based on the facts of the country's economic position'. In its short and chequered life the post-war gold pound had to face three serious crises, in 1926-7, 1929, and 1931. Although these were of increasing intensity, only the last proved fatal. In the intervening periods there is little evidence of serious pressure on the exchange. Since it throws some light on the course which internal monetary and debt policy were forced to take, it will be worth our while to examine very briefly the forces at work during these crises. Funds —whether owned by its own nationals or not—move in and out of a country both for causes that are international and for those that are internal to the country. The same factors do not necessarily affect funds owned by British nationalists and by foreigners. It is therefore necessary to distinguish those affecting both types of funds.

The basis of the crisis of 1926-7 was the serious upset to the British balance of payments caused by the sudden drop in exports after the industrial troubles of 1926. These troubles in themselves stimulated a desire to seek more remunerative use for British funds outside the country. It happened that there was abroad a growing volume of foreign securities of an official nature. These offered what appeared to be an ideal combination of high yield and security. It is clear that from the summer of 1926 serious apprehensions were felt at the volume of foreign issues, and there was talk of re-establishing the embargo.[3] A further cause of

---

[1] Cf. *Committee on Finance and Industry*, pp. 110 ff.
[2] Cf. *Economist*, loc. cit.
[3] Cf. *Economist*, 'Capital in the third quarter of 1926'.

pressure on the pound came from America, where gold imports were being assiduously sterilized with a view to restraining boom conditions. Once, however, the strain in the industrial situation was relieved, the crisis soon passed. The execution of postponed orders stimulated production and improved the balance of payments. In the second quarter of 1927 new stock-exchange borrowing on home account constituted a record of 75 per cent.[1] The situation had therefore substantially righted itself even before (in the autumn of 1927) America reverted to an easy credit policy and began to lose gold steadily.

The crisis of 1929 was similarly compounded of a stimulus for the export of British funds and the existence of greater attractions elsewhere for foreign funds. The American boom provided a steady attraction for capital, both before and after the federal reserve discount rate was raised to 5 per cent. (in July 1929). From the time of the legal stabilization of the franc (in June 1928) France also began to draw funds on a large scale. In neither of these cases did the 'reversing mechanism' of the gold standard work efficiently. The pressure on the pound from external events was therefore continuous. On the other hand, the prospects of British industry were much more favourable than they had been in 1926. Nevertheless, the heavies were still lagging behind, and German exports, stimulated by the necessity of paying reparations, were becoming increasingly competitive with them.[2] A new external demand for capital was, moreover, arising. Once the most pressing currency troubles had been righted, the less fortunate belligerents found themselves in urgent need of funds to rebuild their economic equipment. Simultaneously the basis on which this demand might be met with security had been enlarged in two ways. First, reserves of countries working the gold exchange standard were being entrusted to England. This increased the internal supply of funds.[3] Secondly, increasing amounts of war debt were becoming available for use as collateral to loans as they approached maturity.[4] The passage of time was increasing the inflationary aspect of the debt and no adequate steps were being taken to restore its former composition. Thus foreign lending at this

[1] Of new issues cf. *Economist*, 'Quarter's review of capital'.

[2] Cf. Bresciani-Turroni (trans. Sayers), *The Economics of Inflation*.

[3] On the assumption (which appears to be well founded) that foreigners held British short-term debt, which they pledged as collateral.

[4] Cf. N. F. Hall, op. cit., chap. ii.

period was mainly the work of financial interests,[1] and did not lead to a large number of foreign issues on the stock exchange. It was less conspicuous, but as afterwards proved, more dangerous, because the amount of British liabilities was unknown. In 1929 the situation was considerably more critical than it had been in 1926. The reserve was reduced to £140 m. Nevertheless, at the time apprehension was felt not so much because the standard was considered to be in danger, as that the high rates necessary to secure a return of funds would be seriously detrimental to home industry.[2] In the event the situation was saved by the Wall Street collapse and the return of funds from America.

During 1931 the earlier causes of weakness of sterling persisted, but they were overshadowed by new developments. There was, indeed, no immediate reason for America to draw funds. The pressure on the pound was, moreover, increasingly being relieved as the world depression deepened by the cheaper prices of British imports in terms of her exports. But these alleviating factors were more than compensated for by the sudden withdrawal of European funds to cover losses in the banking crises of Austria, Germany, and France. Even more serious, the European banking collapse prevented the counter-withdrawal of British funds. Thus British short-term borrowing came to an abrupt end while its lending became indefinitely prolonged. It only required the withdrawal of foreign reserve and 'safety first' balances to complete the discomfiture of the pound. Given the psychology of the European situation, it is not in the least surprising that the disregarded Treasury warning on British expenditure, and the alarmist revelations of the May report, sent foreign balances headlong back to their owners. The British gold standard had been founded on an import of capital and it was destroyed by a reverse movement. In vain had rates of interest been kept above the level desired by British industry in order to retain foreign funds.

The weak point of the British gold standard was throughout the failure to build up an adequate and secure reserve. Had a lower parity been adopted for the pound the prospects of doing this would certainly have been improved. The competitive chances of the export industries would have been greater, and a better trade balance would have helped the reserve. Less unemployment

---

[1] It is generally considered that much of it took the form of acceptances of foreign bills. [2] Cf. *Economist*, 'Money in 1929'.

would have set free funds required for the maintenance of the unemployed. Higher tax revenue would have lightened the burden
of the debt. These improvements could not fail to have impressed
foreigners and so increased the reliability of 'borrowed' reserves.
On the other hand, there were inescapable technical and economic
changes standing in the way of any considerable expansion of coal
and cotton, the two pillars of the pre-war export trade. Further,
the necessity for Germany to force on world markets goods which
were highly competitive with British products depended on international politics, and was beyond the control of Great Britain.
Hence it is quite possible that a moderate devaluation of the pound
would not have led to a marked increase in British exports. The
pressure to export British capital was fundamentally due to the
far greater urgency of the demand for funds externally than at
home. Other countries required fundamental reconstruction of
their equipment. Britain appeared as relatively overstocked. This
being so, the British gold standard could only have been maintained if the government had been prepared to introduce some sort
of exchange control. This was certainly true at the chosen parity.
It is quite possible that it would also have been true at a moderately
depreciated parity. In the political circumstances of the day any
such heroic measures as exchange control were probably ruled
out of account, even if they had been technically feasible.

Concentration on the troubles of Great Britain has sometimes
tended to obscure the fact that her experience was by no means
unique, but was shared by other countries who also returned to
gold at an early date, whatever their industrial experience. Sweden
is a particularly good example of this. In spite of the unprecedented development of her metal and timber industries, the
pressure on the Krone became increasingly severe as the post-war
decade passed. It was with genuine relief that Sweden seized the
opportunity of the freeing of the sterling to follow suit with the
Krone.[1] On the other hand, the countries which rejoined the gold
standard at later dates did so with currencies substantially depreciated, not merely below their pre-war levels, but in many
cases below the levels which they held at the time of the early
stabilizations.

This suggests that the overvaluation of sterling in terms of gold

[1] Cf. Lindahl, 'Der Übergang zur Papierwährung in Schweden, 1931',
Weltwirtschaftliches Archiv, 1936.

was the reflection not so much of a mistake on the part of the British authorities as of a world under-valuation of gold. That is to say, there was a general tendency for currencies to be fixed too high in relation to gold. The existing stock of the metal was insufficient for the work it was required to do, and there was nothing in the post-war gold standard to stimulate its expansion. This explanation would go some way to account for the increasing severity of successive crises of the pound, *pari passu* with the extension of the field to be covered by the world's gold stock. It does, however, raise the question whether the post-war gold standard was worth saving. To attempt to answer it is obviously beyond the scope of our inquiry. It is plain, however, that post-war experience revealed weaknesses in the gold standard mechanism which were not previously realized. It is quite possible that British financial opinion held an unduly favourable view of the workability of the pre-war gold standard, induced by intensive study of the immediate pre-war period. It is not without significance that the chairman of the committee whose report was the basis of the policy of return had been governor of the Bank of England just before the war.[1]

The maldistribution of gold in the post-war world due to the failure of the 'reversing mechanism' had mainly a political foundation. At least a partial remedy for this appears to have been found in the technique of exchange accounts. An uncertain part of it, however, was due to economic causes. This has a (perhaps unexpected) relevancy to our inquiry since it represents essentially the problem of the depressed area. In the case of the depressed area the existence of a single national currency implies that the 'exchange' will necessarily be kept fixed, and that changes in productivity will be fully reflected by changes in relative price and income levels. If the staple industries of (say) south Wales decay, wealth will leave the district, her incomes will fall and her condition progressively deteriorate, at least until her costs have fallen and other advantages increased sufficiently to stimulate the spontaneous introduction of new industries. Before that point is reached a long tale of hardship must be endured, unless the rest of the country is prepared to come to her assistance. What British policy for the depressed areas essentially amounts to is, on the one hand, a reversal of the currency flow by direct subsidy, and on the

[1] Cf. Sayers, *Bank of England Operations, 1890–1914*, p. 137.

other, a restoration of technical advantages by the (partially artificial) calling into existence of new industries. In international relations, however, such benevolent conduct is rare.[1] An international standard which provides no mechanism for varying exchanges will always have this difficulty to face.[2]

Internal monetary and financial policy during the gold standard period was inevitably determined by two factors—acute budgetary stringency on the one hand, and the precarious condition of the exchanges on the other. We have already examined the contribution of expanding social expenditure to the problem of balancing the budget. To this was added the heavy demands of a debt service fixed in money terms. The needs of the Treasury and the real burden of the debt alike demanded low interest rates. On the other hand, the necessities of the exchange required that the short-term rate should be kept high enough to maintain such foreign demand for sterling as might from time to time be necessary to support the pound. In practice this meant that after the unfortunate experience of 1925 Bank Rate was kept at least up to $4\frac{1}{2}$ per cent. There was thus a fundamental dilemma in British finances, only capable of solution by heroic measures.

The main obstacle to the reduction of the real burden of the debt was the failure of the rate on long-term government securities to fall. To this a number of causes contributed. Among the more important were first the rough relation between short- and long-term rates which the possibility of arbitrage necessarily maintains except in the very short period. It is noticeable, however, that the fixity of gilt-edged rates was greater than that on commercial long-term borrowing. Chart II shows that while the rate at which industrial debentures could be floated improved progressively from the middle of 1921 (excepting for the brief panic period of 1931), the yield on long-term government bonds remained obstinately rigid. This was no doubt partly due to the renewed public borrowing at the end of the decade. Apart from internal causes, however, the very high rates ruling abroad must have contributed to keeping up British rates. Under the circumstances, the absence of a large

---

[1] Ireland has nevertheless managed to support herself to a considerable extent on payments from abroad in the form of emigrants' remittances.

[2] A variable standard is not a cure for secular movements. But to let the exchange fall spreads the burden by altering incomes without altering their relation. It may be a quicker way of stimulating production than waiting for costs to fall, since prices all move (in relation to other currencies).

volume of direct long-term foreign lending was somewhat misleading.

Since conversion was precluded by the continuance of high interest rates, debt management in the gold standard period was roughly an extension of the policy of 1920-4, except that in the absence of budget surpluses net repayment was negligible. Two considerable funding operations were undertaken:

Year	Issue	Cash	Conversions	Total
		£ m.	£ m.	£ m.
1927	4 % consols	32·6	133·8	166·4 (later increased to £400 m.)
1929	5 % conversion	154·0	179·0	333·0

(From Hargreaves, loc. cit.)

The need for funding appeared even more urgent than it had been earlier. Firstly, it was desirable to keep down the Treasury bill issue, both on grounds of economy and because the existence of a large basis for advances in the money market as the short-term debt matured materially added to the difficulties of official control. Secondly, as time wore on the objectionable features of the big loans became increasingly apparent. The funding operations were not, however, very fortunate. In some cases—conspicuously that of the early $3\frac{1}{2}$ per cent. War Loan—funding still constituted a 'conversion' upwards. Although the 5 per cent. Conversion Loan guaranteed a yield until 1944 practically equal to that of the 5 per cent. War Loan, it did not succeed in inducing many of its holders to transfer. The truth was that the day for breaking up the 5 per cent. was past. It had already gone over to the money market. On the other hand, the 4 per cent. War Loan was got rid of, and with it disappeared the full tax-free concession.

There were thus at least two potentially deflationary elements present throughout the gold standard period: one arising from the height of the long-term interest rate, and the other from the curtailment of the Treasury bill issue. Whatever may in general be the effect of high interest rates on industrial enterprise—and probably few economists would be prepared to deny that it is deflationary—in this period it had a particular effect which is worth mentioning. The intensive refinancing which British industry had undertaken in 1920-1 at high rates of interest had mainly been in shorter term securities than the big government loans. Much of it had been in the form of seven- and ten-year notes which were already maturing before the decade was over. As long as interest rates remained high the conversion of these was impossible. On the other hand, the meagre dividends payable in times of even fairly good trade when the capital structure was 'highly geared' stood in the way of a successful appeal to investors in other forms of borrowing. In this respect British industry was decidedly worse off than American, where the opportunity of the boom was widely seized to secure voluntary 'conversions' of bonds into common stock. The enormous spate of industrial conversions when interest rates fell was partly accountable for by the damning up of the outlet until 1932.

The effect of debt management on the money market at this time is both complicated and obscure. The majority of witnesses before the Colwyn Committee were inclined to deplore the curtailment of the bill issue, and to urge upon the government the attraction of keeping as large a proportion of the debt as possible in floating form, as long as the three months' rate was below other rates. This was partly out of tender regard for the taxpayer's pocket. Whether the reduction of the volume of outstanding bills could have embarrassed discount houses or traders at this time depends on the extent to which they were prepared to use other forms of government debt as a substitute. The mere fact of having to use an unaccustomed medium may perhaps have introduced a certain awkwardness. And in the middle years of the decade it is quite possible that there was a genuine shortage of debt of convenient maturity.

On the other hand, when the large maturities began to fall in, the situation seems to have been completely reversed. Just as the existence of a large volume of securities on which capital depreciation was ruled out provided a safe basis for foreign lending, it tended to stimulate lending at home. The stock exchange boom was no doubt partly the effect of this.[1] It was natural that the result should be especially obvious in the case of rather speculative issues, since, as suggested above, a large part of the established industrial field was not in a position again to borrow extensively. How considerable the inflationary effect of this more or less accidental factor was, is difficult to determine. There are other

[1] As boom conditions developed, the willingness of the banks to accept collateral without inquiring too deeply into fundamental prospects would probably tend to increase.

354 THE GOLD STANDARD AND THE DEBT, 1925-31

more fundamental possible explanations of the stock exchange boom. The effect of the debt can hardly have been so great as has sometimes been supposed, since the really large maturity—the 5 per cent. War Loan—was not on the *tapis* until 1929. Even then the date of its conversion in the current budgetary circumstances was, to say the least, highly speculative. Nevertheless, the effect of the maturing debt should evidently be set down as a factor mitigating the effect of deflationary forces.

There were also other mitigating factors. The authorities frequently attempted to offset gold losses by open-market policy, thus damping down the effect on internal prices. Table 1 (p. 360) affords some illustration of this policy by setting changes in the total cash basis (liabilities plus notes in the banking department) against changes in the stock of bullion in the issue department. Since the decrease in cash over the whole gold standard period was greater than the loss of bullion, there would not appear to have been a net expansion.[1] Indeed, policy has more the appearance of an attempt to keep money neutral. This is confirmed by the consideration that bank cash was until 1931 practically unaltered at round about £65 m. From time to time, however, this policy must have afforded some relief. The anti-deflationary effect of accelerated social expenditure must also be borne in mind in this connexion. This operated at least until public apprehension at its volume was aroused. Of this there is little sign before 1930.

The effect of a large volume of outstanding debt on the economy depends primarily on the distribution of holdings between different interests in the community. In the absence of statistics on the distribution of investors we can only estimate what the type of movement in the different demands was likely to be. According to the estimate of Sir Walter Layton, made for the Colwyn Committee, personal holdings amounted to some 35 per cent. of the debt, the bulk of the remainder being institutionally held, but mainly within the country. What little information is available suggests that the institutional share increased at the expense of personal holdings as the post-war decade advanced. Both classes, however, included investors of the rentier and of the more active type. The extreme convenience of long-term government securities

---

[1] It is impossible to say what steps would (or could) have been taken to mitigate the effect of the gold withdrawals of 1931, since Britain left the gold standard before there had been time for any action.

made a particular appeal to rentier investors, but there seems no reason to expect that anything occurred to cause them drastically to reorganize their normal investment policy on account of the opportunities afforded by the debt. What we should rather expect is a gradual acquisition of gilt-edged by both personal and institutional rentiers. As regards the latter, the change was no doubt partly at the expense of mortgages and other forms of medium-term security normally held. But, on the other hand, there is ample evidence of the increase in the total demand of institutional rentiers, due to the extension of working-class savings and of the habit of insurance.

In contrast to the stability of these holders, events certainly suggest that the demands of the more active class of investors were changing rather rapidly, particularly in the last years of the decade. During 1928 and 1929 the banks and financial houses tended to absorb large quantities of floating and maturing debt as a basis for advances. (The latter would readily be exchanged by its former rentier holders for longer term trustee securities.) From the autumn of 1929, when market rates fell, institutional demand, and specially that of the banks, tended to switch over increasingly to long-term gilt-edged. The very important effects of this change, however, belong to the next period. It remains to consider the movement of company holdings.

With the onset of depression companies hastened to invest their reserves in government stock. While this tendency is normal to depression, there were particular reasons in 1930-1 serving to accentuate it. In the first place, such an immense opportunity for buying the safest form of security had not existed before the war. Although this condition had already been present in the depression of 1921, there was then considerable uncertainty as to the future course of interest rates. Hence the motive of expected capital appreciation was relatively unimportant. On the other hand, in 1930 not merely was the 5 per cent. free from fear of capital depreciation, but the practical certainty of its conversion within a very short period held the hope of a considerable capital gain on long-term stock. The 5 per cent. War Loan was in 1930 particularly attractive from this point of view. In addition the boom had broken with such precipitancy that many firms must have found themselves with extensive liquid funds, the proceeds of recent flotations. Once depression had started they could no longer with confidence invest these in the directions originally intended. It therefore paid them better virtually to turn themselves temporarily into investment trusts, earning their dividends on the high yields offered by war loan rather than by normal production. Conditions remained suitable for this solution of industrial troubles until the fall in interest rates in 1932. The existence of the debt thus probably tended to promote large-scale industrial hoarding in the depression and to intensify general stagnation. In more normal market conditions this must have caused a perceptible fall in the long-term interest rate, and so have promoted recovery, but the peculiar tangle of rates due to the pre-eminence of the now mature 5 per cent. war loan (no doubt assisted by the sales of personal holders) prevented any but a very small decline.

When we turn from the institutional to the personal section of debt holdings we enter the field which was explored most fully by the Colwyn Committee—the fiscal effect of raising revenue for debt service, and the expenditure effect of paying interest. Interest payments on internal debt are only transfers, and do not cause a loss of any portion of the national income, as do interest payments on external debt. They can therefore make no difference to the current national income. Unless, however, receipts of interest were proportionate to tax payments for each tax-payer they may very decidedly affect the volume and direction of spending and investing in the community. In so far as they do so the national income of the future is altered. The effect for the community as a whole depends on the incidence of the real tax burden on the one hand, and on the distribution of debt holdings on the other. The first of these factors does, and the second may, change with changing prices and with the trade cycle.

Unfortunately there is no comprehensive information as to the distribution of personal debt holdings. Broadly speaking, debt must necessarily be held by the richer element in the community, since the poor are not property owners. It appears, however, that war loan was distributed rather more evenly in proportion to income than other forms of property. The figures of estates paying death duty for 1930 illustrate this, and are supported by evidence from other years. This suggests that raising revenue for interest payments was only a net burden at the two ends of the tax structure. The very rich paid highly progressive taxes, but only received proportional interest payments. The poor, on the

Percentages of War Debt and other Securities in the Estates of persons dying in 1930

Estate	£100 to £1,000	£1,000 to £5,000	£5,000 to £10,000	£10,000 to £25,000	£25,000 to £100,000	£100,000 +
War debt	11·0	16·6	14·7	14·4	14·8	17·0
Other securities	5·6	15·6	25·8	33·8	39·3	41·0

other hand, paid regressive taxes and received little or no interest. They thus suffered more from the debt than any one else. This burden should be taken into account in any reckoning of the net effects of public expenditure. On the other hand, it is hardly legitimate to argue, as has sometimes been done, that because the taxes paid by the rich (income and surtax and death duties) roughly equalled the service of the debt, these classes in fact contributed nothing to the expenses of the country. We may either say that rich tax-payers (in so far as they were also debt holders) paid no taxes, but received no interest on their holdings, or that they both received interest and paid taxes. On the other hand, it may be argued that the war created a new type of investment, combining in a unique manner high yield and security, the advantages of which accrued mainly to the rich. But apart from any consideration so remote as what might have happened if there had been no war—it is certainly arguable that if a larger proportion of expenditure had been covered by taxation the position of the rich, as well as of everybody else, would have been better ten years after the end of the war than in fact it was. An attractive investment would have been absent or reduced, but the relative absence of the burden of debt service would have encouraged the expansion of the national income. Ultimately, the important point for both rich and poor is the extent to which debt service (which it must be noted depends not only on borrowing policy but on the management of the debt) held down the national income by discouraging investment and spending. The double burden on the poor probably curtailed the latter. As to the former, there are arguments on both sides, and little opportunity for choosing between them.

Some light might be thrown on the question if we had detailed information as to the distribution of personal debt holders. There is little doubt that the largest original investors in war loan were those entrepreneurs whose incomes had risen most as a result of the war. War borrowing was notable, however, for the success of the appeal to the small investor, and this probably accounts for its relatively proportionate distribution in estates. It is generally agreed that as the years passed the larger holdings tended to pass out of the hands of entrepreneurs. Either the war entrepreneurs themselves retired as rentiers or they exchanged their war loan for more active investments. Thus there was probably an increasing transfer, in money terms, from the more to the less active members of the community. Apart from the cyclical incentive, this change appears a very natural sequel to a period of heavy borrowing, and is probably inevitable. It constitutes a strong argument in favour of shortening the second phase as much as possible. In the case of the war debt the effect of this movement was very much aggravated by the rise in the real burden of the debt. As prices fell the percentage of the national income absorbed by debt service rose steadily (Table 2) (p. 360), reaching a maximum of 8·26 per cent. in 1932. The deflationary effect increased *pari passu*. Moreover, the burden bore with increasing weight on that part of the community whose incomes were not fixed in money terms, just at the moment when their taxable capacity was reduced by the depression. This danger provides one of the most powerful arguments for getting rid of the effects of borrowing as quickly as possible.

The conclusion of the majority of the Colwyn Committee that the economic effects of the debt were not of very great importance was reasonably justifiable, given the course of events up to 1926. The apprehensions of the minority as to the growth of the burden with falling prices were, however, only too well grounded. The difficulties which might arise in connexion with the maturity of short-term debt were at least in part foreseen as far back as 1920.[1] All these judgements, however, were made without the experience of the important developments of the effects of the debt which were crowded into the last few years of the post-war decade. It seems an inescapable conclusion that the hazards of a large accumulation of deadweight debt are even greater than had commonly been supposed.

Monetary and financial policy in the gold standard period presents a depressing story of opposing forces and frustrated effort. Low interest rates were particularly desired, yet they could not be enjoyed. The effects of a programme of social expenditure so great

[1] Cf. the reference in Austen Chamberlain's budget speech to the importance of an energetic funding policy.

that it strained the financial resources of the country were largely
nullified by falling incomes and increasing unemployment. The deflationary effect of the debt could not be side-stepped, yet it turned
out to have inflationary effects just where they were not wanted.[1]
It is not strictly true to say that the monetary situation could not
have been controlled, but the necessary measures would have been
drastic. They could hardly have failed to have increased deflationary influences in the short run. And that could ill be afforded.

In two ways, however, the period is of more general interest
than its very special conditions would suggest. In the first place, it
was significant of a change that was taking place in monetary control. Both the long- and the short-term markets were dominated
by government debt. While the rate on industrial debentures
might show some small measure of independence, by and large it
was compelled to toe the line. In the money market the potency of
Bank Rate changes was very much lessened as compared with the
pre-war position. As long as floating debt had been issued at fixed
rates it was, of course, completely inoperative. But even after
tender issues were restored the large amount of funds available to
the market very much reduced responsiveness to changes in Bank
Rate. The relative importance of government and Bank action
implicitly demanded a situation in which the government and not
the Bank should take conscious control of policy. But the time for
such a change was not yet.

Secondly, the period is interesting as an illustration of the relative impotency of public finance when monetary policy is not in
a position to support it. For many purposes these two types of
policy are weapons out of the same armoury. Both can be usefully
brought to bear on the problem of social and economic betterment.
The monetary weapon is, however, normally the more powerful.
At a touch it can change the size of the national income for years
to come. But for many purposes it is the blunter tool; its action is
clumsy and unrefined. The changes in relative incomes which it
brings about (for instance between rentiers and entrepreneurs) are
not those which are normally desired. And in any case so many of
its effects are indirect that they are always difficult to foretell, both
as to time and degree. It is these characteristics of monetary
management which constitute both the attraction and the danger
of its use as a tool of social policy.

[1] By stimulating foreign lending and stock exchange borrowing in 1929.

C c

TABLE 1

(£ m.)

Year	Cash Basis (Changes in liabilities + notes in Banking Department)	Gold Movement (Changes in Bullion in Issue Department)
1925	− 7·1	−13·6
1926	− 9·7	+ 4·4
1927	− 0·7	− 1·7
1928	− 8·5	+11·2
1929	−14·7	−27·0
1930	+ 3·9	+24·4
1931 (1st three quarters)	− 1·2	−15·7
Net movement	−38·0	−18·0

TABLE 2

Change in the Burden of the National Debt, 1924–35

(£ m.)

Year	(1) National Income (net) calendar years*	(2) Debt service financial years	(2) as percentage of (1)
1924	4,035	312·2	7·70
1925	4,357	308·2	6·80
1926	4,173	318·6	7·60
1927	4,359	313·8	7·16
1928	4,339	311·5	7·20
1929	4,384	312·0	7·20
1930	4,318	293·2	6·80
1931	3,889	298·9	7·65
1932	3,844	318·0	8·26
1933	3,962	216·3	5·45
1934	4,238	211·7	5·00
1935	4,530	210·9	4·65

Estimated change, 1920–3†

(£ m.)

Year	(1) Layton's estimate of total National Income	(2) Internal Debt Interest	(2) as percentage of (1)
1920	5,600	309	5·5
1921	3,900	286	7·3
1922	3,500	266	7·6
1923	3,800	270	7·1

* Mr. C. G. Clark's calculation.   † Colwyn Report, p. 66.

XXIII

CONVERSION AND EASY MONEY, 1932-6

THE collapse of the pound necessitated a fresh start in British finances. The situation was fundamentally a good deal less serious that it had been eleven years previously, but psychologically it was hardly any better. Three major financial problems faced the 'National' government: to restore confidence, to free the internal monetary system from dependence on foreign balances, and to convert the 5 per cent. War Loan. This last was an urgent matter, both as a step to lightening the fiscal burden and to facilitate the restoration of control in the money market. No time was lost in putting the financial house in order. The first problem was attended to in the second budget of 1931. The announcement of the establishment of the Exchange Equalization Fund in the budget of 1932 made provision for the second, and the conversion of the war loan announced in April 1932 was carried through in the summer of the same year. Monetary policy in the next five years followed from, and arose out of, these three steps.

It is interesting to compare the measures taken to restore confidence with the deflation of 1920-1. Naturally the ingredients were similar—heavy increases in tax rates, economy, and a rise of Bank Rate. In several respects, however, the brew concocted in 1931-2 was stronger than that served out by Austen Chamberlain.[1] Not only was the entire tax structure raised, more or less proportionately, from end to end, but social insurance contributions were increased and benefits cut down. The resulting tax structure was considerably higher than any of its predecessors.[2] Salary cuts and rigid economy at the centre were backed up by the enforcement of the most severe retrenchment in local government. Economy circulars of an almost mandatory tone were sent round. Public works grants were abruptly discontinued. An (unofficial) embargo was placed on local borrowing on the stock exchange. The fall in rate-receipts due to the depression and the activities of local economy committees, their nerves completely shattered by the magnitude of the disaster, caused an even greater collapse of local

---

[1] This does not imply that total deflation was not greater in 1921, but merely that official deflation was less.　　　　　　　　　　　[2] Cf. Chap. XVI.

than of central spending. Finally, measures were taken to improve the foreign balance—a general tariff on the one side and an (also unofficial) embargo on foreign lending on the other. Only in the purely monetary field does the deflation appear to have been less drastic than in 1920–1. Bank Rate was kept at a repressive level for less than five months instead of over twelve. In contrast to the reduction of floating debt in 1920–1, conditions in the money market remained easy throughout.

Familiar as these very recent events are, it is only by bringing them together that their scope can be realized. The reform of 1931–2 was a colossal effort. On the face it was wildly deflationary. There is no doubt, however, of two things. In the first place it was completely successful in attaining its object. The confidence of foreigners, and to a considerable extent also of the British public itself, in British finances had been rudely shaken by the events of 1931. Both were restored in an extraordinarily short space of time. More important still, the confidence of the British public in itself had been gradually undermined during the five years when every other country appeared to be doing better than England. After 1931 a spirit of imperturbable self-confidence, almost of complacency, took the place of apprehension and distrust. And there is no doubt that the measures taken had the full support of the public. The extraordinary voluntary acceleration in tax payments and the correspondence quoted by Snowden in the budget debate[1] are sufficient evidence of this.

Whether, or to what extent, the effort was unnecessarily great and hence wasteful can hardly be demonstrated. The devil to be exorcized was mainly psychological, and the force of mass psychology is imponderable. It is at least evident that, like the reform of 1920, the initial effect was stimulating rather than deflationary. In some respects, however, it does appear that the deflationary measures, if not too drastic, were at least too prolonged, and hence tended to retard recovery. A 6 per cent. Bank Rate was maintained for some months after it was evident that confidence had been restored. This led to some recrudescence of the foreign fund import nuisance. It also increased the inducement for corporate investment in gilt-edged, by adding the attraction of an almost certain capital appreciation. It thus fostered the acquisition of securities at a moment when it might have been possible to

[1] Cf. Chap. I, p. 14.

stimulate new investment. The sudden restriction of local spending caused a considerable loss on works planned or actually started. By this economy also the contribution which public investment might have made towards hastening recovery was irrevocably lost. Moreover, many of the works were of a fairly urgent nature—or they would not originally have qualified for grant—so that their postponement must have caused some inconvenience. Assistance to complete works suspended at this time was only very grudgingly awarded over the next five years. It is hard to believe that such a degree of local economy was necessary. The steadiness of municipal stocks through the crisis refutes the idea of any loss of confidence in local finances. The main trouble was that most of the works depended on exchequer contributions, and in the circumstances these could not be forthcoming.

In the spring of 1932 it seems to have been perceived rather suddenly that at any rate on monetary grounds a somewhat sharp reversal of policy was desirable. The high Bank Rate was probably encouraging the new influx of foreign funds, and was certainly disliked at home. More important, the magnitude of the deflation caused abroad by the fall of the pound was becoming apparent. There was a world-wide demand to raise prices, by artificial if not by natural economic means. There was also the coming conversion to consider. If interest rates could first be lowered a very much better bargain might be struck with debt holders. Accordingly Bank Rate was brought down in a series of rapid steps, reaching $2\frac{1}{2}$ per cent. in April 1932. Also dating from April, a steady enlargement of the cash basis was secured by open-market policy. Reversal in the monetary field was not, however, in any sense a general return to expansionary policy. Practically the only relaxation in public finance was the gradual restoration of salary and insurance cuts. Income tax was not lowered until the 1934 budget.[1]

The change in monetary policy was justified by its results within a very short time. A $3\frac{1}{2}$ per cent. conversion rate was not merely obtained, but the new loan was prevented from falling to a discount. The extent to which artificial conditions had been created in order to reach such a result can be guessed from the figure of £25·9 m. appearing in the Accounts for expenses in connexion with the conversion of the 5 per cent. War Loan.[2] Although the

[1] Although in 1933 there was some relaxation, as the quota payable in January was restored to one-half.   [2] Mainly for the payment of commissions.

publicity and commission methods adopted were crude and perhaps wasteful, the affair is interesting as a foretaste of the new technique for securing cheap borrowing which was later developed. Once the 5 per cent. was removed the way was cleared not merely for the conversion of other blocks of unfunded debt as they matured, but also for a similar cleansing of company finances. Even local authorities, although hampered by their less astute borrowing policy, and by the periodic embargo on stock-exchange borrowing, considerably improved their financial structure during the next five years.[1]

Low interest rates thus emerged as a by-product of the conversion and the depression. It was clearly to the interest of the Treasury to keep them low. And it soon became clear that they were proving a real advantage to industry. Besides facilitating conversions they were proving a direct stimulus to the building trade. It is not easy to determine the relative importance of the factors which set going the building boom. An important part, however, must be ascribed to the easier terms on which advances could be obtained, owing to the fall in the yield on gilt-edged. In particular the building societies, which had not reduced their interest rates, received a considerable influx of funds. Competition among them to secure business led, if not to an actual reduction in rates, at least to a greater flexibility in terms. While the banks themselves may not have relaxed their conditions, it is probable that other financial institutions followed the example of the building societies. Thus it came about that the desideratum of the Treasury was assumed as a virtue. Low interest rates and easy money became the explicit aim of British policy.

An extraordinary change had come over the monetary situation. Bank Rate remained steady at 2 per cent. after June 1932. Even at this low point, however, it was quite out of touch with the market, where the three months' rate was consistently below 1 per cent. except for a brief period at the end of 1933. The rate on consols fell steadily to a point not much above $2\frac{1}{2}$ per cent. in December 1934, and thereafter climbed out of the pit only very slowly and reluctantly. The interpretation of such recent events is necessarily very hazardous, more particularly in the monetary sphere, where it is frequently impossible to check up hypotheses adequately from published figures. The changes which appear to

[1] Cf. Chap. VII, pp. 123 ff.

have been taking place, however, are of such considerable importance from the point of view of monetary control that it seems worth making the attempt to investigate those on which there is some measure of agreement among experts. These concern in the first place the technique for keeping down interest rates, and secondly that for securing a good reception in the market for government issues.

The first seems, like cheap money policy, to have arisen as a by-product of an entirely different change. Since the war the volume of funds passing through government departments has enormously increased. This fact creates for the government an opportunity of satisfying directly from public balances a greater proportion of its temporary needs than formerly. This it can do by issuing Treasury bills on tap to the departments. Hence the proportion of the total issue sold on tap has increased steadily in relation to the proportion offered by tender to the market. In part, perhaps mainly, this appears to be a development of the war-time practice of using the spare balances of the departments. The opportunity for the increasing adoption of the policy has arisen partly from the extension of the sphere of administrative activity in general, but especially from the growth of the public savings banks and the social insurance funds. In addition, owing to the more or less accidental circumstance that the Exchange Fund receives its resources in the form of Treasury bills, a further opportunity for temporary borrowing has arisen since 1932. Since it is possible to have a fair idea in advance what the market demand for bills is likely to be—it is largely a conventional demand, depending on well-known seasonal, &c., movements—it is a simple matter for the government to distribute its needs for funds between the tap and tender issues in such a way as to fix the price of the latter at any desired point, within fairly wide limits.

It would greatly facilitate the task of interpreting monetary history and policy if it were possible to ascertain the extent and timing of the use of this technique. From the date of the establishment of the Exchange Fund to that of the divulgation of its holding in June 1937 the published figures of Treasury bill issues were practically meaningless unless some means could be found of estimating the volume of tap bills. The successive issues to the Exchange Fund are clearly visible in 1932 and 1933 at the time of issue (cf. Chap. XXI, Chart II), but not beyond. An ingenious device was invented by economists[1] for estimating the relative size of the tap and tender issues at any time. Chart I shows the estimated movements of the two forms of bills from the spring of 1932.

The importance in the policy of control of the price of Treasury bills lies not only in its money-market effect but also in the opportunity it gives for exerting direct control over long-term rates. As long as the three months' rate is very low the banks with their rigid costs have an almost overwhelming need to buy gilt-edged in order to replace the income lost on their bill portfolios. The extent to which they have responded to this stimulus is shown by series (B), Chart II (p. 368). The corresponding movement in the long-term interest rate is clearly traceable in the yield on consols (Chap. XX, Chart I). The success of this policy depends on the existing distribution of the holdings of the banks. In the first place they must have the requisite cash for the purchase. This can be supplied by open-market operations. It appears, however, that to ensure the purchase of long-term securities it may be considered necessary by the banks to maintain not merely the cash but the cash plus bills ratio. Thus in the early part of 1934 the absorption of gilt-edged by the banks slowed up very considerably. The reason would seem to have been the shortage of market Treasury bills. At the end of the year this was made good, and the banks at once began to buy gilt-edged at an accelerated pace.

The technique for assuring a good reception for long-term loans is also to a considerable extent a by-product of the enlargement of the funds held by public departments. In the main it consists of three processes. First, the public departments dispose of their holdings of bills and increase their deposits at the Bank. Secondly, they buy up enough of the loan when it is issued to ensure its success. Thirdly, they dispose of their holdings to the public, gradually, at the best terms the government broker can arrange. Thus the financial balance of the departments is restored and they are once more free to play the government's game in the bill market. As an additional precaution a temporary embargo on municipal issues has been used to limit the number of possible competitors. The effect which this manipulation of the Treasury bill issue may be expected to have is first a sharp fall in the tap issue, as the departments clear the decks, followed by a more gradual rise as they get rid of the new stock. The first movement can be clearly

[1] The method is described in the *Economist*, 21 March 1936.

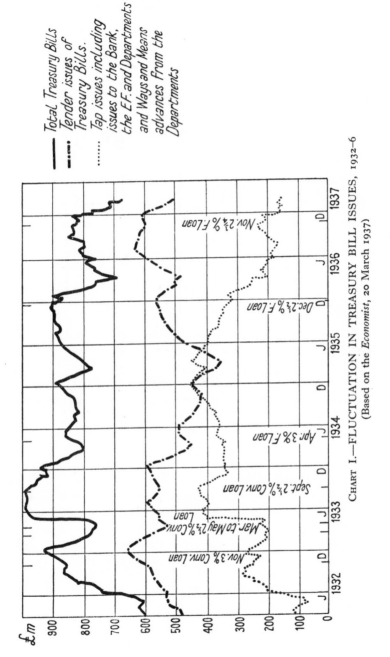

Total Treasury Bills
Tender issues of Treasury Bills.
Tap issues including issues to the Bank, the E.F. and Departments and Ways and Means advances from the Departments

CHART I.—FLUCTUATION IN TREASURY BILL ISSUES, 1932–6

(Based on the *Economist*, 20 March 1937)

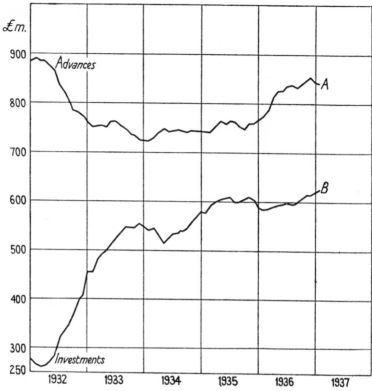

CHART II.—CLEARING BANK ADVANCES AND INVESTMENTS
1932–6
(Nine Clearing Banks)
(From London and Cambridge Economic Service)

traced on Chart I, where the dates of the chief funding operations are shown. The second is less obvious, because it may be spread over a considerable period, and may also be concealed by other movements, such as changes in the tap-tender relation.

It is a point of extreme interest to inquire how far these methods of monetary control are likely to be generally available. There can be little doubt that the period in which they were developed was exceptionally favourable for their use. The ability of the departments to take up either bills or loans depends on their internal finances. As far as the Exchange Fund is concerned, this depends on the free margin in excess of its holdings of gold and foreign exchange. Its total funds are limited to its statutory resources and those acquired in the course of its trading in currencies. There have pretty evidently been occasions in recent years when it has had practically no free reserves. One way out has been found by allowing it to hand over some of its gold to the Bank. In the absence of a reversal of the capital import movement the only other appears to be to enlarge its statutory resources. It would not appear, however, that either method could be carried on indefinitely.

The position of other possible contributors to the policy of internal flotation is more complicated. Normally the regular government departments can have only a small amount of free funds, although no doubt during the war these were considerably extended with the larger volume of business passing through their hands. The part played by the extra-budgetary funds is undoubtedly the dominant feature. Since their inception these funds have regularly been invested in government securities. In the case of the Post Office Savings Bank this policy is seventy-five years old. It is the double contingency of the post-war growth of the funds and of the government's refinancing necessities which has created their importance for monetary policy. In 1936 the amounts standing to the credit of the larger funds were roughly as follows:

	£ m.
Post Office Savings Bank	451
Trustee Savings Banks	130
National Health Insurance Fund	136
Unemployment Insurance Fund	43
Treasury Pensions Fund	19
Post Office Fund	3
Total	782

These were practically all invested in government securities. The addition of a number of smaller funds is estimated to bring the total to almost £800 m. It may even be possible for the government also to make use of the £200 m. backing of the fiduciary issue, but presumably this would hardly be available for long-term investments.

An estimate has been made[1] of the distribution of holdings of the various classes of government securities between these funds. It appears from this that substantial percentages of certain issues are held by public departments. In the case of the 2½ per cent. and 3 per cent. guaranteed stock (of which approximately 39 per cent. and 74 per cent. are so held) there is nothing peculiar or doubtful about the holdings. Similarly it has always been understood that it was the practice to invest Post Office Savings Bank funds in Local Loans stock. Since this forms the basis of the Public Works Loans Board advances, small savers thus have the opportunity of assisting indirectly, if not directly, the resources which the smaller local authorities applied to social expenditure, while at the same time safeguarding their own savings. It seems, however, that the National Health Insurance Fund holds some £75 m. Local Loans stock—nearly twice as much as the savings bank. At one time it appeared very probable that this stock would be converted, and it is pertinent to ask what effect this would have had on the income of the funds. Would a reputable trustee have allowed these funds to retain such large amounts of a vulnerable stock?

More significant still is the holding of 36·2 per cent. of 1 per cent. Treasury Bonds (£29·8 m.) by the Unemployment Fund. This is an issue made after the turn in the trend of interest rates. It appears that an abnormally large holding had to remain in the Fund because of the difficulty of unloading it on the market. There is thus a possibility that the continuance of a policy which worked without difficulty during the period of falling interest rates may land the departments in an absolute loss. This is particularly serious in the case of the social insurance funds, since (at least if a rational budget-balancing policy were followed) they would necessarily have to realize most of their funds in each recession. Nearly 75 per cent. of the total reserves of the

[1] Cf. the *Economist*, 6 Nov. 1937, based on the pioneer work of Prof. N. F. Hall.

Unemployment Fund appears to be tied up in what must, from the point of view of the fund, be regarded as a malinvestment. If the public interest, as represented by the needs of the Treasury, is to have priority over the rights of the insured, it is at least desirable to know what steps would be taken to compensate the funds for losses sustained in the manœuvres of borrowing policy.

The task of keeping interest rates low is an easy matter in depression, because there is little demand to borrow. Institutions with money to lend must be prepared to relax their terms very considerably. For the banks this is a difficult matter. Experience of the last few years has shown that even a very large increase of deposits does not necessarily create a situation in which the banks can safely increase their advances. For instance, although deposits expanded rapidly in 1932-3, time deposits were altogether outrun by the increase in current accounts, withdrawable without notice. A further heavy increase in deposits in 1935-6 mainly represented refugee money from the gold bloc, and similarly could not be used as a basis for expansion. In 1935, however, the demand for advances began to expand rather suddenly in two directions. On the one hand, British local authorities became active borrowers from the banks. It is easy to surmise the genesis of this demand. As far as the larger municipalities were concerned, the embargo on stock-exchange issues probably meant that those far down the queue had to satisfy their immediate needs by borrowing an unusually large amount from the banks. On the other hand, the smaller authorities probably found bank advances cheaper than borrowing from the Public Loans Works Board. (It will be remembered that it had proved impossible to convert the Local Loans Stock from which it chiefly derives its funds.) Secondly, an opportunity arose of lending to the French government. The terms were remunerative, and there was the additional satisfaction of helping the franc. The effect of these two demands on bank advances was considerable (cf. series A, Chart II).

It is not surprising to find, therefore, that the long-term interest rate began gradually to rise from about December 1934. The movement was extremely slow, at any rate up to the end of 1936.[1] Nevertheless, the trend appears to have been definitely established by 1936. It is clearly evident in the case of municipal issues, for

---

[1] After that date a considerable allowance has to be made for mainly psychological fears connected with taxation, gold scares, and the international situation.

instance. The government was at no particular pains to rig the market for them. On the other hand, the issues were spaced by the Treasury in such a way as to avoid choking the market with this particular type of security. Table 1 (p. 378) shows the terms of the chief local issues (England and Wales) 1935–7 and their spacing. It seems to have been found that every time a more favourable rate was set, a number of issues could be floated successfully. After an interval, however, it became necessary to make a further concession to lenders.[1]

Recovery from the depression of 1931 was financed by an unexpectedly small volume of bank advances. One reason for this was no doubt that companies had abnormally large holdings of gilt edged. It was cheaper to dispose of these to the banks than to take advances. But it will be remembered that the phenomenon also caused surprise in 1922–3. Possibly the extent to which additional profits are available for financing development in the upswing has not been fully realized. As long as shareholders receive an appetizing increase of dividend they are easily persuaded that it is to their best interests to plough the rest back into the business. Other factors working in the same direction have arisen since 1923. Among the most important are probably the great extension of company integration, and especially the financial economies possible under the holding company system. Weight must also be given to the substitution of advances from other institutions, who in the fierce light of competition have tended to be more forward than the banks in relaxing their terms. The result of these factors has been that recovery has been able to make considerable progress without the banks having to part with large amounts of their gilt-edged holdings.

There is thus a reasonable hope that the benefit of relatively low interest rates may continue to be enjoyed by British industry.[2] The danger is not ruled out, however, of a serious conflict of interest between the Treasury, on the one hand, and both the departments and industrial interests on the other, if the government were to persist with a technique which was no longer suitable, or to attempt to maintain low rates by inflationary measures. It ap-

---

[1] Allowance must also be made for subsidiary factors such as the amount of issue, as well as for passing conditions in the market. The trend is clear, but the rise in the yields offered is not unbroken.

[2] Apart of course from war risks.

peared, however, in 1935 and 1936, that the authorities were prepared to pay some regard to the general tendencies of the market.
The Funding Loans of 1935 and 1936 (and the National Defence
Loan of the spring of 1937)[1] were floated on progressively more
favourable terms to the lenders. But it is noticeable that they
were progressively less successful. This suggests that at least the
first of these dangers is a very real one.

Looking back over the monetary policy of the years from 1932
to 1936, the long tale of solid achievements is very striking. Between 1925 and 1931 it proved impossible to build up any adequate
reserve. In the next five years a cover of more than 100 per cent.
of the note issue was achieved.[2] The external effects of the Exchange Fund do not concern us in detail, but it is evident that it
successfully acted as a buffer to the economy against an enormous
capital import. The extent to which it is possible to write the
monetary history of the period purely in terms of the internal
situation is proof of the success of the experiment.[3] Interest rates
were lowered, and kept at a rate which proved stimulating to investment. Perhaps the most satisfactory change of all, however,
was in the burden of the debt. The fact that we have not come up
against it at an earlier stage in our investigation of the period is an
indication of the secondary place in British finances to which the
war debt was relegated. Extensive funding-conversion operations
between 1932 and 1936 reduced the annual charge on the main part

[1] The terms offered were as follows (it will be noted that the Defence Loan
runs for only half the period of the 1935 Funding Loan):

Date of issue	Loan	Amount	Issue price	Nominal interest	Yield to Redemption	
					Earliest	Latest
Dec. 1935	Funding	£ m. 200	96½	2½	£2 14s. 7d. (20 yrs.)	£2 13s. 10d. (25 yrs.)
Nov. 1936	Funding	100	98½	2¾	£2 17s. 4d. (15½ yrs.)	£2 17s. 0d. (20½ yrs.)
May 1937	Nat. Defence Bonds	100	99½	2½	£2 11s. 6d. (7½ yrs.)	£2 11s. 0d. (12½ yrs.)

[2] Whether this will ultimately prove serviceable depends on the future world
price of gold. As a result of widespread devaluation since 1931 the situation
described in Chapter XXII has been completely reversed. It is not inconceivable that gold in its turn may have to be devalued.

[3] In saying this I do not in the least want to undervalue the appalling external
effects of the collapse of the pound; cf. Robbins, *The Great Depression*.

of the debt by some £55·5 m. But this is not the whole of the saving in interest achieved at this time (Table 2, p. 379). Interest on Treasury bills fell by £16·9 m., and on Savings Certificates by £14·3 m. In the case of the former the saving was almost entirely due to the low rate of interest, since the volume of market bills has remained roughly constant. Savings Certificates have, however, steadily increased in volume. (It must be remembered, however, that recovery years tend to be years of low encashment.) Still, the most important point is that the biggest saving was made on the longer term debt. This is a gain which cannot be taken away by any rise in interest rates. It was a most satisfactory contrast to all previous experience of the war debt.

It is true that the pre-war relation between funded and unfunded debt was far from having been regained. But except for a small group of Treasury bonds—mostly bearing very low rates of interest—all the unfunded debt had been put into long-term form. The position was therefore not too unfavourable for a renewal of borrowing. There are, however, two points of some importance concerning the old debt. £211 m. is still all too heavy an item in the budget for a kind of expenditure which contains at any rate some features in direct conflict with the social programme. Secondly, it appears that even after the experience of the war debt, sufficient care was not taken in arranging maturities. It is certainly to be hoped that rates of interest will be low round about 1957. It is obvious that an exceptional amount of both central and local debt comes to maturity at that time.[1] If rearmament borrowing is allowed to add its weight to these years, the situation might become very awkward.

In contemplating the achievements of monetary policy in the latest period it is as well to bear in mind also items on the other side of the account. During the late twenties economic physicians might doubt as to whether they had to prescribe for a boom or a depression. In the early thirties the diagnosis was entirely unambiguous. An exceptionally deep depression was followed by a very considerable measure of recovery. Conditions clearly called for some relaxation of deflation the moment confidence was restored, and probably for a certain amount of damping down at a later stage.

---

[1] The terms of issue usually allow of repayment (with six or nine months notice) some years in advance of the final date. This is shown in Table 1 (p. 378) where it occurs.

It appears that exactly the opposite policy was followed. Income and capital taxation was maintained at crisis rates after the crisis had passed, and was only partially relaxed after 1934.[1] Public expenditure swung over from the social to the economic side, i.e. as far as the community as a whole was concerned, from an income-raising to a price-raising policy. At first local investment was severely restricted, but later a more expansive policy took its place. An extended programme of road building was decided upon, including two expensive Thames bridges.[2] The expansion of public utilities was also stimulated after general recovery was well on the way. (The first instalment of the London Electric Transport Finance Corporation was not issued until June 1935.) This change of policy is reflected in the steady increase of local public issues on the stock exchange. In 1931 these totalled £8 m., by 1934 they had risen to £36 m. In 1935 they reached £51·1 m., and in 1936 the very considerable figure of £79·5 m. It is not surprising that in 1936 the Ministry of Health sanctioned local expenditure of a capital nature amounting to £96 m.[3]—almost a record for our period.

While such an extension of public investment may well be very desirable on long-run grounds, it would surely have been more appropriate in 1932–3 than in 1935–6. On the other hand, the fact that public investment is once more stirring is not without hope for the immediate future. An extension of contemplated expenditure implies that planning is actively proceeding. There are still immense arrears of road building and railway electrification—to mention only two obvious outlets. The extent of rearmament expenditure should imply that the *tempo* of total expenditure is more under the control of the government than is usual in periods of prosperity. It should not therefore be beyond its powers to encourage planning, but to restrict the commencement of schemes until the peak of armament expenditure has been passed. In this way the peak of public works expenditure should fall somewhere about what would otherwise have been the depression.

The position of the foreign balance, though less conspicuous, is probably more serious, particularly as there are scant grounds for optimism in this direction. The decline in international trade which was a natural accompaniment of the depression inflicted a

[1] Cf. Chap. XIV.   [2] Cf. Chap. VII, p. 129.
[3] As recorded in *The Times*, 18 Nov. 1937.

heavy loss in income on British industry. Nevertheless, the contraction in trade was not so great as it appeared, since the measurement is made in value terms which necessarily declined sharply with the fall in prices. Since prices only rose very slowly this factor has also partly concealed the extent of subsequent recovery. Had it been possible to obtain some relief of tariffs and import restrictions, recovery would undoubtedly have been very much greater. Apart, however, from the policy of other countries, it is clear that for Britain to relax restrictions in certain important lines of imports would have conflicted directly with the economic policy of the 'national' government.

The general tariff was ostensibly sanctioned in 1931-2, not to subsidize particular British interests, but to protect the balance of payments. Since that date the tariff, on the one hand, and the embargo on foreign issues on the London stock exchange, on the other, have been steadily kept in force for that purpose. Both returning prosperity and the necessities of rearmament expenditure have led to an enormous increase of imports. But it appears that the fear of the Adverse Balance has faded from the news. It would, however, be unsafe to conclude that the measures in question have been either particularly useful or particularly successful. On the one hand, the tariff has contributed indirectly to curtailing British exports, and is thus a two-edged weapon as far as the balance of payments is concerned. On the other, the embargo on foreign issues did not prevent the export of considerable amounts of British capital to take part in the American stock-exchange boom.[1] This is not the type of foreign lending which is likely to have any favourable repercussions on British exports. It merely serves to emphasize the fact that default on the American debt has played a part in assisting the stability of the British balance of payments. A still more important contribution has been made by the repayment of British loans by foreign and Empire borrowers.[2] Even more urgently than a recovery of freer trade, a restoration of the normal channels of foreign lending is required as a guarantee of long-run stability, and of a steady income.

The want of attention to economic considerations in the period

---

[1] Estimated by American authorities at £484 m. during 1935 and 1936. Cf. *Economist*, 30 Oct. 1937.

[2] According to Sir Robert Kindersley's calculations net repayments of principal in 1935-6 totalled £76 m.

1932–6 is the more disturbing because the evidence of effective government control is very much greater than at any other time since the war. This increase in control has aroused wide comment, and we have had to refer to it in detail in every aspect of public finance. It has received less notice in the purely monetary sphere. But here, too, there has been a startling change in emphasis. The change in the responsibility for policy which we noted as implicit in the relation between public borrowing and the market in the earlier post-war period seems now to be generally acknowledged. The government has become the monetary authority.

This change in monetary leadership has come about so gradually that it is not easy to date, but it may be evidenced repeatedly in monetary debates in the House. It was acknowledged more formally in the British statement in the Tripartite Currency Agreement of October 1936. His Majesty's Government then welcomed the 'opportunity to reaffirm *their* purpose to continue the policy which *they* have pursued in recent years'.[1] What is even more striking than the assumption of responsibility by the government is the complete acceptance of the new relation by the Bank and the public. On the occasion of the annual Mansion House dinner[2] the governor of the Bank of England referred with something like pride to the directed freedom which British financial institutions now enjoyed, and proceeded:

'I assure the Ministers that if they will make known through the appropriate channels what they wish us to do in the furtherance of their policies, they will at all times find us as willing with goodwill and loyalty to do what they direct, as though we were under legal compulsion.'

This implies a change of attitude which is full of presage for the future.[3] It may be that a monetary policy directly under the control of the government is more capable of supporting public finance than one which is not consciously integrated with it. But it will not be an easy tool to handle.

[1] Cf. *Economist*, 3 Oct. 1936.   [2] Cf. *The Times*, 7 Oct. 1936.
[3] For a fuller discussion of monetary policy, 1931–7, cf. Crick, *Bankers' Magazine*, Feb. 1938.

TABLE I

Principal borrowing on the Stock Exchange by Local Authorities (England and Wales) (1935–7)

1935

Authority	Date (week ending)	Amount	Price of issue	Nominal interest	Maturity (optional and final)	Result of issue
		(£m.)				
London C.C.	Jan. 12	10·0	100	2¾	1960–70	55 per cent. left
Bristol .	,, 12	2·8	99	2¾	1955–65	Oversubscribed
Hull . .	,, 26	1·2	98½	2¾	1960–70	Discount
Blackburn .	Feb. 2	1·0	98¾	2¾	1960–5	97 per cent. left
Ilford .	,, 9	0·5	99	2¾	1955–65	33 per cent. left
Manchester .	June 8	4·0	99	3	1952–5	Oversubscribed
Cardiff .	,, 15	1·5	99	3	1952–5	,,
Birkenhead .	,, 22	1·0	99	3	1952–5	Mod. oversub.
Leeds . .	,, 29	4·0	99½	3	1955–8	Premium
Liverpool .	,, 29	3·0	99½	3	1955–8	,,
West Brom- wich.	Aug. 3	0·6	100	3	1954–6	Slight premium
Sunderland .	Nov. 23	1·0	99½	3	1955–8	Heavy oversub.
Brighton .	,, 30	0·5	101	3	1955–8	Discount, then premium

1936

Authority	Date (week ending)	Amount	Price of issue	Nominal interest	Maturity (optional and final)	Result of issue
Smethwick .	Jan.	0·5	101	3	1956–8	Lists left open
Luton . .	,,	1·0	100½	3	1958	95 per cent. left
Coventry .	Feb.	1·0	100	3	1956–8	Just subscribed
Middx. C.C .	,,	2·5	100	3	1961–6	Oversubscribed
Blackpool .	,,	1·5	100	3	1957	,,
York . .	,,	0·5	100	3	1955–95	,,
Surrey C.C.	Mar.	1·5	100	3	1961–6	61 per cent. left
Walsall .	,,	0·4	100	3	1957	65 per cent. left
Southgate .	,,	0·55	100	3	1956–61	67 per cent. left
Birmingham	Apr. 20	4·9	99	3	1956–8	Lists left open
Croydon .	,, 24	1·5	99	3	1956–8	Fully sub.
Bradford .	,, 28	1·7	99	3	1956–8	Lists left open
Cardiff .	,, 28	1·4	99	3	1956–8	,,
Rochdale .	May 8	1·0	99	3	1956–8	Fully sub.
South Shields	,, 8	0·5	99	3	1956–8	Oversubscribed

1936 (*cont.*)

Authority	Date (week ending)	Amount	Price of issue	Nominal interest	Maturity (optional and final)	Result of issue
		£ m.				
Sheffield	May 14	2·5	99	3	1956–8	48 per cent. left
Huddersfield	,, 19	1·0	99	3	1956–8	Oversubscribed
Stockton/Tees	,, 19	0·9	99	3	1956–8	85 per cent. left
Newcastle	,, 30	1·5	99	3	1957	78 per cent. left
Salford	,, 30	1·25	98½	3	1954–6	Oversubscribed
Birkenhead	July 18	1·0	99	3	1957	Good
Nottingham	,, 18	1·75	99	3	1957	,,
Plymouth	,, 25	0·75	99	3	1956	,,
London C.C.	Sept. 26	10·0	99½	3	1958–63	Oversubscribed
Manchester	Oct. 10	5·0	99½	3	1958–63	Good, but fell
Bristol	,, 10	3·0	99½	3	1958–63	,,
Leicester	,, 10	1·5	99½	3	1958–63	76 per cent. left
Southampton	Nov. 7	1·25	99½	3	1958–63	Fair
Dewsbury	,, 7	0·85	99½	3	1958–63	Immediate discount

1937 (1st half)

Authority	Date (week ending)	Amount	Price of issue	Nominal interest	Maturity (optional and final)	Result of issue
Leeds	May 29	4·0	101	3½	1957–60	Oversubscribed
W. Riding	June 1	1·0	100½	3½	1957	Satisfactory
London C.C.	,, 26	10·0	100½	3½	1952–62	Bad

TABLE 2

National Debt interest (£ m.)

Year	Treas. Bills	Savings Certs.	Other interest	Management and expenses	Total interest Management expenses
1931–2	20·7	23·7*	251·6	1·9	297·9*
1932–3	5·9	17·7*	259·2	2·1†	284·9*
1933–4	4·1	11·1	200·0	1·1	216·3
1934–5	3·5	9·0	198·1	1·0	211·6
1935–6	3·5	8·9	198·1	1·0	211·5
1936–7	3·8	9·4	196·1	1·1	210·4

(*Economist*, Budget Supplement, 1938)

* Including funds borrowed for payment of interest on savings certificates.
† Excluding expenses of the conversion operation.

APPENDICES

TABLE I

Total Public Expenditure (Great Britain)
(£ m.)

	1913	1920	1921	1922	1923	1924	1925	1926	1927	1928	1929	1930	1931	1932	1933	1934	1935	1936
National Debt Services*	24.5	349.6	332.3	324.0	347.3	357.2	358.6	378.6	378.8	369.0	355.0	360.0	322.0	308.5	224.0	224.0	224.0	224.0
Military Expenditure	77.2	689.6	418.8	256.2	197.9	194.3	193.0	185.2	180.8	171.7	168.7	164.0	158.2	153.0	153.1	159.3	180.6	229.4
Civil Government	20.2	55.3	63.8	48.5	56.2	49.7	48.7	50.6	51.1	49.8	51.6	50.8	50.7	56.2	57.1	57.1	61.0	62.4
Social Expenditure	118.5	312.5	344.1	315.5	307.9	331.4	345.3	375.0	384.3	380.3	421.8	483.1	503.3	475.5	472.7	475.7	491.6	498.6
Economic Expenditure	101.8	289.5	279.0	222.5	223.2	228.5	258.5	262.0	257.0	258.0	274.7	282.2	280.2	272.0	274.3	288.0	298.8	308.6
Total	342.2	1696.5	1437.9	1166.7	1132.5	1161.1	1204.1	1251.4	1252.2	1228.8	1271.8	1340.1	1314.4	1265.2	1181.2	1204.1	1256.0	1323.0

* Budget charge—for actual cost of the debt see Chapter XXII, Table 2, p. 360.

TABLE 2

Military Expenditure
(£ m.)

	1913	1920	1921	1922	1923	1924	1925	1926	1927	1928	1929	1930	1931	1932	1933	1934	1935	1936
Army, Navy, and Air Force (less Civil Aviation)	77.2	291.9	189.0	110.7	105.6	114.5	119.1	116.3	117.1	113.1	112.9	110.2	106.9	102.5	107.4	113.4	136.5	185.5
Middle East Services	..	27.0	0.8	7.2	5.3	4.8	4.0	2.9	0.8	0.8	1.0	1.0	0.0	0.4	0.3	0.3	..	1.7
War Pensions*	..	106.4	95.8	80.6	72.6	69.9	67.3	63.6	60.2	57.1	54.5	52.1	49.8	49.5	46.8	45.1	43.3	41.7
Imperial War Graves Commission	..	1.4	0.5	0.4	0.8	1.0	0.8	1.0	0.5	0.7	0.5	0.6	0.5	0.5	0.5	0.5	0.5	..
Resettlement of ex-service men	..	13.1	10.2	7.4	4.1	1.8	0.9	0.2	0.1	..	..	..	..	..	..	..	..	..
Relief of war victims	..	0.1	..	0.1	..	1.8	0.04	0.04	0.1	0.03	0.03	0.03	0.01	..	..	..	..	..
Unclassified War Expenditure	..	276.7	96.3	47.2	7.6	0.1	0.02	0.03	..	..	..	..	..	..	..	..	..	..
Total	77.2	689.6	418.8	256.2	197.9	194.3	193.0	185.2	180.8	171.7	168.7	164.0	158.2	153.0	155.1	159.3	180.6	229.4

* Includes Ministry of Pensions Vote and Merchant Seamen's War Pensions. It is therefore more inclusive than the figure in Chapter III, Diagram I.

(For notes, see p. 382.)

TABLE 3
Expenditure on Civil Government
(£ m.)

	1913	1920	1921	1922	1923	1924	1925	1926	1927	1928	1929	1930	1931	1932	1933	1934	1935	1936
Central Government and Finance	1·1	2·2	2·0	2·4	2·7	2·2	2·3	2·0	1·7	1·7	1·8	1·7	1·6	1·6	1·7	1·8	2·0	2·2
Imperial and Foreign Administration, &c.	1·6	5·1	4·5	3·7	10·7	2·7	2·8	2·0	2·7	2·7	2·9	2·3	2·7	6·6	7·1	6·6	6·8	6·1
Home Department, Law and Justice, &c.	0·2	5·5	5·5	3·0	3·8	2·8	2·9	2·8	2·8	2·2	2·3	2·1	2·1	2·1	2·0	2·1	2·1	3·2
Local Expenditure on Police, Justice, and Fire Brigades	10·3	26·2	27·0	24·2	24·1	25·0	25·7	26·2	27·1	27·3	27·8	28·6	28·0	28·0	28·1	28·3	28·6	29·0
Civil Pensions (non-social)	0·8	1·2	1·6	1·2	1·3	1·3	1·3	1·4	1·4	1·5	1·5	1·5	1·5	1·9	2·0	2·0	1·8	1·9
Emergency and Temporary Expenditure	..	2·0	7·1	..	..	2·3	..	1·8	..	..	..	..	..	..	..	..	..	..
Miscellaneous Consolidated Fund Expenditure*	6·2	13·1	16·1	14·0	13·6	13·4	13·7	14·4	15·4	14·4	15·3	14·6	14·8	16·0	16·2	16·3	19·7	20·0
Total	20·2	55·3	63·8	48·5	56·2	49·7	48·7	50·6	51·1	49·8	51·6	50·8	50·7	56·2	57·1	57·1	61·0	62·4

* Including cost of Customs and Excise Administration.

TABLE 4
Economic Expenditure*
(£ m.)

	1913	1920	1921	1922	1923	1924	1925	1926	1927	1928	1929	1930	1931	1932	1933	1934	1935	1936
1. Aid to Industry and Trade†	1·2	56·1	15·9	9·5	5·4	2·4	21·9	8·6	4·7	5·1	4·5	5·2	4·5	5·0	5·7	5·3	9·0	7·7
2. Aid to Agriculture‡		15·5	28·3	4·9	8·4	5·8	6·6	9·1	9·7	8·4	10·5	12·3	8·3	12·7	14·9	22·8	19·8	18·0
3. Local Trading Services	54·1	117·3	115·2	103·1	103·6	107·2	110·4	123·4	118·4	121·0	125·9	130·0	130·8	131·1	134·4	137·0	140·0	145·0‖
4. Roads§	21·9	46·9	53·6	55·1	56·0	62·7	65·6	66·9	67·4	66·3	74·9	75·7	78·6	63·9	60·4	61·1	63·9	66·0‖
5. Post Office**	24·6	53·7	66·0	49·9	49·8	50·4	54·0	54·0	56·8	57·2	58·9	59·0	58·0	59·3	59·3	61·8	66·1	71·9
Total	101·8	289·5	279·0	222·5	223·2	228·5	258·5	262·0	257·0	258·0	274·7	282·2	280·2	272·0	274·3	288·0	298·0	308·6

* Certain small trading services operated by central departments (mainly the Ministry of Agriculture) have been omitted, also the services of the Stationery Office.
† Cf. Chapter IV, Table I, p. 66.   ‡ Cf. Chapter V, Table I, p. 190.
§ From Road Fund Accounts, Total Expenditure, excluding loans, but including loan charges.   ‖ Estimate.   ** Excluding loans.

TABLE 5

Social Expenditure

(£ m.)

	1913	1920	1921	1922	1923	1924	1925	1926	1927	1928	1929	1930	1931	1932	1933	1934	1935	1936
Central Education Services	2·5	5·7	7·6	5·0	5·3	6·2	6·7	9·7	10·0	4·0	4·7	5·2	6·0	6·9	6·9	6·8	6·6	7·5
Central Health and Labour Services	18·0	61·0	49·9	41·0	43·8	46·2	49·4	52·7	57·4	57·7	65·9	88·8	105·1	95·0	89·4	88·9	106·0	107·0
Social Expenditure of Local Authorities.	86·3	198·3	219·5	212·9	268·1	216·0	228·3	348·1	347·7	248·3	264·9	269·8	271·5	272·5	277·2	282·6	286·5	293·0
Social Insurance, less State Contribution	11·7	47·3	65·5	57·0	50·5	62·4	60·7	64·9	69·3	70·2	86·1	119·9	120·5	100·9	99·1	91·8	92·3	90·9
Miscellaneous Social Services, central*	..	0·2	1·6	0·3	0·2	0·4	0·2	0·1	0·1	0·1	0·2	0·4	0·2	0·2	0·1	0·1	0·2	0·2
Total	118·5	312·5	344·1	315·5	307·9	331·4	345·3	375·0	384·3	380·3	421·8	484·1	503·3	475·5	472·7	470·2	491·6	498·6

* Including Friendly Societies Deficiency Grant and Unemployment Relief Works.

General Notes to Tables 1–5 (Chapter II, Diagram 1)

1. The figures are for financial years, and capital expenditure has been excluded as far as possible.
2. Sources: Appropriation Accounts and *Statistical Abstract*.
3. Irish figures are excluded throughout.
4. Expenditure by local authorities includes government grants. Local figures for 1935 and 1936 are estimates only.
5. Figures for Appropriation Accounts are net issues (see also note 1 to Table 1, Chapter IV, p. 66). Local and Post Office expenditure are total issues, other than out of loan.

TABLE 6

Expenditure on Social Services—Gross and Transfer*
(exclusive of Expenditure out of Loan)—Great Britain
(Chapter III, Diagrams I and III)

(£ m.)

I. GROSS

	1890	1900	1910	1920	1921	1922	1923	1924	1925	1926	1927	1928	1929	1930	1931	1932	1933	1934	1935	1936†
Education	11·5	19·3	33·5	88·9	93·9	89·6	87·4	89·4	92·0	93·2	94·4	97·0	100·5	104·2	103·3	100·8	101·7	105·7	111·7	115·3
Public Health (including Mental Health)	1·4	2·8	4·7	40·6	42·5	42·2	44·4	46·5	51·1	56·6	53·1	55·9	55·4	55·6	56·9	58·7	58·6	60·5	63·5	65·0
Housing	0·2	0·5	1·5	1·9	5·2	11·7	16·5	18·4	20·0	22·8	26·8	31·6	35·6	37·5	40·2	42·6	44·8	46·1	48·2	49·0
Unemployment and Public Assistance	9·1	12·3	16·1	46·4	118·1	96·2	90·0	91·0	93·8	111·3	88·3	97·7	98·4	144·1	164·0	161·8	147·6	148·3	150·8	137·9
Civil Pensions	..	..	7·4	20·7	23·0	22·4	23·0	25·7	29·6	38·4	45·1	57·7	62·2	72·1	78·3	81·2	83·9	85·6	88·4	89·2
War Pensions	..	..	..	100·9	88·9	76·0	69·3	65·4	63·9	60·2	56·0	53·9	51·4	49·2	47·0	44·5	42·8	41·2	40·5	39·4
Total Gross	22·2	34·9	63·2	299·5	371·6	338·1	330·6	336·4	350·4	382·5	363·7	393·8	403·5	462·7	489·7	489·6	479·4	487·4	503·1	495·8

II. TRANSFER

	1890	1900	1910	1920	1921	1922	1923	1924	1925	1926	1927	1928	1929	1930	1931	1932	1933	1934	1935	1936†
Education	Not available		31·8	84·6	89·3	85·5	80·9	82·3	84·8	85·4	86·7	88·8	92·2	95·5	94·6	92·6	93·1	97·1	102·9	Not available
Public Health			4·3	26·7	30·9	29·6	31·3	32·9	37·3	44·4	39·9	43·0	42·4	42·6	44·0	45·6	45·7	46·3	47·0	
Housing			0·9	0·8	2·6	6·7	9·1	9·6	10·1	11·3	13·0	14·3	15·4	16·4	17·5	18·1	18·6	18·6	19·7	
Unemployment and Public Assistance			15·3	35·1	101·6	77·9	76·7	74·2	85·5	95·8	73·2	82·4	83·8	128·0	145·0	142·5	120·7	124·0	125·7	
Civil Pensions			7·4	20·7	23·0	22·4	23·0	25·7	29·6	38·4	32·2	46·1	50·6	60·1	66·6	69·8	72·0	74·0	76·5	76·4
War Pensions			..	100·9	88·9	76·0	69·3	65·4	63·9	60·2	56·0	53·9	51·4	49·2	47·0	44·5	42·8	41·2	40·5	39·4
Total Transfer			59·7	268·8	336·3	298·1	290·3	290·1	311·2	335·5	301·0	328·5	335·5	391·8	414·7	413·1	392·1	401·2	412·3	

* From *Annual Returns of Social Services*. A small amount of miscellaneous expenditure has been omitted.

† Estimates.

TABLE 7

The Yield of Income and Capital Taxes (Chap. XIV, Diagram I (1))

(£ m.)

	1913	1920	1921	1922	1923	1924	1925	1926	1927	1928	1929	1930	1931	1932	1933	1934	1935	1936
Income Tax	43·9	340·6	334·9	314·4	271·4	273·8	258·1	230·1	253·5	237·3	237·9	255·3	287·4	251·5	228·9	228·9	238·1	257·0
Super (Sur) Tax	3·3	55·7	61·4	63·9	61·7	62·7	67·8	66·3	60·1	56·2	56·6	67·8	76·7	60·7	52·6	51·2	51·0	53·4
Estate, &c., Duties	27·4	47·2	52·5	56·5	57·6	59·5	61·3	67·4	77·1	81·0	79·2	83·1	65·0	77·1	85·3	81·4	87·9	87·9
Stamp Duties	10·0	26·5	19·6	21·9	21·6	22·8	25·1	24·9	26·9	30·1	25·3	20·3	17·1	19·2	22·7	24·1	25·8	29·0
Miscellaneous Inland Revenue*	3·4	221·7	30·4	22·8	28·0	22·3	15·1	9·3	2·9	2·8	3·1	3·5	2·1	3·0	2·6	3·1	2·1	1·7
Total	88·0	691·7	498·8	479·5	440·3	441·1	427·4	398·0	420·5	407·4	402·1	430·0	448·3	411·5	392·1	388·7	404·9	429·0

* Including War Profits Taxes.

(Source: Statistical Abstract.)

TABLE 8

The Yield of Commodity Taxes (Chap. XIV, Diagram I (2))

(£ m.)

	1913	1920	1921	1922	1923	1924	1925	1926	1927	1928	1929	1930	1931	1932	1933	1934	1935	1936
Alcohol Duties*	43·2	201·2	192·1	153·2	143·4	141·4	140·5	136·6	139·4	130·1	129·3	125·0	118·4	111·5	100·8	99·8	104·6	109·0
Tobacco Duties	18·3	55·5	55·2	53·4	51·9	53·5	53·5	53·9	58·1	59·1	62·8	64·1	63·3	67·2	67·5	70·7	75·0	77·3
'Breakfast Table' Duties†	9·8	50·5	57·8	54·4	51·6	28·1	26·7	26·3	26·0	22·5	14·9	16·5	18·3	18·3	18·6	18·1	17·9	22·3
Motor and Oil Duties‡	0·8	10·4	11·3	12·6	14·6	16·5	18·5	21·5	24·7	38·5	41·6	43·7	56·6	63·3	71·5	73·2	76·0	80·5
Miscellaneous Revenue Duties§	3·8	18·6	16·8	15·2	15·4	12·2	11·6	12·7	15·3	15·9	13·9	13·8	13·7	13·1	13·0	13·8	13·2	13·2
Protective Duties‖		5·5	1·7	3·0	2·4	3·1	4·7	9·8	11·4	11·8	11·7	11·1	11·9	34·9	44·5	43·9	47·2	50·0
Total	75·9	341·7	334·9	291·8	279·2	253·2	255·5	260·8	274·9	278·1	274·2	274·2	282·2	308·3	315·9	319·5	333·9	352·3

(Source: Statistical Abstract.)

* Including taxes on spirits, beer, wine, and liquor licences.
† Including tea, cocoa, coffee, &c., sugar, dried fruits, and table waters.
‡ Including motor vehicle licences, motor spirit duty (to 1921), and hydrocarbon oils duty (from 1928) (only some 75 per cent. of the last is imputable to motoring).
§ Including matches, &c., entertainments, miscellaneous duties and licences, and betting.
‖ Including the 'McKenna' duties, 1932 import duties, Irish Free State, and miscellaneous import duties.

TABLE 9

The Yield of Miscellaneous Levies (Chap. XIV, Diagram I (3))

(£ m.)

	1913	1920	1921	1922	1923	1924	1925	1926	1927	1928	1929	1930	1931	1932	1933	1934	1935	1936
Local Rates (U.K.)	79·7	172·4	192·2	177·0	163·1	162·1	169·4	181·6	190·7	190·6	177·4	171·1	168·1	166·5	170·0	175·9	188·6	196·5
Social Insurance Contributions*	16·8	31·6	56·5	59·4	63·3	64·5	61·5	45·1	83·4	79·8	80·2	79·8	82·8	86·3	88·2	92·3	95·2	92·0
Post Office Contribution†	3·4	..	..	4·5	5·3	5·4	6·7	5·8	7·6	9·0	9·4	9·2	10·6	11·1	12·3	11·9	11·7	11·1
Processing Tax (Wheat Quota)	..	..	..	..	..	..	..	..	..	..	..	..	..	4·5	7·2	6·8	5·6	2·4
Total	99·9	204·0	248·7	240·9	231·7	232·0	237·6	232·5	281·7	279·4	267·0	260·1	261·5	268·4	277·7	286·9	301·1	302·0

(Source: Statistical Abstract.)

* Unemployment Insurance not included in 1913, 9 months only, in 1921 and 1926.
† The P.O. figure for 1920 is not comparable. In 1921 a deficit was realized.

TABLE 10

Calculations of the Distribution of the Tax Structure*

	(1) 1903-4		(2) 1913-14		(3) 1918-19		(4) 1925-6		(5) 1930-1	
Income £	All earned	Half earned, half investment†	All earned	Half earned, half investment†	All earned	Half earned, half investment†	All earned	Half earned, half investment†	All earned	Wholly from investments†
					Taxation‡ as a percentage of Income					
50	8·7	9·5	8·0	8·8	..	..	..	..	..	..
100	5·6	6·8	5·4	6·6	9·9	11·1	11·6	13·0	10·9	13·1
150	4·5	5·7	4·4	5·6	9·0	10·2	11·6	12·7	11·3	13·2
200	4·8	6·0	4·0	5·3	7·9	9·1	10·2	11·3	9·6	11·7
500	5·3	6·5	4·4	7·1	10·2	13·5	6·2	8·4	5·1	10·1
1,000	6·1	7·8	5·2	8·3	16·9	20·6	11·0	14·4	10·9	20·7
2,000	5·7	7·4	4·9	8·4	24·0	28·1	15·2	19·3	17·5	30·8
5,000	5·5	7·5	6·7	9·6	36·6	39·2	23·2	29·5	28·2	47·7
10,000	5·0	7·6	8·0	11·8	42·5	46·3	31·2	40·1	37·6	63·8
20,000	4·9	7·7	8·3	13·0	47·6	52·3	37·5	48·7	45·3	83·4
50,000	4·8	8·0	8·4	13·6	50·6	58·2	44·4	57·7	53·2	117·9

* Chapter XVI, Diagram I, 1-4, Colwyn Committee; 5, Sandral, J.R.S.S. cit. The taxpayer is in all cases assumed to be married and to have three children under 16.
† Including death duties.
‡ For differences in the taxes on which the calculations are based, cp. p. 271.

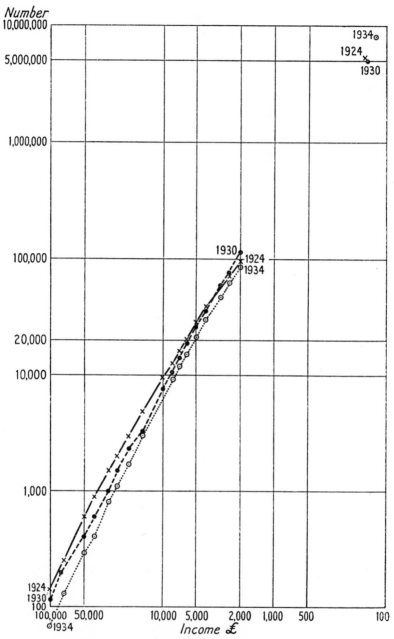

THE DISTRIBUTION OF THE NATIONAL INCOME
(Surtax Years) 1924, 1930, 1934

The trend towards greater equalization (steeper slope) is slightly disturbed in 1930 by the existence of boom incomes (making for greater inequality), and slightly exaggerated in 1934 by the fact that surtax assessments are not quite complete. Also cf. p. 266, fn.

No attempt is made to interpolate between the surtax minimum and total liability to income tax. For such an attempt (for 1929 and 1932) cf. Colin Clark, *National Income and Outlay*, pp. 105 ff.

INDEX